THE COMPLETE

PERSEPOLIS

THE COMPLETE

PERSEPOLIS

MARJANE SATRAPI

PANTHEON

The Complete Persepolis was originally published in the United States in two separate volumes:

Persepolis was originally published in France in two volumes as *Persepolis 1* and *Persepolis 2* by L'Association, Paris, in 2000 and 2001, respectively. This translation was originally published in hardcover by Pantheon Books, a division of Random House, Inc., New York, in 2003.

Persepolis 2 was originally published in France in two volumes as *Persepolis 3* and *Persepolis 4* by L'Association, Paris, in 2002 and 2003, respectively. This translation was originally published in hardcover by Pantheon Books, a division of Random House, Inc., New York, in 2004.

L'Association

Library of Congress Cataloging-in-Publication Data
Satrapi, Marjane, [date]
[Persepolis, English]
The complete Persepolis / Marjane Satrapi.
p. cm.
Contains the author's Persepolis (2003) and Persepolis 2 (2004)
ISBN 978-0-375-71483-2
1. Satrapi, Marjane, [date]–Comic books, strips, etc. I. Satrapi, Marjane, [date] Persepolis 2. English. II. Title.
PN6747.S245P4713 2007
955.05'42092–dc22
[B] 2007060106

www.pantheonbooks.com
Printed in India
First Edition

35th Printing

To my parents

INTRODUCTION

In the second millennium B.C., while the Elam nation was developing a civilization alongside Babylon, Indo-European invaders gave their name to the immense Iranian plateau where they settled. The word "Iran" was derived from "Ayryana Vaejo," which means "the origin of the Aryans." These people were semi-nomads whose descendants were the Medes and the Persians. The Medes founded the first Iranian nation in the seventh century B.C.; it was later destroyed by Cyrus the Great. He established what became one of the largest empires of the ancient world, the Persian Empire, in the sixth century B.C. Iran was referred to as Persia – its Greek name – until 1935 when Reza Shah, the father of the last Shah of Iran, asked everyone to call the country Iran.

Iran was rich. Because of its wealth and its geographic location, it invited attacks: From Alexander the Great, from its Arab neighbors to the west, from Turkish and Mongolian conquerors, Iran was often subject to foreign domination. Yet the Persian language and culture withstood these invasions. The invaders assimilated into this strong culture, and in some ways they became Iranians themselves.

In the twentieth century, Iran entered a new phase. Reza Shah decided to modernize and westernize the country, but meanwhile a fresh source of wealth was discovered: oil. And with the oil came another invasion. The West, particularly Great Britain, wielded a strong influence on the Iranian economy. During the Second World War, the British, Soviets, and Americans asked Reza Shah to ally himself with them against Germany. But Reza Shah, who sympathized with the Germans, declared Iran a neutral zone. So the Allies invaded and occupied Iran. Reza Shah was sent into exile and was succeeded by his son, Mohammad Reza Pahlavi, who was known simply as the Shah.

In 1951, Mohammed Mossadeq, then prime minister of Iran, nationalized the oil industry. In retaliation, Great Britain organized an embargo on all exports of oil from Iran. In 1953, the CIA, with the help of British intelligence, organized a coup against him. Mossadeq was overthrown and the Shah, who had earlier escaped from the country, returned to power. The Shah stayed on the throne until 1979, when he fled Iran to escape the Islamic revolution.

Since then, this old and great civilization has been discussed mostly in connection with fundamentalism, fanaticism, and terrorism. As an Iranian who has lived more than half of my life in Iran, I know that this image is far from the truth. This is why writing *Persepolis* was so important to me. I believe that an entire nation should not be judged by the wrongdoings of a few extremists. I also don't want those Iranians who lost their lives in prisons defending freedom, who died in the war against Iraq, who suffered under various repressive regimes, or who were forced to leave their families and flee their homeland to be forgotten.

One can forgive but one should never forget.

Marjane Satrapi
Paris, September 2002

THE COMPLETE

PERSEPOLIS

THE VEIL

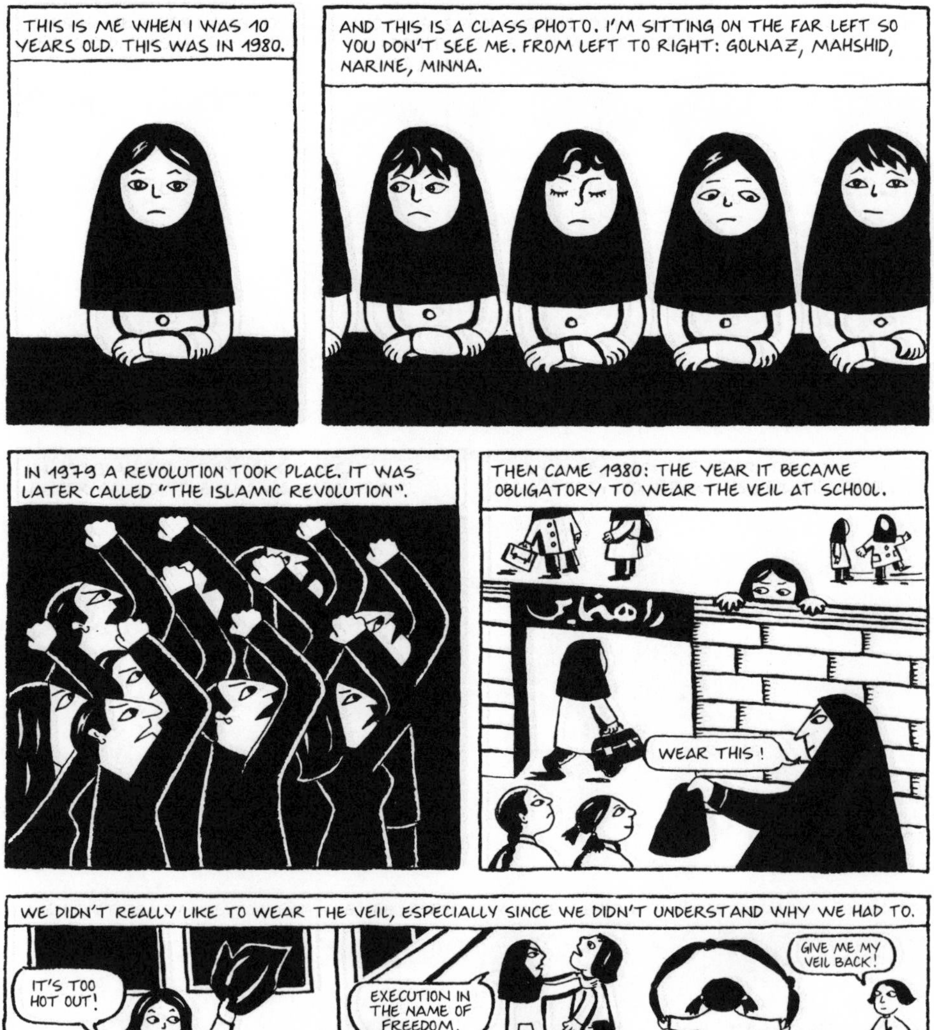
THIS IS ME WHEN I WAS 10 YEARS OLD. THIS WAS IN 1980.
AND THIS IS A CLASS PHOTO. I'M SITTING ON THE FAR LEFT SO YOU DON'T SEE ME. FROM LEFT TO RIGHT: GOLNAZ, MAHSHID, NARINE, MINNA.
IN 1979 A REVOLUTION TOOK PLACE. IT WAS LATER CALLED "THE ISLAMIC REVOLUTION".
THEN CAME 1980: THE YEAR IT BECAME OBLIGATORY TO WEAR THE VEIL AT SCHOOL.
WEAR THIS!
WE DIDN'T REALLY LIKE TO WEAR THE VEIL, ESPECIALLY SINCE WE DIDN'T UNDERSTAND WHY WE HAD TO.
IT'S TOO HOT OUT!
EXECUTION IN THE NAME OF FREEDOM.
GIVE ME MY VEIL BACK!
YOU'LL HAVE TO LICK MY FEET!
OOH! I'M THE MONSTER OF DARKNESS.
GIDDYAP!

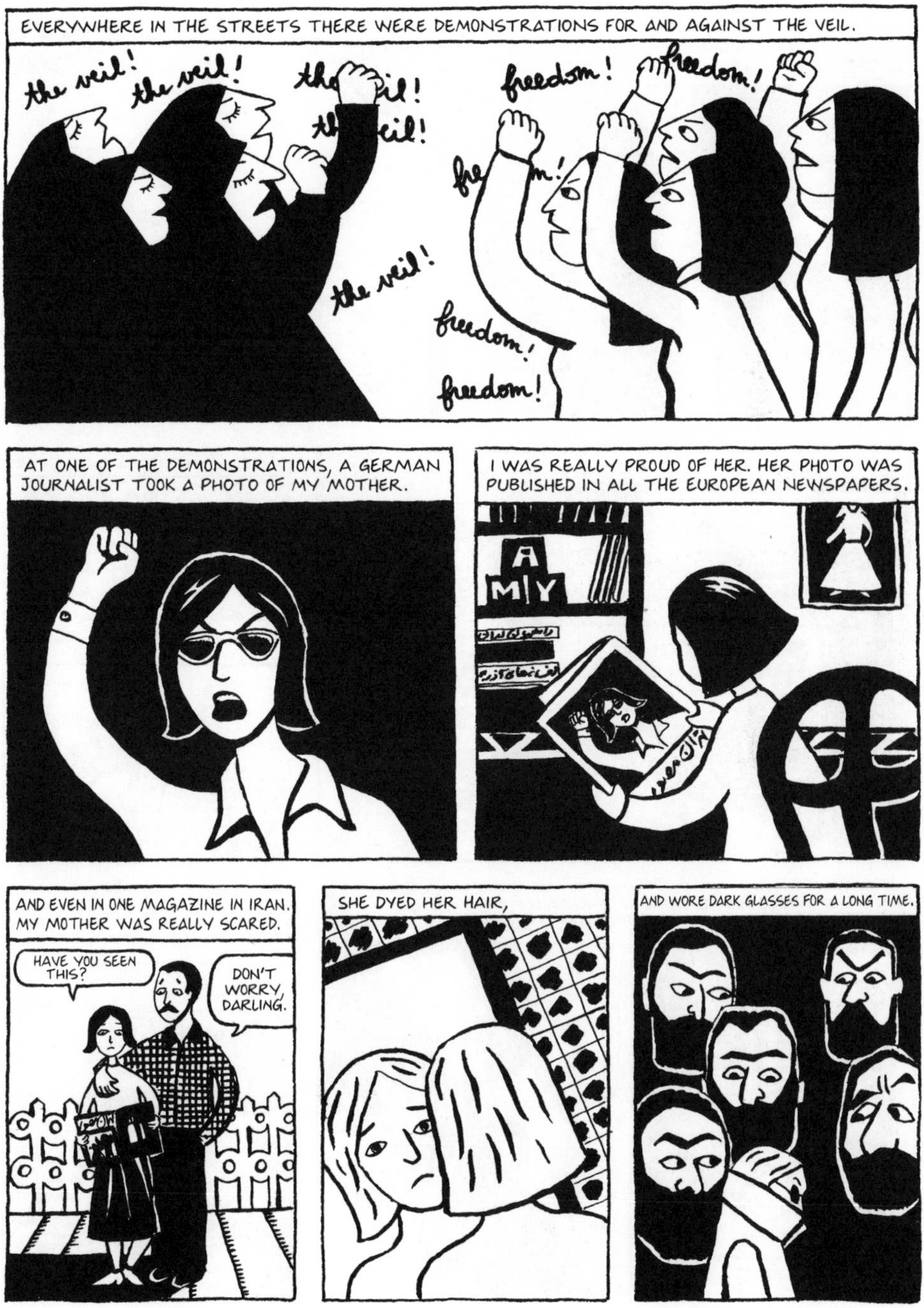
EVERYWHERE IN THE STREETS THERE WERE DEMONSTRATIONS FOR AND AGAINST THE VEIL.
the veil!
the veil!
the veil!
freedom!
freedom!
the veil!
freedom!
freedom!
AT ONE OF THE DEMONSTRATIONS, A GERMAN JOURNALIST TOOK A PHOTO OF MY MOTHER.
I WAS REALLY PROUD OF HER. HER PHOTO WAS PUBLISHED IN ALL THE EUROPEAN NEWSPAPERS.
AND EVEN IN ONE MAGAZINE IN IRAN. MY MOTHER WAS REALLY SCARED.
HAVE YOU SEEN THIS?
DON'T WORRY, DARLING.
SHE DYED HER HAIR,
AND WORE DARK GLASSES FOR A LONG TIME.

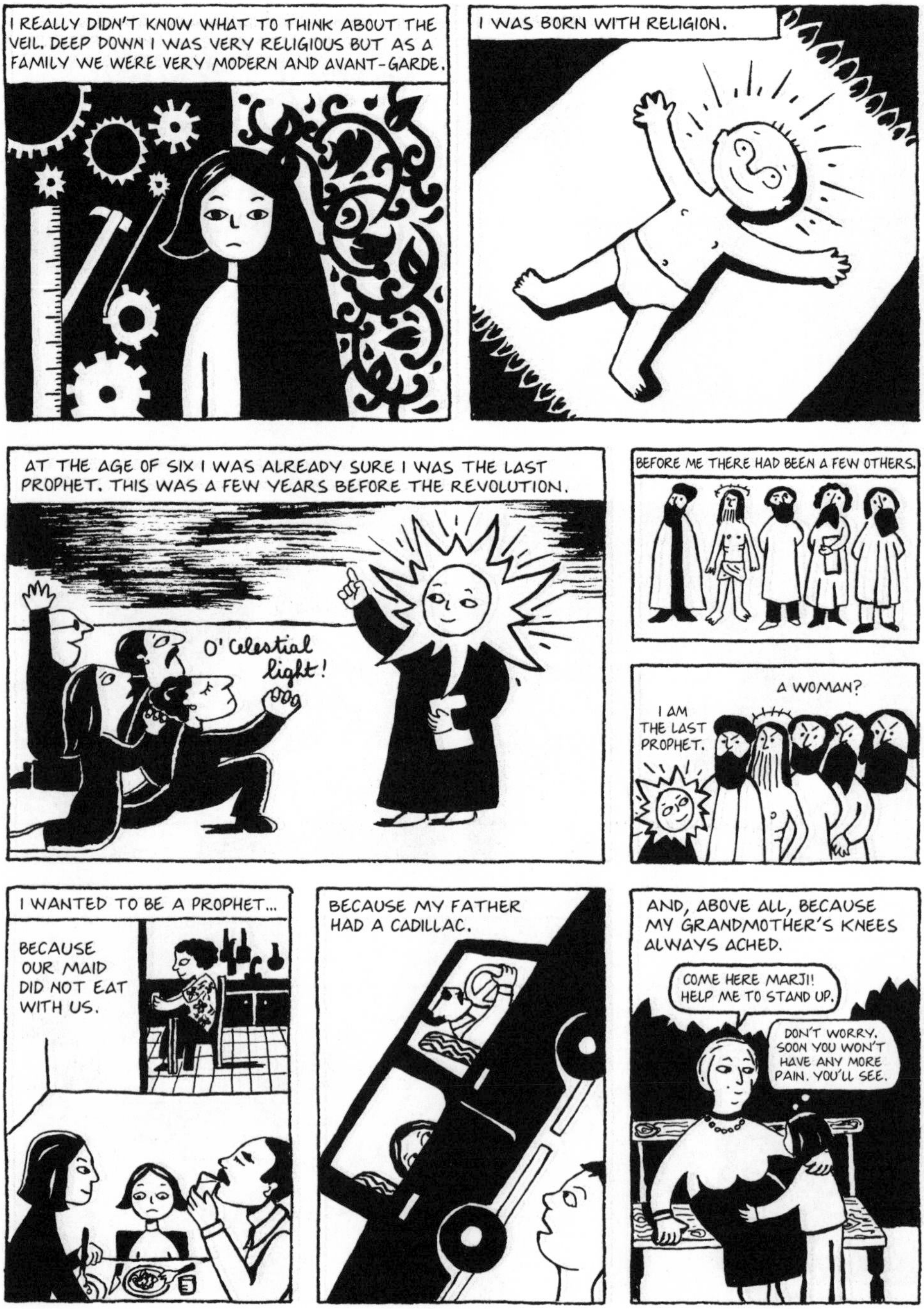
I REALLY DIDN'T KNOW WHAT TO THINK ABOUT THE VEIL. DEEP DOWN I WAS VERY RELIGIOUS BUT AS A FAMILY WE WERE VERY MODERN AND AVANT-GARDE.
I WAS BORN WITH RELIGION.
AT THE AGE OF SIX I WAS ALREADY SURE I WAS THE LAST PROPHET. THIS WAS A FEW YEARS BEFORE THE REVOLUTION.
O' Celestial light!
BEFORE ME THERE HAD BEEN A FEW OTHERS.
I AM THE LAST PROPHET.
A WOMAN?
I WANTED TO BE A PROPHET...
BECAUSE OUR MAID DID NOT EAT WITH US.
BECAUSE MY FATHER HAD A CADILLAC.
AND, ABOVE ALL, BECAUSE MY GRANDMOTHER'S KNEES ALWAYS ACHED.
COME HERE MARJI! HELP ME TO STAND UP.
DON'T WORRY. SOON YOU WON'T HAVE ANY MORE PAIN. YOU'LL SEE.

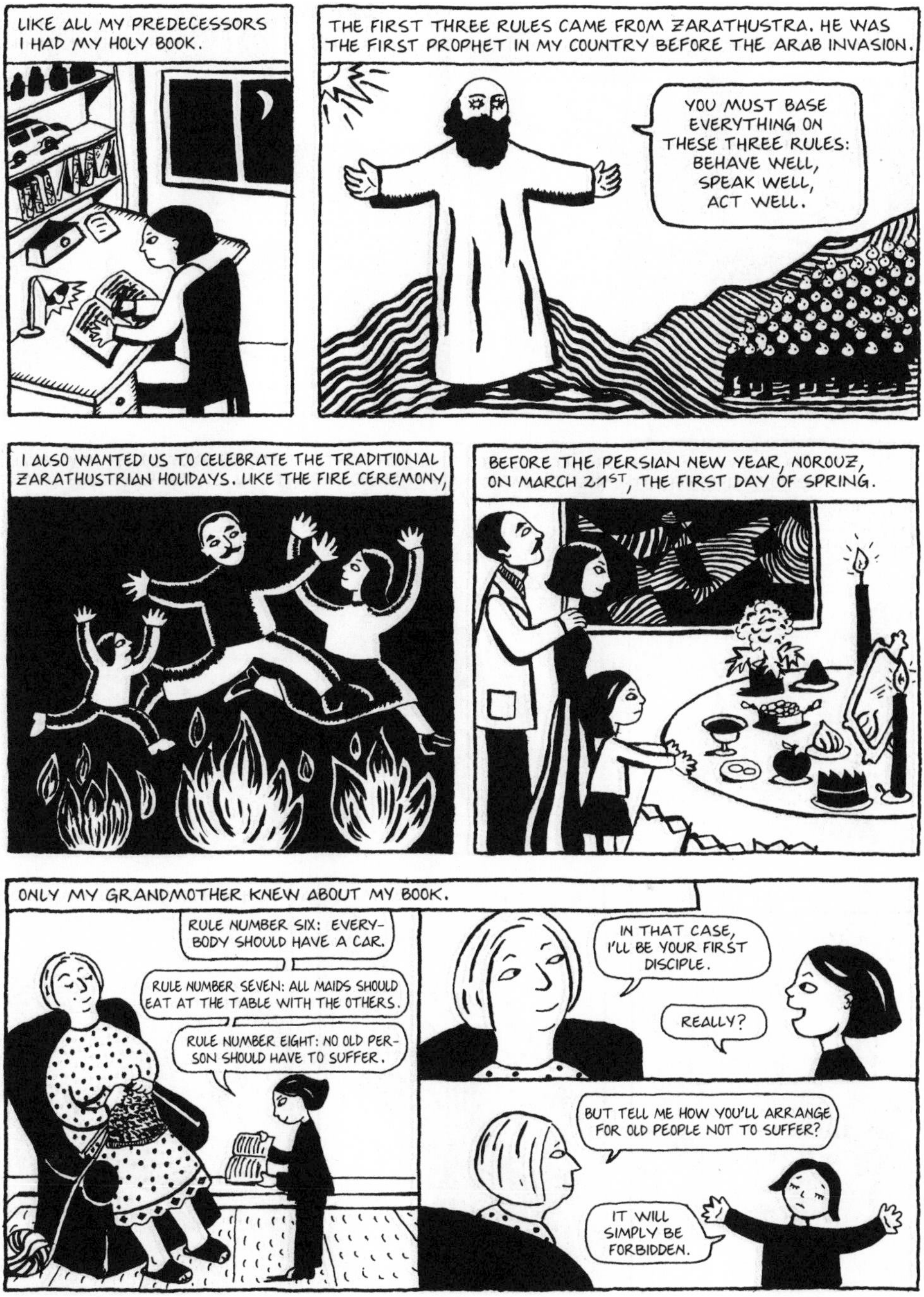
LIKE ALL MY PREDECESSORS I HAD MY HOLY BOOK.
THE FIRST THREE RULES CAME FROM ZARATHUSTRA. HE WAS THE FIRST PROPHET IN MY COUNTRY BEFORE THE ARAB INVASION.
YOU MUST BASE EVERYTHING ON THESE THREE RULES: BEHAVE WELL, SPEAK WELL, ACT WELL.
I ALSO WANTED US TO CELEBRATE THE TRADITIONAL ZARATHUSTRIAN HOLIDAYS. LIKE THE FIRE CEREMONY,
BEFORE THE PERSIAN NEW YEAR, NOROUZ, ON MARCH 21ST, THE FIRST DAY OF SPRING.
ONLY MY GRANDMOTHER KNEW ABOUT MY BOOK.
RULE NUMBER SIX: EVERYBODY SHOULD HAVE A CAR.
RULE NUMBER SEVEN: ALL MAIDS SHOULD EAT AT THE TABLE WITH THE OTHERS.
RULE NUMBER EIGHT: NO OLD PERSON SHOULD HAVE TO SUFFER.
IN THAT CASE, I'LL BE YOUR FIRST DISCIPLE.
REALLY?
BUT TELL ME HOW YOU'LL ARRANGE FOR OLD PEOPLE NOT TO SUFFER?
IT WILL SIMPLY BE FORBIDDEN.

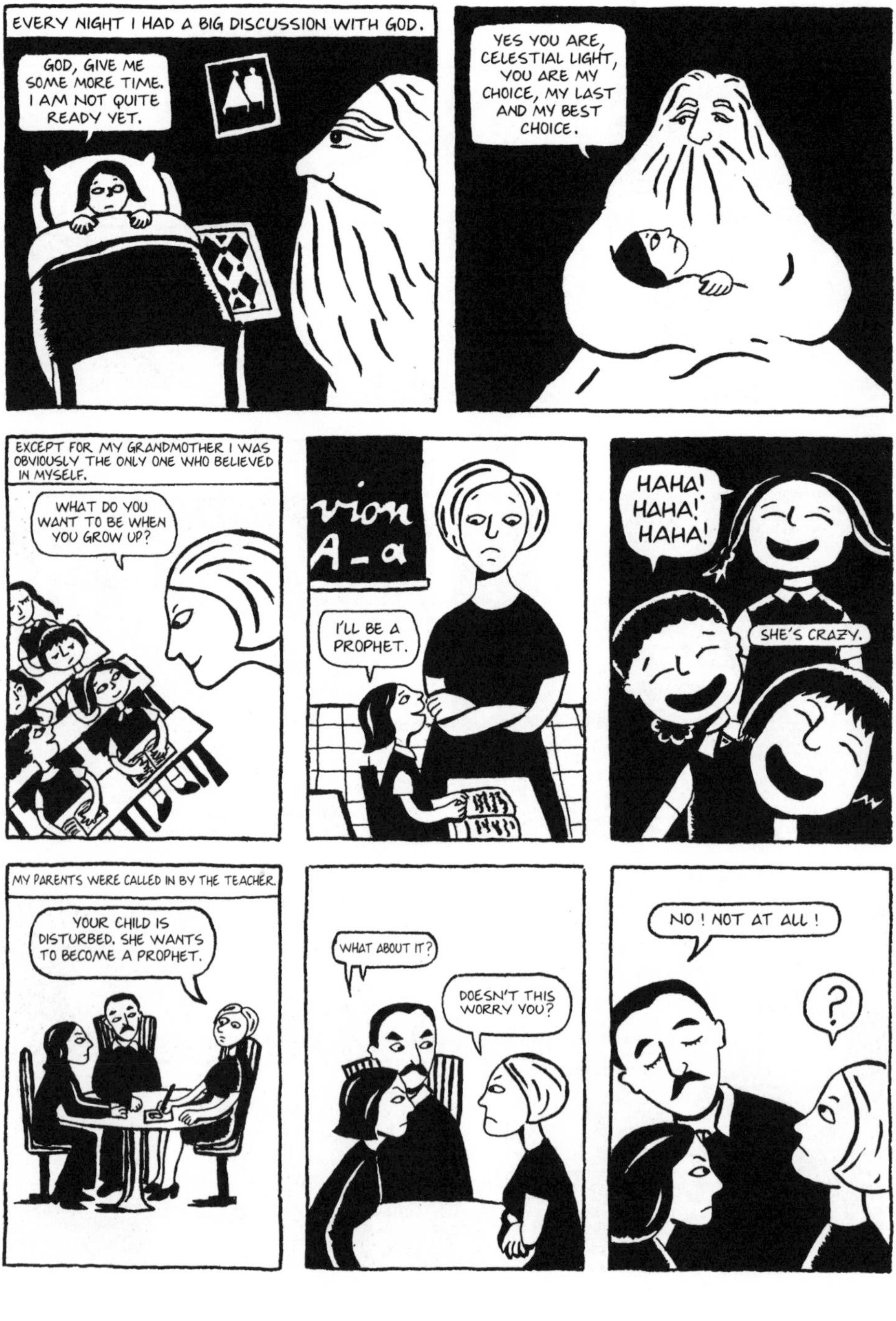
EVERY NIGHT I HAD A BIG DISCUSSION WITH GOD.
GOD, GIVE ME SOME MORE TIME. I AM NOT QUITE READY YET.
YES YOU ARE, CELESTIAL LIGHT, YOU ARE MY CHOICE, MY LAST AND MY BEST CHOICE.
EXCEPT FOR MY GRANDMOTHER I WAS OBVIOUSLY THE ONLY ONE WHO BELIEVED IN MYSELF.
WHAT DO YOU WANT TO BE WHEN YOU GROW UP?
vion
A - a
I'LL BE A PROPHET.
HAHA! HAHA! HAHA!
SHE'S CRAZY.
MY PARENTS WERE CALLED IN BY THE TEACHER.
YOUR CHILD IS DISTURBED. SHE WANTS TO BECOME A PROPHET.
WHAT ABOUT IT?
DOESN'T THIS WORRY YOU?
NO ! NOT AT ALL !
?

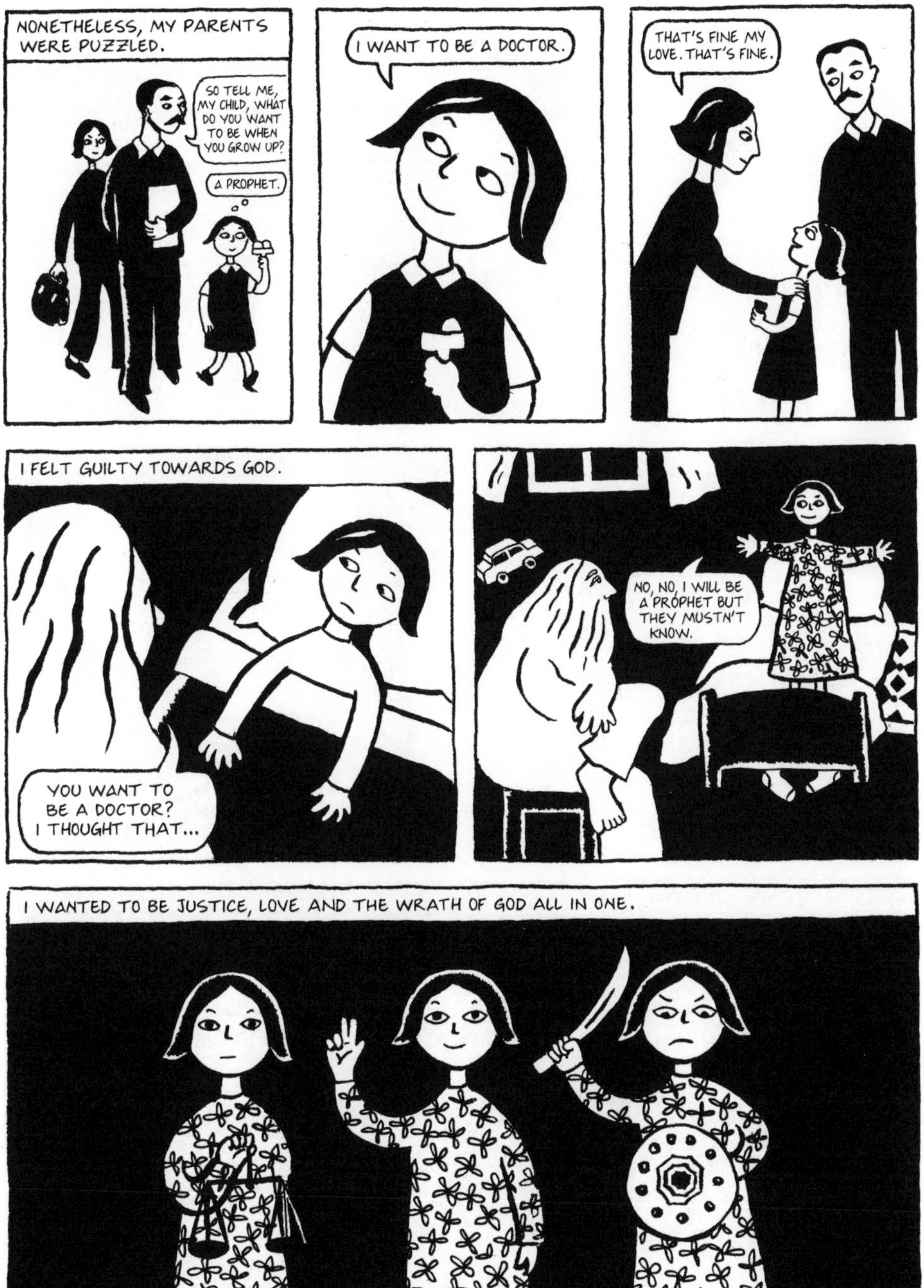
NONETHELESS, MY PARENTS WERE PUZZLED.
SO TELL ME, MY CHILD, WHAT DO YOU WANT TO BE WHEN YOU GROW UP?
A PROPHET.
I WANT TO BE A DOCTOR.
THAT'S FINE MY LOVE. THAT'S FINE.
I FELT GUILTY TOWARDS GOD.
YOU WANT TO BE A DOCTOR? I THOUGHT THAT...
NO, NO, I WILL BE A PROPHET BUT THEY MUSTN'T KNOW.
I WANTED TO BE JUSTICE, LOVE AND THE WRATH OF GOD ALL IN ONE.

THE BICYCLE

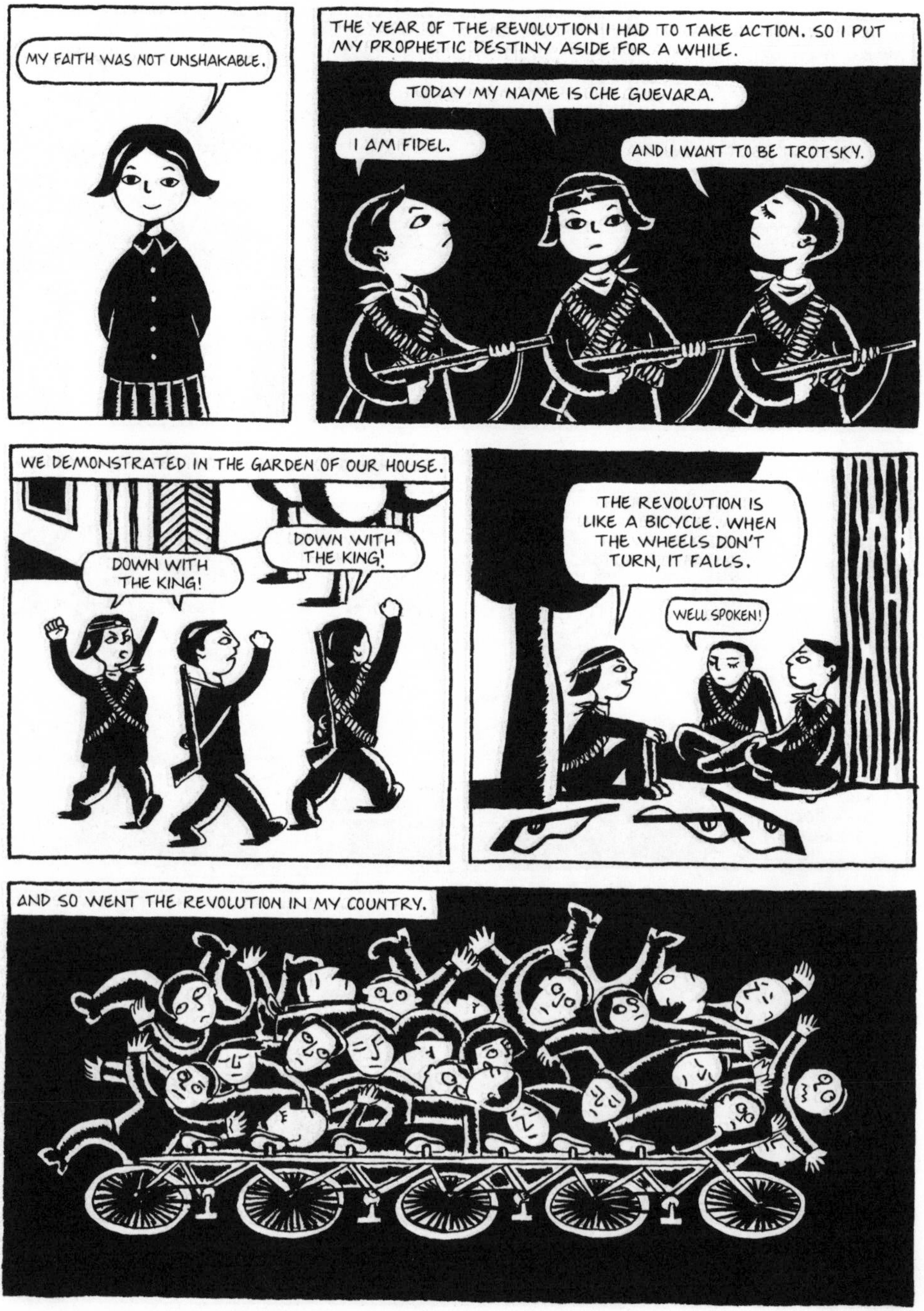

MY FAITH WAS NOT UNSHAKABLE.
THE YEAR OF THE REVOLUTION I HAD TO TAKE ACTION. SO I PUT MY PROPHETIC DESTINY ASIDE FOR A WHILE.
TODAY MY NAME IS CHE GUEVARA.
I AM FIDEL.
AND I WANT TO BE TROTSKY.
WE DEMONSTRATED IN THE GARDEN OF OUR HOUSE.
DOWN WITH THE KING!
DOWN WITH THE KING!
THE REVOLUTION IS LIKE A BICYCLE. WHEN THE WHEELS DON'T TURN, IT FALLS.
WELL SPOKEN!
AND SO WENT THE REVOLUTION IN MY COUNTRY.

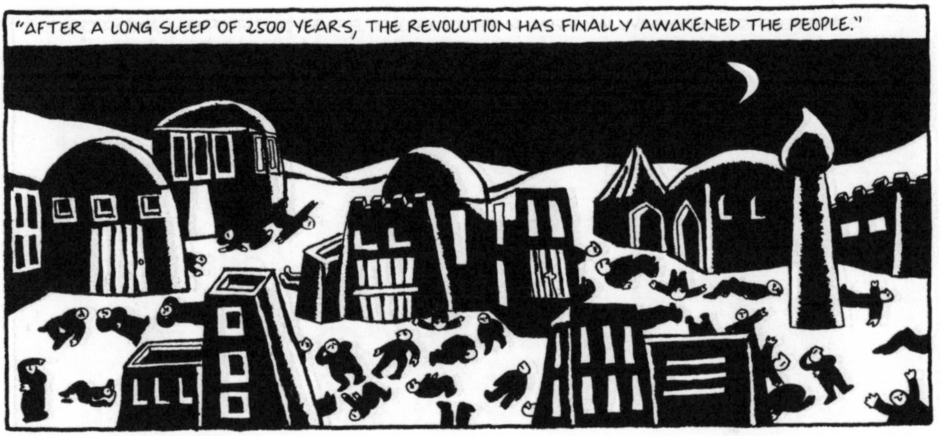
"AFTER A LONG SLEEP OF 2500 YEARS, THE REVOLUTION HAS FINALLY AWAKENED THE PEOPLE."

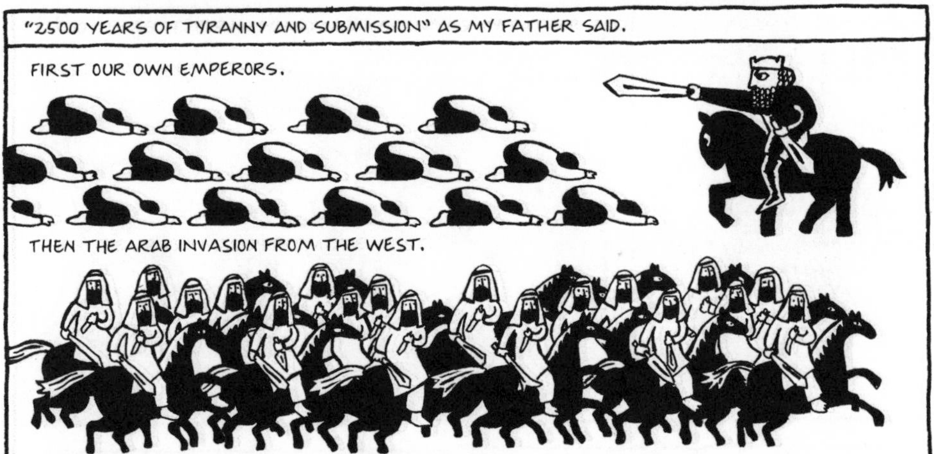
"2500 YEARS OF TYRANNY AND SUBMISSION" AS MY FATHER SAID.
FIRST OUR OWN EMPERORS.
THEN THE ARAB INVASION FROM THE WEST.
FOLLOWED BY THE MONGOLIAN INVASION FROM THE EAST.
AND FINALLY MODERN IMPERIALISM.

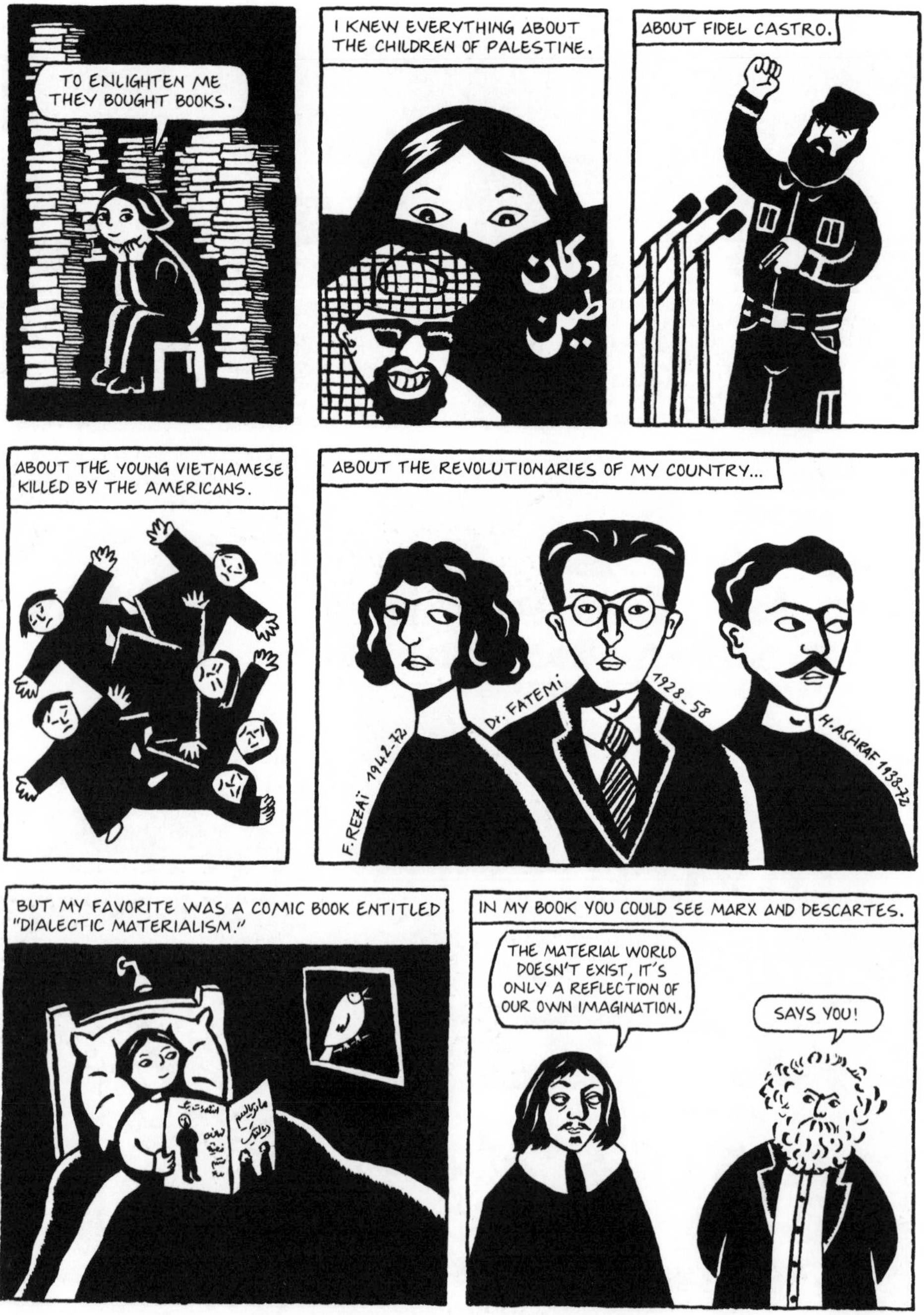
TO ENLIGHTEN ME THEY BOUGHT BOOKS.
I KNEW EVERYTHING ABOUT THE CHILDREN OF PALESTINE.
ABOUT FIDEL CASTRO.
ABOUT THE YOUNG VIETNAMESE KILLED BY THE AMERICANS.
ABOUT THE REVOLUTIONARIES OF MY COUNTRY...
F. REZAÏ 1942-72
Dr. FATEMI
1928-58
H. ASHRAF 1938-72
BUT MY FAVORITE WAS A COMIC BOOK ENTITLED "DIALECTIC MATERIALISM."
IN MY BOOK YOU COULD SEE MARX AND DESCARTES.
THE MATERIAL WORLD DOESN'T EXIST, IT'S ONLY A REFLECTION OF OUR OWN IMAGINATION.
SAYS YOU!

13

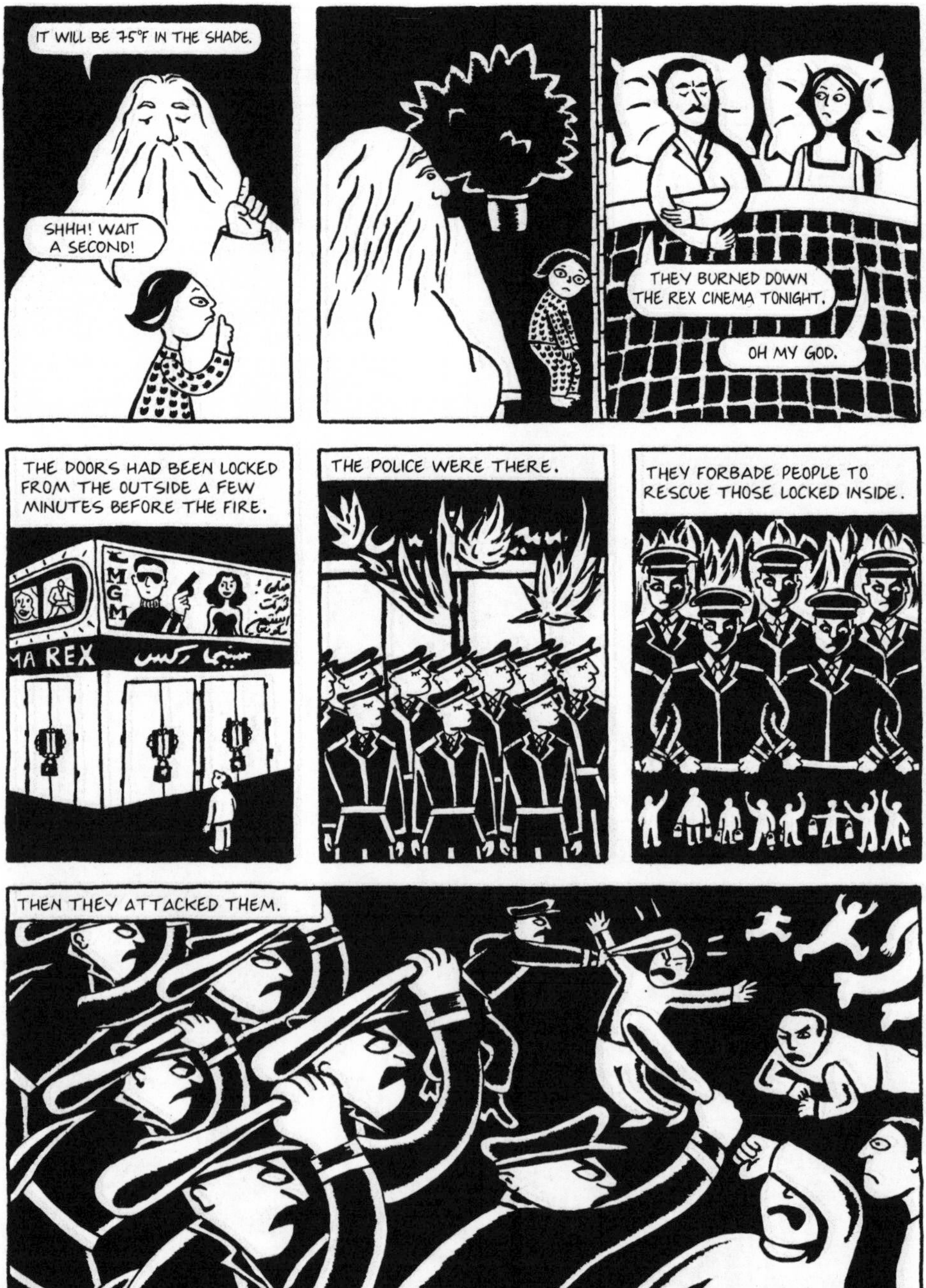

IT WILL BE 75°F IN THE SHADE.
SHHH! WAIT A SECOND!
THEY BURNED DOWN THE REX CINEMA TONIGHT.
OH MY GOD.
THE DOORS HAD BEEN LOCKED FROM THE OUTSIDE A FEW MINUTES BEFORE THE FIRE.
MGM
MA REX
THE POLICE WERE THERE.
THEY FORBADE PEOPLE TO RESCUE THOSE LOCKED INSIDE.
THEN THEY ATTACKED THEM.

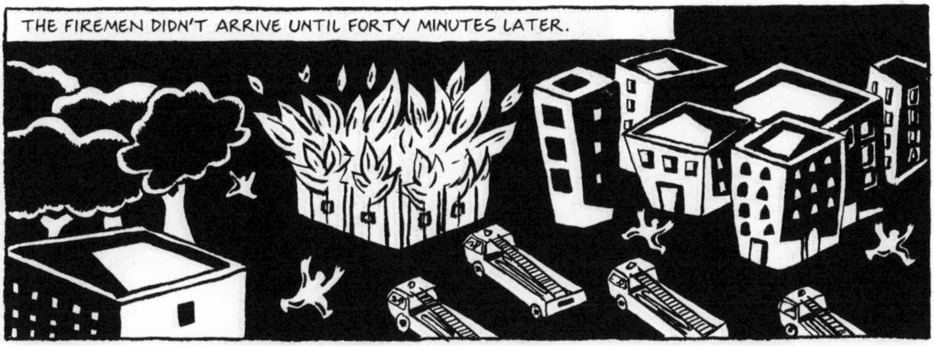
THE FIREMEN DIDN'T ARRIVE UNTIL FORTY MINUTES LATER.

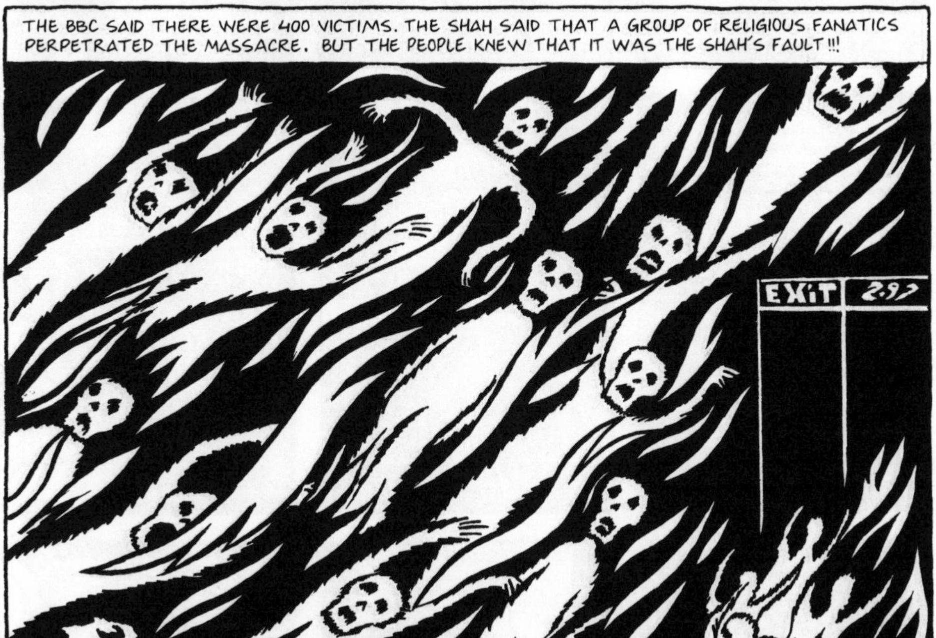
THE BBC SAID THERE WERE 400 VICTIMS. THE SHAH SAID THAT A GROUP OF RELIGIOUS FANATICS PERPETRATED THE MASSACRE. BUT THE PEOPLE KNEW THAT IT WAS THE SHAH'S FAULT!!!
EXIT

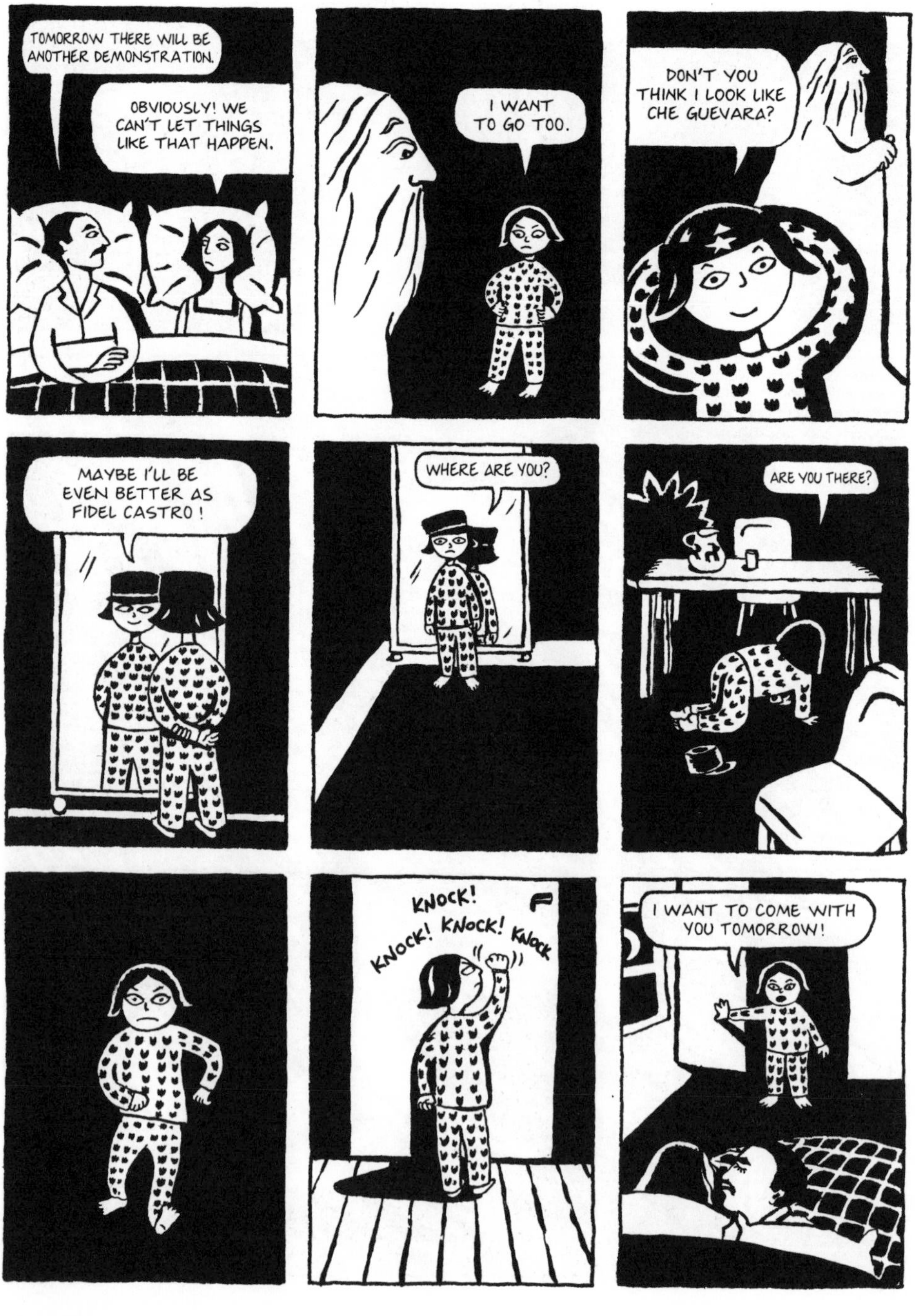

TOMORROW THERE WILL BE ANOTHER DEMONSTRATION.
OBVIOUSLY! WE CAN'T LET THINGS LIKE THAT HAPPEN.
I WANT TO GO TOO.
DON'T YOU THINK I LOOK LIKE CHE GUEVARA?
MAYBE I'LL BE EVEN BETTER AS FIDEL CASTRO !
WHERE ARE YOU?
ARE YOU THERE?
KNOCK!
KNOCK! KNOCK! KNOCK
I WANT TO COME WITH YOU TOMORROW!

THE WATER CELL

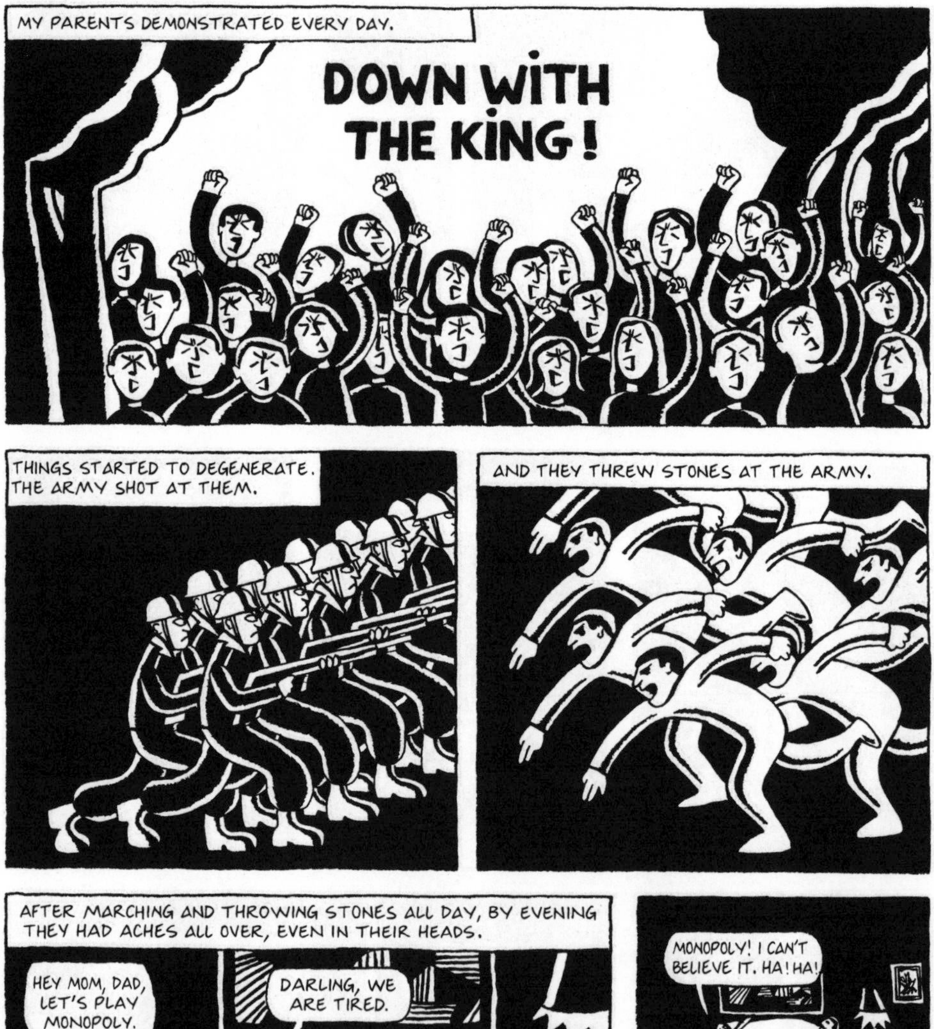

MY PARENTS DEMONSTRATED EVERY DAY.
DOWN WITH THE KING!
THINGS STARTED TO DEGENERATE. THE ARMY SHOT AT THEM.
AND THEY THREW STONES AT THE ARMY.
AFTER MARCHING AND THROWING STONES ALL DAY, BY EVENING THEY HAD ACHES ALL OVER, EVEN IN THEIR HEADS.
HEY MOM, DAD, LET'S PLAY MONOPOLY.
DARLING, WE ARE TIRED.
NOW IS NOT THE RIGHT TIME.
MONOPOLY! I CAN'T BELIEVE IT. HA! HA!
IT IS NEVER THE RIGHT TIME!

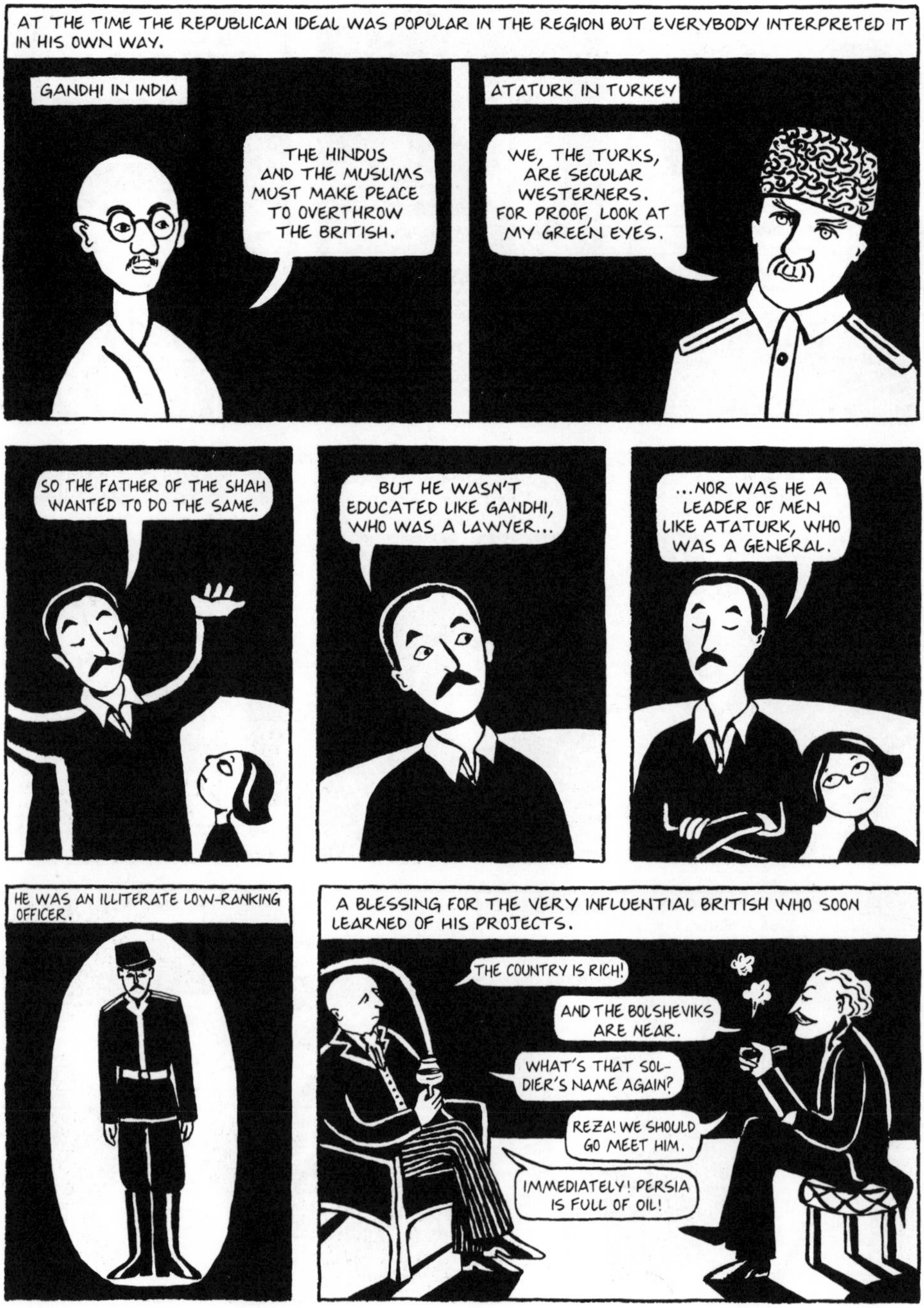

AT THE TIME THE REPUBLICAN IDEAL WAS POPULAR IN THE REGION BUT EVERYBODY INTERPRETED IT IN HIS OWN WAY.
GANDHI IN INDIA
THE HINDUS AND THE MUSLIMS MUST MAKE PEACE TO OVERTHROW THE BRITISH.
ATATURK IN TURKEY
WE, THE TURKS, ARE SECULAR WESTERNERS. FOR PROOF, LOOK AT MY GREEN EYES.
SO THE FATHER OF THE SHAH WANTED TO DO THE SAME.
BUT HE WASN'T EDUCATED LIKE GANDHI, WHO WAS A LAWYER...
...NOR WAS HE A LEADER OF MEN LIKE ATATURK, WHO WAS A GENERAL.
HE WAS AN ILLITERATE LOW-RANKING OFFICER.
A BLESSING FOR THE VERY INFLUENTIAL BRITISH WHO SOON LEARNED OF HIS PROJECTS.
THE COUNTRY IS RICH!
AND THE BOLSHEVIKS ARE NEAR.
WHAT'S THAT SOLDIER'S NAME AGAIN?
REZA! WE SHOULD GO MEET HIM.
IMMEDIATELY! PERSIA IS FULL OF OIL!

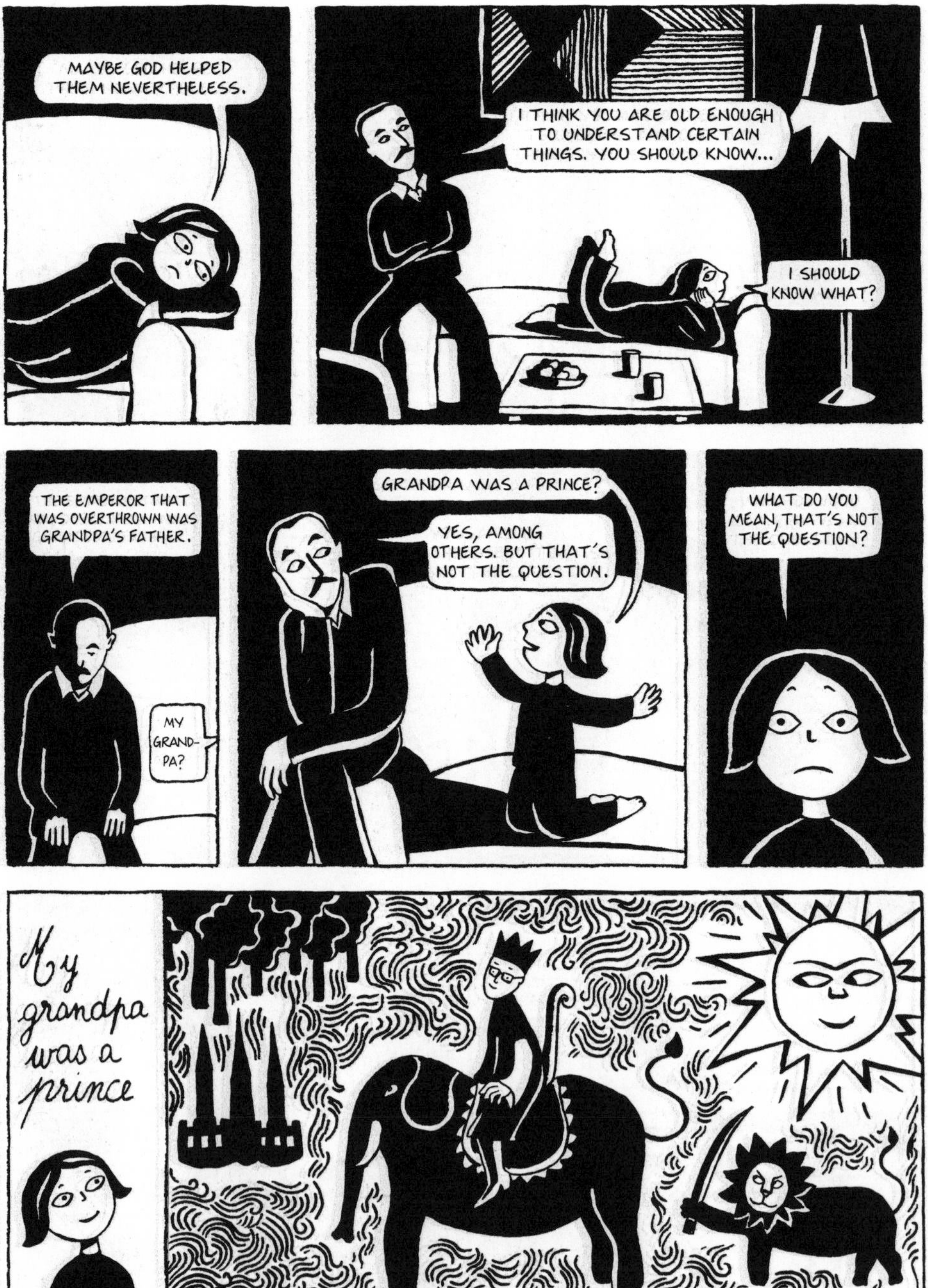
MAYBE GOD HELPED THEM NEVERTHELESS.
I THINK YOU ARE OLD ENOUGH TO UNDERSTAND CERTAIN THINGS. YOU SHOULD KNOW...
I SHOULD KNOW WHAT?
THE EMPEROR THAT WAS OVERTHROWN WAS GRANDPA'S FATHER.
MY GRAND-PA?
GRANDPA WAS A PRINCE?
YES, AMONG OTHERS. BUT THAT'S NOT THE QUESTION.
WHAT DO YOU MEAN, THAT'S NOT THE QUESTION?
My grandpa was a prince

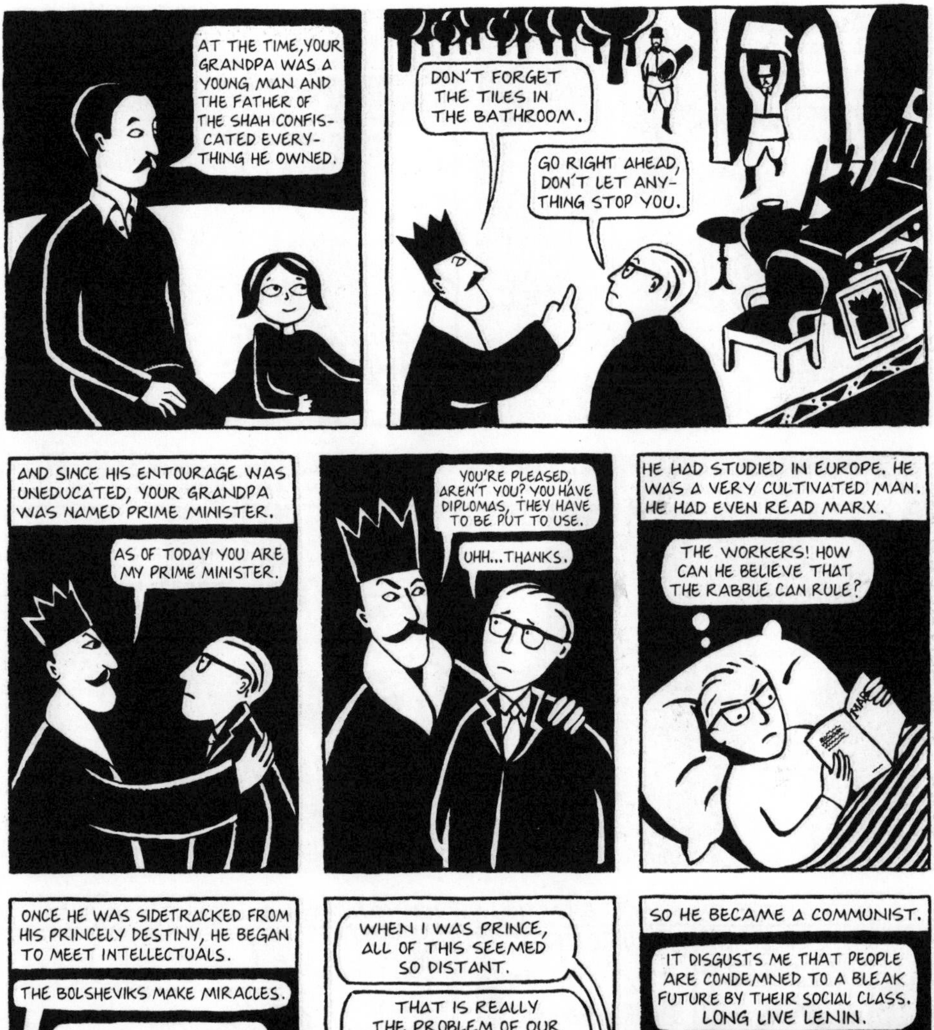
AT THE TIME, YOUR GRANDPA WAS A YOUNG MAN AND THE FATHER OF THE SHAH CONFISCATED EVERYTHING HE OWNED.
DON'T FORGET THE TILES IN THE BATHROOM.
GO RIGHT AHEAD, DON'T LET ANYTHING STOP YOU.
AND SINCE HIS ENTOURAGE WAS UNEDUCATED, YOUR GRANDPA WAS NAMED PRIME MINISTER.
AS OF TODAY YOU ARE MY PRIME MINISTER.
YOU'RE PLEASED, AREN'T YOU? YOU HAVE DIPLOMAS, THEY HAVE TO BE PUT TO USE.
UHH...THANKS.
HE HAD STUDIED IN EUROPE. HE WAS A VERY CULTIVATED MAN. HE HAD EVEN READ MARX.
THE WORKERS! HOW CAN HE BELIEVE THAT THE RABBLE CAN RULE?
ONCE HE WAS SIDETRACKED FROM HIS PRINCELY DESTINY, HE BEGAN TO MEET INTELLECTUALS.
THE BOLSHEVIKS MAKE MIRACLES.
THE EMPEROR OF PERSIA IS NOT REZA SHAH BUT THE KING OF ENGLAND.
WHEN I WAS PRINCE, ALL OF THIS SEEMED SO DISTANT.
THAT IS REALLY THE PROBLEM OF OUR COUNTRY: ONLY A PRINCE CAN ALLOW HIMSELF TO HAVE A CONSCIENCE.
SO HE BECAME A COMMUNIST.
IT DISGUSTS ME THAT PEOPLE ARE CONDEMNED TO A BLEAK FUTURE BY THEIR SOCIAL CLASS. LONG LIVE LENIN.

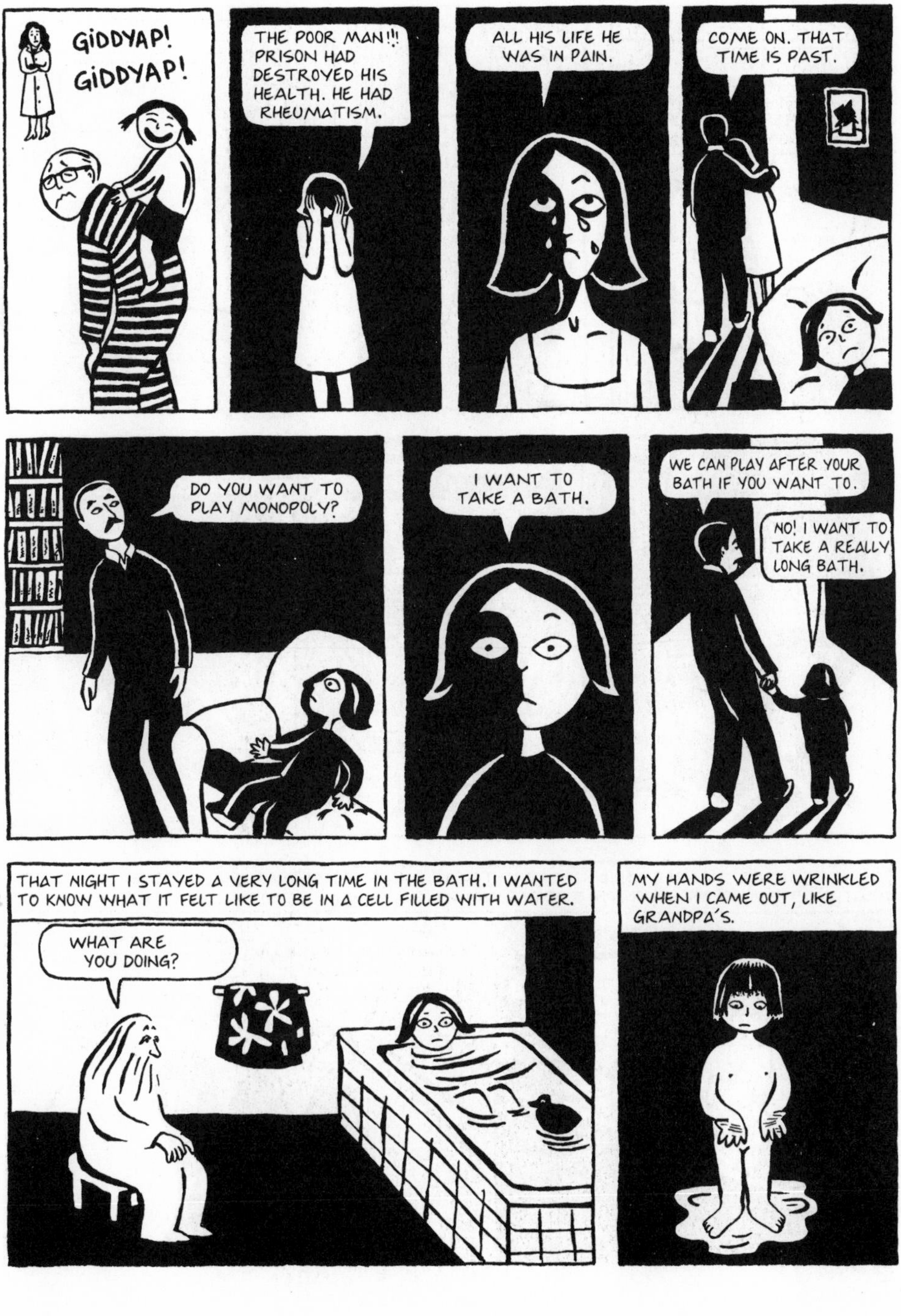
GIDDYAP! GIDDYAP!
THE POOR MAN!!! PRISON HAD DESTROYED HIS HEALTH. HE HAD RHEUMATISM.
ALL HIS LIFE HE WAS IN PAIN.
COME ON. THAT TIME IS PAST.
DO YOU WANT TO PLAY MONOPOLY?
I WANT TO TAKE A BATH.
WE CAN PLAY AFTER YOUR BATH IF YOU WANT TO.
NO! I WANT TO TAKE A REALLY LONG BATH.
THAT NIGHT I STAYED A VERY LONG TIME IN THE BATH. I WANTED TO KNOW WHAT IT FELT LIKE TO BE IN A CELL FILLED WITH WATER.
WHAT ARE YOU DOING?
MY HANDS WERE WRINKLED WHEN I CAME OUT, LIKE GRANDPA'S.

PERSEPOLIS

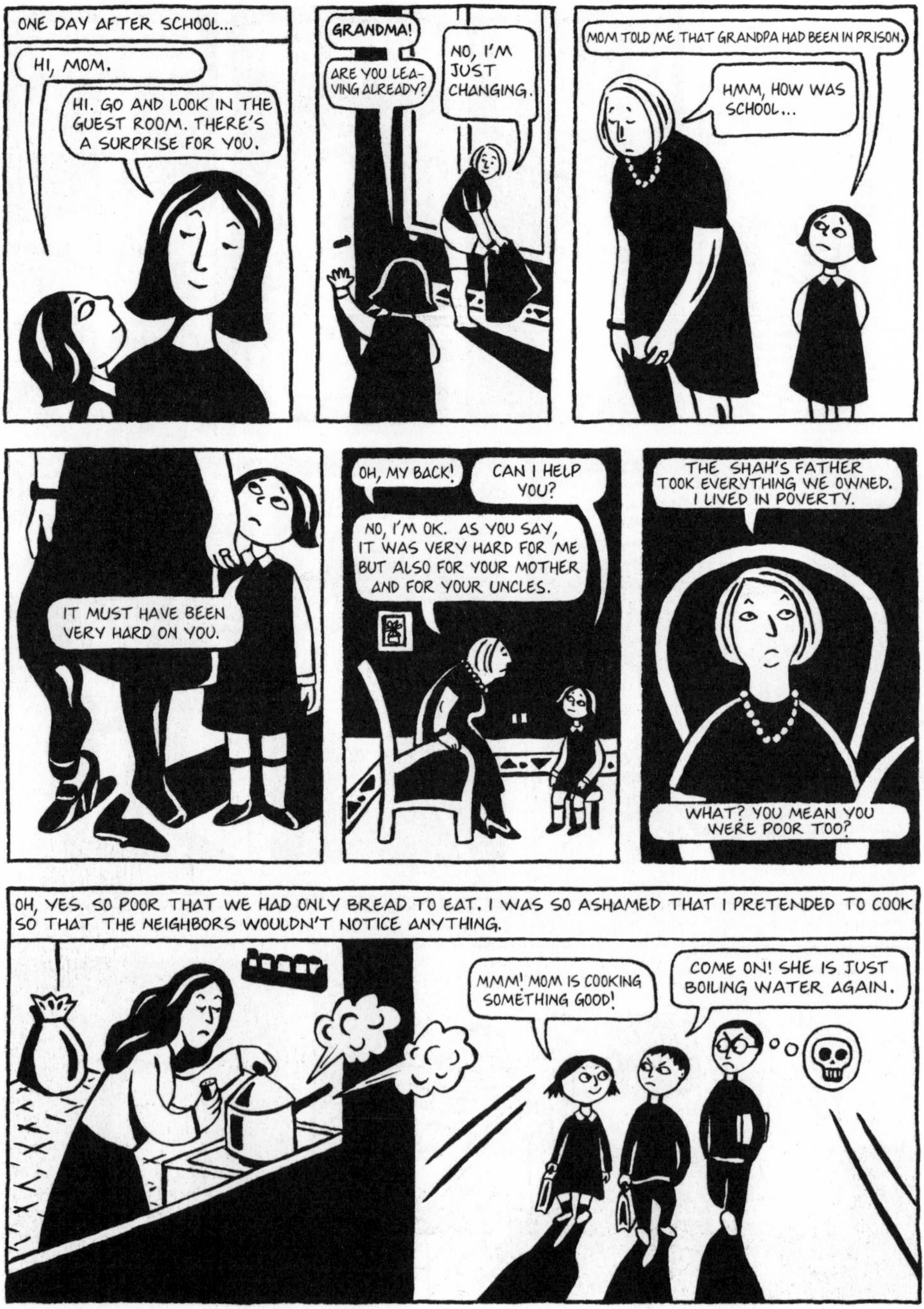

ONE DAY AFTER SCHOOL...
HI, MOM.
HI. GO AND LOOK IN THE GUEST ROOM. THERE'S A SURPRISE FOR YOU.
GRANDMA!
ARE YOU LEAVING ALREADY?
NO, I'M JUST CHANGING.
MOM TOLD ME THAT GRANDPA HAD BEEN IN PRISON.
HMM, HOW WAS SCHOOL...
IT MUST HAVE BEEN VERY HARD ON YOU.
OH, MY BACK!
CAN I HELP YOU?
NO, I'M OK. AS YOU SAY, IT WAS VERY HARD FOR ME BUT ALSO FOR YOUR MOTHER AND FOR YOUR UNCLES.
THE SHAH'S FATHER TOOK EVERYTHING WE OWNED. I LIVED IN POVERTY.
WHAT? YOU MEAN YOU WERE POOR TOO?
OH, YES. SO POOR THAT WE HAD ONLY BREAD TO EAT. I WAS SO ASHAMED THAT I PRETENDED TO COOK SO THAT THE NEIGHBORS WOULDN'T NOTICE ANYTHING.
MMM! MOM IS COOKING SOMETHING GOOD!
COME ON! SHE IS JUST BOILING WATER AGAIN.

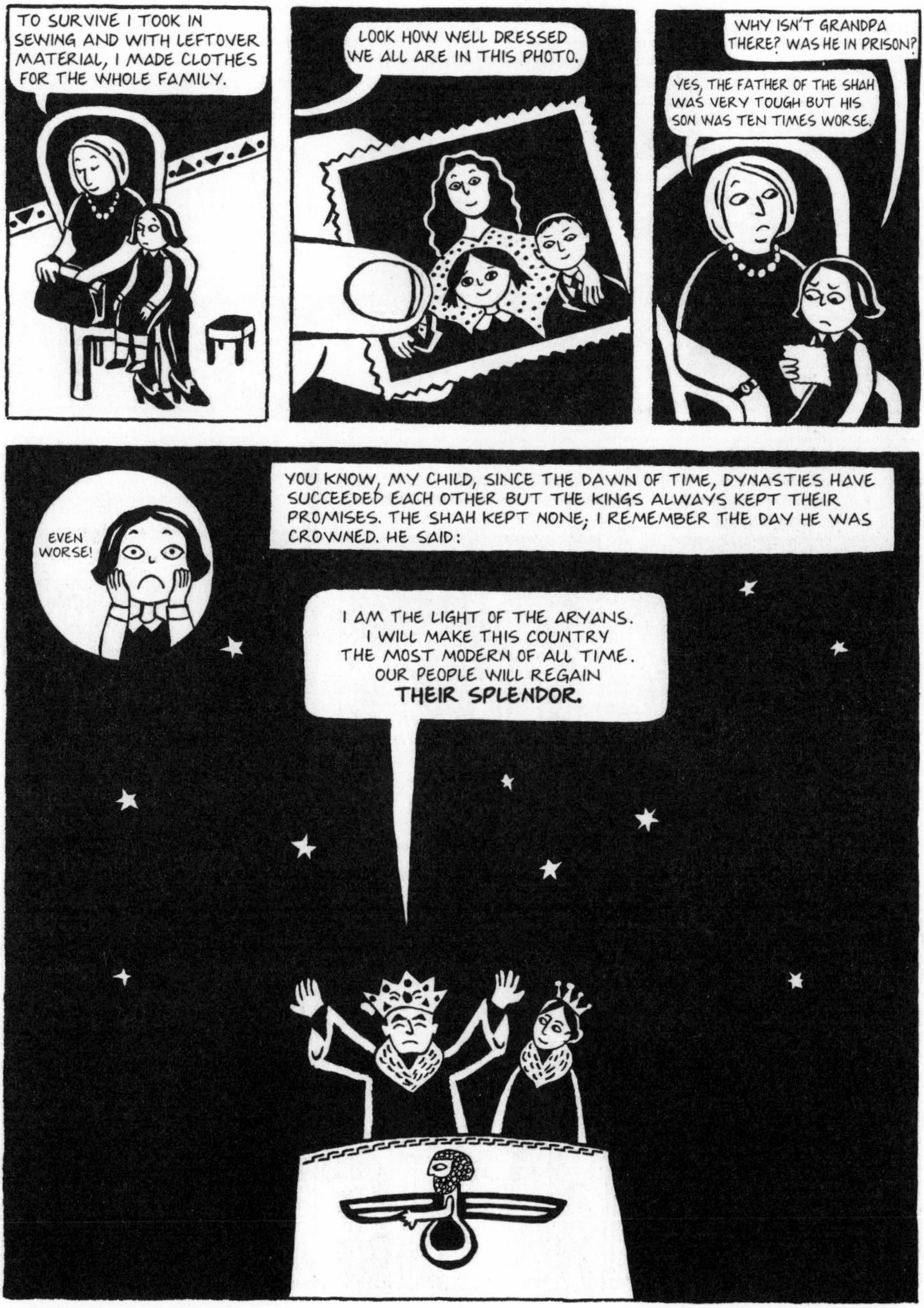
TO SURVIVE I TOOK IN SEWING AND WITH LEFTOVER MATERIAL, I MADE CLOTHES FOR THE WHOLE FAMILY.
LOOK HOW WELL DRESSED WE ALL ARE IN THIS PHOTO.
WHY ISN'T GRANDPA THERE? WAS HE IN PRISON?
YES, THE FATHER OF THE SHAH WAS VERY TOUGH BUT HIS SON WAS TEN TIMES WORSE.
EVEN WORSE!
YOU KNOW, MY CHILD, SINCE THE DAWN OF TIME, DYNASTIES HAVE SUCCEEDED EACH OTHER BUT THE KINGS ALWAYS KEPT THEIR PROMISES. THE SHAH KEPT NONE; I REMEMBER THE DAY HE WAS CROWNED. HE SAID:
I AM THE LIGHT OF THE ARYANS. I WILL MAKE THIS COUNTRY THE MOST MODERN OF ALL TIME. OUR PEOPLE WILL REGAIN **THEIR SPLENDOR.**

HE TOOK PHOTOS EVERY DAY. IT WAS STRICTLY FORBIDDEN. HE HAD EVEN BEEN ARRESTED ONCE BUT ESCAPED AT THE LAST MINUTE.

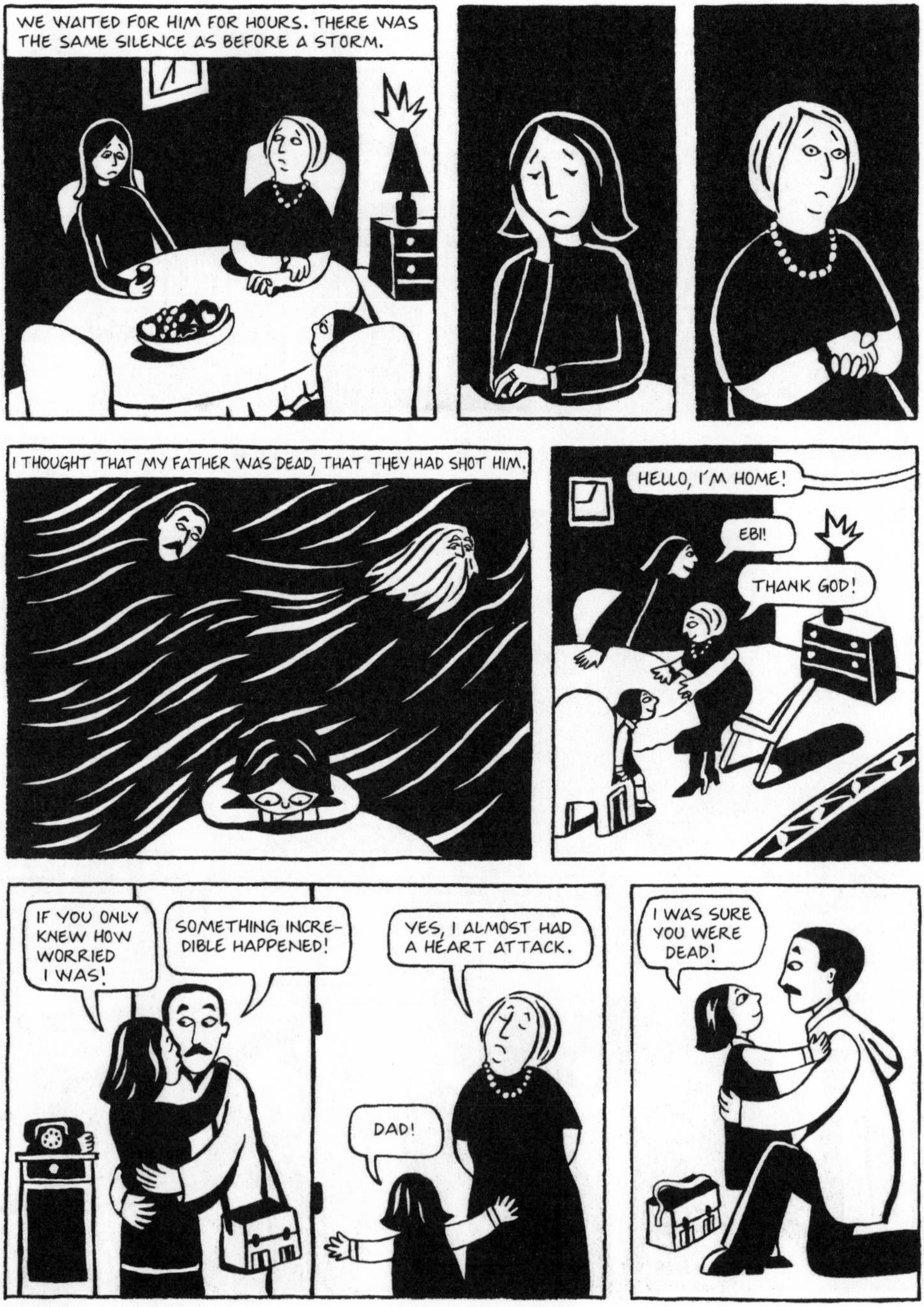
WE WAITED FOR HIM FOR HOURS. THERE WAS THE SAME SILENCE AS BEFORE A STORM.
I THOUGHT THAT MY FATHER WAS DEAD, THAT THEY HAD SHOT HIM.
HELLO, I'M HOME!
EBI!
THANK GOD!
IF YOU ONLY KNEW HOW WORRIED I WAS!
SOMETHING INCREDIBLE HAPPENED!
YES, I ALMOST HAD A HEART ATTACK.
DAD!
I WAS SURE YOU WERE DEAD!

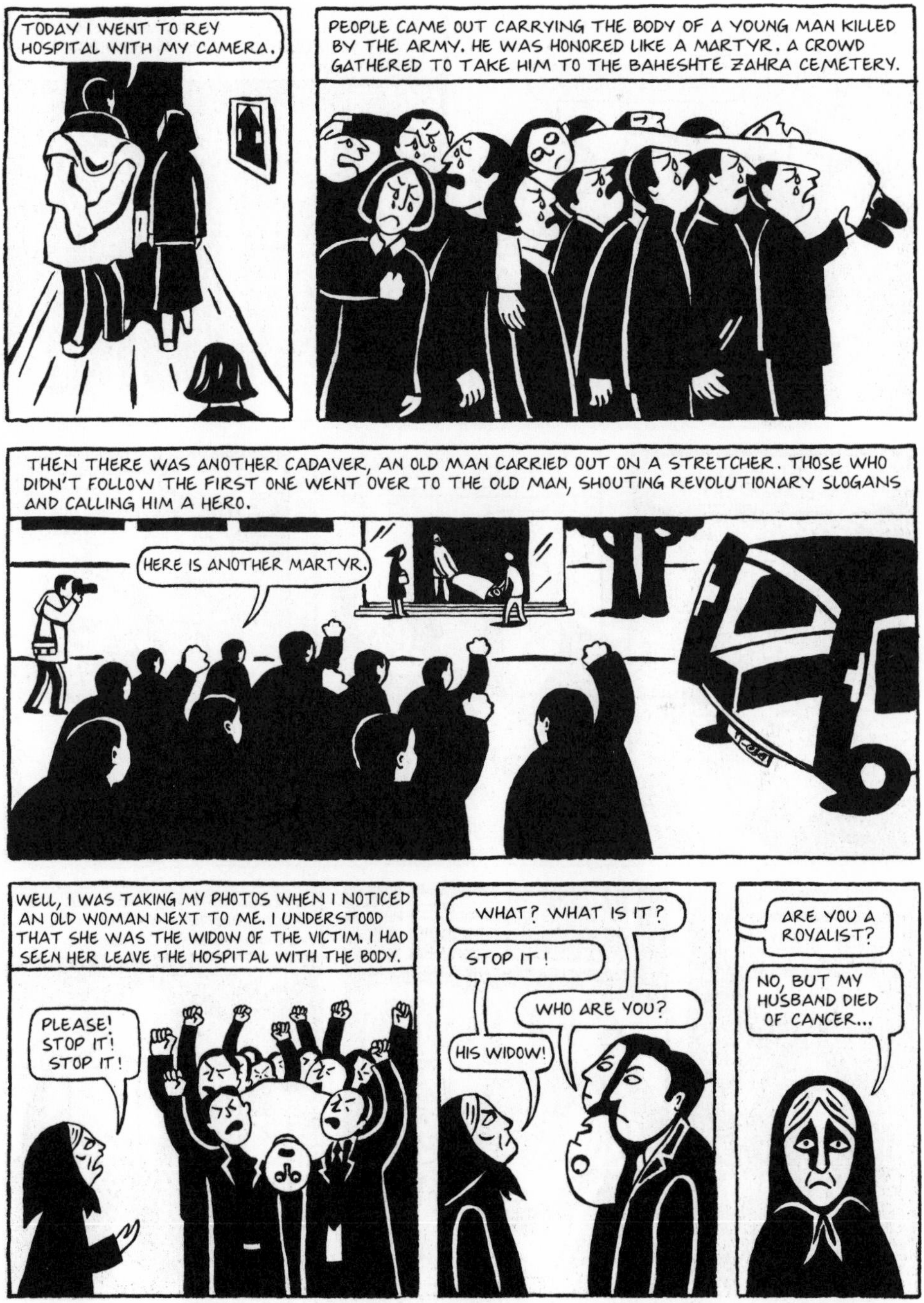
TODAY I WENT TO REY HOSPITAL WITH MY CAMERA.
PEOPLE CAME OUT CARRYING THE BODY OF A YOUNG MAN KILLED BY THE ARMY. HE WAS HONORED LIKE A MARTYR. A CROWD GATHERED TO TAKE HIM TO THE BAHESHTE ZAHRA CEMETERY.
THEN THERE WAS ANOTHER CADAVER, AN OLD MAN CARRIED OUT ON A STRETCHER. THOSE WHO DIDN'T FOLLOW THE FIRST ONE WENT OVER TO THE OLD MAN, SHOUTING REVOLUTIONARY SLOGANS AND CALLING HIM A HERO.
HERE IS ANOTHER MARTYR.
WELL, I WAS TAKING MY PHOTOS WHEN I NOTICED AN OLD WOMAN NEXT TO ME. I UNDERSTOOD THAT SHE WAS THE WIDOW OF THE VICTIM. I HAD SEEN HER LEAVE THE HOSPITAL WITH THE BODY.
PLEASE! STOP IT! STOP IT!
WHAT? WHAT IS IT?
STOP IT!
WHO ARE YOU?
HIS WIDOW!
ARE YOU A ROYALIST?
NO, BUT MY HUSBAND DIED OF CANCER...

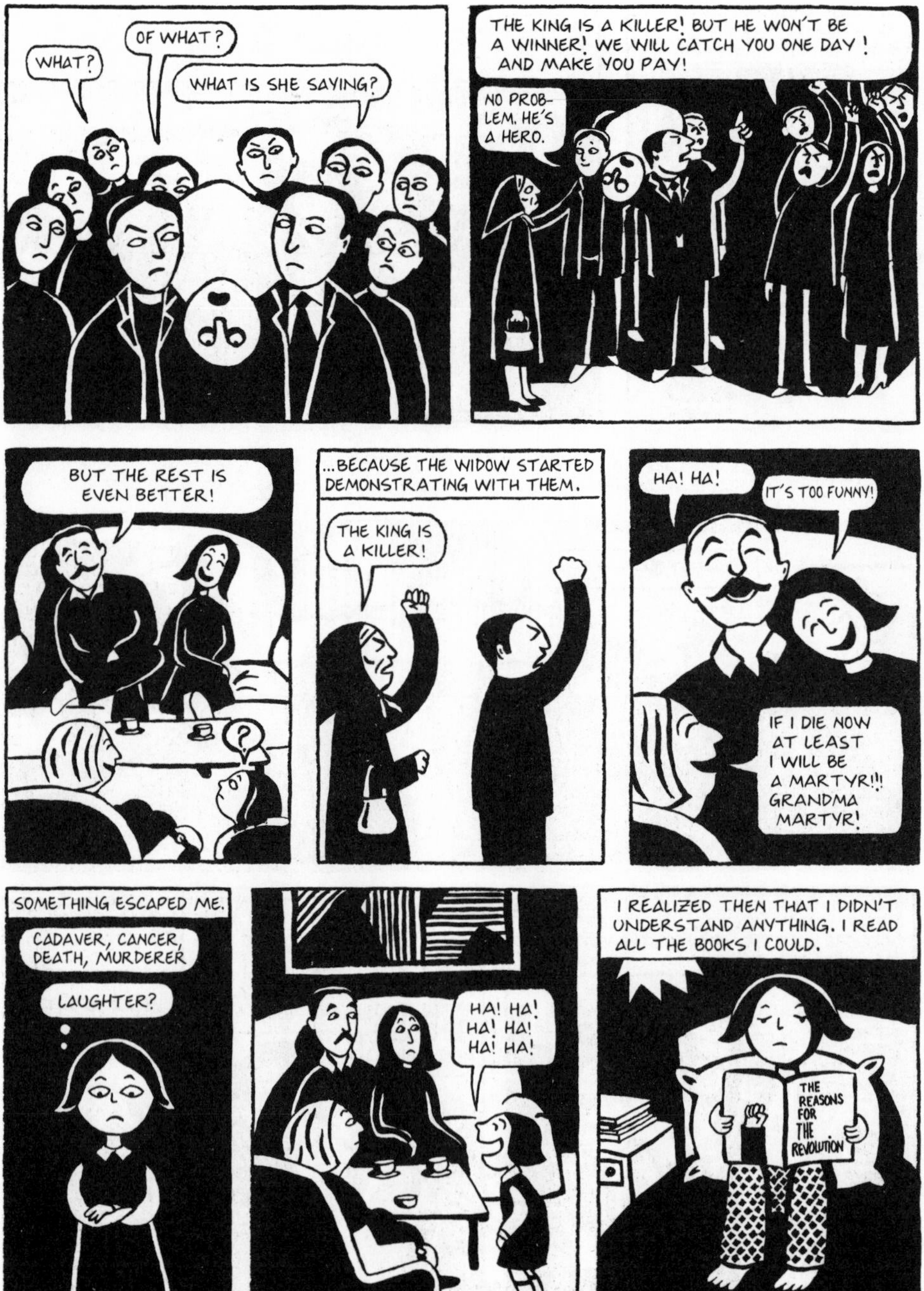
WHAT?
OF WHAT?
WHAT IS SHE SAYING?
THE KING IS A KILLER! BUT HE WON'T BE A WINNER! WE WILL CATCH YOU ONE DAY! AND MAKE YOU PAY!
NO PROBLEM. HE'S A HERO.
BUT THE REST IS EVEN BETTER!
?
...BECAUSE THE WIDOW STARTED DEMONSTRATING WITH THEM.
THE KING IS A KILLER!
HA! HA!
IT'S TOO FUNNY!
IF I DIE NOW AT LEAST I WILL BE A MARTYR!!! GRANDMA MARTYR!
SOMETHING ESCAPED ME.
CADAVER, CANCER, DEATH, MURDERER
LAUGHTER?
HA! HA! HA! HA! HA! HA!
I REALIZED THEN THAT I DIDN'T UNDERSTAND ANYTHING. I READ ALL THE BOOKS I COULD.
THE REASONS FOR THE REVOLUTION

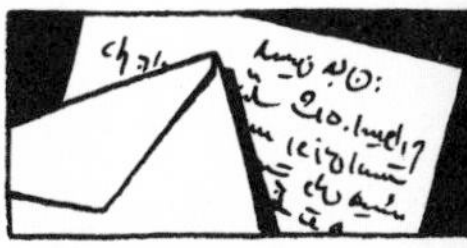

THE LETTER

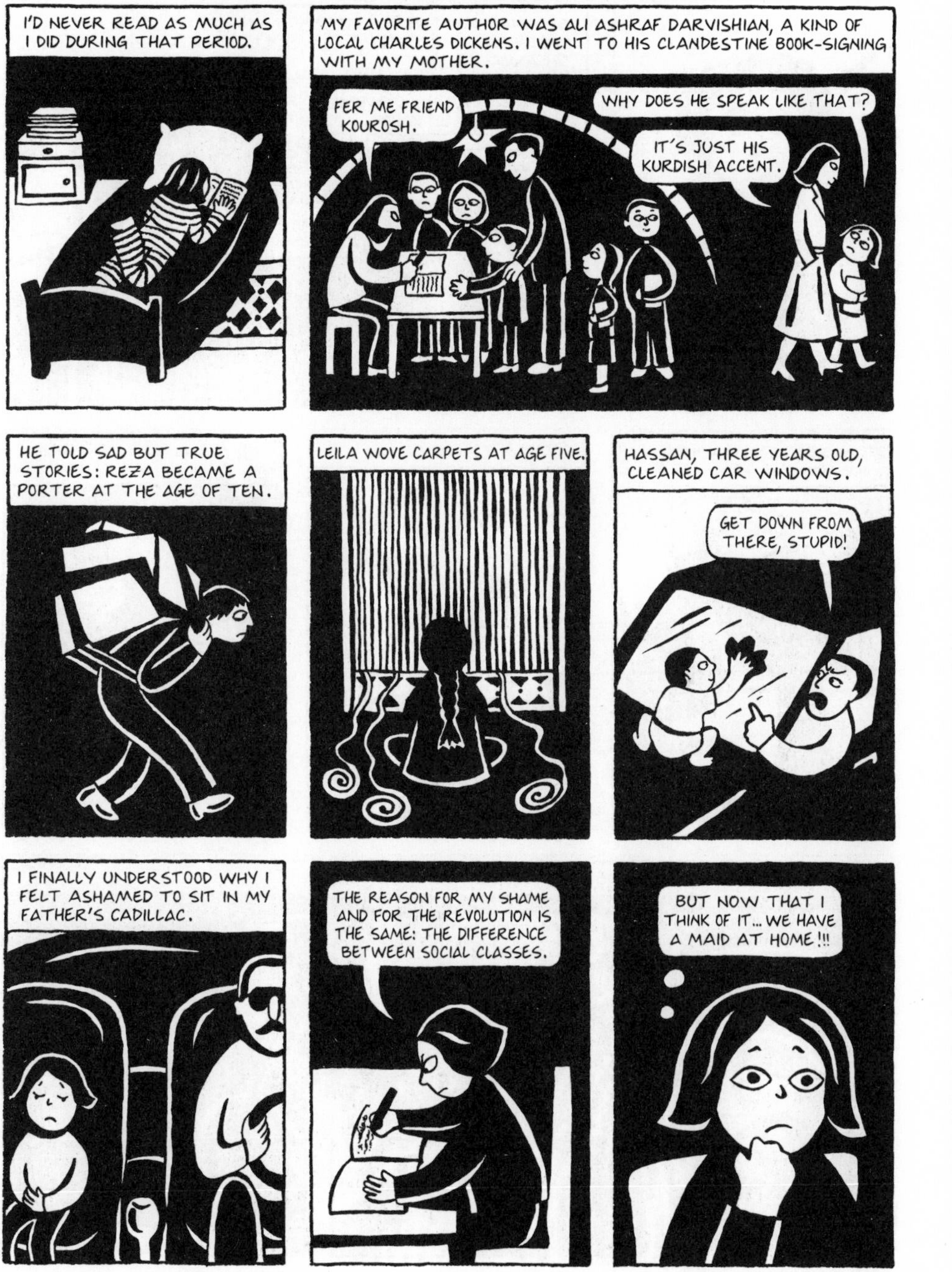

I'D NEVER READ AS MUCH AS I DID DURING THAT PERIOD.
MY FAVORITE AUTHOR WAS ALI ASHRAF DARVISHIAN, A KIND OF LOCAL CHARLES DICKENS. I WENT TO HIS CLANDESTINE BOOK-SIGNING WITH MY MOTHER.
FER ME FRIEND KOUROSH.
WHY DOES HE SPEAK LIKE THAT?
IT'S JUST HIS KURDISH ACCENT.
HE TOLD SAD BUT TRUE STORIES: REZA BECAME A PORTER AT THE AGE OF TEN.
LEILA WOVE CARPETS AT AGE FIVE.
HASSAN, THREE YEARS OLD, CLEANED CAR WINDOWS.
GET DOWN FROM THERE, STUPID!
I FINALLY UNDERSTOOD WHY I FELT ASHAMED TO SIT IN MY FATHER'S CADILLAC.
THE REASON FOR MY SHAME AND FOR THE REVOLUTION IS THE SAME: THE DIFFERENCE BETWEEN SOCIAL CLASSES.
BUT NOW THAT I THINK OF IT... WE HAVE A MAID AT HOME!!!

HER

THIS IS MEHRI.

SHE WAS EIGHT YEARS OLD WHEN SHE HAD TO LEAVE HER PARENTS' HOME TO COME TO WORK FOR US. JUST LIKE REZA, LEILA AND HASSAN.

WE HAVE TOO MANY CHILDREN, 14 OR 15 INCLUDING HER.

SHE WILL EAT WELL AT YOUR HOUSE.

WE WILL TAKE CARE OF HER.

SHE WAS JUST TEN YEARS OLD WHEN I WAS BORN...SHE TOOK CARE OF ME.

SHE PLAYED WITH ME.

AND SHE ALWAYS FINISHED MY FOOD.

SHE ALSO TOLD ME STORIES ABOUT JACKALS THAT SCARED ME.

AND IT CAME CLOSER! AND IT CAME CLOSER!

IN OTHER WORDS, WE GOT ALONG WELL.

35

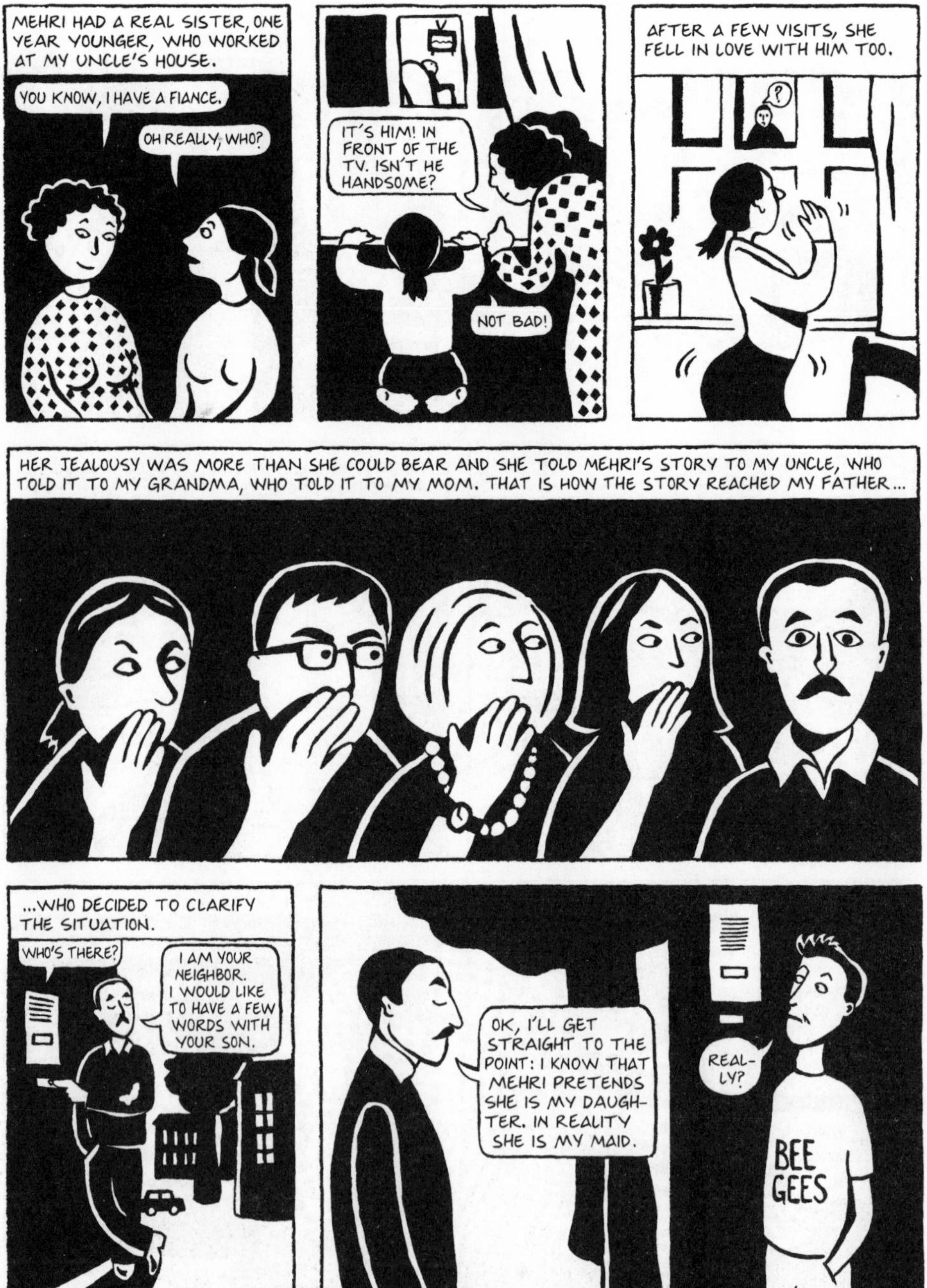
MEHRI HAD A REAL SISTER, ONE YEAR YOUNGER, WHO WORKED AT MY UNCLE'S HOUSE.
YOU KNOW, I HAVE A FIANCE.
OH REALLY, WHO?
IT'S HIM! IN FRONT OF THE TV. ISN'T HE HANDSOME?
NOT BAD!
AFTER A FEW VISITS, SHE FELL IN LOVE WITH HIM TOO.
?
HER JEALOUSY WAS MORE THAN SHE COULD BEAR AND SHE TOLD MEHRI'S STORY TO MY UNCLE, WHO TOLD IT TO MY GRANDMA, WHO TOLD IT TO MY MOM. THAT IS HOW THE STORY REACHED MY FATHER...
...WHO DECIDED TO CLARIFY THE SITUATION.
WHO'S THERE?
I AM YOUR NEIGHBOR. I WOULD LIKE TO HAVE A FEW WORDS WITH YOUR SON.
OK, I'LL GET STRAIGHT TO THE POINT: I KNOW THAT MEHRI PRETENDS SHE IS MY DAUGHTER. IN REALITY SHE IS MY MAID.
REAL-LY?
BEE GEES

38

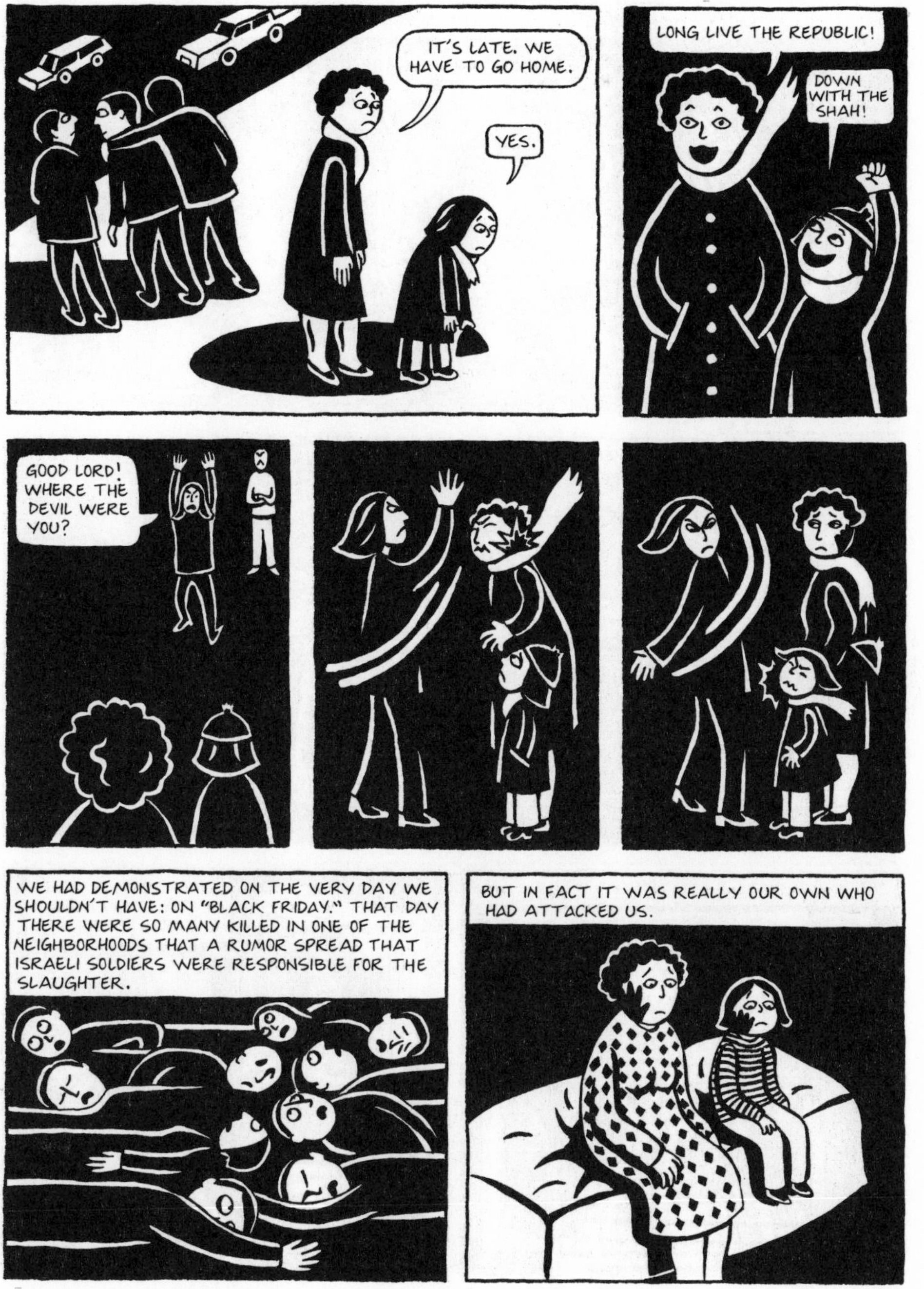
IT'S LATE. WE HAVE TO GO HOME.
YES.
LONG LIVE THE REPUBLIC!
DOWN WITH THE SHAH!
GOOD LORD! WHERE THE DEVIL WERE YOU?
WE HAD DEMONSTRATED ON THE VERY DAY WE SHOULDN'T HAVE: ON "BLACK FRIDAY." THAT DAY THERE WERE SO MANY KILLED IN ONE OF THE NEIGHBORHOODS THAT A RUMOR SPREAD THAT ISRAELI SOLDIERS WERE RESPONSIBLE FOR THE SLAUGHTER.
BUT IN FACT IT WAS REALLY OUR OWN WHO HAD ATTACKED US.

THE PARTY

AFTER BLACK FRIDAY, THERE WAS ONE MASSACRE AFTER ANOTHER. MANY PEOPLE WERE KILLED.

THE END OF THE SHAH'S REIGN WAS NEAR.

ONE DAY HE MADE A DECLARATION ON TV.

I UNDERSTAND YOUR REVOLT.

TOGETHER WE WILL TRY TO MARCH TOWARDS DEMOCRACY.

AFTER ALL THAT HE HAS DONE!

QUIET!

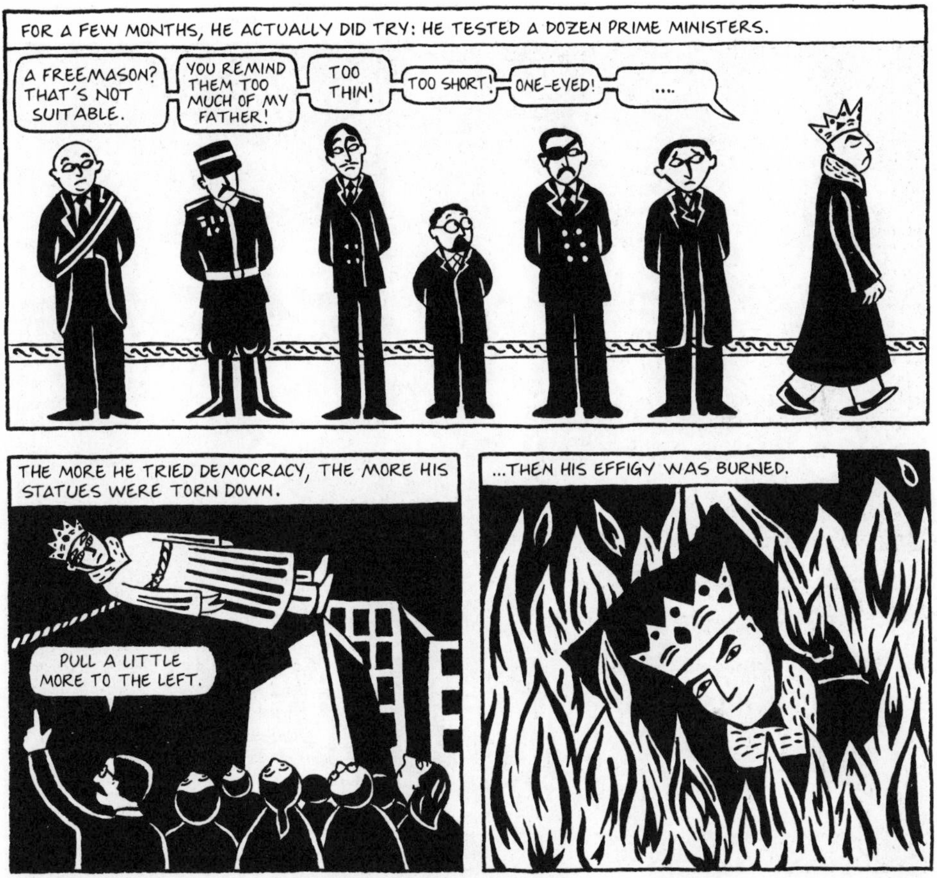
FOR A FEW MONTHS, HE ACTUALLY DID TRY: HE TESTED A DOZEN PRIME MINISTERS.
A FREEMASON? THAT'S NOT SUITABLE.
YOU REMIND THEM TOO MUCH OF MY FATHER!
TOO THIN!
TOO SHORT!
ONE-EYED!
....
THE MORE HE TRIED DEMOCRACY, THE MORE HIS STATUES WERE TORN DOWN.
PULL A LITTLE MORE TO THE LEFT.
...THEN HIS EFFIGY WAS BURNED.
THE PEOPLE WANTED ONLY ONE THING: HIS DEPARTURE! SO FINALLY...
OUT!
OUT!
OUT!
WE WILL NEVER FOR-GET YOU!

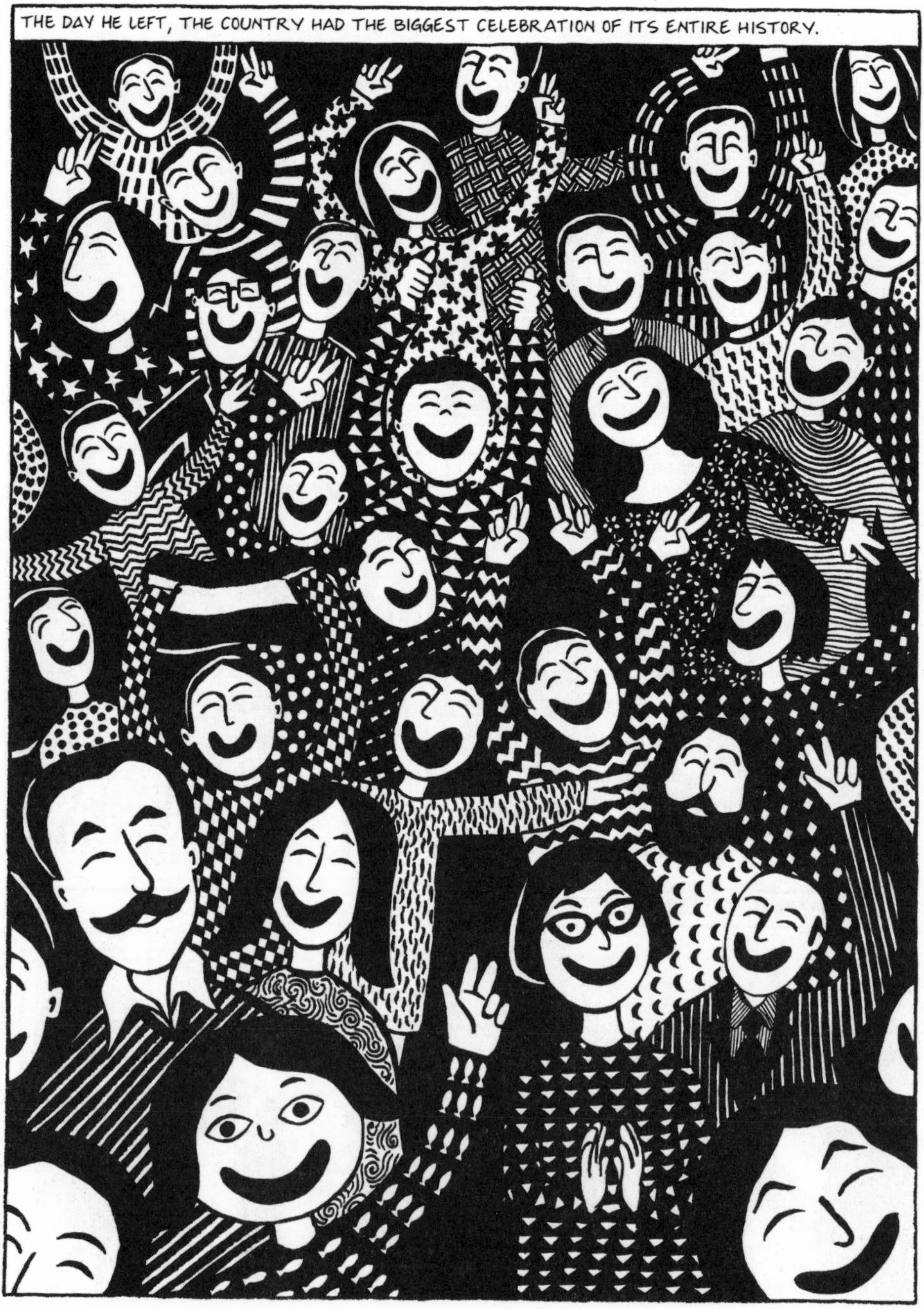
THE DAY HE LEFT, THE COUNTRY HAD THE BIGGEST CELEBRATION OF ITS ENTIRE HISTORY.

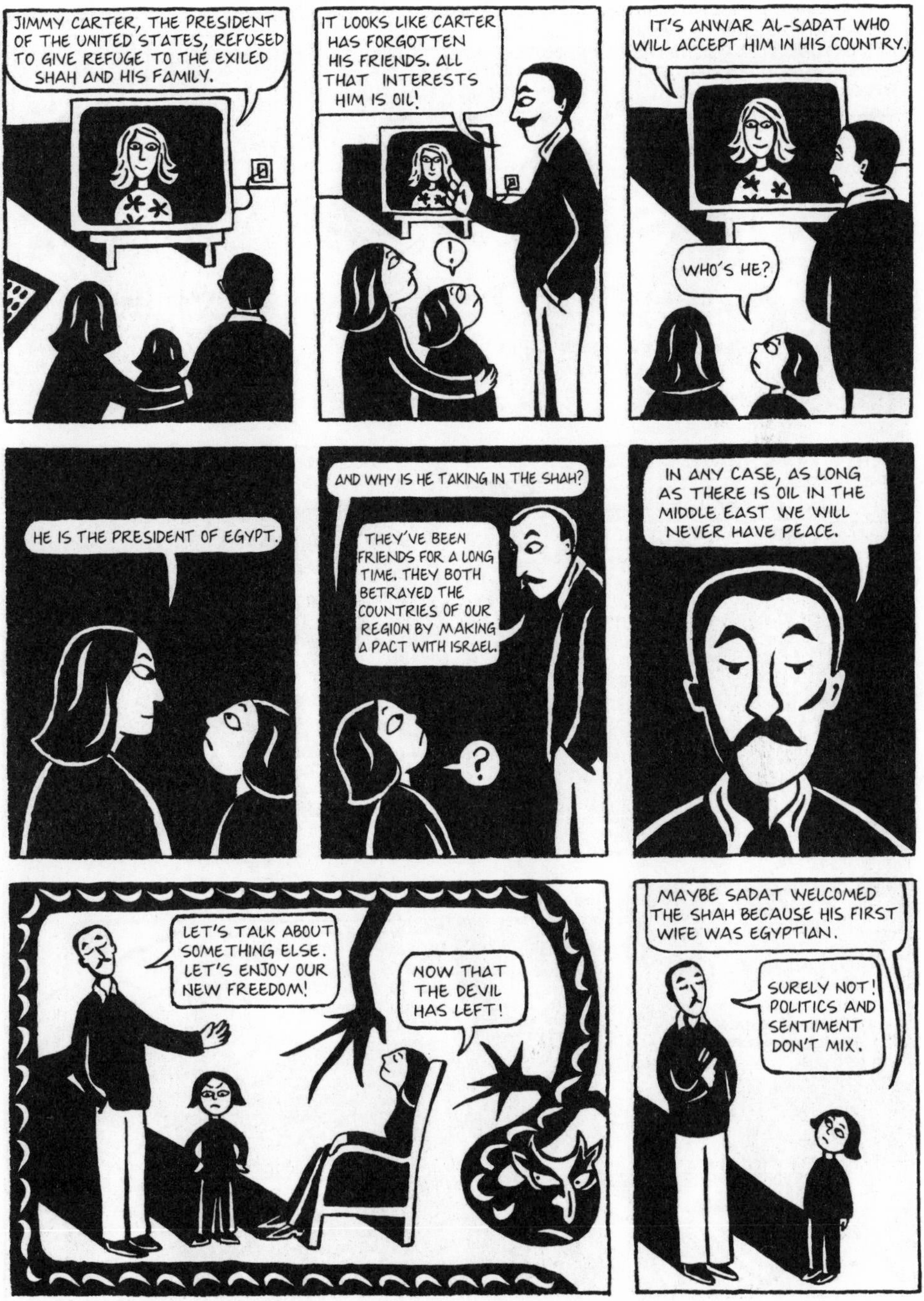

JIMMY CARTER, THE PRESIDENT OF THE UNITED STATES, REFUSED TO GIVE REFUGE TO THE EXILED SHAH AND HIS FAMILY.
IT LOOKS LIKE CARTER HAS FORGOTTEN HIS FRIENDS. ALL THAT INTERESTS HIM IS OIL!
!
IT'S ANWAR AL-SADAT WHO WILL ACCEPT HIM IN HIS COUNTRY.
WHO'S HE?
HE IS THE PRESIDENT OF EGYPT.
AND WHY IS HE TAKING IN THE SHAH?
THEY'VE BEEN FRIENDS FOR A LONG TIME. THEY BOTH BETRAYED THE COUNTRIES OF OUR REGION BY MAKING A PACT WITH ISRAEL.
?
IN ANY CASE, AS LONG AS THERE IS OIL IN THE MIDDLE EAST WE WILL NEVER HAVE PEACE.
LET'S TALK ABOUT SOMETHING ELSE. LET'S ENJOY OUR NEW FREEDOM!
NOW THAT THE DEVIL HAS LEFT!
MAYBE SADAT WELCOMED THE SHAH BECAUSE HIS FIRST WIFE WAS EGYPTIAN.
SURELY NOT! POLITICS AND SENTIMENT DON'T MIX.

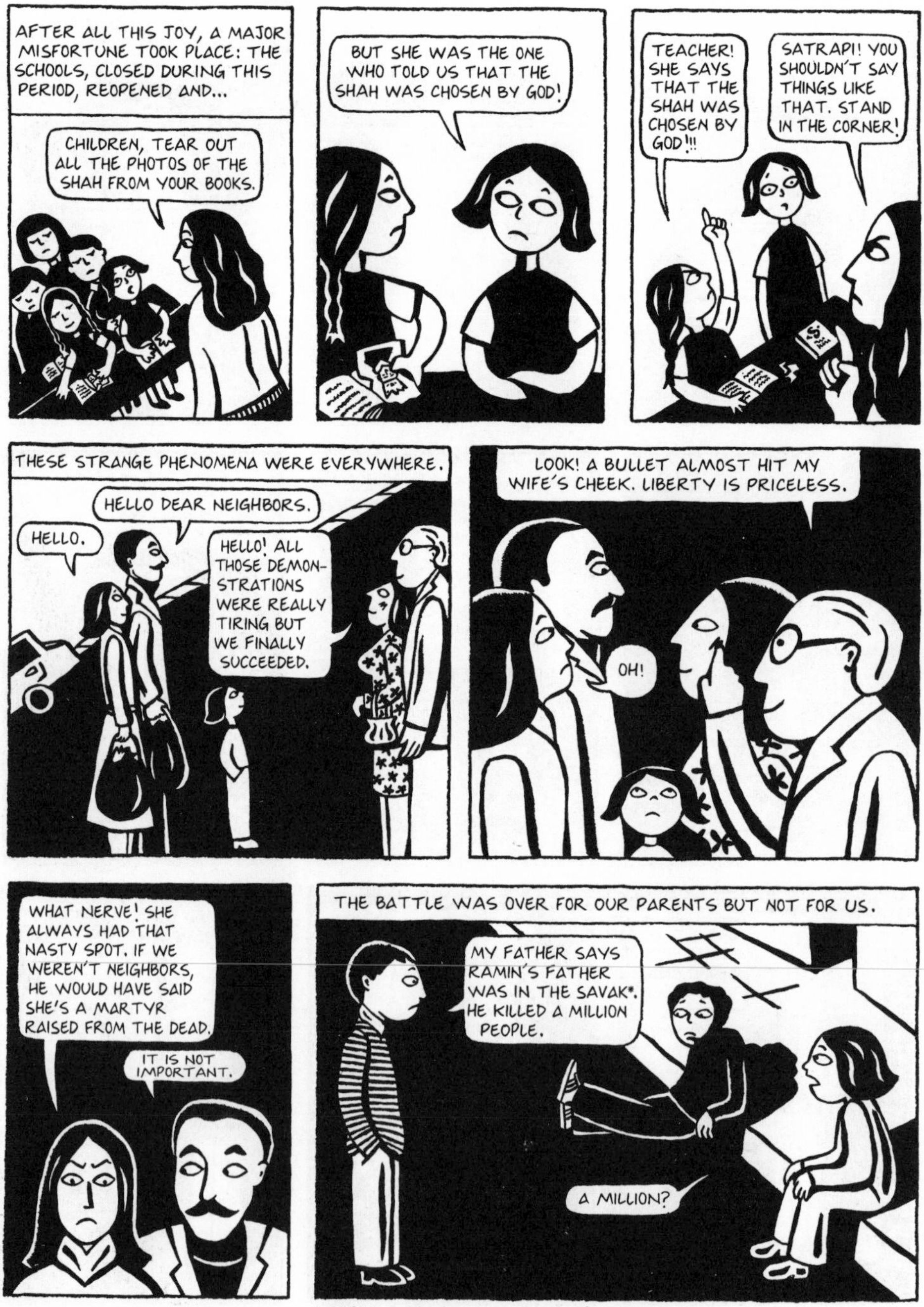
AFTER ALL THIS JOY, A MAJOR MISFORTUNE TOOK PLACE: THE SCHOOLS, CLOSED DURING THIS PERIOD, REOPENED AND...
CHILDREN, TEAR OUT ALL THE PHOTOS OF THE SHAH FROM YOUR BOOKS.
BUT SHE WAS THE ONE WHO TOLD US THAT THE SHAH WAS CHOSEN BY GOD!
TEACHER! SHE SAYS THAT THE SHAH WAS CHOSEN BY GOD!!!
SATRAPI! YOU SHOULDN'T SAY THINGS LIKE THAT. STAND IN THE CORNER!
THESE STRANGE PHENOMENA WERE EVERYWHERE.
HELLO DEAR NEIGHBORS.
HELLO.
HELLO! ALL THOSE DEMONSTRATIONS WERE REALLY TIRING BUT WE FINALLY SUCCEEDED.
LOOK! A BULLET ALMOST HIT MY WIFE'S CHEEK. LIBERTY IS PRICELESS.
OH!
WHAT NERVE! SHE ALWAYS HAD THAT NASTY SPOT. IF WE WEREN'T NEIGHBORS, HE WOULD HAVE SAID SHE'S A MARTYR RAISED FROM THE DEAD.
IT IS NOT IMPORTANT.
THE BATTLE WAS OVER FOR OUR PARENTS BUT NOT FOR US.
MY FATHER SAYS RAMIN'S FATHER WAS IN THE SAVAK*. HE KILLED A MILLION PEOPLE.
A MILLION?

* SECRET POLICE OF THE SHAH'S REGIME.

45

46

THE HEROES

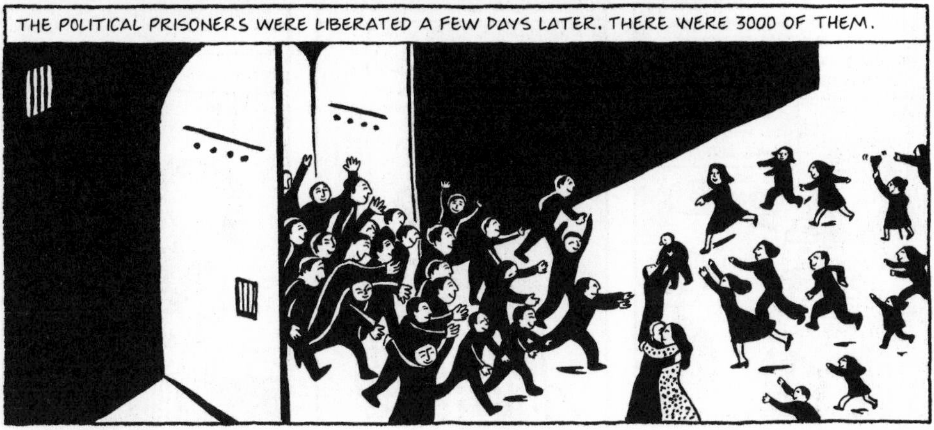
THE POLITICAL PRISONERS WERE LIBERATED A FEW DAYS LATER. THERE WERE 3000 OF THEM.

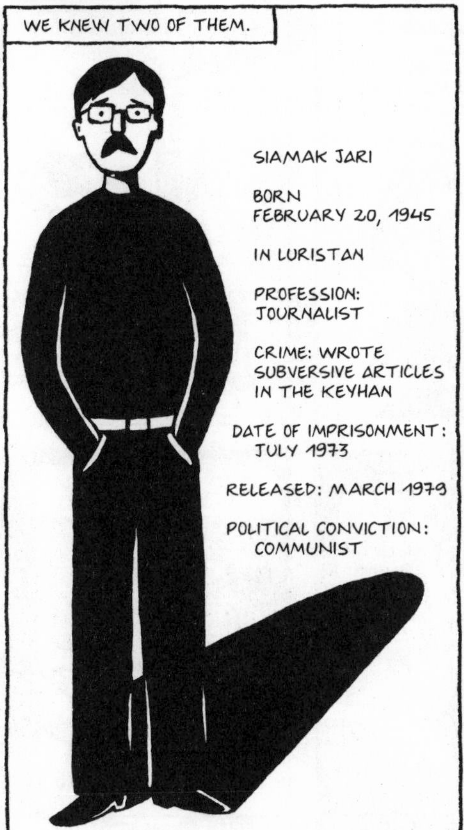
WE KNEW TWO OF THEM.
SIAMAK JARI
BORN
FEBRUARY 20, 1945
IN LURISTAN
PROFESSION:
JOURNALIST
CRIME: WROTE
SUBVERSIVE ARTICLES
IN THE KEYHAN
DATE OF IMPRISONMENT:
JULY 1973
RELEASED: MARCH 1979
POLITICAL CONVICTION:
COMMUNIST

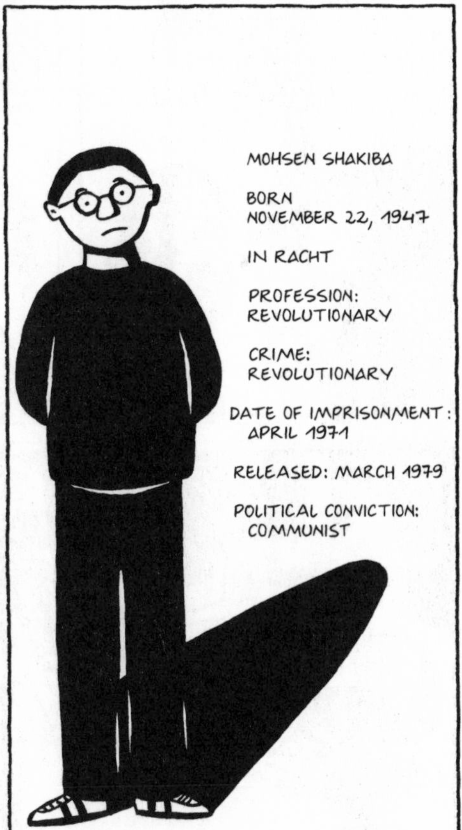
MOHSEN SHAKIBA
BORN
NOVEMBER 22, 1947
IN RACHT
PROFESSION:
REVOLUTIONARY
CRIME:
REVOLUTIONARY
DATE OF IMPRISONMENT:
APRIL 1971
RELEASED: MARCH 1979
POLITICAL CONVICTION:
COMMUNIST

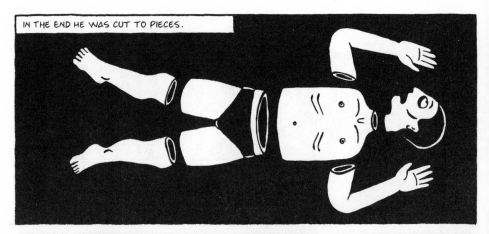

IN THE END HE WAS CUT TO PIECES.

HE WAS IN MY CLASS AT THE UNIVERSITY.

IT'S A GOOD THING THEY DIDN'T KILL YOUR FATHER IN PRISON.

BUT YOU HAVE TO ADMIT I WASN'T COMPLETELY WRONG WHEN I SAID HE WAS NOT ON A TRIP.

MAYBE, BUT MY FATHER IS A HERO!

ALL TORTURERS SHOULD BE MASSACRED!

MY FATHER WAS NOT A HERO, MY MOTHER WANTED TO KILL PEOPLE...SO I WENT OUT TO PLAY IN THE STREET.

MOSCOW

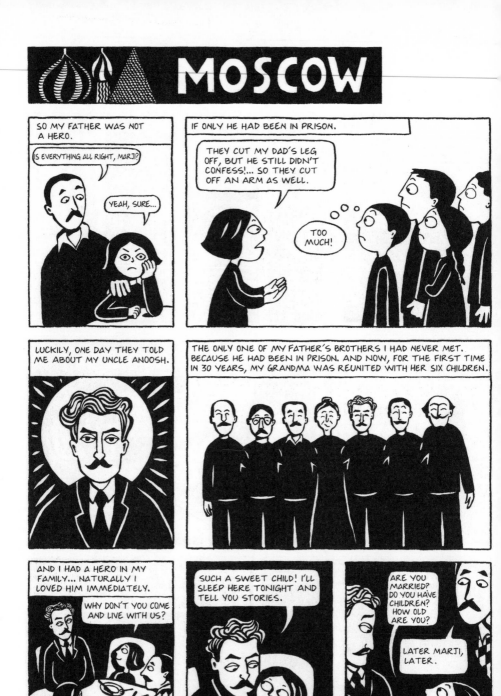

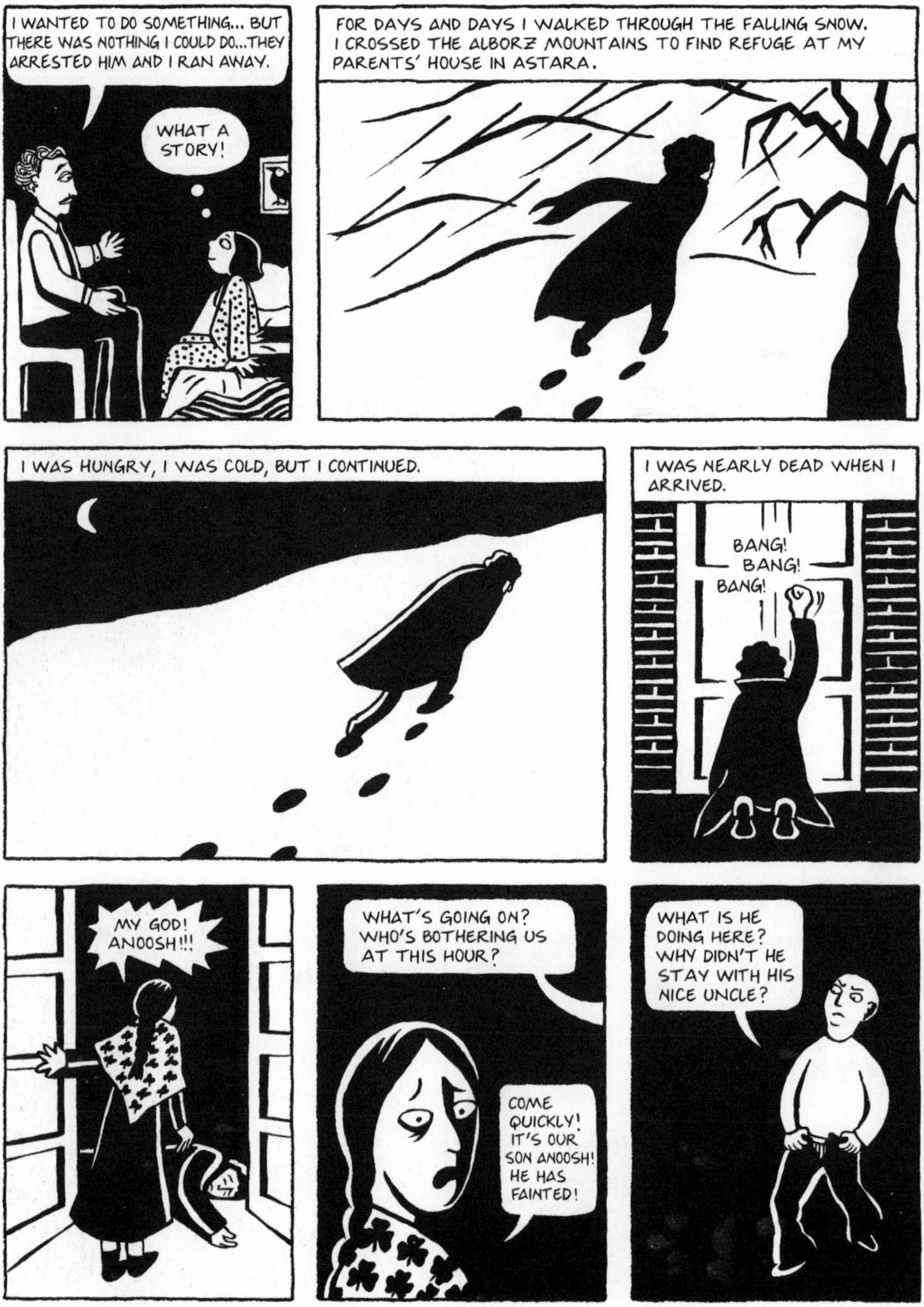
I WANTED TO DO SOMETHING... BUT THERE WAS NOTHING I COULD DO...THEY ARRESTED HIM AND I RAN AWAY.
WHAT A STORY!
FOR DAYS AND DAYS I WALKED THROUGH THE FALLING SNOW. I CROSSED THE ALBORZ MOUNTAINS TO FIND REFUGE AT MY PARENTS' HOUSE IN ASTARA.
I WAS HUNGRY, I WAS COLD, BUT I CONTINUED.
I WAS NEARLY DEAD WHEN I ARRIVED.
BANG! BANG! BANG!
MY GOD! ANOOSH!!!
WHAT'S GOING ON? WHO'S BOTHERING US AT THIS HOUR?
COME QUICKLY! IT'S OUR SON ANOOSH! HE HAS FAINTED!
WHAT IS HE DOING HERE? WHY DIDN'T HE STAY WITH HIS NICE UNCLE?

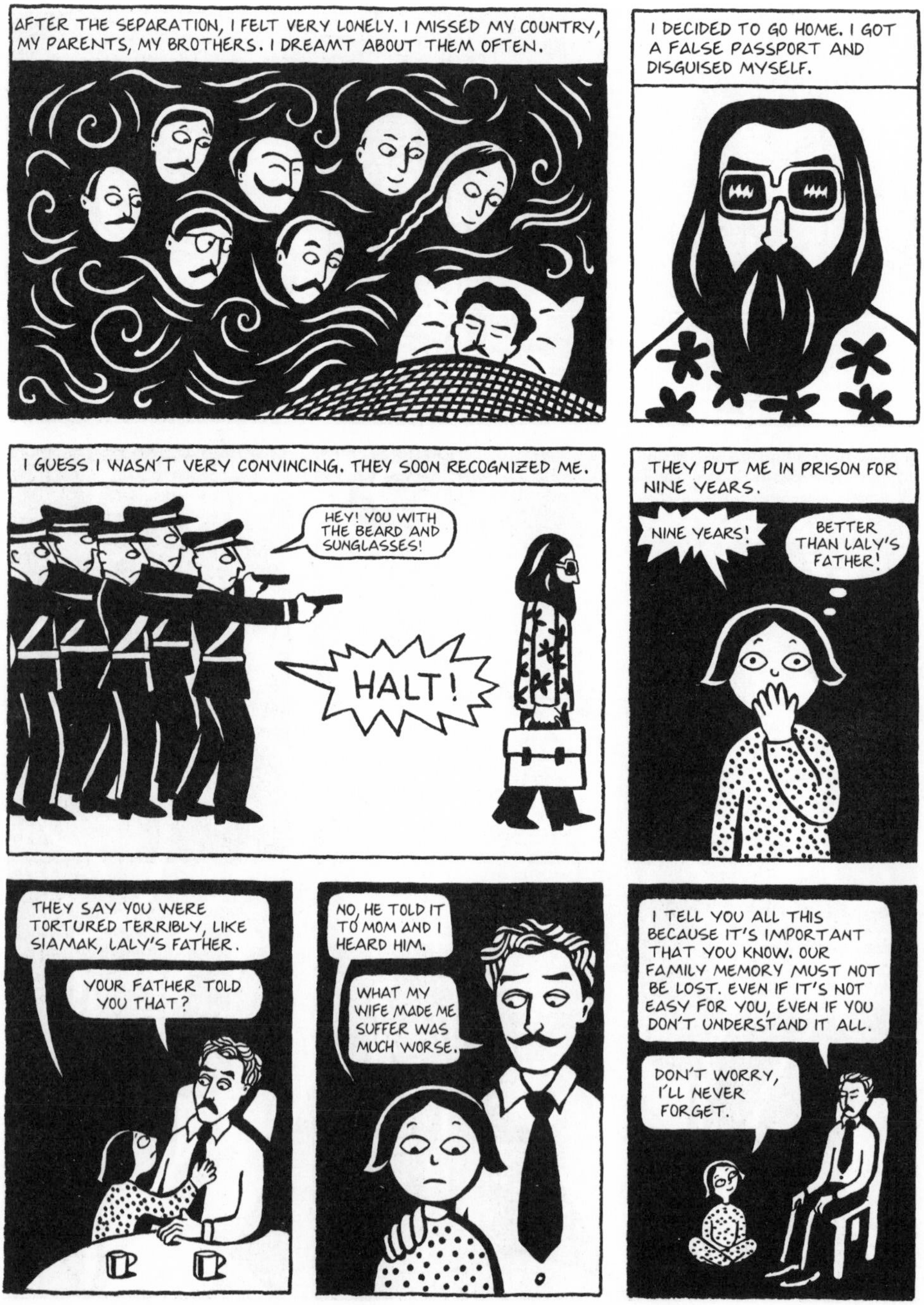
AFTER THE SEPARATION, I FELT VERY LONELY. I MISSED MY COUNTRY, MY PARENTS, MY BROTHERS. I DREAMT ABOUT THEM OFTEN.
I DECIDED TO GO HOME. I GOT A FALSE PASSPORT AND DISGUISED MYSELF.
I GUESS I WASN'T VERY CONVINCING. THEY SOON RECOGNIZED ME.
HEY! YOU WITH THE BEARD AND SUNGLASSES!
HALT!
THEY PUT ME IN PRISON FOR NINE YEARS.
NINE YEARS!
BETTER THAN LALY'S FATHER!
THEY SAY YOU WERE TORTURED TERRIBLY, LIKE SIAMAK, LALY'S FATHER.
YOUR FATHER TOLD YOU THAT?
NO, HE TOLD IT TO MOM AND I HEARD HIM.
WHAT MY WIFE MADE ME SUFFER WAS MUCH WORSE.
I TELL YOU ALL THIS BECAUSE IT'S IMPORTANT THAT YOU KNOW. OUR FAMILY MEMORY MUST NOT BE LOST. EVEN IF IT'S NOT EASY FOR YOU, EVEN IF YOU DON'T UNDERSTAND IT ALL.
DON'T WORRY, I'LL NEVER FORGET.

 # THE SHEEP

DURING THE TIME ANOOSH STAYED WITH US I HEARD POLITICAL DISCUSSIONS OF THE HIGHEST ORDER.

IT'S INCREDIBLE. THE REVOLUTION IS A LEFTIST REVOLUTION AND THE REPUBLIC WANTS TO BE CALLED ISLAMIC.

IT'S NOT IMPORTANT. EVERYTHING WILL TURN OUT FINE. IN A COUNTRY WHERE HALF THE POPULATION IS ILLITERATE YOU CANNOT UNITE THE PEOPLE AROUND MARX. THE ONLY THING THAT CAN REALLY UNITE THEM IS NATIONALISM OR A RELIGIOUS ETHIC...

BUT THE RELIGIOUS LEADERS DON'T KNOW HOW TO GOVERN. THEY WILL RETURN TO THEIR MOSQUES. THE PROLETARIAT SHALL RULE! IT'S INEVITABLE!!! THAT'S JUST WHAT LENIN EXPLAINED IN "THE STATE AND THE REVOLUTION."

SOMETIMES I EVEN TOLD THEM MY OPINION...

ON TV THEY SAY THAT 99.99% OF THE POPULATION VOTED FOR THE ISLAMIC REPUBLIC.

DID YOU HEAR THAT, ANOOSH? DO YOU REALIZE HOW IGNORANT OUR PEOPLE ARE? THE ELECTIONS WERE FAKED AND THEY BELIEVE THE RESULTS: 99.99%!! AS FOR ME, I DON'T KNOW A SINGLE PERSON WHO VOTED FOR THE ISLAMIC REPUBLIC. WHERE DID THAT FIGURE COME FROM? FROM THEIR ASSES, THAT'S WHERE!

BUT IT'S NOT MY FAULT! IT'S THE TV!! BOO HOO!!!

CALM DOWN EBI, SHE'S JUST A CHILD WHO REPEATS WHAT SHE HEARS!

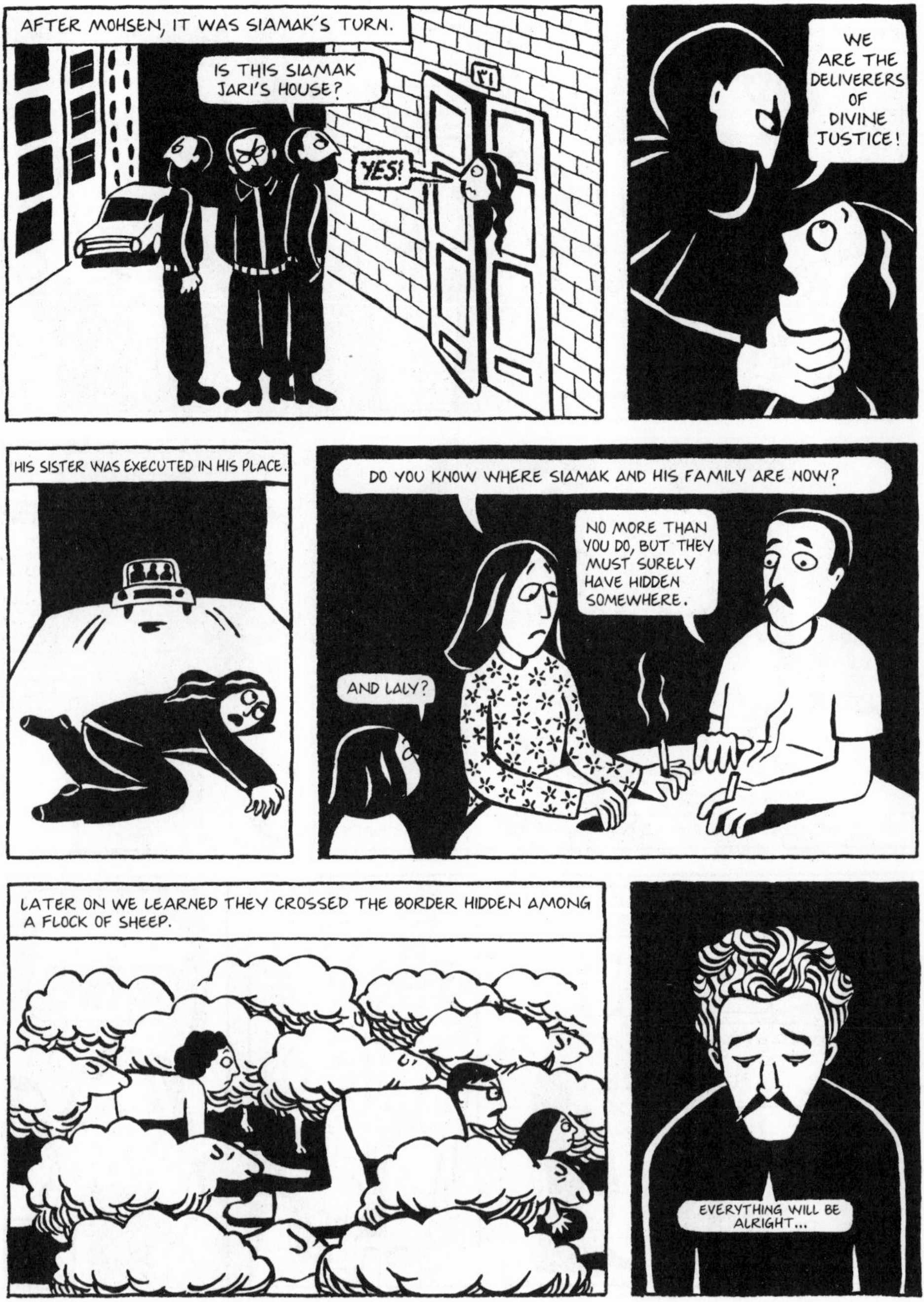
AFTER MOHSEN, IT WAS SIAMAK'S TURN.
IS THIS SIAMAK JARI'S HOUSE?
YES!
WE ARE THE DELIVERERS OF DIVINE JUSTICE!
HIS SISTER WAS EXECUTED IN HIS PLACE.
DO YOU KNOW WHERE SIAMAK AND HIS FAMILY ARE NOW?
NO MORE THAN YOU DO, BUT THEY MUST SURELY HAVE HIDDEN SOMEWHERE.
AND LALY?
LATER ON WE LEARNED THEY CROSSED THE BORDER HIDDEN AMONG A FLOCK OF SHEEP.
EVERYTHING WILL BE ALRIGHT...

68

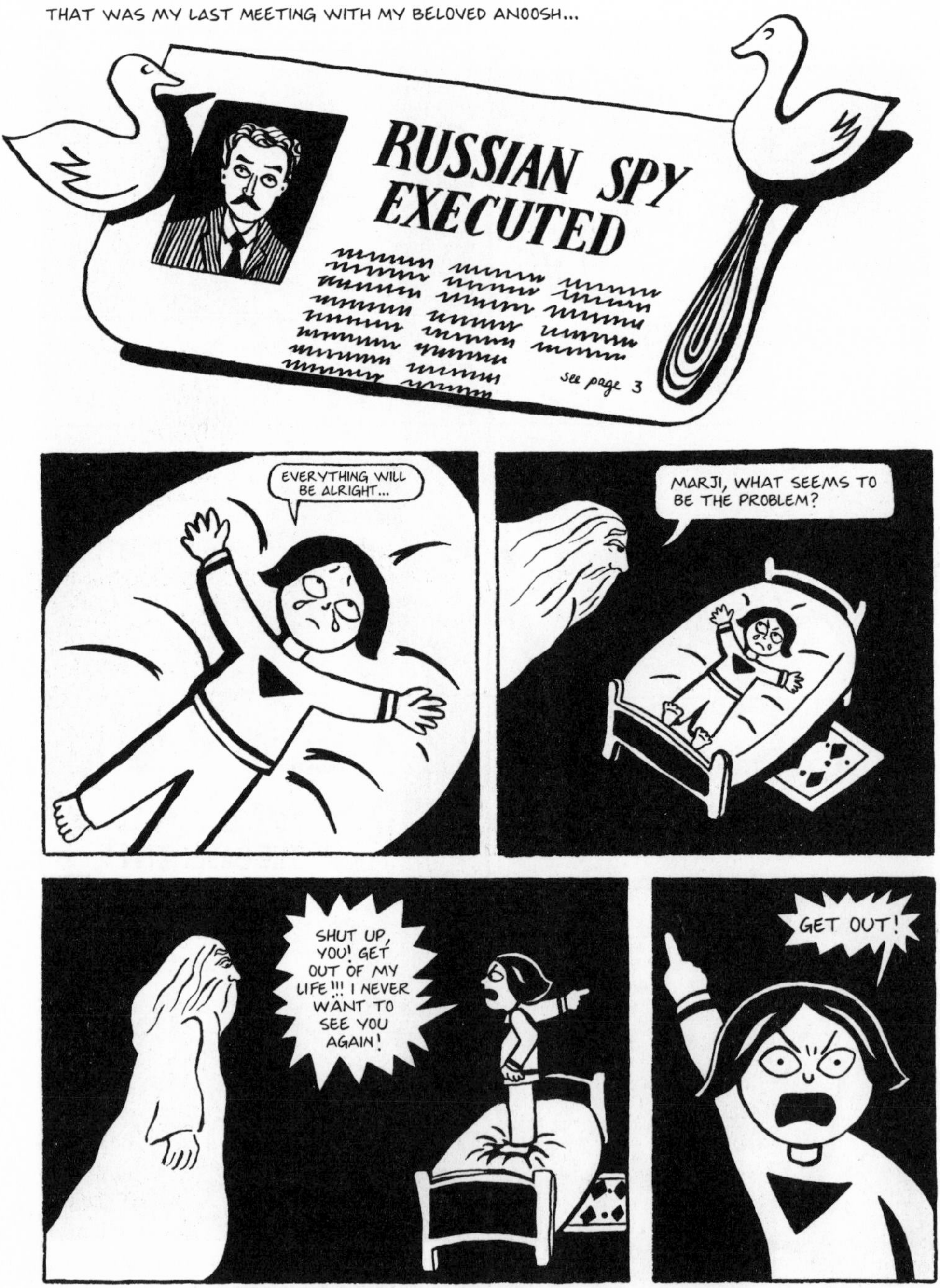
THAT WAS MY LAST MEETING WITH MY BELOVED ANOOSH...
RUSSIAN SPY EXECUTED
see page 3
EVERYTHING WILL BE ALRIGHT...
MARJI, WHAT SEEMS TO BE THE PROBLEM?
SHUT UP, YOU! GET OUT OF MY LIFE!!! I NEVER WANT TO SEE YOU AGAIN!
GET OUT!

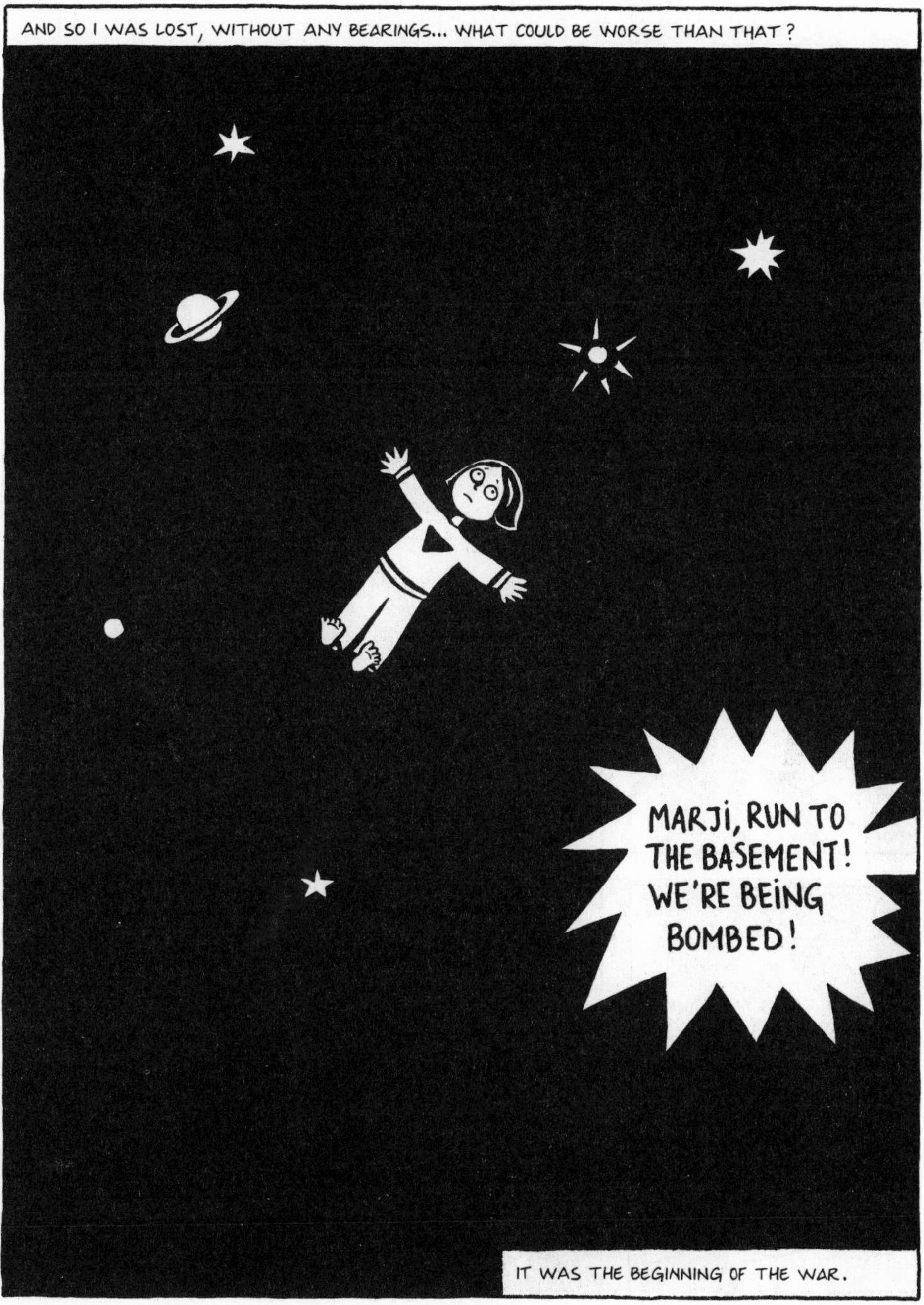
AND SO I WAS LOST, WITHOUT ANY BEARINGS... WHAT COULD BE WORSE THAN THAT?
MARJI, RUN TO THE BASEMENT! WE'RE BEING BOMBED!
IT WAS THE BEGINNING OF THE WAR.

73

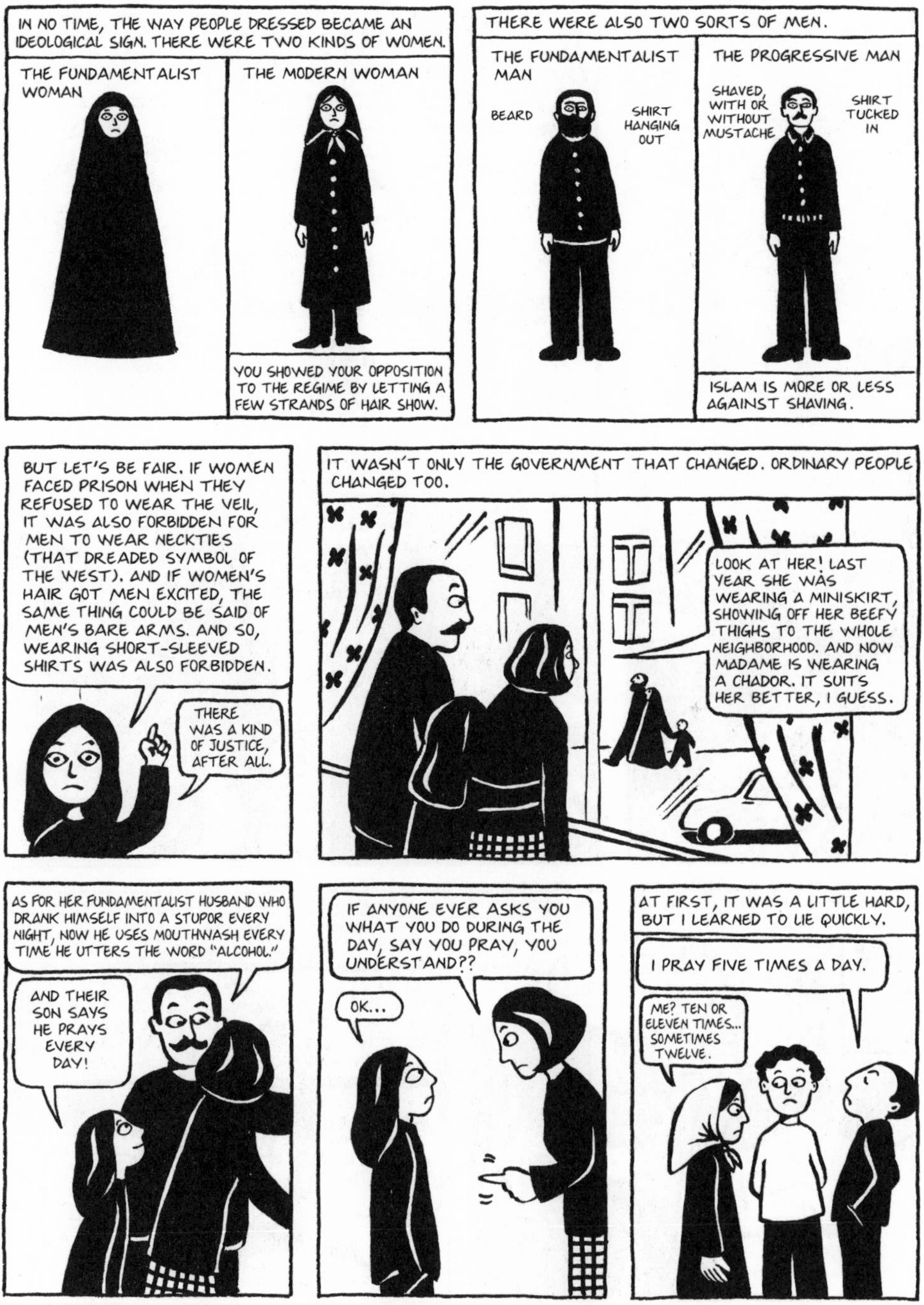
IN NO TIME, THE WAY PEOPLE DRESSED BECAME AN IDEOLOGICAL SIGN. THERE WERE TWO KINDS OF WOMEN.
THE FUNDAMENTALIST WOMAN
THE MODERN WOMAN
YOU SHOWED YOUR OPPOSITION TO THE REGIME BY LETTING A FEW STRANDS OF HAIR SHOW.
THERE WERE ALSO TWO SORTS OF MEN.
THE FUNDAMENTALIST MAN
BEARD
SHIRT HANGING OUT
THE PROGRESSIVE MAN
SHAVED, WITH OR WITHOUT MUSTACHE
SHIRT TUCKED IN
ISLAM IS MORE OR LESS AGAINST SHAVING.
BUT LET'S BE FAIR. IF WOMEN FACED PRISON WHEN THEY REFUSED TO WEAR THE VEIL, IT WAS ALSO FORBIDDEN FOR MEN TO WEAR NECKTIES (THAT DREADED SYMBOL OF THE WEST). AND IF WOMEN'S HAIR GOT MEN EXCITED, THE SAME THING COULD BE SAID OF MEN'S BARE ARMS. AND SO, WEARING SHORT-SLEEVED SHIRTS WAS ALSO FORBIDDEN.
THERE WAS A KIND OF JUSTICE, AFTER ALL.
IT WASN'T ONLY THE GOVERNMENT THAT CHANGED. ORDINARY PEOPLE CHANGED TOO.
LOOK AT HER! LAST YEAR SHE WAS WEARING A MINISKIRT, SHOWING OFF HER BEEFY THIGHS TO THE WHOLE NEIGHBORHOOD. AND NOW MADAME IS WEARING A CHADOR. IT SUITS HER BETTER, I GUESS.
AS FOR HER FUNDAMENTALIST HUSBAND WHO DRANK HIMSELF INTO A STUPOR EVERY NIGHT, NOW HE USES MOUTHWASH EVERY TIME HE UTTERS THE WORD "ALCOHOL."
AND THEIR SON SAYS HE PRAYS EVERY DAY!
IF ANYONE EVER ASKS YOU WHAT YOU DO DURING THE DAY, SAY YOU PRAY, YOU UNDERSTAND??
OK...
AT FIRST, IT WAS A LITTLE HARD, BUT I LEARNED TO LIE QUICKLY.
I PRAY FIVE TIMES A DAY.
ME? TEN OR ELEVEN TIMES... SOMETIMES TWELVE.

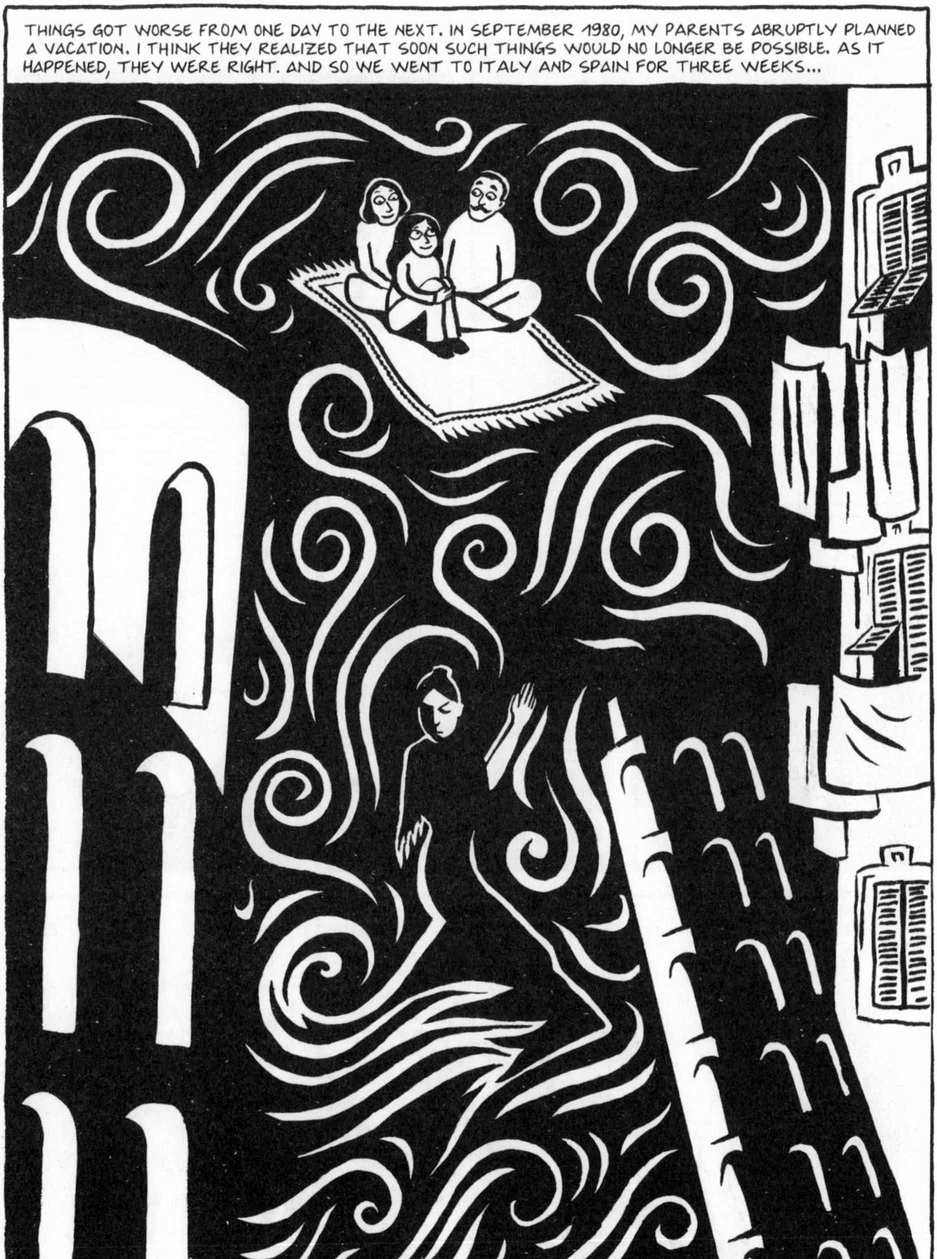
THINGS GOT WORSE FROM ONE DAY TO THE NEXT. IN SEPTEMBER 1980, MY PARENTS ABRUPTLY PLANNED A VACATION. I THINK THEY REALIZED THAT SOON SUCH THINGS WOULD NO LONGER BE POSSIBLE. AS IT HAPPENED, THEY WERE RIGHT. AND SO WE WENT TO ITALY AND SPAIN FOR THREE WEEKS...
...IT WAS WONDERFUL.

81

86

THE JEWELS

AFTER ABADAN, EVERY BORDER TOWN WAS TARGETED BY BOMBERS. MOST OF THE PEOPLE LIVING IN THOSE AREAS HAD TO FLEE NORTHWARD, FAR FROM THE IRAQI MISSILES.

THE KEY

THE IRAQI ARMY HAD CONQUERED THE CITY OF KHORRAMSHAHR. THEIR ARMS WERE MODERN, BUT WHERE IRAQ HAD QUALITY, WE HAD QUANTITY. COMPARED TO IRAQ, IRAN HAD A HUGE RESERVOIR OF POTENTIAL SOLDIERS. THE NUMBER OF WAR MARTYRS EMPHASIZED THAT DIFFERENCE.

CAN YOU HELP ME STYLE MY HAIR?

HAVE YOU SEEN ALL THESE CASUALTIES?

HOW CAN I NOT SEE? THEY'RE DOING ALL THEY CAN TO SHOW HOW MANY PEOPLE HAVE DIED. THE STREETS ARE PACKED WITH NUPTIAL CHAMBERS.

ACCORDING TO SHIITE TRADITION, WHEN AN UNMARRIED MAN DIES, A NUPTIAL CHAMBER IS BUILT FOR HIM. THAT WAY, THE DEAD MAN CAN SYMBOLICALLY ATTAIN CARNAL KNOWLEDGE.

IT WAS OBVIOUS THAT MANY OF THE FIGHTERS DIED VIRGINS.

VRUUUUUUU

MOM, DON'T ALL THESE DEAD MEAN ANYTHING TO YOU?

OF COURSE THEY MEAN SOMETHING TO ME! BUT WE ARE STILL LIVING!

OUR COUNTRY HAS ALWAYS KNOWN WAR AND MARTYRS. SO, LIKE MY FATHER SAID: "WHEN A BIG WAVE COMES, LOWER YOUR HEAD AND LET IT PASS!"

THAT'S VERY PERSIAN. THE PHILOSOPHY OF RESIGNATION.

I AGREED WITH MY MOTHER. I TOO TRIED TO THINK ONLY OF LIFE. HOWEVER, IT WASN'T ALWAYS EASY: AT SCHOOL, THEY LINED US UP TWICE A DAY TO MOURN THE WAR DEAD. THEY PUT ON FUNERAL MARCHES, AND WE HAD TO BEAT OUR BREASTS.

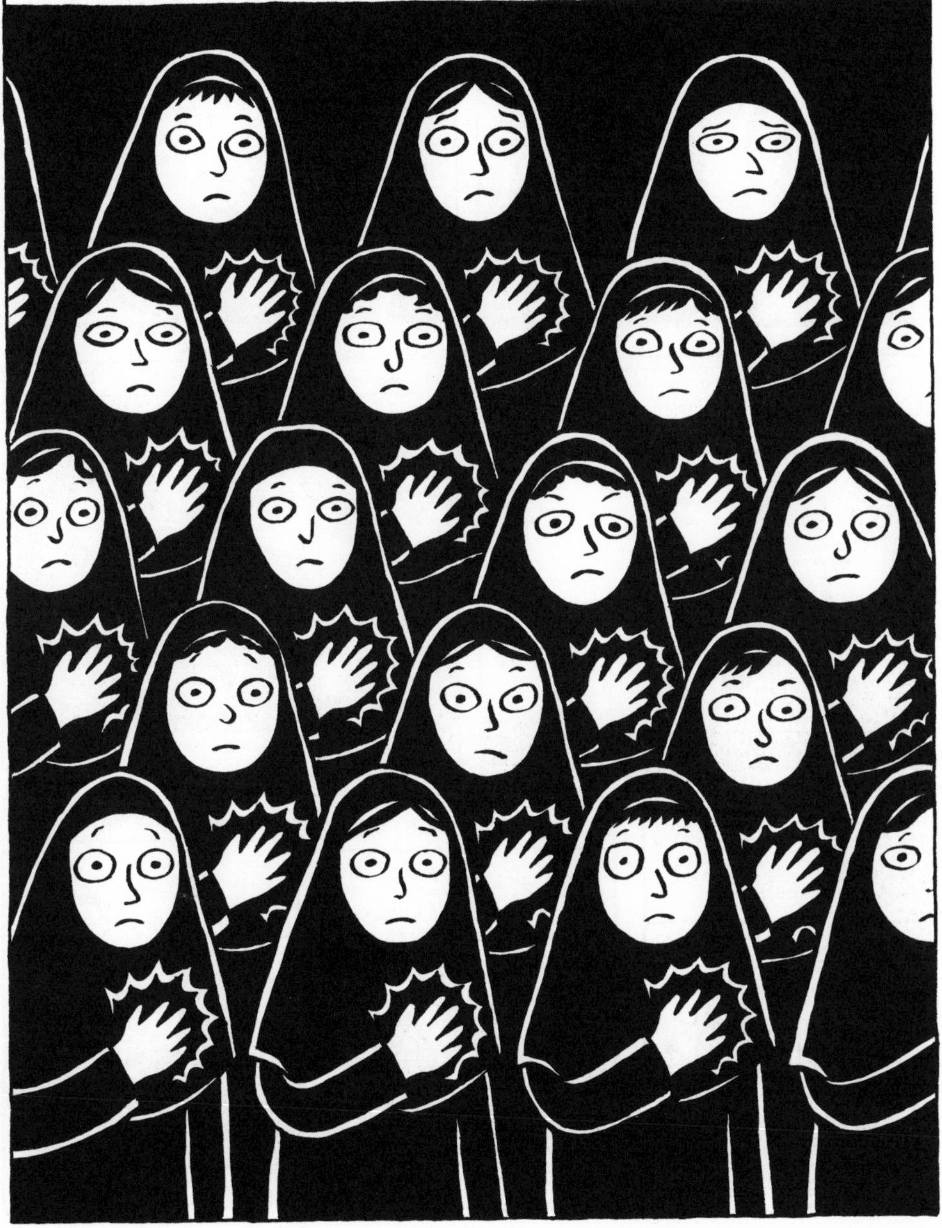

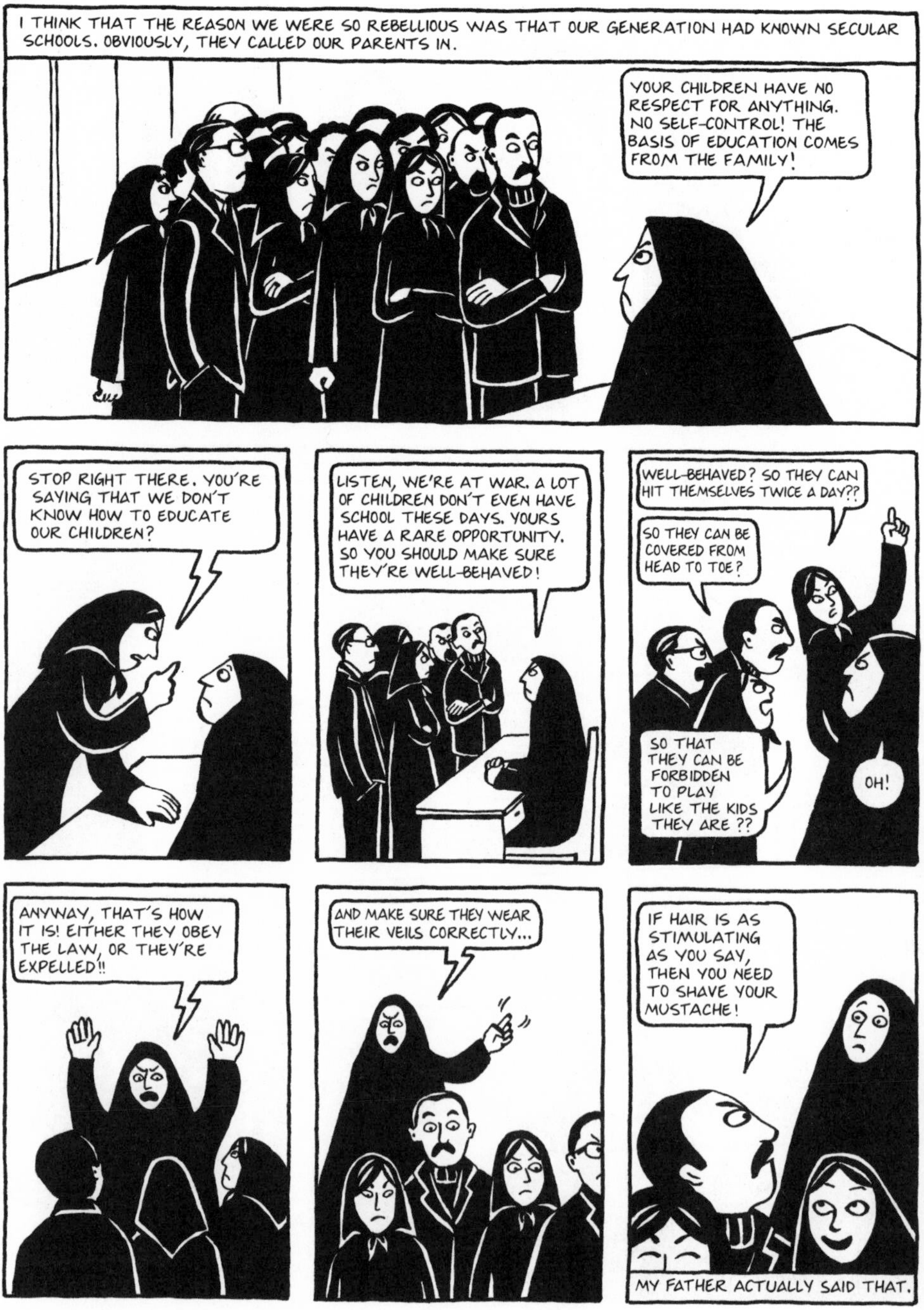
I THINK THAT THE REASON WE WERE SO REBELLIOUS WAS THAT OUR GENERATION HAD KNOWN SECULAR SCHOOLS. OBVIOUSLY, THEY CALLED OUR PARENTS IN.
YOUR CHILDREN HAVE NO RESPECT FOR ANYTHING. NO SELF-CONTROL! THE BASIS OF EDUCATION COMES FROM THE FAMILY!
STOP RIGHT THERE. YOU'RE SAYING THAT WE DON'T KNOW HOW TO EDUCATE OUR CHILDREN?
LISTEN, WE'RE AT WAR. A LOT OF CHILDREN DON'T EVEN HAVE SCHOOL THESE DAYS. YOURS HAVE A RARE OPPORTUNITY. SO YOU SHOULD MAKE SURE THEY'RE WELL-BEHAVED!
WELL-BEHAVED? SO THEY CAN HIT THEMSELVES TWICE A DAY??
SO THEY CAN BE COVERED FROM HEAD TO TOE?
SO THAT THEY CAN BE FORBIDDEN TO PLAY LIKE THE KIDS THEY ARE ??
OH!
ANYWAY, THAT'S HOW IT IS! EITHER THEY OBEY THE LAW, OR THEY'RE EXPELLED!!
AND MAKE SURE THEY WEAR THEIR VEILS CORRECTLY...
IF HAIR IS AS STIMULATING AS YOU SAY, THEN YOU NEED TO SHAVE YOUR MUSTACHE!
MY FATHER ACTUALLY SAID THAT.

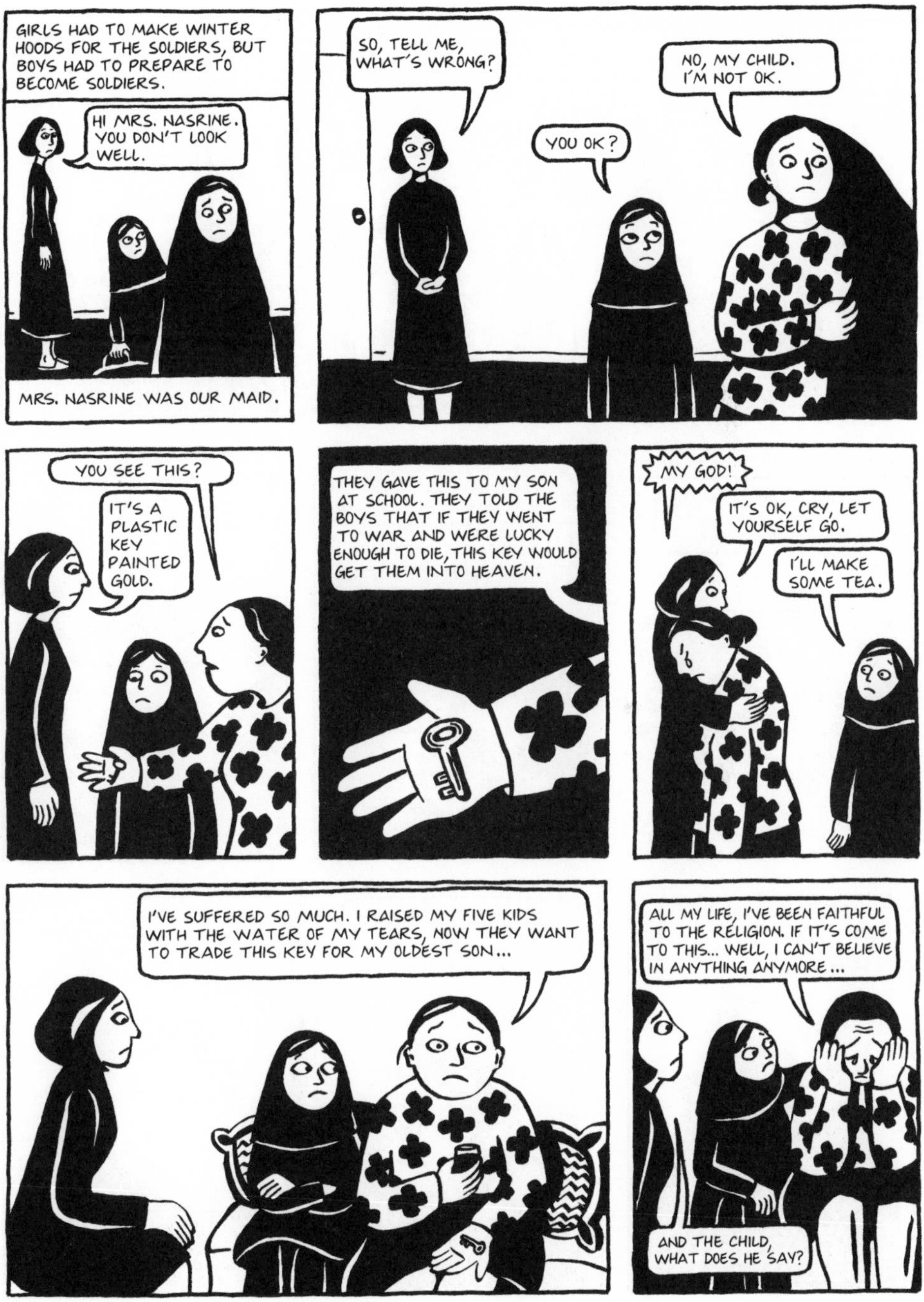
GIRLS HAD TO MAKE WINTER HOODS FOR THE SOLDIERS, BUT BOYS HAD TO PREPARE TO BECOME SOLDIERS.
HI MRS. NASRINE. YOU DON'T LOOK WELL.
MRS. NASRINE WAS OUR MAID.
SO, TELL ME, WHAT'S WRONG?
YOU OK?
NO, MY CHILD. I'M NOT OK.
YOU SEE THIS?
IT'S A PLASTIC KEY PAINTED GOLD.
THEY GAVE THIS TO MY SON AT SCHOOL. THEY TOLD THE BOYS THAT IF THEY WENT TO WAR AND WERE LUCKY ENOUGH TO DIE, THIS KEY WOULD GET THEM INTO HEAVEN.
MY GOD!
IT'S OK, CRY, LET YOURSELF GO.
I'LL MAKE SOME TEA.
I'VE SUFFERED SO MUCH. I RAISED MY FIVE KIDS WITH THE WATER OF MY TEARS, NOW THEY WANT TO TRADE THIS KEY FOR MY OLDEST SON...
ALL MY LIFE, I'VE BEEN FAITHFUL TO THE RELIGION. IF IT'S COME TO THIS... WELL, I CAN'T BELIEVE IN ANYTHING ANYMORE...
AND THE CHILD, WHAT DOES HE SAY?

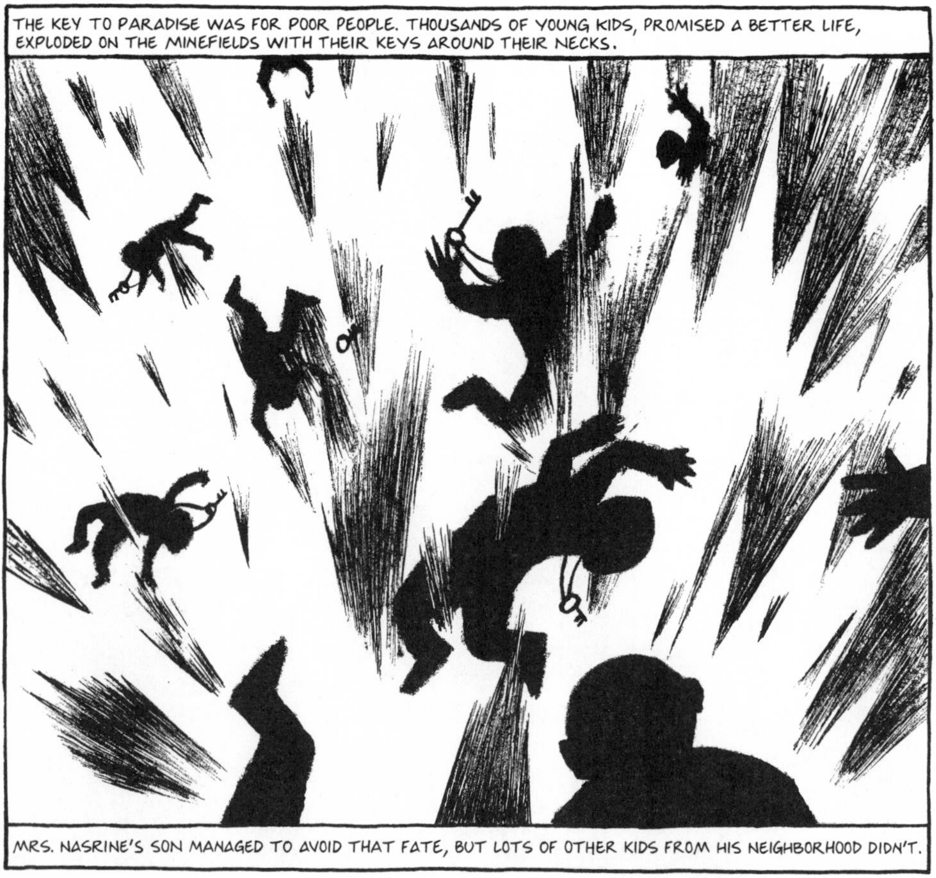
THE KEY TO PARADISE WAS FOR POOR PEOPLE. THOUSANDS OF YOUNG KIDS, PROMISED A BETTER LIFE, EXPLODED ON THE MINEFIELDS WITH THEIR KEYS AROUND THEIR NECKS.
MRS. NASRINE'S SON MANAGED TO AVOID THAT FATE, BUT LOTS OF OTHER KIDS FROM HIS NEIGHBORHOOD DIDN'T.

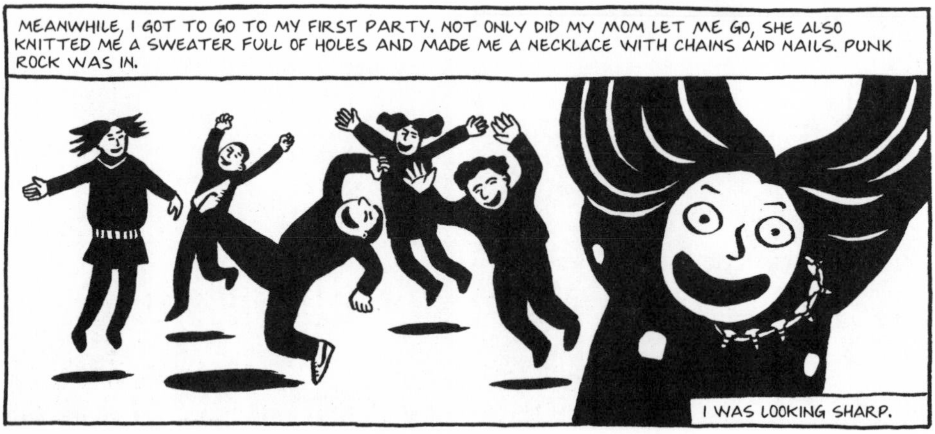
MEANWHILE, I GOT TO GO TO MY FIRST PARTY. NOT ONLY DID MY MOM LET ME GO, SHE ALSO KNITTED ME A SWEATER FULL OF HOLES AND MADE ME A NECKLACE WITH CHAINS AND NAILS. PUNK ROCK WAS IN.
I WAS LOOKING SHARP.

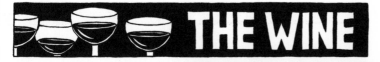

THE WINE

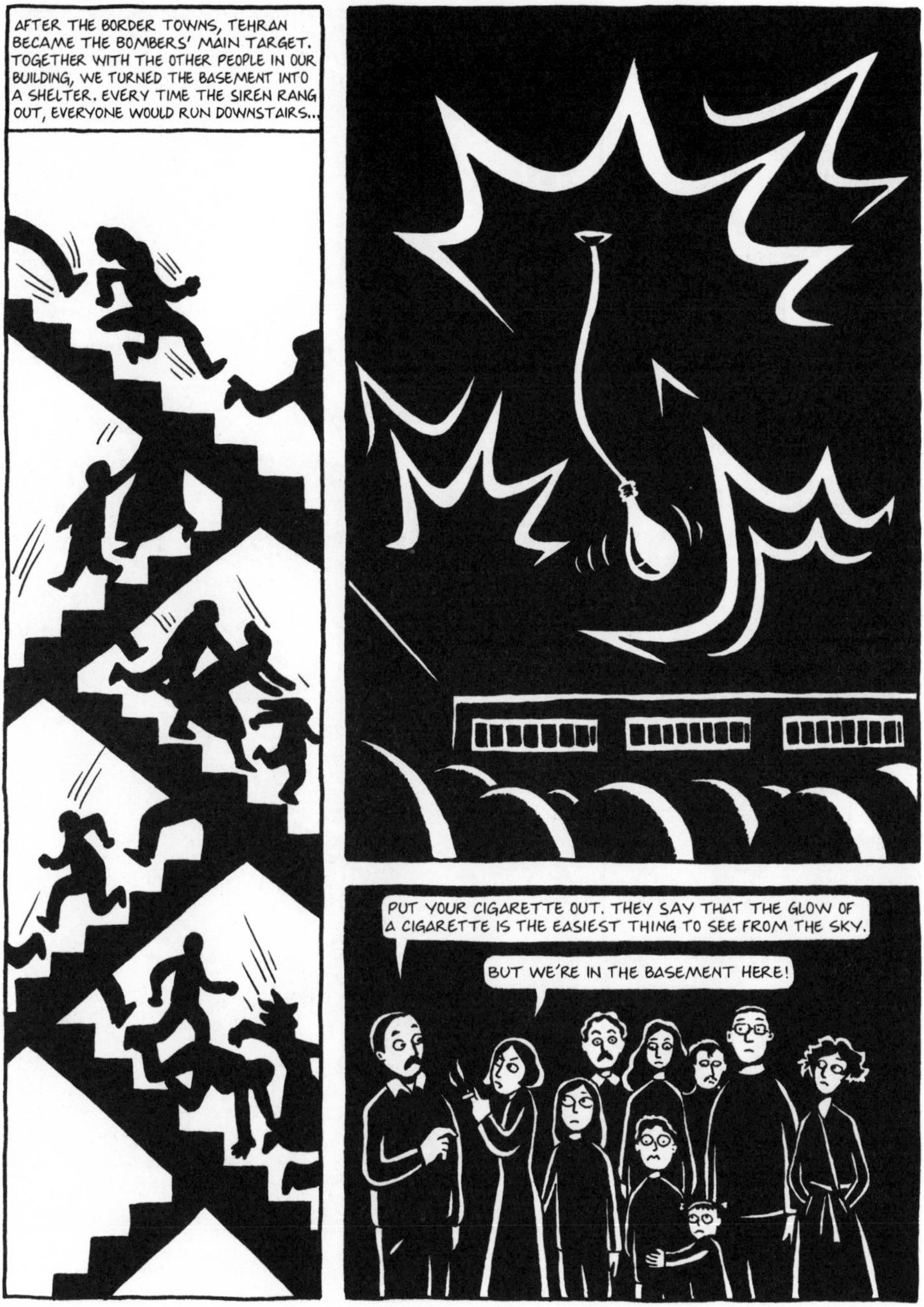
AFTER THE BORDER TOWNS, TEHRAN BECAME THE BOMBERS' MAIN TARGET. TOGETHER WITH THE OTHER PEOPLE IN OUR BUILDING, WE TURNED THE BASEMENT INTO A SHELTER. EVERY TIME THE SIREN RANG OUT, EVERYONE WOULD RUN DOWNSTAIRS...
PUT YOUR CIGARETTE OUT. THEY SAY THAT THE GLOW OF A CIGARETTE IS THE EASIEST THING TO SEE FROM THE SKY.
BUT WE'RE IN THE BASEMENT HERE!

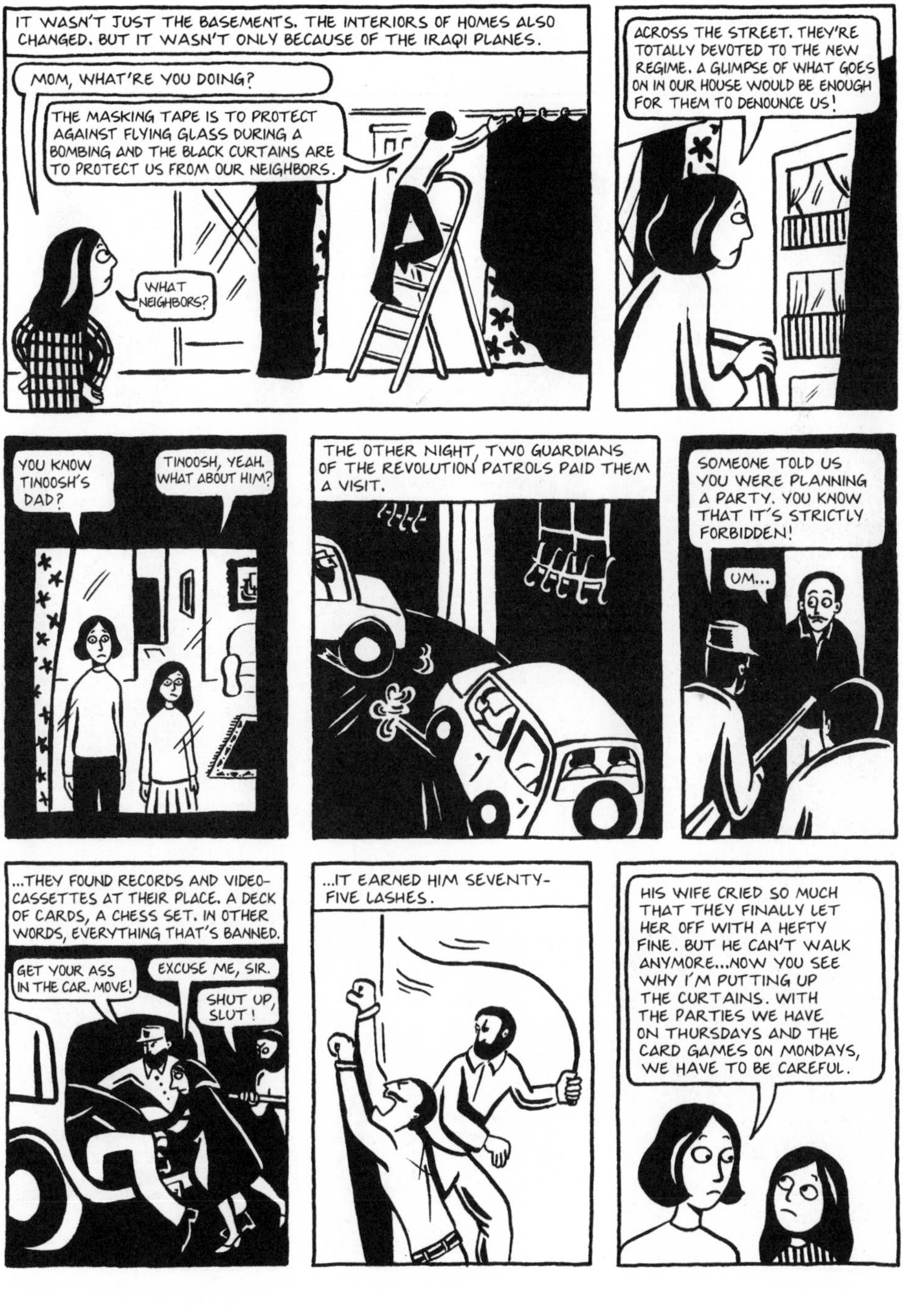
IT WASN'T JUST THE BASEMENTS. THE INTERIORS OF HOMES ALSO CHANGED. BUT IT WASN'T ONLY BECAUSE OF THE IRAQI PLANES.
MOM, WHAT'RE YOU DOING?
THE MASKING TAPE IS TO PROTECT AGAINST FLYING GLASS DURING A BOMBING AND THE BLACK CURTAINS ARE TO PROTECT US FROM OUR NEIGHBORS.
WHAT NEIGHBORS?
ACROSS THE STREET. THEY'RE TOTALLY DEVOTED TO THE NEW REGIME. A GLIMPSE OF WHAT GOES ON IN OUR HOUSE WOULD BE ENOUGH FOR THEM TO DENOUNCE US!
YOU KNOW TINOOSH'S DAD?
TINOOSH, YEAH. WHAT ABOUT HIM?
THE OTHER NIGHT, TWO GUARDIANS OF THE REVOLUTION PATROLS PAID THEM A VISIT.
SOMEONE TOLD US YOU WERE PLANNING A PARTY. YOU KNOW THAT IT'S STRICTLY FORBIDDEN!
UM...
...THEY FOUND RECORDS AND VIDEO-CASSETTES AT THEIR PLACE. A DECK OF CARDS, A CHESS SET. IN OTHER WORDS, EVERYTHING THAT'S BANNED.
GET YOUR ASS IN THE CAR. MOVE!
EXCUSE ME, SIR.
SHUT UP, SLUT!
...IT EARNED HIM SEVENTY-FIVE LASHES.
HIS WIFE CRIED SO MUCH THAT THEY FINALLY LET HER OFF WITH A HEFTY FINE. BUT HE CAN'T WALK ANYMORE...NOW YOU SEE WHY I'M PUTTING UP THE CURTAINS. WITH THE PARTIES WE HAVE ON THURSDAYS AND THE CARD GAMES ON MONDAYS, WE HAVE TO BE CAREFUL.

IN SPITE OF ALL THE DANGERS, THE PARTIES WENT ON. "WITHOUT THEM IT WOULDN'T BE PSYCHOLOGI-CALLY BEARABLE," SOME SAID. "WITHOUT PARTIES, WE MIGHT AS WELL JUST BURY OURSELVES NOW," ADDED THE OTHERS. MY UNCLE INVITED US TO HIS HOUSE TO CELEBRATE THE BIRTH OF MY COUSIN. EVERYONE WAS THERE. EVEN GRANDMA WAS DANCING.

DAMN! POWER OUTAGE!!

BE CAREFUL WHERE YOU STEP!!!

AWWW! NO MORE MUSIC!

DON'T WORRY ABOUT IT! I'LL GO GET THE ZARB.

A ZARB IS A KIND OF DRUM. MY FATHER PLAYED IT VERY WELL. LIKE A PRO.

WE HAD EVERYTHING. WELL, EVERYTHING THAT WAS FORBIDDEN. EVEN ALCOHOL, GALLONS OF IT.

MY UNCLE WAS THE VINTNER. HE HAD BUILT A GENUINE WINE-MAKING LAB IN HIS BASEMENT.

MRS. NASRINE, WHO WAS ALSO HIS CLEANING LADY, CRUSHED THE GRAPES.

GOD FORGIVE ME! GOD FORGIVE ME!

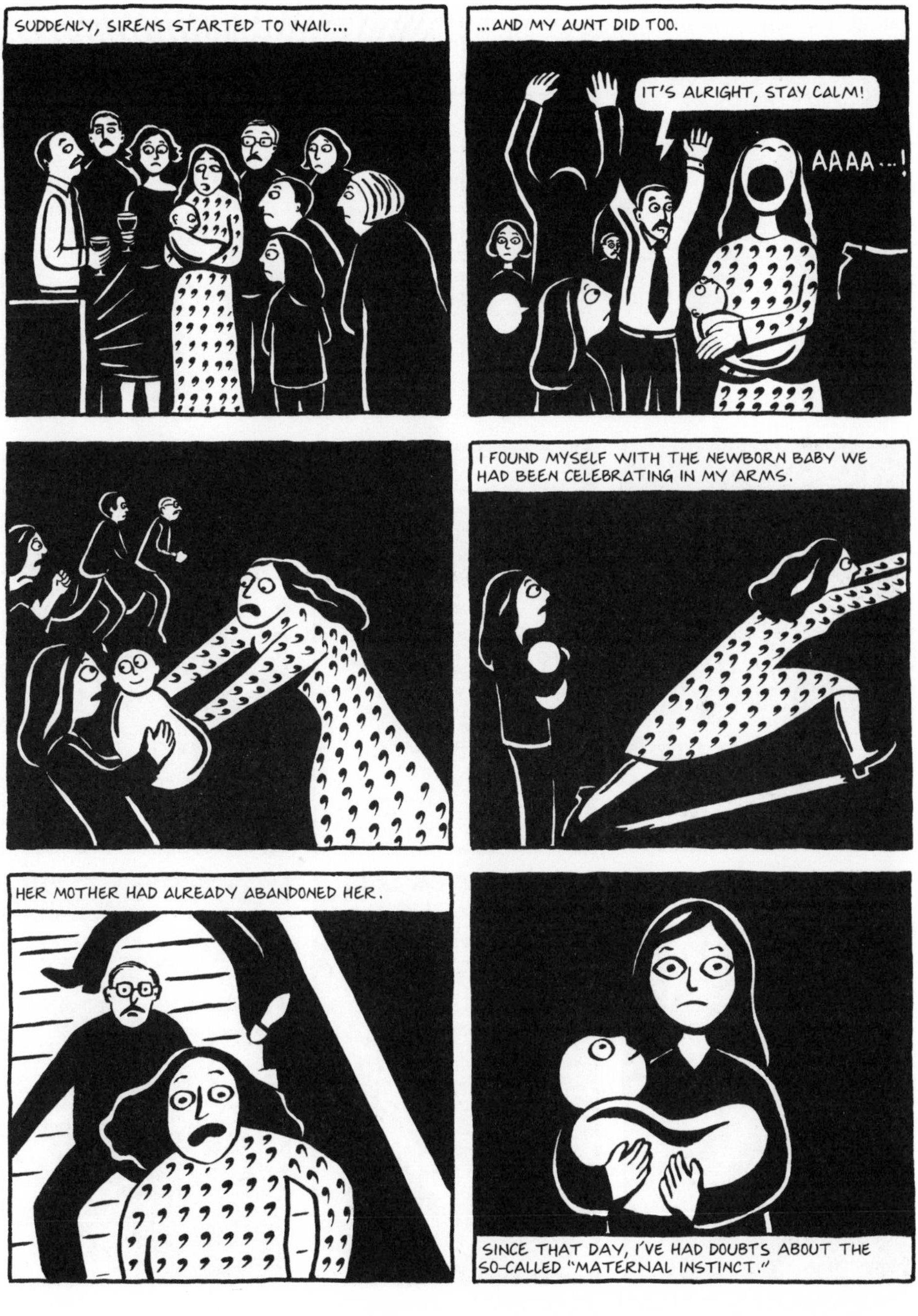

SUDDENLY, SIRENS STARTED TO WAIL...
...AND MY AUNT DID TOO.
IT'S ALRIGHT, STAY CALM!
AAAA...!
I FOUND MYSELF WITH THE NEWBORN BABY WE HAD BEEN CELEBRATING IN MY ARMS.
HER MOTHER HAD ALREADY ABANDONED HER.
SINCE THAT DAY, I'VE HAD DOUBTS ABOUT THE SO-CALLED "MATERNAL INSTINCT."

108

110

JORDAN AVENUE WAS WHERE THE TEENAGERS FROM NORTH TEHRAN (THE NICE NEIGHBORHOODS) HUNG OUT. KANSAS WAS ITS TEMPLE.

IF SOME PUBLIC PLACES HAD SURVIVED THE REGIME'S REPRESSION, EITHER IT WAS TO LEAVE US A LITTLE FREE SPACE, OR ELSE IT WAS OUT OF IGNORANCE. PERSONALLY, THE LATTER THEORY SOUNDED MORE LIKELY: THEY PROBABLY HADN'T THE SLIGHTEST IDEA WHAT "KANSAS" WAS.

DID YOU SEE HIS HAIR? JUST LIKE ROD STEWART!

STOP

KANS

YEAH, IF HE GETS CAUGHT, HE'LL GET A BUZZ CUT!

...IN SPITE OF EVERYTHING, KIDS WERE TRYING TO LOOK HIP, EVEN UNDER RISK OF ARREST.

MY FRIENDS WEREN'T ACTUALLY THAT INTERESTED IN THE HAMBURGERS...

WE LET THE BOYS KNOW THAT THEY COULD FOLLOW US BY A FEW SIGNS.

FOLLOW THE OTHERS, I MEAN. I WAS TOO YOUNG TO INTEREST THEM.

WOOOOO

...THE SIRENS WENT OFF.

WHAT THE HELL ARE YOU DOING??

HIT THE DIRT!

?

?

?

WE HAD BEEN TOLD THAT IF WE WERE IN THE STREET DURING A BOMBING, WE SHOULD LIE DOWN IN THE GUTTER FOR SAFETY.

HA! YOU CHICKEN!

112

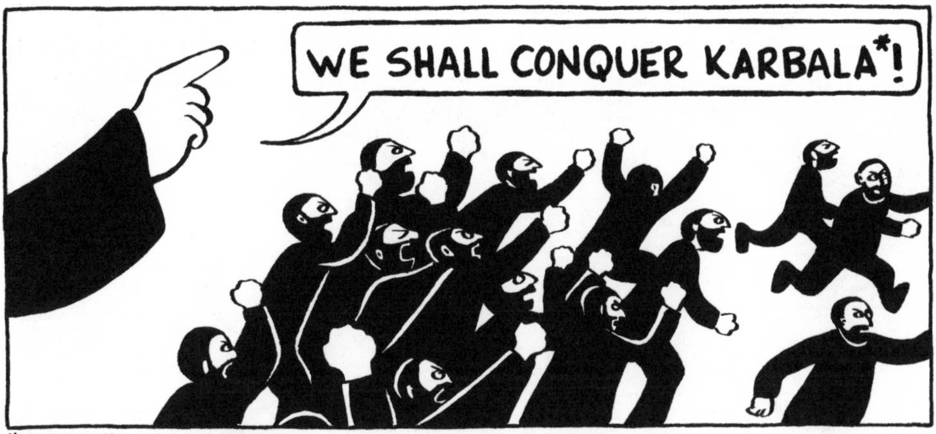
WE SHALL CONQUER KARBALA*!

* A SHIITE HOLY CITY IN IRAQ

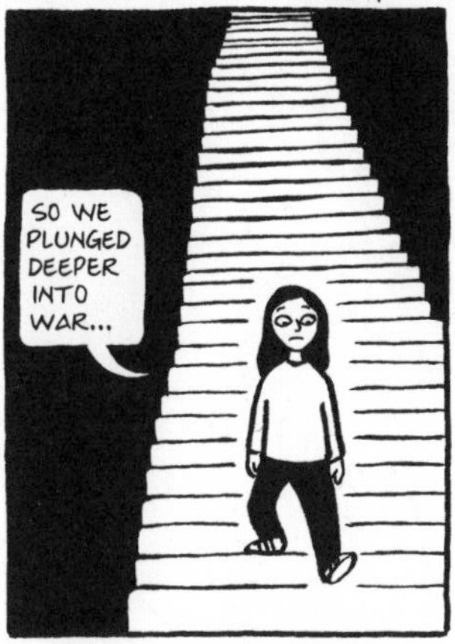
SO WE PLUNGED DEEPER INTO WAR...

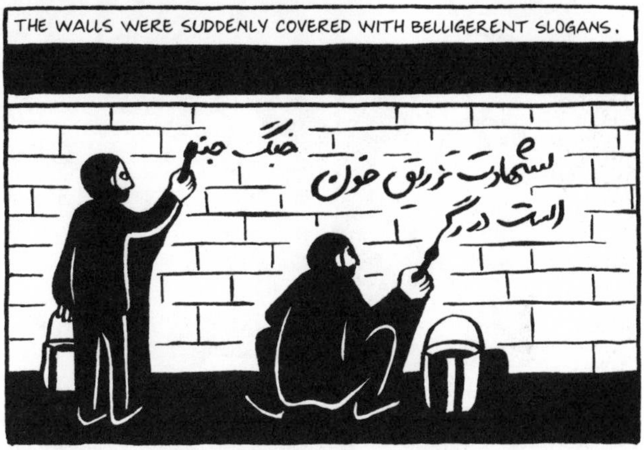
THE WALLS WERE SUDDENLY COVERED WITH BELLIGERENT SLOGANS.

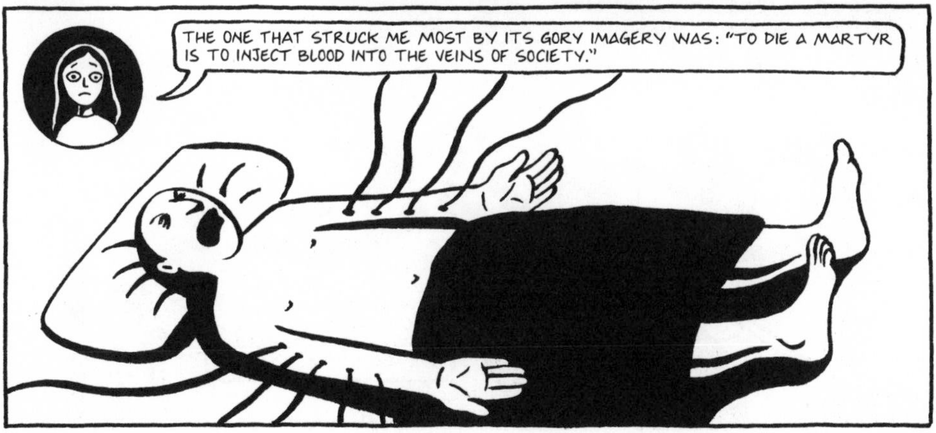
THE ONE THAT STRUCK ME MOST BY ITS GORY IMAGERY WAS: "TO DIE A MARTYR IS TO INJECT BLOOD INTO THE VEINS OF SOCIETY."

116

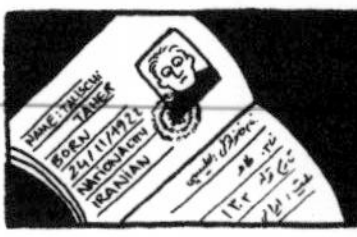

THE PASSPORT

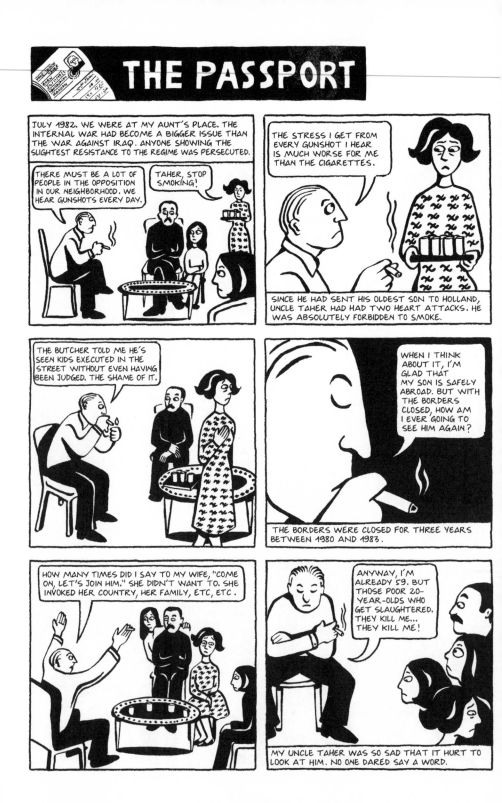

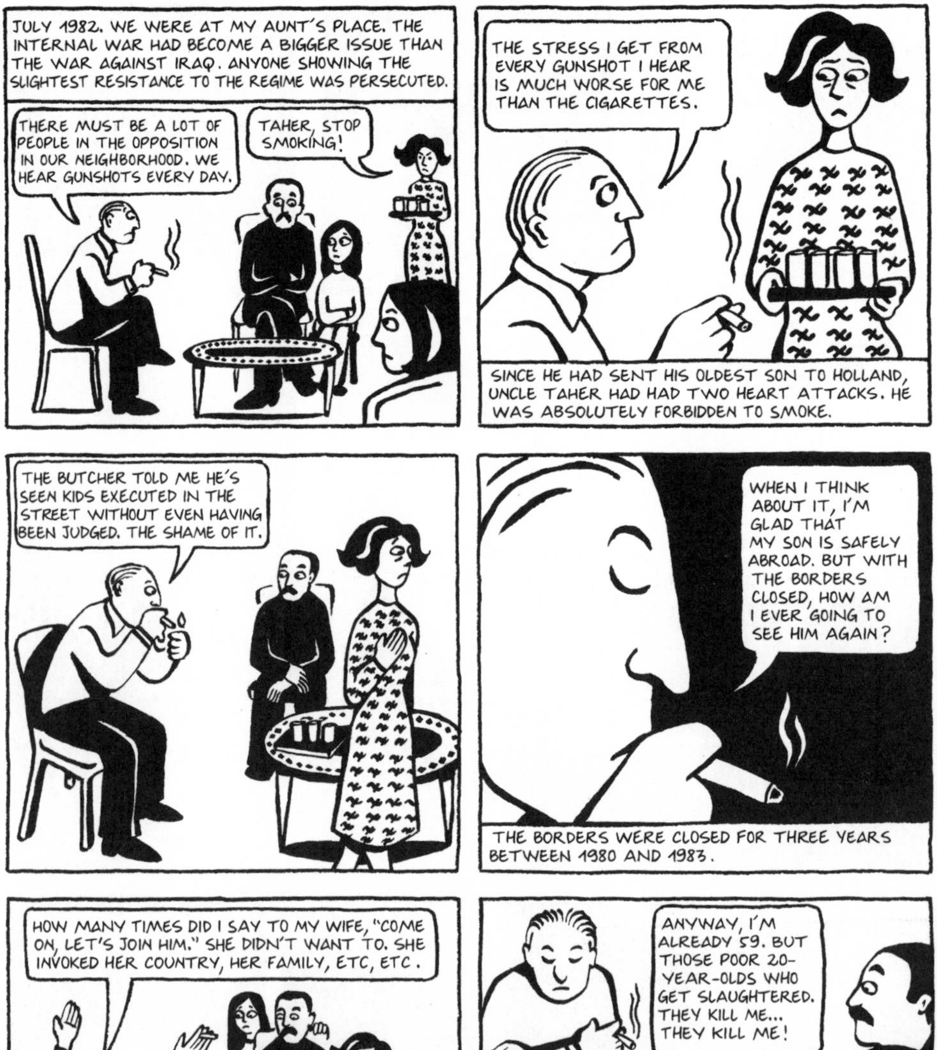
JULY 1982. WE WERE AT MY AUNT'S PLACE. THE INTERNAL WAR HAD BECOME A BIGGER ISSUE THAN THE WAR AGAINST IRAQ. ANYONE SHOWING THE SLIGHTEST RESISTANCE TO THE REGIME WAS PERSECUTED.
THERE MUST BE A LOT OF PEOPLE IN THE OPPOSITION IN OUR NEIGHBORHOOD. WE HEAR GUNSHOTS EVERY DAY.
TAHER, STOP SMOKING!
THE STRESS I GET FROM EVERY GUNSHOT I HEAR IS MUCH WORSE FOR ME THAN THE CIGARETTES.
SINCE HE HAD SENT HIS OLDEST SON TO HOLLAND, UNCLE TAHER HAD HAD TWO HEART ATTACKS. HE WAS ABSOLUTELY FORBIDDEN TO SMOKE.
THE BUTCHER TOLD ME HE'S SEEN KIDS EXECUTED IN THE STREET WITHOUT EVEN HAVING BEEN JUDGED. THE SHAME OF IT.
WHEN I THINK ABOUT IT, I'M GLAD THAT MY SON IS SAFELY ABROAD. BUT WITH THE BORDERS CLOSED, HOW AM I EVER GOING TO SEE HIM AGAIN?
THE BORDERS WERE CLOSED FOR THREE YEARS BETWEEN 1980 AND 1983.
HOW MANY TIMES DID I SAY TO MY WIFE, "COME ON, LET'S JOIN HIM." SHE DIDN'T WANT TO. SHE INVOKED HER COUNTRY, HER FAMILY, ETC, ETC.
ANYWAY, I'M ALREADY 59. BUT THOSE POOR 20-YEAR-OLDS WHO GET SLAUGHTERED. THEY KILL ME... THEY KILL ME!
MY UNCLE TAHER WAS SO SAD THAT IT HURT TO LOOK AT HIM. NO ONE DARED SAY A WORD.

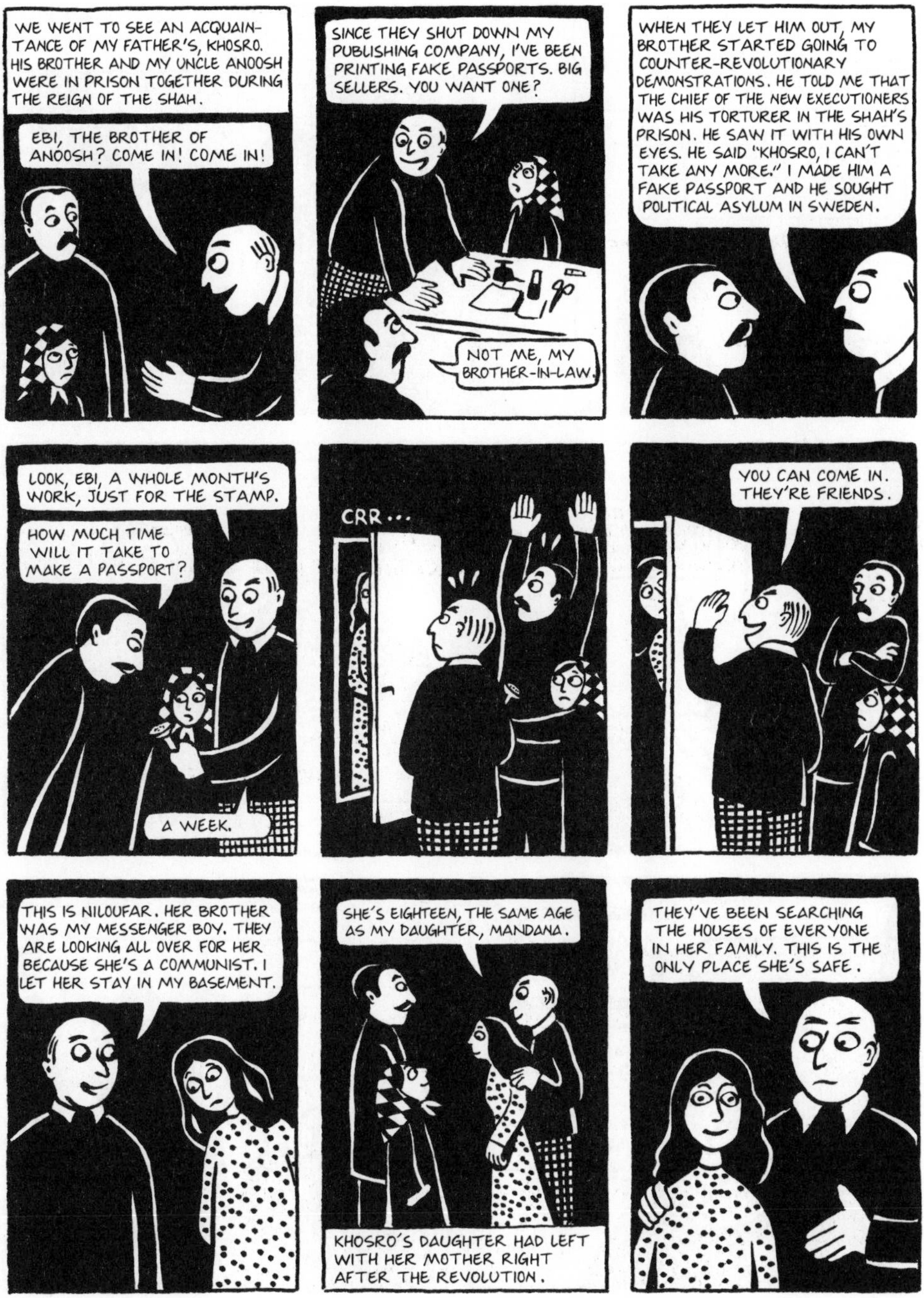
WE WENT TO SEE AN ACQUAINTANCE OF MY FATHER'S, KHOSRO. HIS BROTHER AND MY UNCLE ANOOSH WERE IN PRISON TOGETHER DURING THE REIGN OF THE SHAH.
EBI, THE BROTHER OF ANOOSH? COME IN! COME IN!
SINCE THEY SHUT DOWN MY PUBLISHING COMPANY, I'VE BEEN PRINTING FAKE PASSPORTS. BIG SELLERS. YOU WANT ONE?
NOT ME, MY BROTHER-IN-LAW.
WHEN THEY LET HIM OUT, MY BROTHER STARTED GOING TO COUNTER-REVOLUTIONARY DEMONSTRATIONS. HE TOLD ME THAT THE CHIEF OF THE NEW EXECUTIONERS WAS HIS TORTURER IN THE SHAH'S PRISON. HE SAW IT WITH HIS OWN EYES. HE SAID "KHOSRO, I CAN'T TAKE ANY MORE." I MADE HIM A FAKE PASSPORT AND HE SOUGHT POLITICAL ASYLUM IN SWEDEN.
LOOK, EBI, A WHOLE MONTH'S WORK, JUST FOR THE STAMP.
HOW MUCH TIME WILL IT TAKE TO MAKE A PASSPORT?
A WEEK.
CRR...
YOU CAN COME IN. THEY'RE FRIENDS.
THIS IS NILOUFAR. HER BROTHER WAS MY MESSENGER BOY. THEY ARE LOOKING ALL OVER FOR HER BECAUSE SHE'S A COMMUNIST. I LET HER STAY IN MY BASEMENT.
SHE'S EIGHTEEN, THE SAME AGE AS MY DAUGHTER, MANDANA.
KHOSRO'S DAUGHTER HAD LEFT WITH HER MOTHER RIGHT AFTER THE REVOLUTION.
THEY'VE BEEN SEARCHING THE HOUSES OF EVERYONE IN HER FAMILY. THIS IS THE ONLY PLACE SHE'S SAFE.

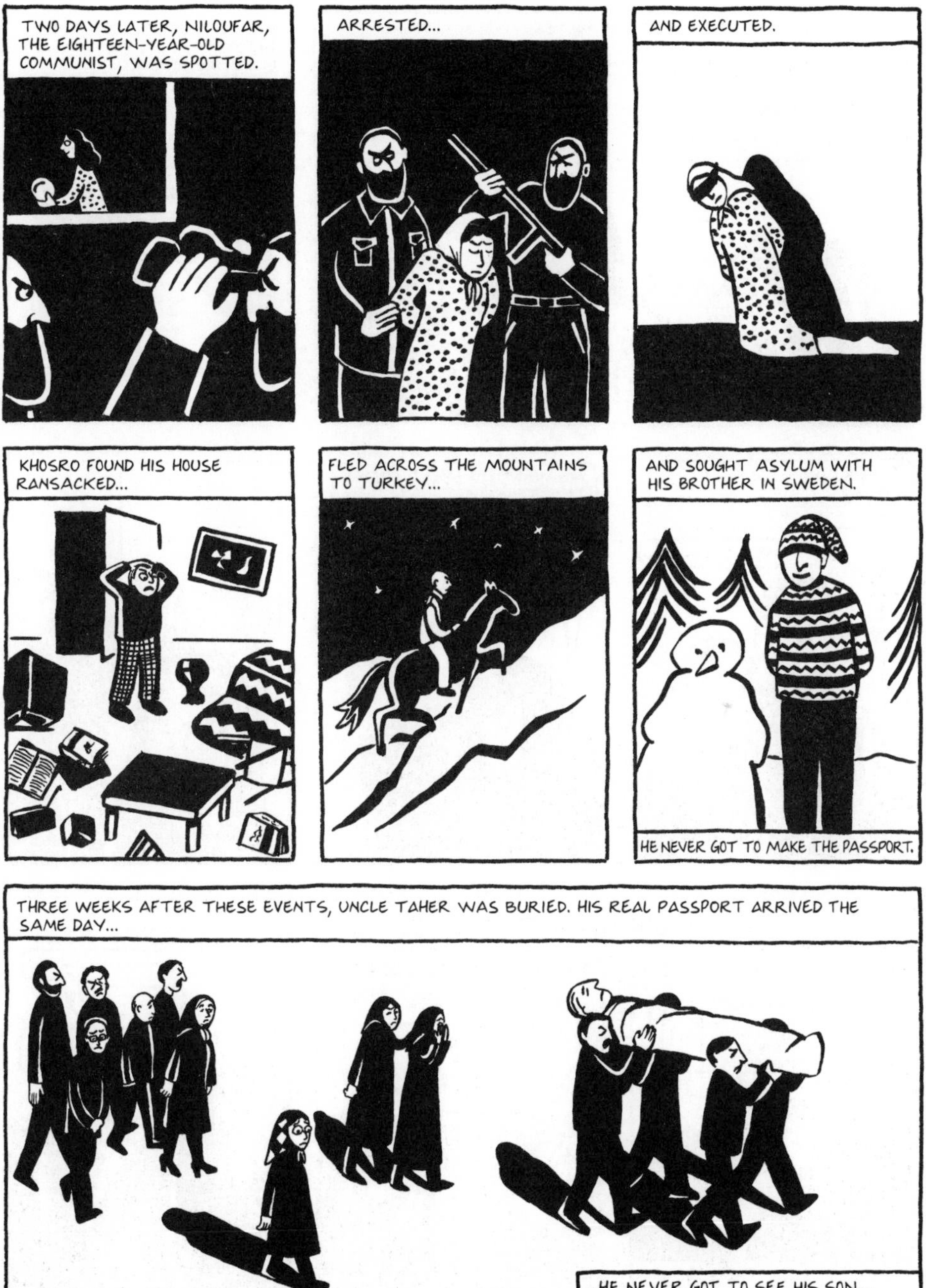
TWO DAYS LATER, NILOUFAR, THE EIGHTEEN-YEAR-OLD COMMUNIST, WAS SPOTTED.
ARRESTED...
AND EXECUTED.
KHOSRO FOUND HIS HOUSE RANSACKED...
FLED ACROSS THE MOUNTAINS TO TURKEY...
AND SOUGHT ASYLUM WITH HIS BROTHER IN SWEDEN.
HE NEVER GOT TO MAKE THE PASSPORT.
THREE WEEKS AFTER THESE EVENTS, UNCLE TAHER WAS BURIED. HIS REAL PASSPORT ARRIVED THE SAME DAY...
...HE NEVER GOT TO SEE HIS SON...

126

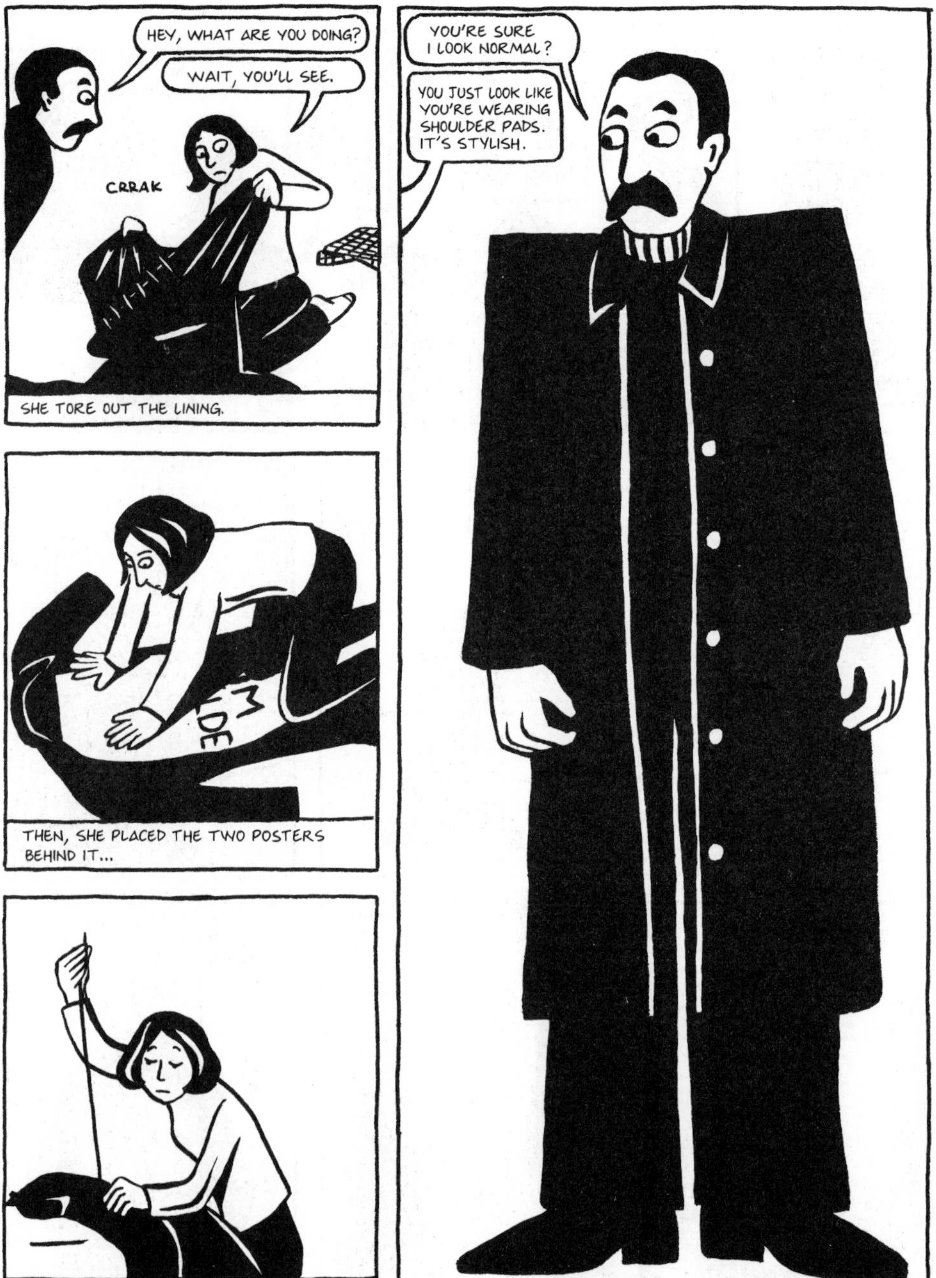
HEY, WHAT ARE YOU DOING?
WAIT, YOU'LL SEE.
CRRAK
SHE TORE OUT THE LINING.
M
DE
THEN, SHE PLACED THE TWO POSTERS BEHIND IT...
...AND THEN SEWED IT BACK IN.
YOU'RE SURE I LOOK NORMAL?
YOU JUST LOOK LIKE YOU'RE WEARING SHOULDER PADS. IT'S STYLISH.

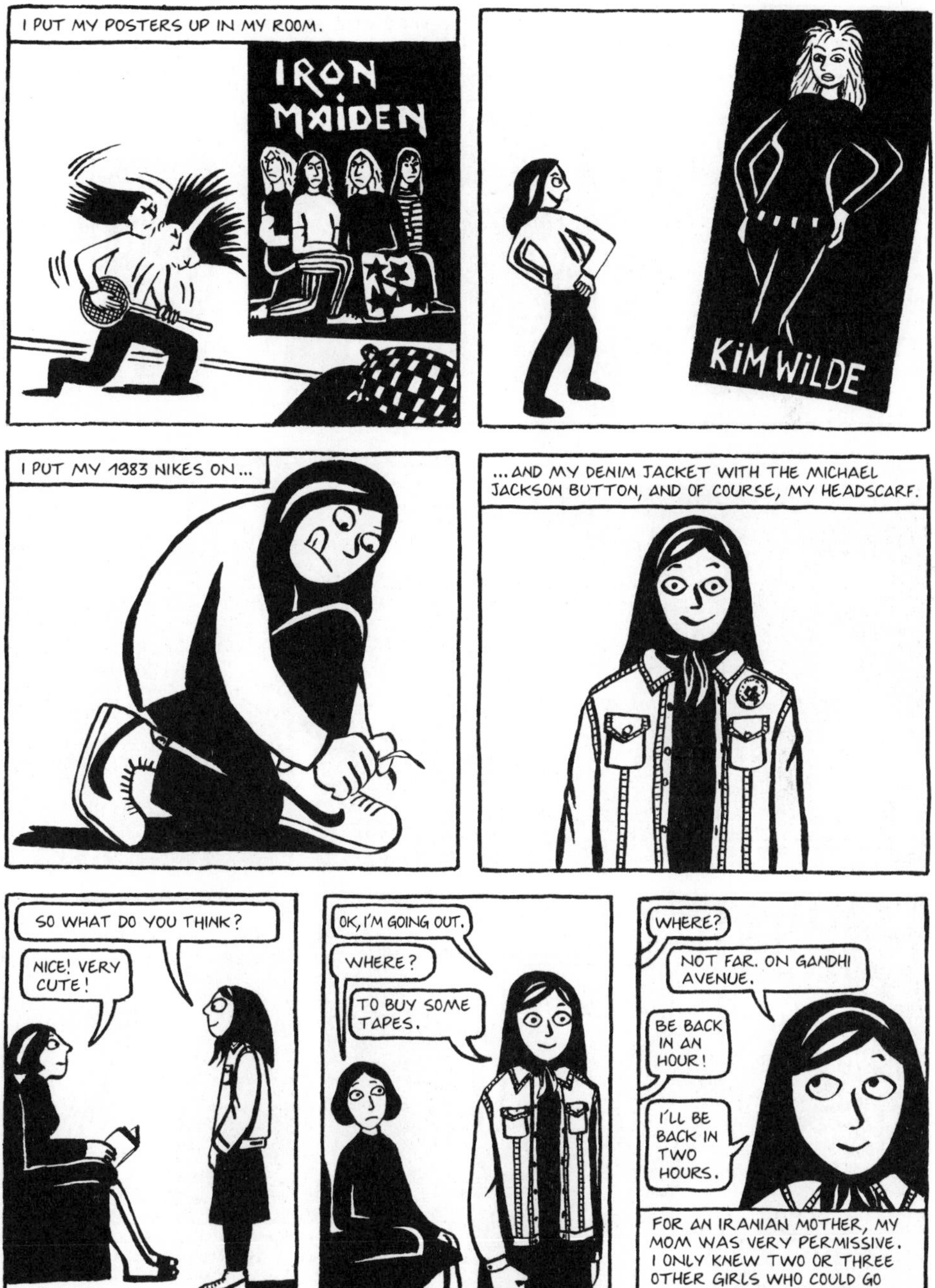
I PUT MY POSTERS UP IN MY ROOM.
IRON MAIDEN
KIM WILDE
I PUT MY 1983 NIKES ON...
...AND MY DENIM JACKET WITH THE MICHAEL JACKSON BUTTON, AND OF COURSE, MY HEADSCARF.
SO WHAT DO YOU THINK?
NICE! VERY CUTE!
OK, I'M GOING OUT.
WHERE?
TO BUY SOME TAPES.
WHERE?
NOT FAR. ON GANDHI AVENUE.
BE BACK IN AN HOUR!
I'LL BE BACK IN TWO HOURS.
FOR AN IRANIAN MOTHER, MY MOM WAS VERY PERMISSIVE. I ONLY KNEW TWO OR THREE OTHER GIRLS WHO COULD GO OUT ALONE AT THIRTEEN.

FOR A YEAR NOW, THE FOOD SHORTAGE HAD BEEN RESOLVED BY THE GROWTH OF THE BLACK MARKET. HOWEVER, FINDING TAPES WAS A LITTLE MORE COMPLICATED. ON GANDHI AVENUE YOU COULD FIND THEM SOMETIMES.

ABBA, BEE GEES

YAZOO

JULIO IGLESIAS

JIKAEL MACKSON

ESTEVIE VONDER

PINK FLOYD

VIDEOS, MUSIC, CARDS, LIPSTICK, NAIL POLISH, CHESS SET, PANTYHOSE, CHOCOLATE, ...,...

I BOUGHT TWO TAPES: KIM WILDE AND CAMEL.

HOW MUCH?

110 TUMANS.

♪WE'RE THE KIDS IN AMERICA ♪WHOA...

YOU! STOP!

THEY WERE GUARDIANS OF THE REVOLUTION, THE WOMEN'S BRANCH. THIS GROUP HAD BEEN ADDED IN 1982, TO ARREST WOMEN WHO WERE IMPROPERLY VEILED. (LIKE ME, FOR EXAMPLE.)

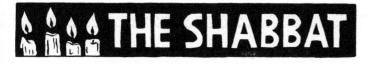

THE SHABBAT

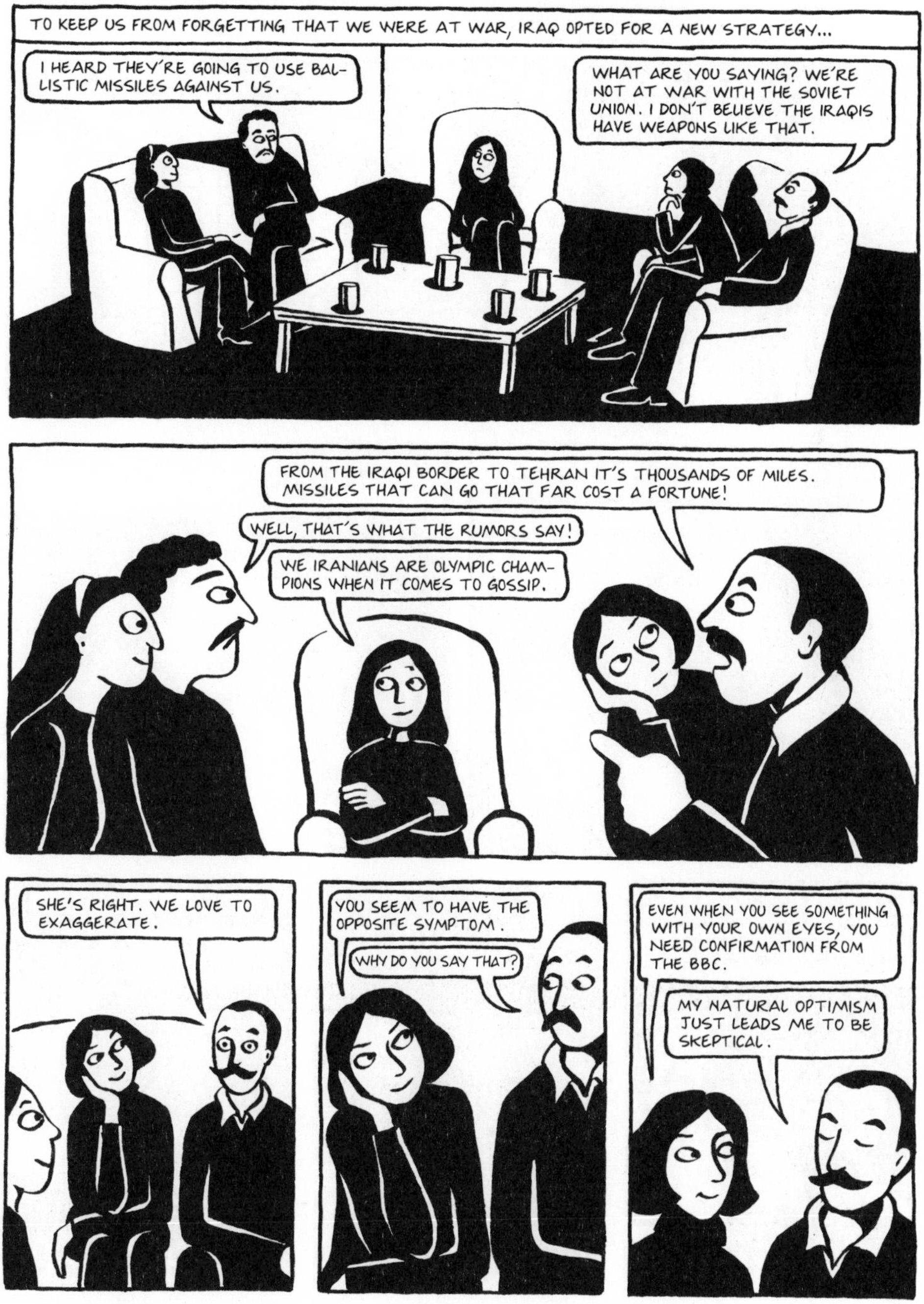
TO KEEP US FROM FORGETTING THAT WE WERE AT WAR, IRAQ OPTED FOR A NEW STRATEGY...
I HEARD THEY'RE GOING TO USE BALLISTIC MISSILES AGAINST US.
WHAT ARE YOU SAYING? WE'RE NOT AT WAR WITH THE SOVIET UNION. I DON'T BELIEVE THE IRAQIS HAVE WEAPONS LIKE THAT.
FROM THE IRAQI BORDER TO TEHRAN IT'S THOUSANDS OF MILES. MISSILES THAT CAN GO THAT FAR COST A FORTUNE!
WELL, THAT'S WHAT THE RUMORS SAY!
WE IRANIANS ARE OLYMPIC CHAMPIONS WHEN IT COMES TO GOSSIP.
SHE'S RIGHT. WE LOVE TO EXAGGERATE.
YOU SEEM TO HAVE THE OPPOSITE SYMPTOM.
WHY DO YOU SAY THAT?
EVEN WHEN YOU SEE SOMETHING WITH YOUR OWN EYES, YOU NEED CONFIRMATION FROM THE BBC.
MY NATURAL OPTIMISM JUST LEADS ME TO BE SKEPTICAL.

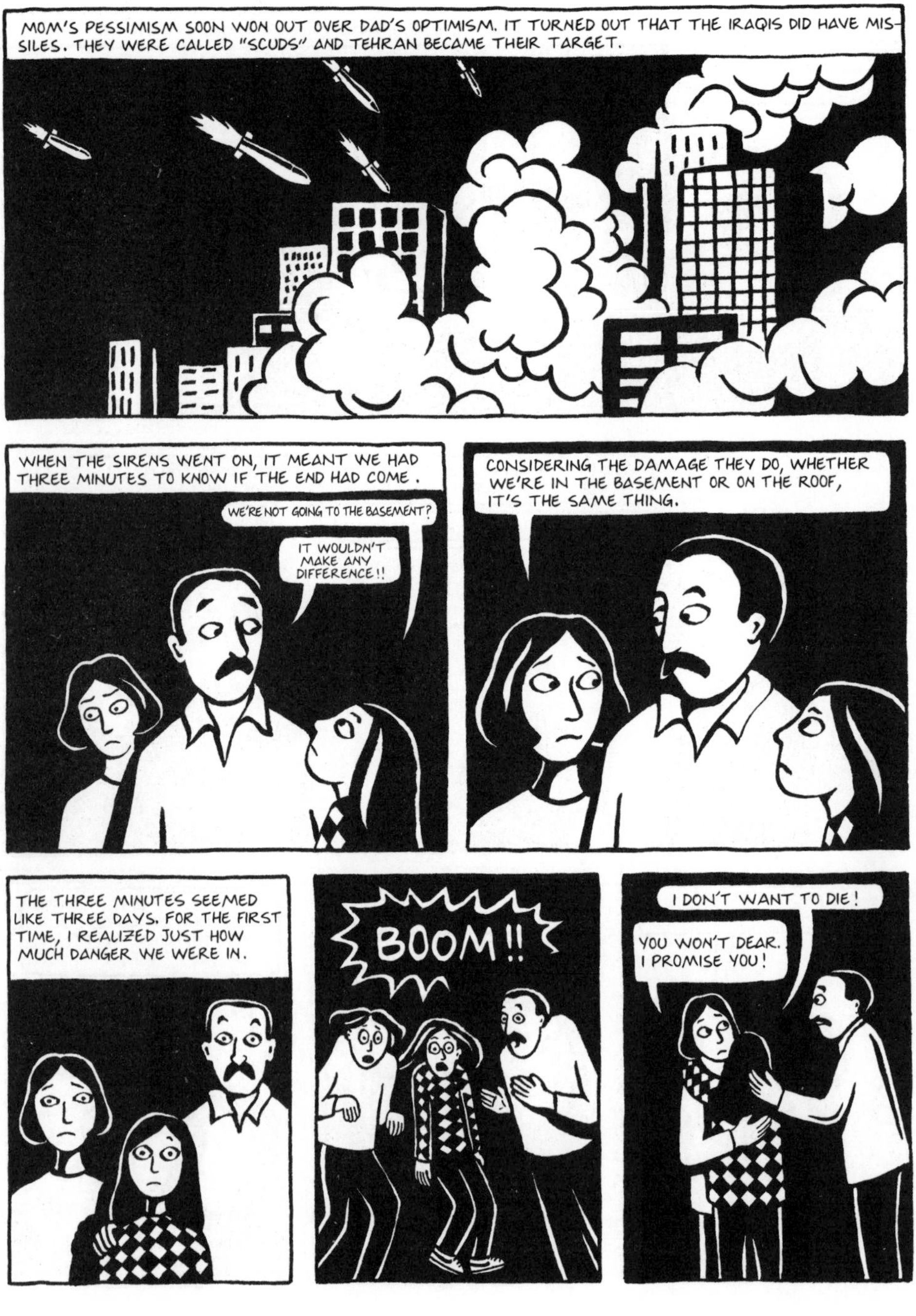
MOM'S PESSIMISM SOON WON OUT OVER DAD'S OPTIMISM. IT TURNED OUT THAT THE IRAQIS DID HAVE MISSILES. THEY WERE CALLED "SCUDS" AND TEHRAN BECAME THEIR TARGET.
WHEN THE SIRENS WENT ON, IT MEANT WE HAD THREE MINUTES TO KNOW IF THE END HAD COME.
WE'RE NOT GOING TO THE BASEMENT?
IT WOULDN'T MAKE ANY DIFFERENCE!!
CONSIDERING THE DAMAGE THEY DO, WHETHER WE'RE IN THE BASEMENT OR ON THE ROOF, IT'S THE SAME THING.
THE THREE MINUTES SEEMED LIKE THREE DAYS. FOR THE FIRST TIME, I REALIZED JUST HOW MUCH DANGER WE WERE IN.
BOOM!!
I DON'T WANT TO DIE!
YOU WON'T DEAR. I PROMISE YOU!

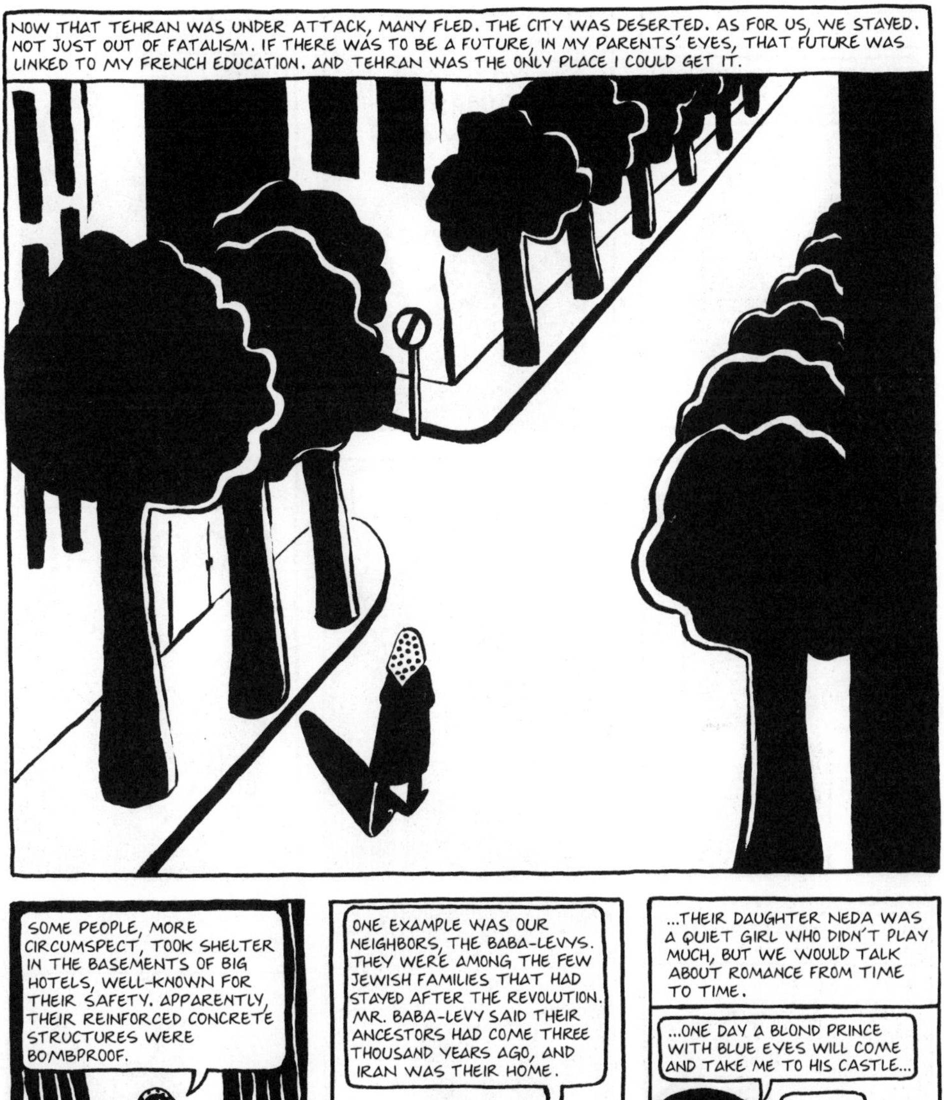
NOW THAT TEHRAN WAS UNDER ATTACK, MANY FLED. THE CITY WAS DESERTED. AS FOR US, WE STAYED. NOT JUST OUT OF FATALISM. IF THERE WAS TO BE A FUTURE, IN MY PARENTS' EYES, THAT FUTURE WAS LINKED TO MY FRENCH EDUCATION. AND TEHRAN WAS THE ONLY PLACE I COULD GET IT.
SOME PEOPLE, MORE CIRCUMSPECT, TOOK SHELTER IN THE BASEMENTS OF BIG HOTELS, WELL-KNOWN FOR THEIR SAFETY. APPARENTLY, THEIR REINFORCED CONCRETE STRUCTURES WERE BOMBPROOF.
ONE EXAMPLE WAS OUR NEIGHBORS, THE BABA-LEVYS. THEY WERE AMONG THE FEW JEWISH FAMILIES THAT HAD STAYED AFTER THE REVOLUTION. MR. BABA-LEVY SAID THEIR ANCESTORS HAD COME THREE THOUSAND YEARS AGO, AND IRAN WAS THEIR HOME.
...THEIR DAUGHTER NEDA WAS A QUIET GIRL WHO DIDN'T PLAY MUCH, BUT WE WOULD TALK ABOUT ROMANCE FROM TIME TO TIME.
...ONE DAY A BLOND PRINCE WITH BLUE EYES WILL COME AND TAKE ME TO HIS CASTLE...
OH YEAH! ME TOO!
SO LIFE WENT ON...

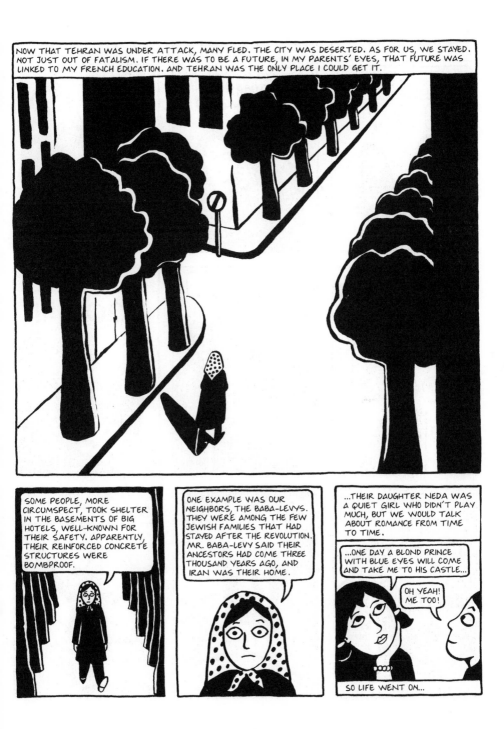

WHEN WE WALKED PAST THE BABA-LEVY'S HOUSE, WHICH WAS COMPLETELY DESTROYED, I COULD FEEL THAT SHE WAS DISCREETLY PULLING ME AWAY. SOMETHING TOLD ME THAT THE BABA-LEVYS HAD BEEN AT HOME. SOMETHING CAUGHT MY ATTENTION.

I SAW A TURQUOISE BRACELET. IT WAS NEDA'S. HER AUNT HAD GIVEN IT TO HER FOR HER FOURTEENTH BIRTHDAY...

THE BRACELET WAS STILL ATTACHED TO... I DON'T KNOW WHAT...

NO SCREAM IN THE WORLD COULD HAVE RELIEVED MY SUFFERING AND MY ANGER.

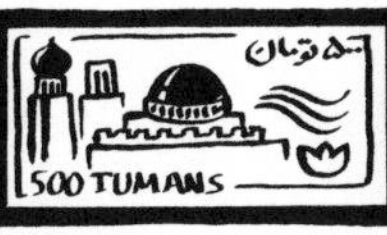
500 TUMANS

THE DOWRY

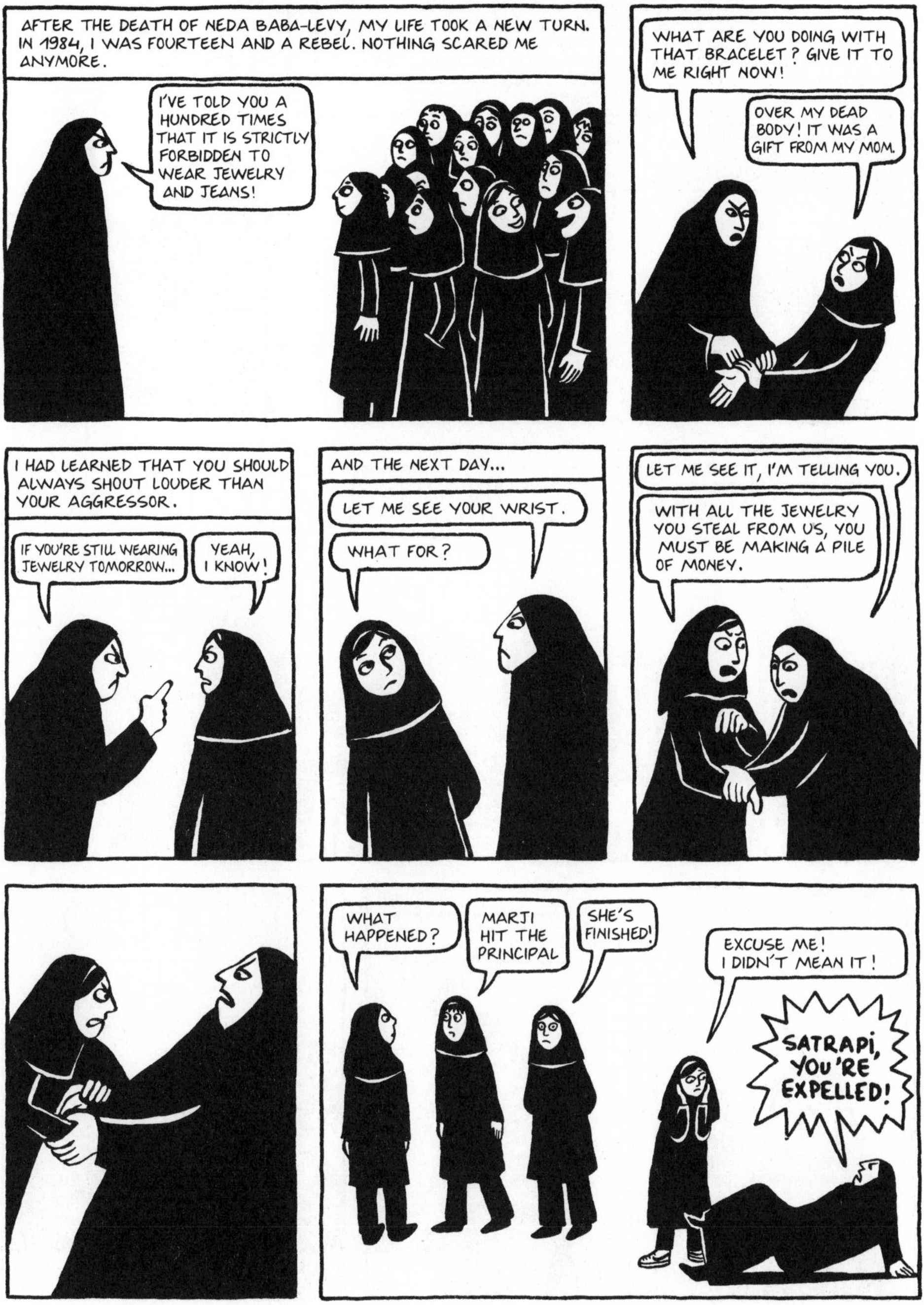
AFTER THE DEATH OF NEDA BABA-LEVY, MY LIFE TOOK A NEW TURN. IN 1984, I WAS FOURTEEN AND A REBEL. NOTHING SCARED ME ANYMORE.
I'VE TOLD YOU A HUNDRED TIMES THAT IT IS STRICTLY FORBIDDEN TO WEAR JEWELRY AND JEANS!
WHAT ARE YOU DOING WITH THAT BRACELET? GIVE IT TO ME RIGHT NOW!
OVER MY DEAD BODY! IT WAS A GIFT FROM MY MOM.
I HAD LEARNED THAT YOU SHOULD ALWAYS SHOUT LOUDER THAN YOUR AGGRESSOR.
IF YOU'RE STILL WEARING JEWELRY TOMORROW...
YEAH, I KNOW!
AND THE NEXT DAY...
LET ME SEE YOUR WRIST.
WHAT FOR?
LET ME SEE IT, I'M TELLING YOU.
WITH ALL THE JEWELRY YOU STEAL FROM US, YOU MUST BE MAKING A PILE OF MONEY.
WHAT HAPPENED?
MARJI HIT THE PRINCIPAL
SHE'S FINISHED!
EXCUSE ME! I DIDN'T MEAN IT!
SATRAPI, YOU'RE EXPELLED!

BUT HOW DO YOU KNOW THAT FOR SURE? MAYBE THEY JUST EXECUTED HER!

NO. YOUR MOTHER'S RIGHT. TRADITIONALLY, WHEN A GIRL GETS MARRIED, THE HUSBAND IS SUPPOSED TO PAY HER A DOWRY.

IF THE GIRL DIES, THE HUSBAND HAS TO GIVE THE DOWRY TO HER FAMILY.

THAT'S WHAT HAPPENED WITH NILOUFAR. AFTER SHE WAS EXECUTED, TO MAKE SURE HER AWFUL FATE WAS UNDERSTOOD, THEY SENT 500 TUMANS* TO HER PARENTS.

500 TUMANS FOR THE LIFE AND VIRGINITY OF AN INNOCENT GIRL.

I HAD NO IDEA.

*EQUIVALENT TO $5.00

ALL NIGHT LONG, I THOUGHT OF THAT PHRASE: "TO DIE A MARTYR IS TO INJECT BLOOD INTO THE VEINS OF SOCIETY." NILOUFAR WAS A REAL MARTYR, AND HER BLOOD CERTAINLY DID NOT FEED OUR SOCIETY'S VEINS.

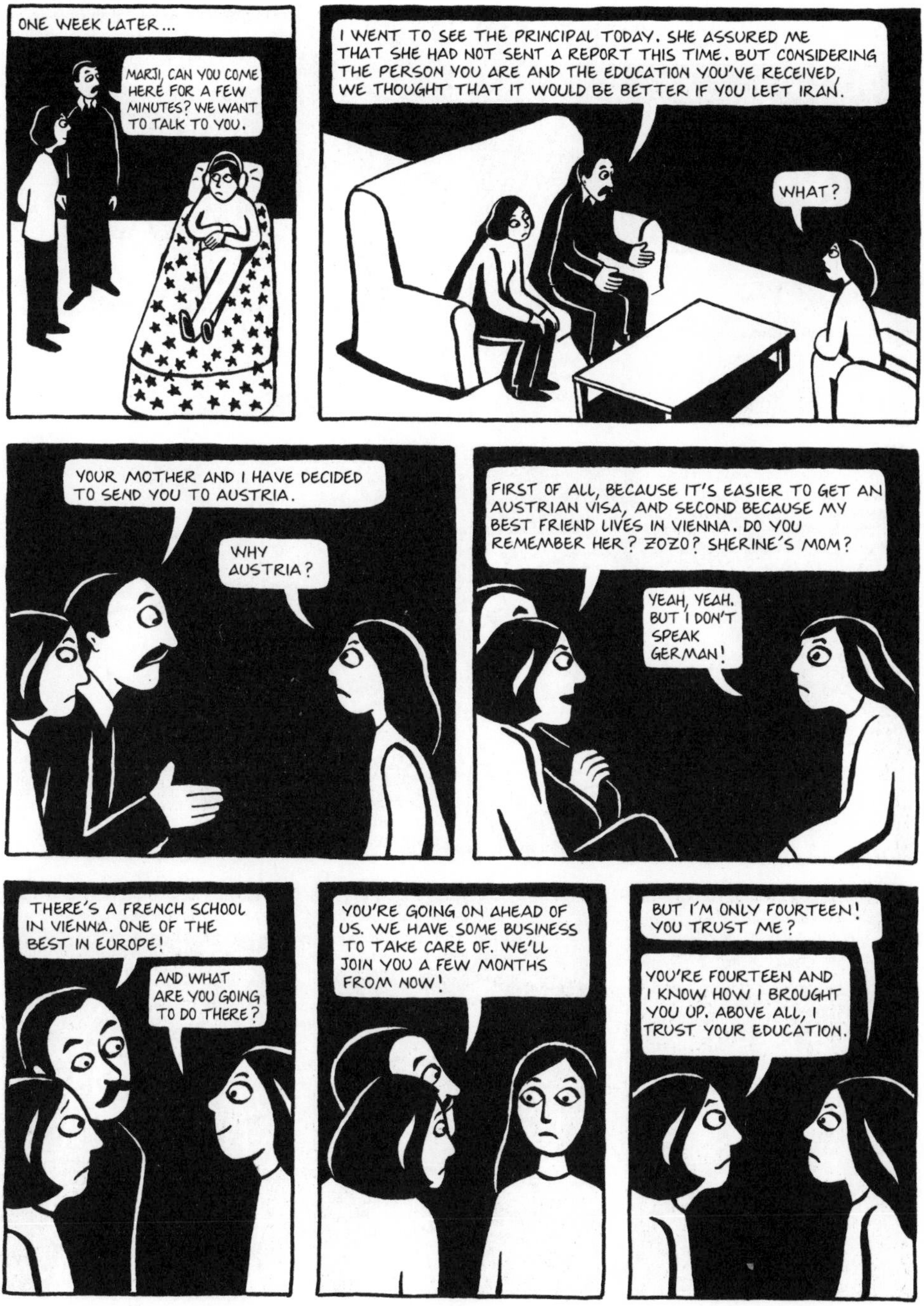
ONE WEEK LATER...
MARJI, CAN YOU COME HERE FOR A FEW MINUTES? WE WANT TO TALK TO YOU.
I WENT TO SEE THE PRINCIPAL TODAY. SHE ASSURED ME THAT SHE HAD NOT SENT A REPORT THIS TIME. BUT CONSIDERING THE PERSON YOU ARE AND THE EDUCATION YOU'VE RECEIVED, WE THOUGHT THAT IT WOULD BE BETTER IF YOU LEFT IRAN.
WHAT?
YOUR MOTHER AND I HAVE DECIDED TO SEND YOU TO AUSTRIA.
WHY AUSTRIA?
FIRST OF ALL, BECAUSE IT'S EASIER TO GET AN AUSTRIAN VISA, AND SECOND BECAUSE MY BEST FRIEND LIVES IN VIENNA. DO YOU REMEMBER HER? ZOZO? SHERINE'S MOM?
YEAH, YEAH. BUT I DON'T SPEAK GERMAN!
THERE'S A FRENCH SCHOOL IN VIENNA. ONE OF THE BEST IN EUROPE!
AND WHAT ARE YOU GOING TO DO THERE?
YOU'RE GOING ON AHEAD OF US. WE HAVE SOME BUSINESS TO TAKE CARE OF. WE'LL JOIN YOU A FEW MONTHS FROM NOW!
BUT I'M ONLY FOURTEEN! YOU TRUST ME?
YOU'RE FOURTEEN AND I KNOW HOW I BROUGHT YOU UP. ABOVE ALL, I TRUST YOUR EDUCATION.

148

149

151

152

NOVEMBER 1984. I AM IN AUSTRIA. I HAD COME HERE WITH THE IDEA OF LEAVING A RELIGIOUS IRAN FOR AN OPEN AND SECULAR EUROPE AND THAT ZOZO, MY MOTHER'S BEST FRIEND, WOULD LOVE ME LIKE HER OWN DAUGHTER.

ONLY HERE I AM! SHE LEFT ME AT A BOARDING HOUSE RUN BY NUNS.

MY ROOM WAS SMALL, AND FOR THE FIRST TIME IN MY LIFE I HAD TO SHARE MY SPACE WITH ANOTHER PERSON.

I HADN'T MET HER YET. I ONLY KNEW THAT HER NAME WAS LUCIA.

I WONDERED WHAT SHE WOULD LOOK LIKE.

EUROPE, THE ALPS, SWITZERLAND, AUSTRIA... FROM THIS I DEDUCED THAT SHE WOULD BE LIKE HEIDI.

THIS WAS OKAY WITH ME. I REALLY LIKED HEIDI.

...I LIVED WITH THEM FOR TEN DAYS. THERE WERE FIGHTS DAILY.

HI SWEETHEART! HERE, THESE ARE FOR YOU!

YOU INCOMPETENT IDIOT! I WORK MYSELF TO THE BONE SO THAT YOU CAN THROW MONEY AWAY ON FLOWERS!

BUT ZOZO, IT'S OUR WEDDING ANNIVERSARY.

YOU CAN GIVE ME WHAT- EVER YOU WANT THE DAY YOU'VE EARNED SOME MONEY. I'VE HAD ENOUGH!!

IN TEHRAN, ZOZO WAS HER HUSBAND HOUSHANG'S SECRETARY,

IN VIENNA, SHE BECAME A HAIRDRESSER.

IT WAS SHE, BY THE WAY, WHO CUT OFF MY LONG HAIR.

AS FOR HOUSHANG, ZOZO'S HUSBAND, HE WAS A CEO IN IRAN,

BUT IN AUSTRIA, HE WAS NOTHING.

THANKS TO A DOZEN BAD INVESTMENTS, HOUSHANG HAD LOST ALL HIS CAPITAL. "YOU GAMBLED IT AWAY!" I HEARD THAT IN THE COURSE OF ONE OF THEIR HABITUAL QUARRELS.

I SAW YOU AT THE CAFÉ WITH THOSE TWO BASTARDS! THEY'D HAVE TO STEAL THE CLOTHES OFF YOUR BACK FOR YOU TO RECOGNIZE THEIR INGRATITUDE!

I WAS ASHAMED. I'D NEVER HEARD MY PARENTS BICKER OVER MONEY.

PROBABLY BECAUSE MY FATHER WASN'T INCOMPETENT ...

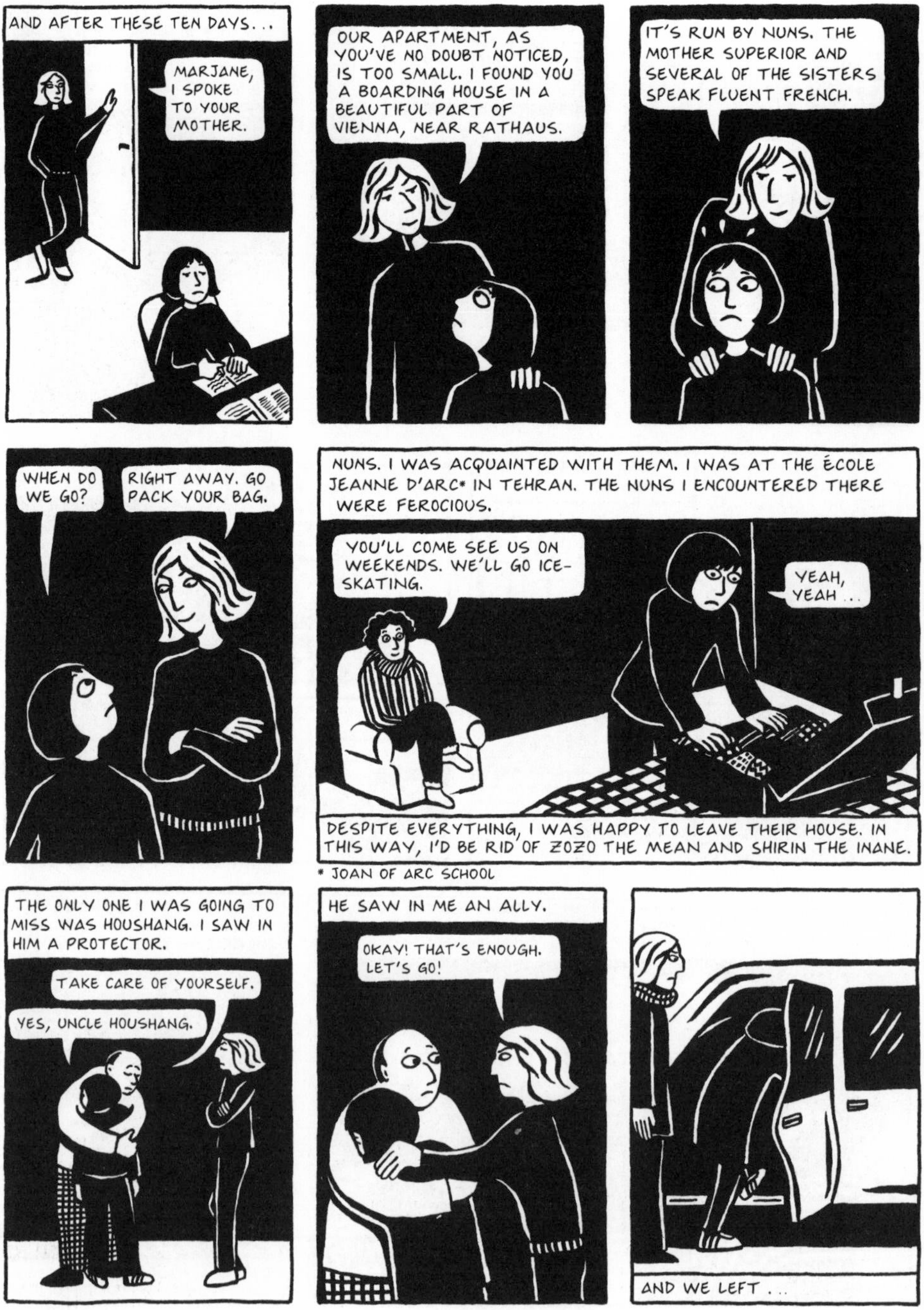
AND AFTER THESE TEN DAYS...
MARJANE, I SPOKE TO YOUR MOTHER.
OUR APARTMENT, AS YOU'VE NO DOUBT NOTICED, IS TOO SMALL. I FOUND YOU A BOARDING HOUSE IN A BEAUTIFUL PART OF VIENNA, NEAR RATHAUS.
IT'S RUN BY NUNS. THE MOTHER SUPERIOR AND SEVERAL OF THE SISTERS SPEAK FLUENT FRENCH.
WHEN DO WE GO?
RIGHT AWAY. GO PACK YOUR BAG.
NUNS. I WAS ACQUAINTED WITH THEM. I WAS AT THE ÉCOLE JEANNE D'ARC* IN TEHRAN. THE NUNS I ENCOUNTERED THERE WERE FEROCIOUS.
YOU'LL COME SEE US ON WEEKENDS. WE'LL GO ICE-SKATING.
YEAH, YEAH...
DESPITE EVERYTHING, I WAS HAPPY TO LEAVE THEIR HOUSE. IN THIS WAY, I'D BE RID OF ZOZO THE MEAN AND SHIRIN THE INANE.
* JOAN OF ARC SCHOOL
THE ONLY ONE I WAS GOING TO MISS WAS HOUSHANG. I SAW IN HIM A PROTECTOR.
TAKE CARE OF YOURSELF.
YES, UNCLE HOUSHANG.
HE SAW IN ME AN ALLY.
OKAY! THAT'S ENOUGH. LET'S GO!
AND WE LEFT...

HERE'S YOUR NEW HOME.

IT'S IMPERATIVE THAT YOU BE BACK BY 9:30. AFTER THAT THE DOOR WILL BE LOCKED.

HERE, MADEMOISELLE. THIS IS YOUR ROOM. YOU'LL SHARE IT WITH LUCIA. SHE'S ARRIVING THIS AFTERNOON.

YOU'LL SEE, YOU'LL BE HAPPY WITH US. WHICH DENOMINATION ARE YOU?

NONE.

OH!

THE SHARED KITCHEN,

THE SHOWERS,

FOR YOUR SHOPPING, YOU CAN GO TO "ALDI." GO OUT AND TURN LEFT, LINKS!*

LINKS!

NOW I HAD A REAL INDEPENDENT ADULT LIFE. I WAS GOING TO FEED MYSELF, DO MY OWN LAUNDRY...

I HEADED STRAIGHT FOR THE SUPERMARKET TO BUY GROCERIES LIKE A WOMAN.

*ALDI IS A SUPERMARKET AND LINKS MEANS LEFT IN GERMAN.

159

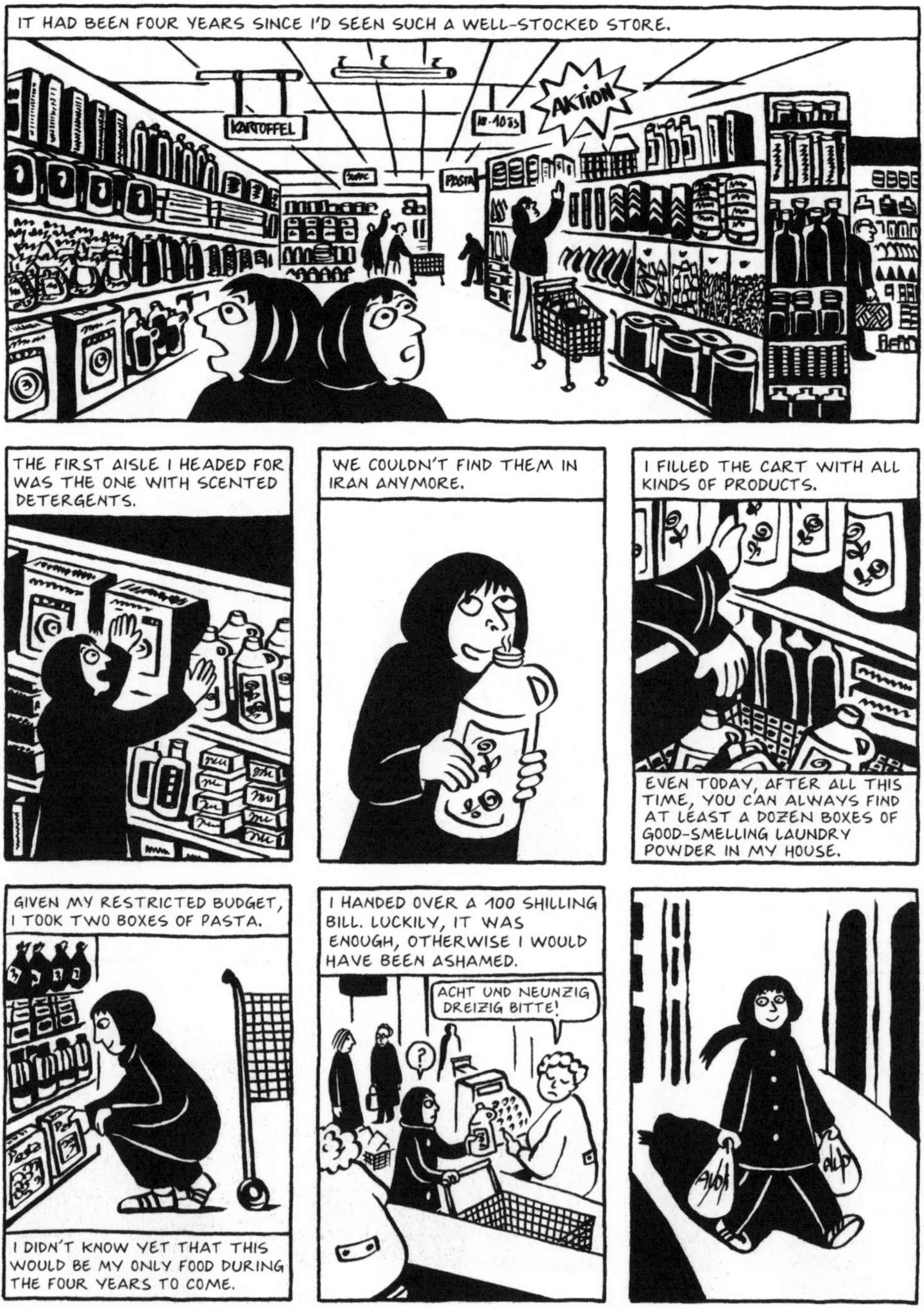
IT HAD BEEN FOUR YEARS SINCE I'D SEEN SUCH A WELL-STOCKED STORE.
KARTOFFEL
AKTION
PASTA
THE FIRST AISLE I HEADED FOR WAS THE ONE WITH SCENTED DETERGENTS.
WE COULDN'T FIND THEM IN IRAN ANYMORE.
I FILLED THE CART WITH ALL KINDS OF PRODUCTS.
EVEN TODAY, AFTER ALL THIS TIME, YOU CAN ALWAYS FIND AT LEAST A DOZEN BOXES OF GOOD-SMELLING LAUNDRY POWDER IN MY HOUSE.
GIVEN MY RESTRICTED BUDGET, I TOOK TWO BOXES OF PASTA.
I DIDN'T KNOW YET THAT THIS WOULD BE MY ONLY FOOD DURING THE FOUR YEARS TO COME.
I HANDED OVER A 100 SHILLING BILL. LUCKILY, IT WAS ENOUGH, OTHERWISE I WOULD HAVE BEEN ASHAMED.
ACHT UND NEUNZIG DREIZIG BITTE!
?

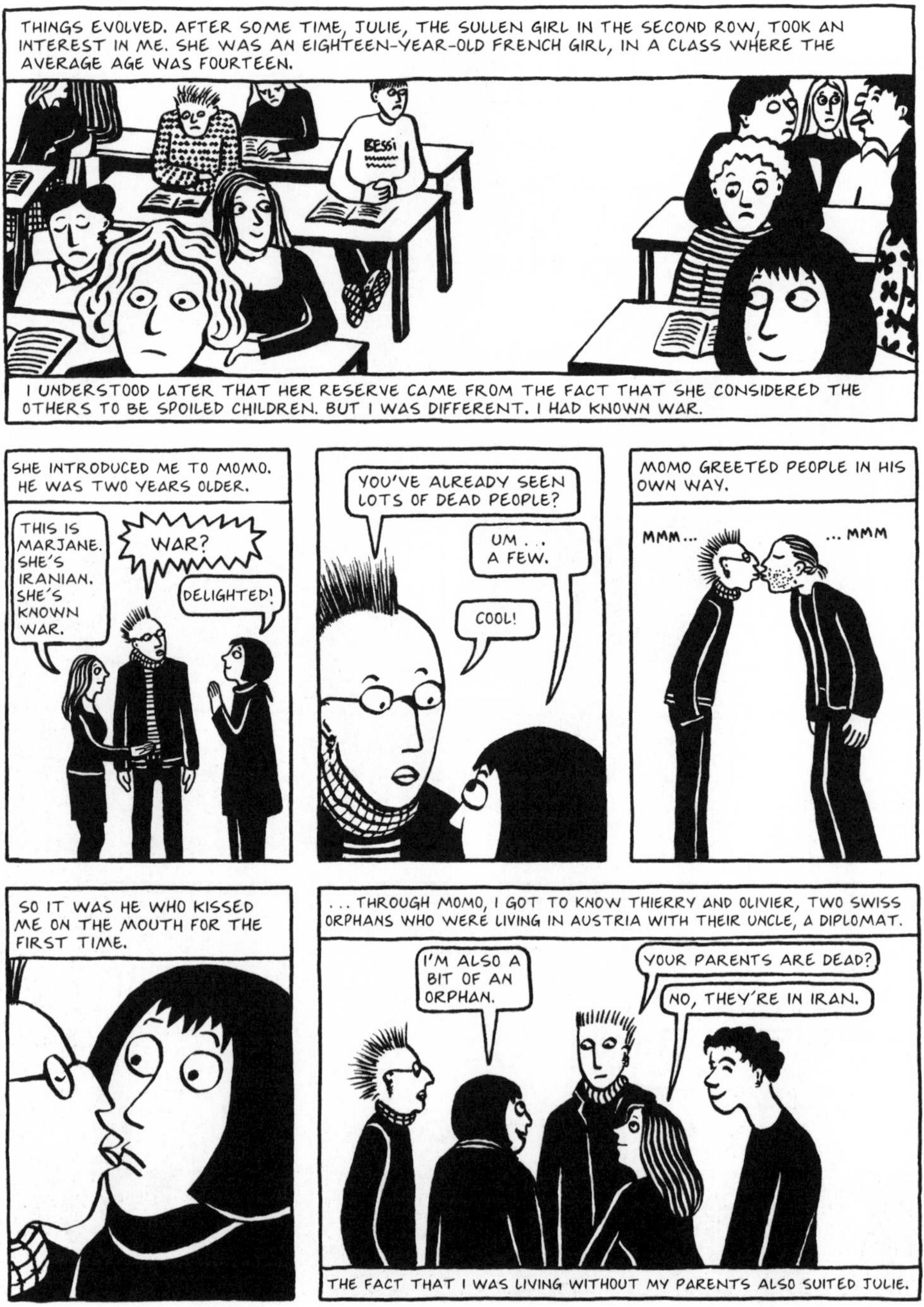
THINGS EVOLVED. AFTER SOME TIME, JULIE, THE SULLEN GIRL IN THE SECOND ROW, TOOK AN INTEREST IN ME. SHE WAS AN EIGHTEEN-YEAR-OLD FRENCH GIRL, IN A CLASS WHERE THE AVERAGE AGE WAS FOURTEEN.
BESSI
I UNDERSTOOD LATER THAT HER RESERVE CAME FROM THE FACT THAT SHE CONSIDERED THE OTHERS TO BE SPOILED CHILDREN. BUT I WAS DIFFERENT. I HAD KNOWN WAR.
SHE INTRODUCED ME TO MOMO. HE WAS TWO YEARS OLDER.
THIS IS MARJANE. SHE'S IRANIAN. SHE'S KNOWN WAR.
WAR?
DELIGHTED!
YOU'VE ALREADY SEEN LOTS OF DEAD PEOPLE?
UM . . . A FEW.
COOL!
MOMO GREETED PEOPLE IN HIS OWN WAY.
MMM...
...MMM
SO IT WAS HE WHO KISSED ME ON THE MOUTH FOR THE FIRST TIME.
. . . THROUGH MOMO, I GOT TO KNOW THIERRY AND OLIVIER, TWO SWISS ORPHANS WHO WERE LIVING IN AUSTRIA WITH THEIR UNCLE, A DIPLOMAT.
I'M ALSO A BIT OF AN ORPHAN.
YOUR PARENTS ARE DEAD?
NO, THEY'RE IN IRAN.
THE FACT THAT I WAS LIVING WITHOUT MY PARENTS ALSO SUITED JULIE.

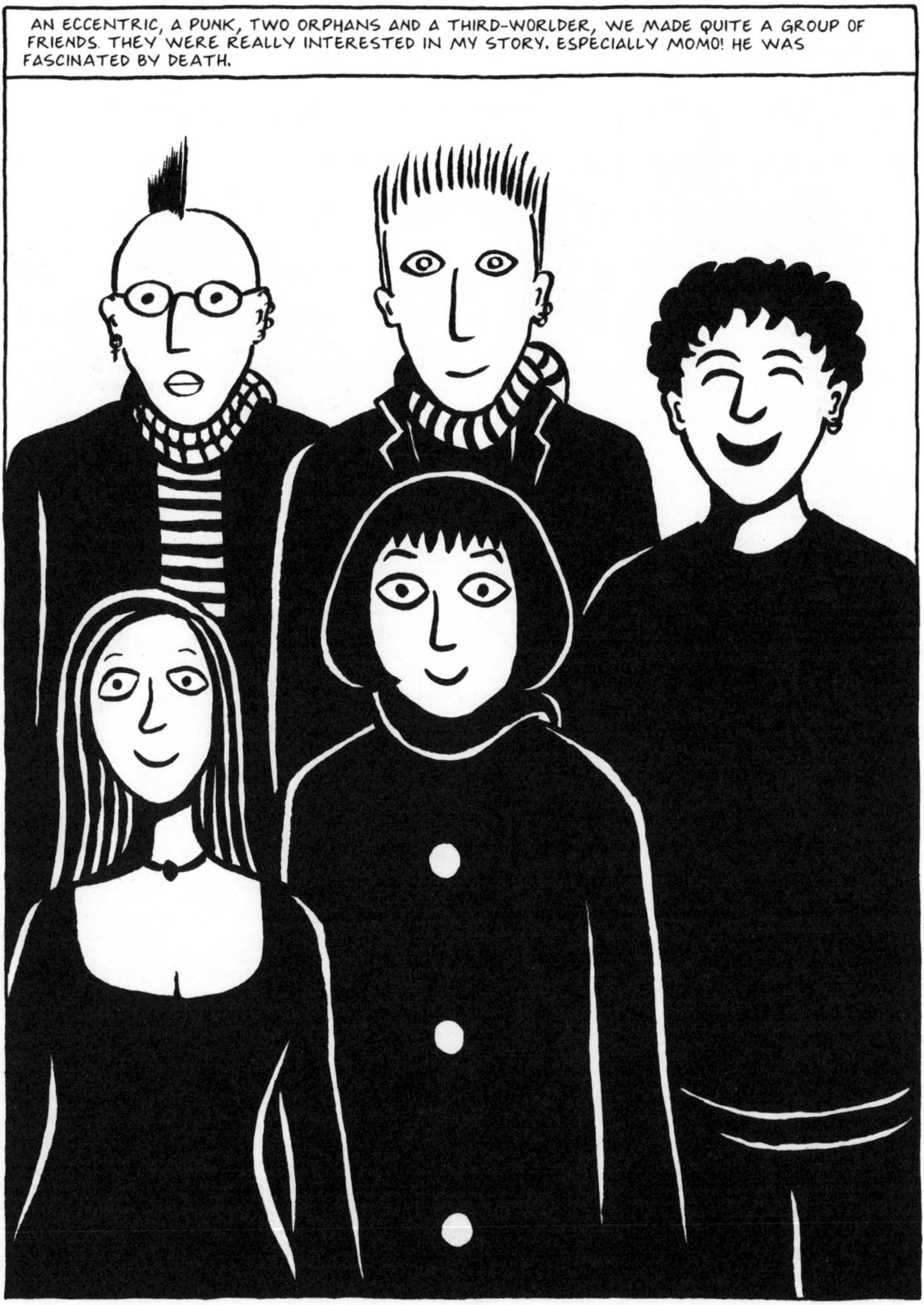
AN ECCENTRIC, A PUNK, TWO ORPHANS AND A THIRD-WORLDER, WE MADE QUITE A GROUP OF FRIENDS. THEY WERE REALLY INTERESTED IN MY STORY. ESPECIALLY MOMO! HE WAS FASCINATED BY DEATH.

168

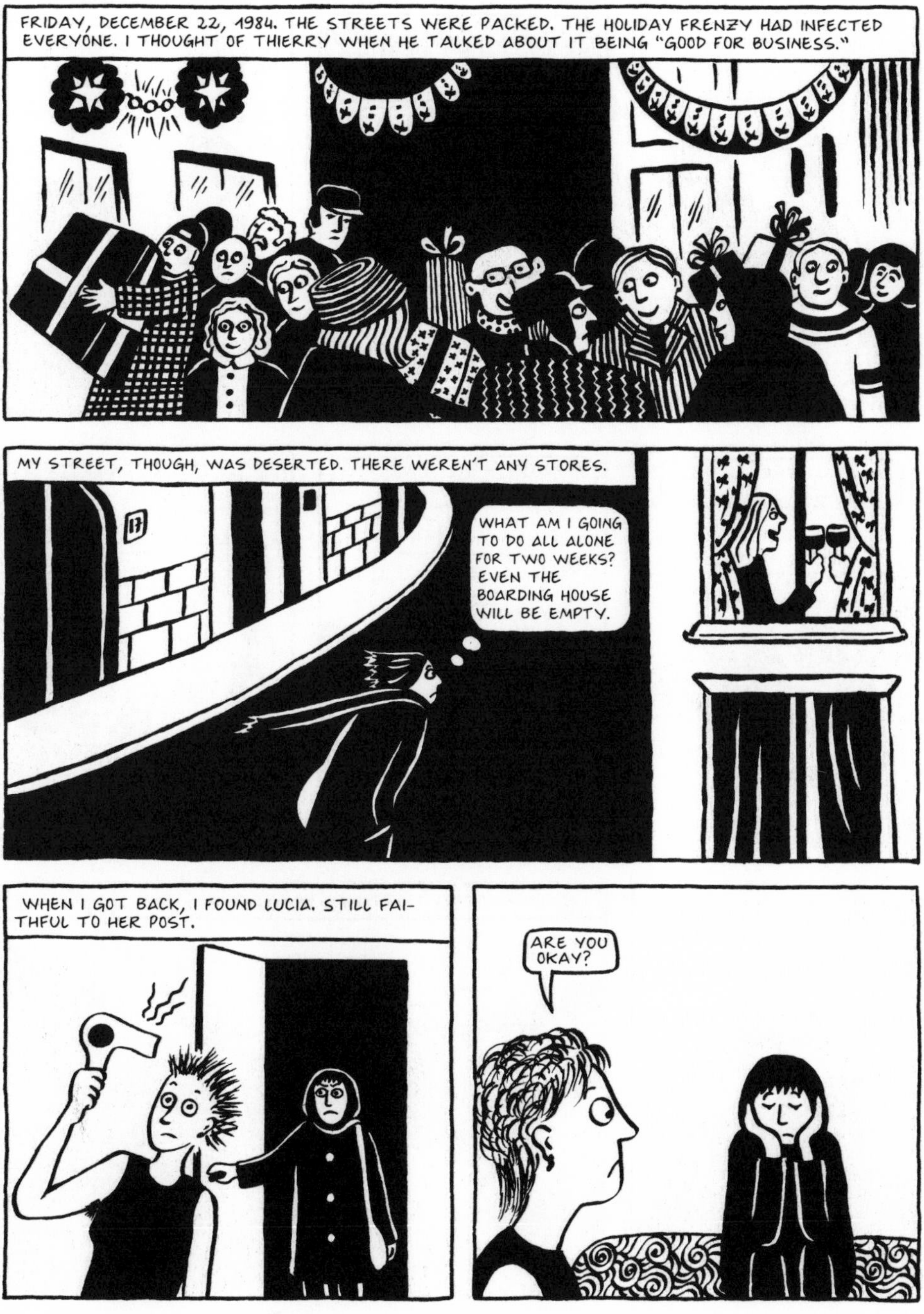
FRIDAY, DECEMBER 22, 1984. THE STREETS WERE PACKED. THE HOLIDAY FRENZY HAD INFECTED EVERYONE. I THOUGHT OF THIERRY WHEN HE TALKED ABOUT IT BEING "GOOD FOR BUSINESS."
MY STREET, THOUGH, WAS DESERTED. THERE WEREN'T ANY STORES.
WHAT AM I GOING TO DO ALL ALONE FOR TWO WEEKS? EVEN THE BOARDING HOUSE WILL BE EMPTY.
WHEN I GOT BACK, I FOUND LUCIA. STILL FAITHFUL TO HER POST.
ARE YOU OKAY?

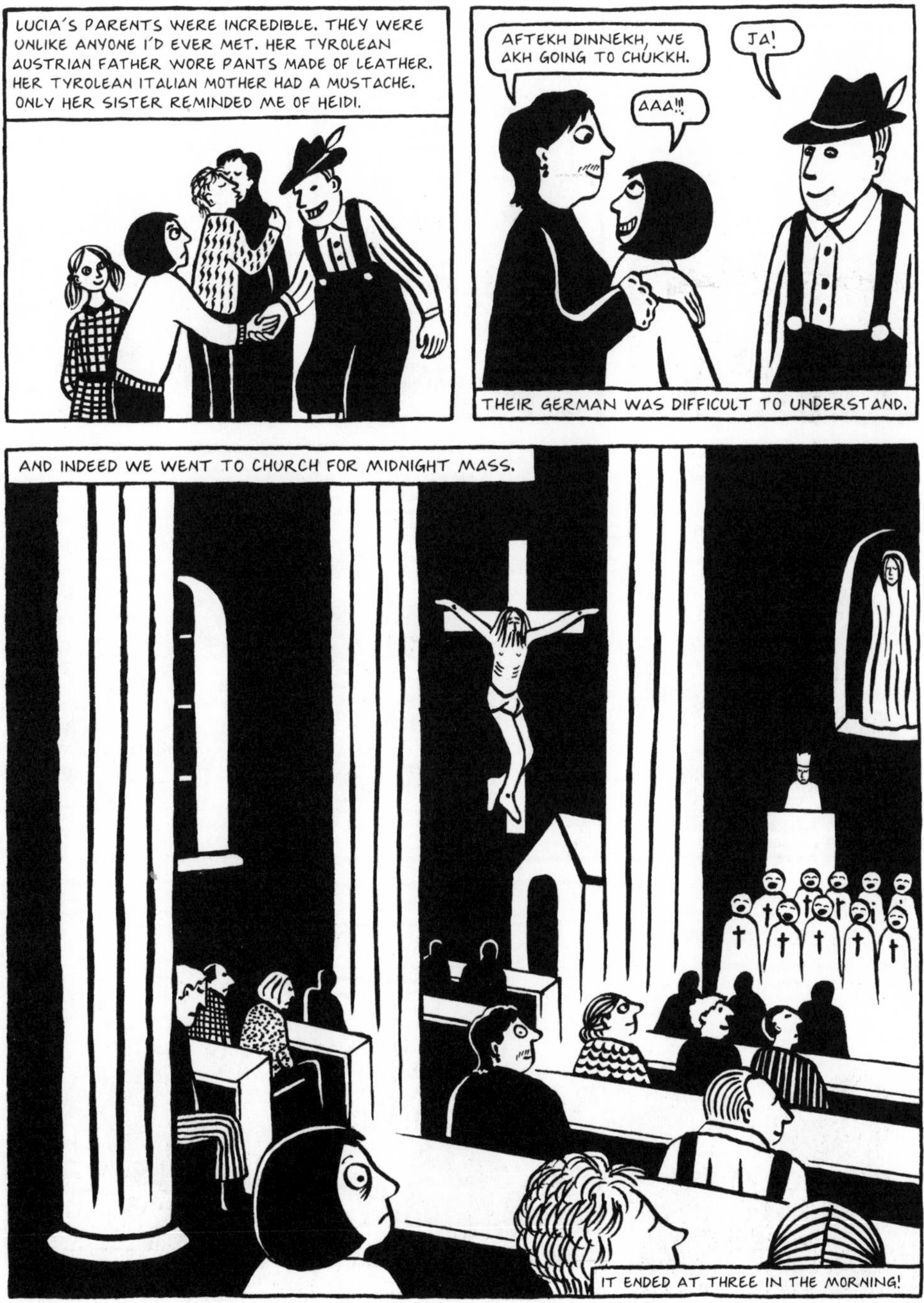
LUCIA'S PARENTS WERE INCREDIBLE. THEY WERE UNLIKE ANYONE I'D EVER MET. HER TYROLEAN AUSTRIAN FATHER WORE PANTS MADE OF LEATHER. HER TYROLEAN ITALIAN MOTHER HAD A MUSTACHE. ONLY HER SISTER REMINDED ME OF HEIDI.
AFTEKH DINNEKH, WE AKH GOING TO CHUKKH.
AAA!!
JA!
THEIR GERMAN WAS DIFFICULT TO UNDERSTAND.
AND INDEED WE WENT TO CHURCH FOR MIDNIGHT MASS.
IT ENDED AT THREE IN THE MORNING!

LUCIA'S FAMILY HAD NEVER SEEN ANY IRANIANS. I WAS THEREFORE INVITED OVER EVERY DAY BY AN UNCLE AND AN AUNT WHO WANTED TO GET TO KNOW ME.

IT'S GOOD? YOU LIKE?

YES.

MY GERMAN WAS RUDIMEN-TARY, THEIRS UNUSUAL. A COUSIN WHO HAD SPENT FOUR YEARS IN FRANCOPHONE SWITZERLAND ENJOYED ACTING AS MY TRANSLATOR.

SHE SAYS THAT SHE ATE WELL.

SHE SAYS THAT SHE LIKES TYROL A LOT.

DESSERT!

SHE SAYS THAT TYROLEANS ARE VERY NICE.

THEY SAY THAT THEY LIKE YOU TOO.

WE SPOKE OF EVERYTHING.

IT'S WONDERFUL TO HAVE INTERNATIONAL FRIENDS.

JAAA

AS OPPOSED TO MY SCHOOL FRIENDS' FAVORITE SUBJECTS OF CONVERSATION, WE NEVER TOUCHED ON WAR, OR DEATH.

FINALLY THE DAY OF DEPARTURE ARRIVED.

YOU KNOW, I'M A CABINETMAKER. I MADE THIS FRAME ESPECIALLY FOR YOU.

SCHATZI,* A CANDIED APPLE AND SOME FRUIT FOR THE ROAD.

I HAD A NEW SET OF PARENTS ...

* DEAR

... LUCIA WAS MY SISTER.

AFTER THIS TRIP, I NEVER COM-PLAINED ABOUT HER HAIR DRYER.

PASTA

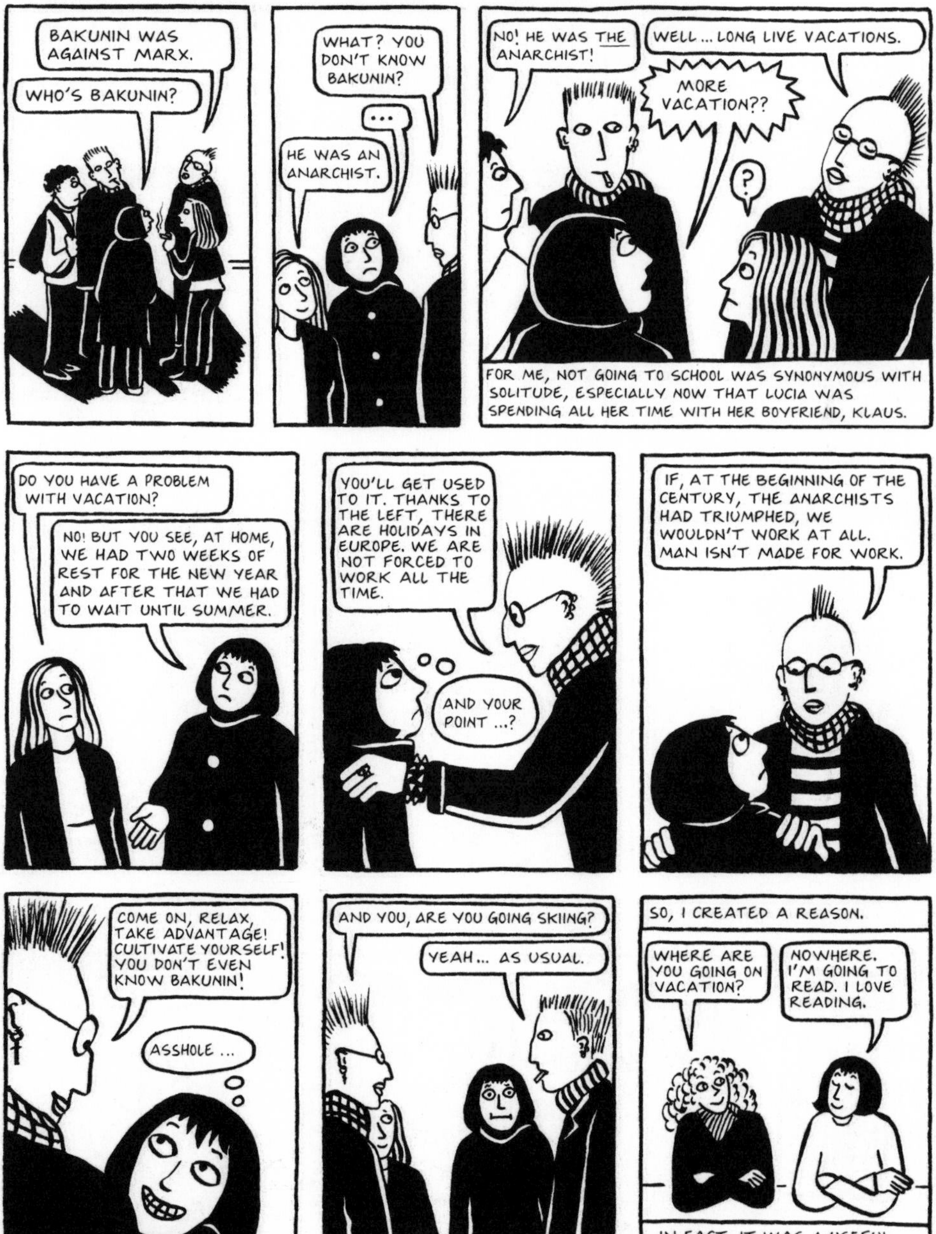

BAKUNIN WAS AGAINST MARX.
WHO'S BAKUNIN?
WHAT? YOU DON'T KNOW BAKUNIN?
...
HE WAS AN ANARCHIST.
NO! HE WAS THE ANARCHIST!
WELL ... LONG LIVE VACATIONS.
MORE VACATION??
?
FOR ME, NOT GOING TO SCHOOL WAS SYNONYMOUS WITH SOLITUDE, ESPECIALLY NOW THAT LUCIA WAS SPENDING ALL HER TIME WITH HER BOYFRIEND, KLAUS.
DO YOU HAVE A PROBLEM WITH VACATION?
NO! BUT YOU SEE, AT HOME, WE HAD TWO WEEKS OF REST FOR THE NEW YEAR AND AFTER THAT WE HAD TO WAIT UNTIL SUMMER.
YOU'LL GET USED TO IT. THANKS TO THE LEFT, THERE ARE HOLIDAYS IN EUROPE. WE ARE NOT FORCED TO WORK ALL THE TIME.
AND YOUR POINT ...?
IF, AT THE BEGINNING OF THE CENTURY, THE ANARCHISTS HAD TRIUMPHED, WE WOULDN'T WORK AT ALL. MAN ISN'T MADE FOR WORK.
COME ON, RELAX, TAKE ADVANTAGE! CULTIVATE YOURSELF! YOU DON'T EVEN KNOW BAKUNIN!
ASSHOLE ...
AND YOU, ARE YOU GOING SKIING?
YEAH... AS USUAL.
THIS CRETIN MOMO WASN'T ALTOGETHER WRONG. I NEEDED TO FIT IN, AND FOR THAT I NEEDED TO EDUCATE MYSELF.
SO, I CREATED A REASON.
WHERE ARE YOU GOING ON VACATION?
NOWHERE. I'M GOING TO READ. I LOVE READING.
IN FACT, IT WAS A USEFUL ANSWER TO THE PERENNIAL QUESTION "WHERE ARE YOU GOING?," ALL THE WHILE GIVING ME A ROLE.

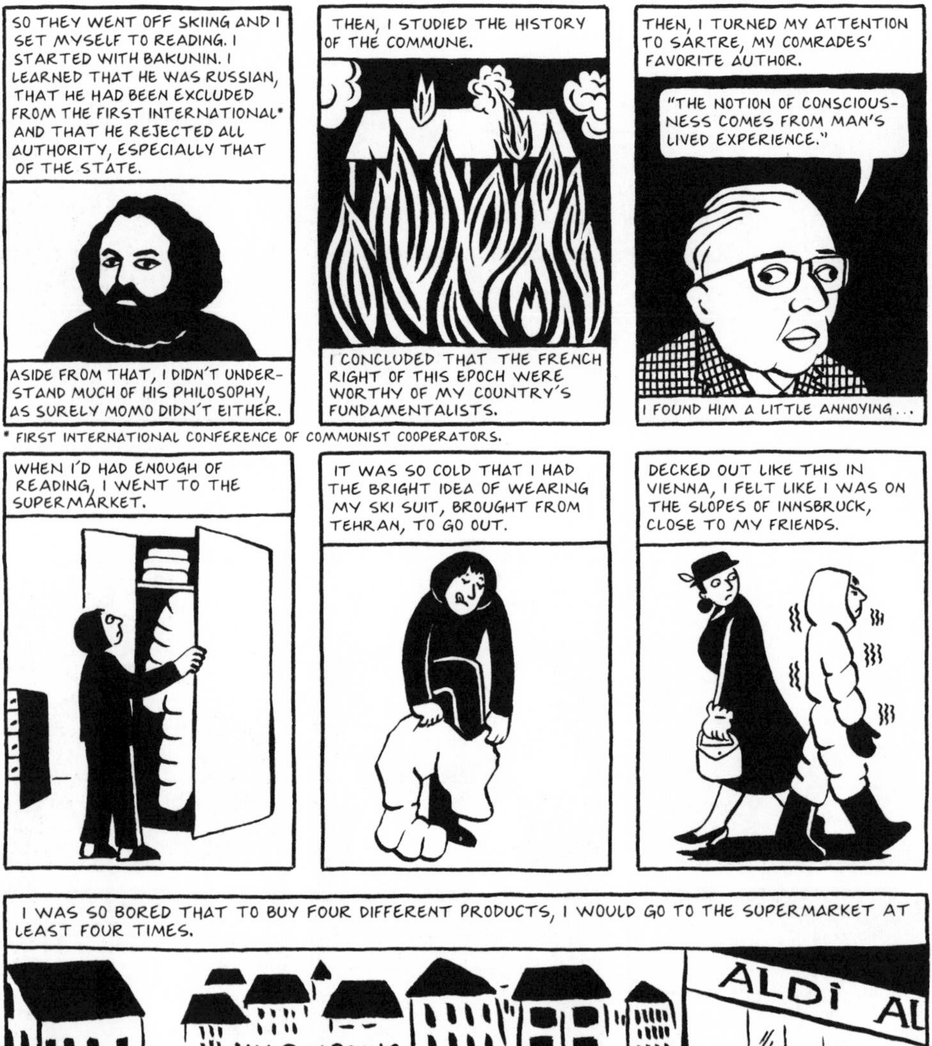
SO THEY WENT OFF SKIING AND I SET MYSELF TO READING. I STARTED WITH BAKUNIN. I LEARNED THAT HE WAS RUSSIAN, THAT HE HAD BEEN EXCLUDED FROM THE FIRST INTERNATIONAL* AND THAT HE REJECTED ALL AUTHORITY, ESPECIALLY THAT OF THE STATE.
ASIDE FROM THAT, I DIDN'T UNDERSTAND MUCH OF HIS PHILOSOPHY, AS SURELY MOMO DIDN'T EITHER.
THEN, I STUDIED THE HISTORY OF THE COMMUNE.
I CONCLUDED THAT THE FRENCH RIGHT OF THIS EPOCH WERE WORTHY OF MY COUNTRY'S FUNDAMENTALISTS.
THEN, I TURNED MY ATTENTION TO SARTRE, MY COMRADES' FAVORITE AUTHOR.
"THE NOTION OF CONSCIOUSNESS COMES FROM MAN'S LIVED EXPERIENCE."
I FOUND HIM A LITTLE ANNOYING...
* FIRST INTERNATIONAL CONFERENCE OF COMMUNIST COOPERATORS.
WHEN I'D HAD ENOUGH OF READING, I WENT TO THE SUPERMARKET.
IT WAS SO COLD THAT I HAD THE BRIGHT IDEA OF WEARING MY SKI SUIT, BROUGHT FROM TEHRAN, TO GO OUT.
DECKED OUT LIKE THIS IN VIENNA, I FELT LIKE I WAS ON THE SLOPES OF INNSBRUCK, CLOSE TO MY FRIENDS.
I WAS SO BORED THAT TO BUY FOUR DIFFERENT PRODUCTS, I WOULD GO TO THE SUPERMARKET AT LEAST FOUR TIMES.
ALDI AL
MY BOARDING HOUSE
THE SUPERMARKET

IF I'D HAD ANYTHING FUN TO DO, I DON'T THINK I WOULD EVER HAVE READ AS MUCH AS I DID.

TO EDUCATE MYSELF, I HAD TO UNDERSTAND EVERYTHING. STARTING WITH MYSELF, ME, MARJI, THE WOMAN. SO I THREW MYSELF INTO READING MY MOTHER'S FAVORITE BOOK.

I READ "THE SECOND SEX." SIMONE EXPLAINED THAT IF WOMEN PEED STANDING UP, THEIR PERCEPTION OF LIFE WOULD CHANGE.

"THE MANDARINS," BY SIMONE DE BAVAR.

NO! BEAUVOIR.

SHE HAD READ ME SOME EXCERPTS, BUT I WAS A LITTLE YOUNG.

...??

SEATED, IT WAS MUCH SIMPLER. AND, AS AN IRANIAN WOMAN, BEFORE LEARNING TO URINATE LIKE A MAN, I NEEDED TO LEARN TO BECOME A LIBERATED AND EMANCIPATED WOMAN.

SO I TRIED. IT RAN LIGHTLY DOWN MY LEFT LEG. IT WAS A LITTLE DISGUSTING.

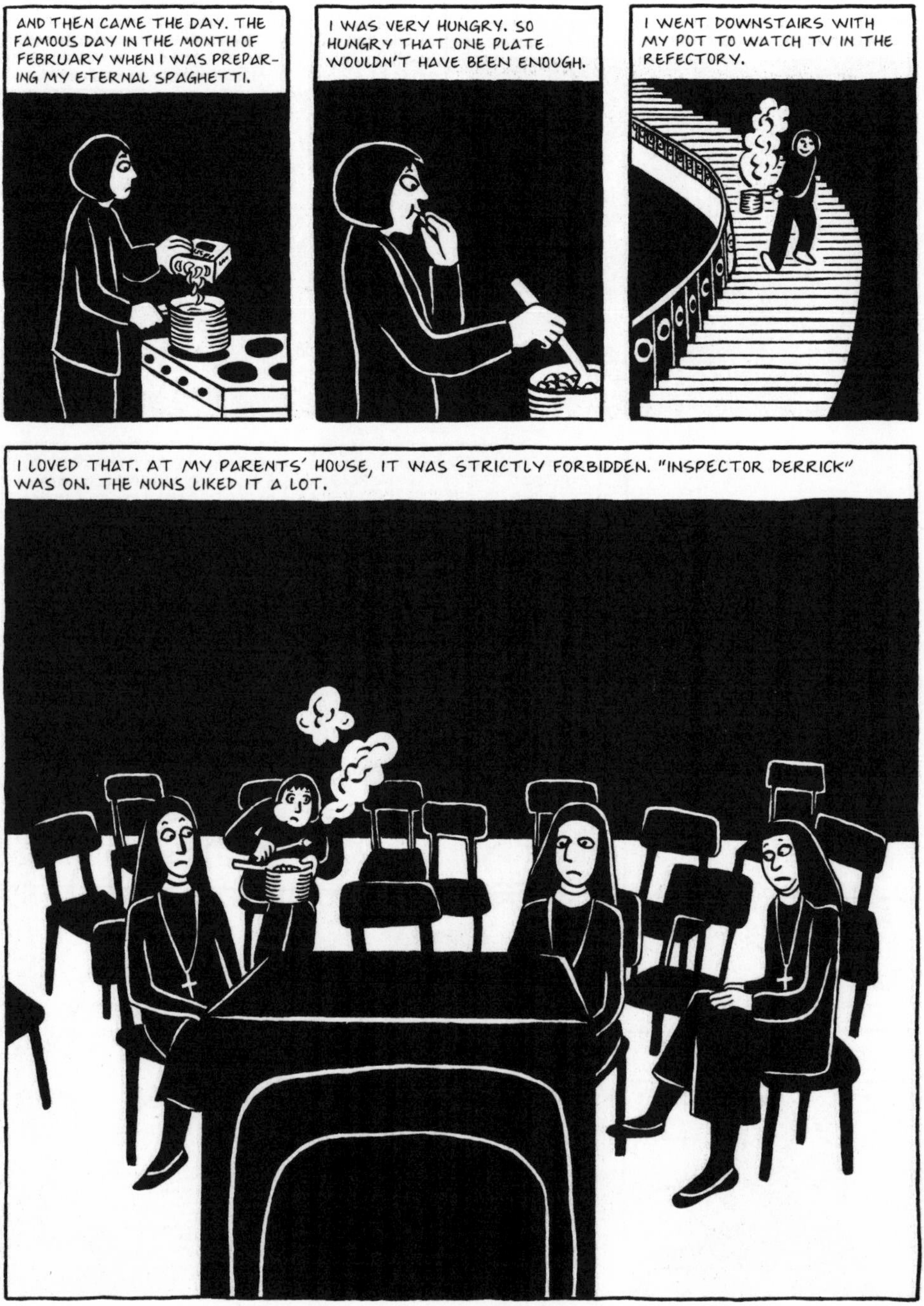
AND THEN CAME THE DAY. THE FAMOUS DAY IN THE MONTH OF FEBRUARY WHEN I WAS PREPARING MY ETERNAL SPAGHETTI.
I WAS VERY HUNGRY. SO HUNGRY THAT ONE PLATE WOULDN'T HAVE BEEN ENOUGH.
I WENT DOWNSTAIRS WITH MY POT TO WATCH TV IN THE REFECTORY.
I LOVED THAT. AT MY PARENTS' HOUSE, IT WAS STRICTLY FORBIDDEN. "INSPECTOR DERRICK" WAS ON. THE NUNS LIKED IT A LOT.

APPROACH!

IT'S UNACCEPTABLE, WHAT YOU SAID TO MOTHER BRIDGET!

AND WHAT SHE SAID TO ME, YOU FIND THAT ACCEPTABLE?

YOU'RE EXPELLED. I'M GOING TO CALL YOUR MOTHER'S FRIEND TO COME GET YOU.

DON'T BOTHER. I HAVE FRIENDS WHO WILL BE HAPPY TO TAKE CARE OF ME.

I WAS THINKING OF JULIE.

YOU SHOULD BE ASHAMED OF YOURSELF!

SO SHOULD YOU!

SHUT UP, YOU INSOLENT GIRL. AS YOU'VE PAID, YOU CAN STAY UNTIL THE END OF THE MONTH.

...

YOU HAVE NOTHING TO SAY TO ME?

...

EXCUSE ME?

I SAID THANK YOU!

IN EVERY RELIGION, YOU FIND THE SAME EXTREMISTS.

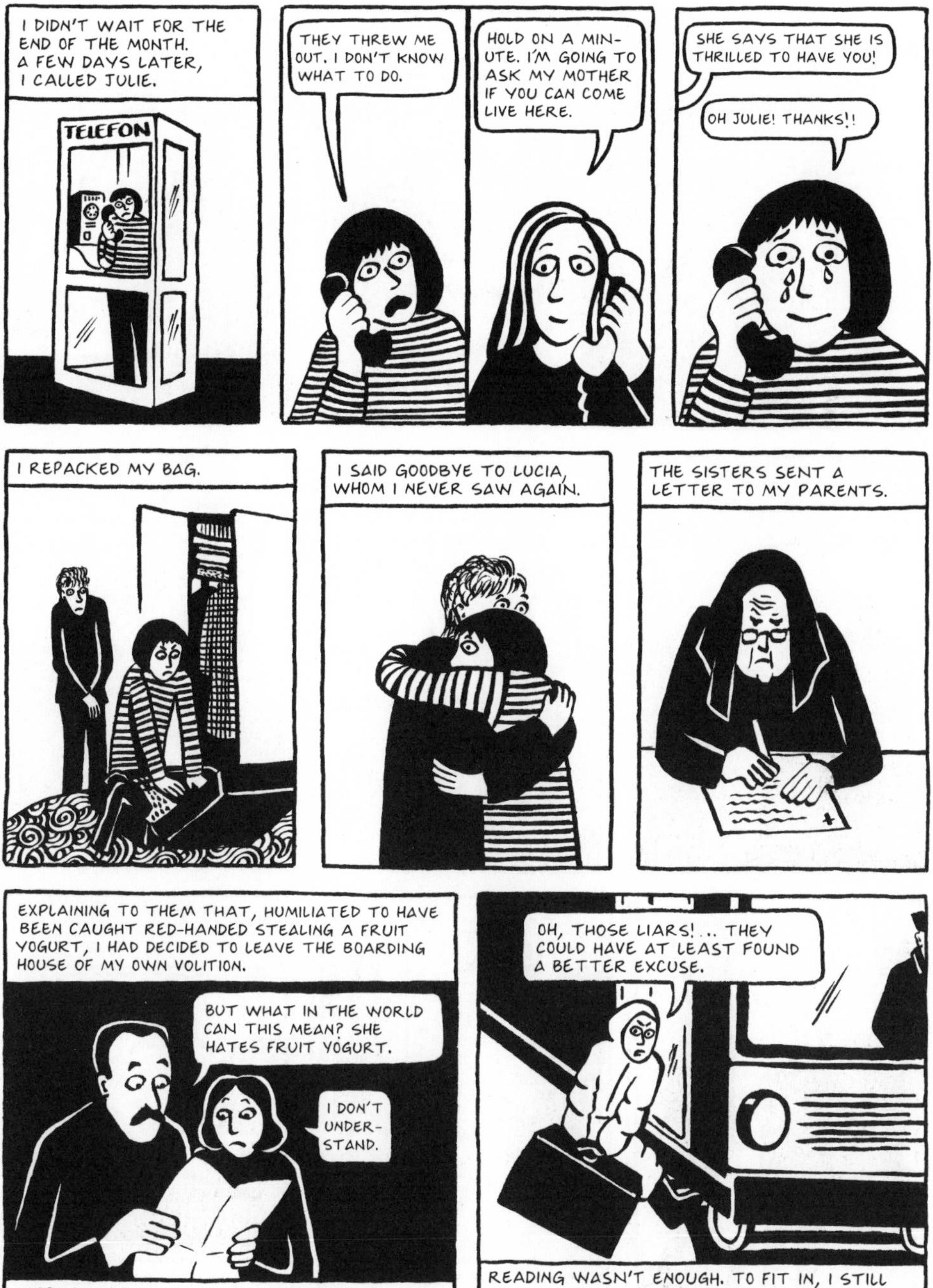
I DIDN'T WAIT FOR THE END OF THE MONTH. A FEW DAYS LATER, I CALLED JULIE.
TELEFON
THEY THREW ME OUT. I DON'T KNOW WHAT TO DO.
HOLD ON A MINUTE. I'M GOING TO ASK MY MOTHER IF YOU CAN COME LIVE HERE.
SHE SAYS THAT SHE IS THRILLED TO HAVE YOU!
OH JULIE! THANKS!!
I REPACKED MY BAG.
I SAID GOODBYE TO LUCIA, WHOM I NEVER SAW AGAIN.
THE SISTERS SENT A LETTER TO MY PARENTS.
EXPLAINING TO THEM THAT, HUMILIATED TO HAVE BEEN CAUGHT RED-HANDED STEALING A FRUIT YOGURT, I HAD DECIDED TO LEAVE THE BOARDING HOUSE OF MY OWN VOLITION.
BUT WHAT IN THE WORLD CAN THIS MEAN? SHE HATES FRUIT YOGURT.
I DON'T UNDERSTAND.
HAPPILY, MY PARENTS KNEW MY TASTES.
OH, THOSE LIARS! ... THEY COULD HAVE AT LEAST FOUND A BETTER EXCUSE.
READING WASN'T ENOUGH. TO FIT IN, I STILL HAD A LONG WAY TO GO.

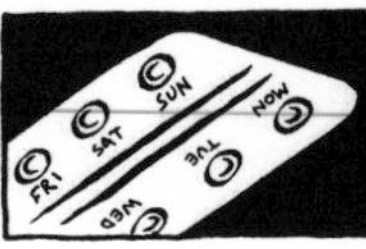
FRI
SAT
SUN
MON
TUE
WED

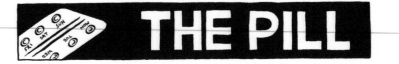

THE PILL

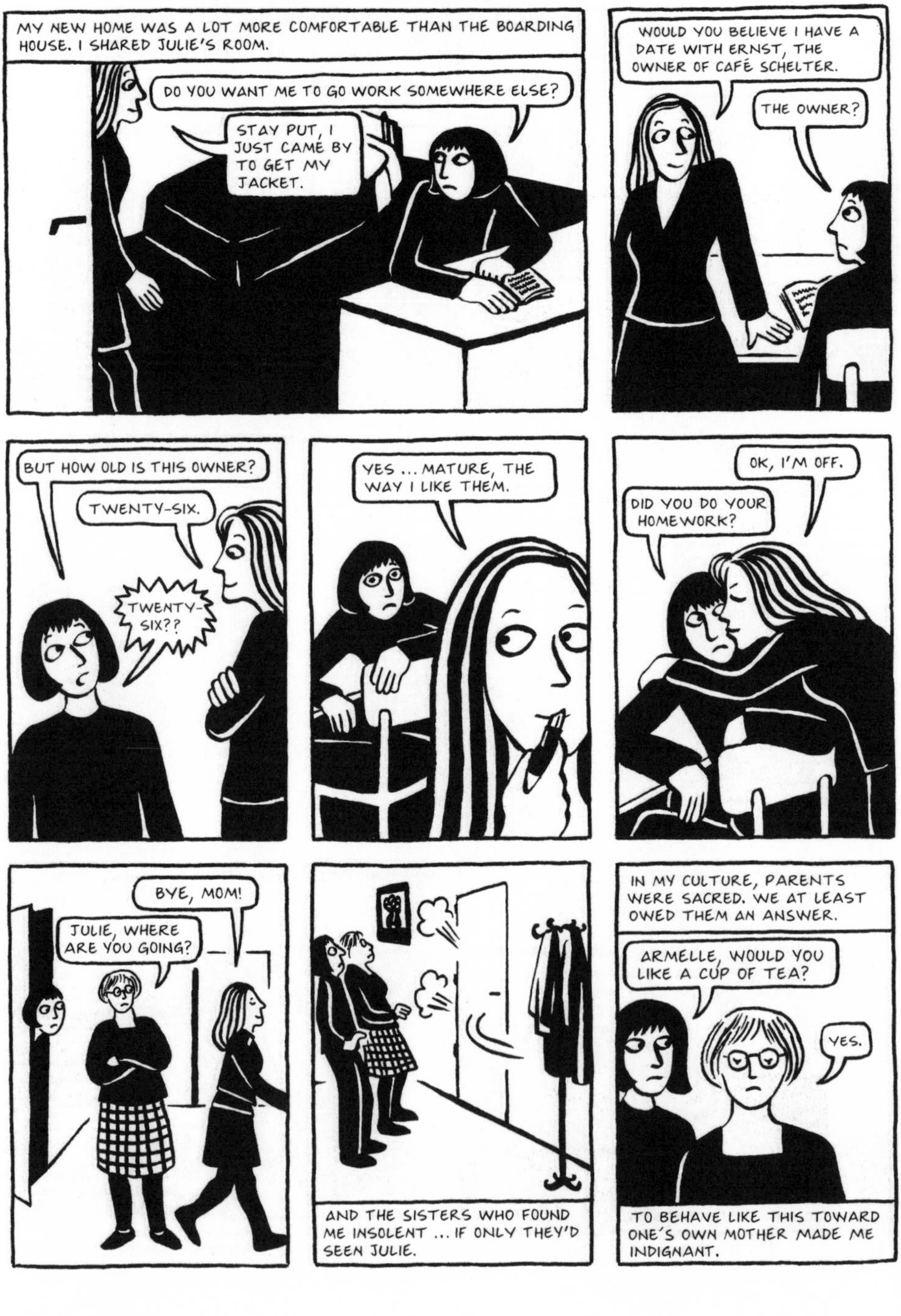
MY NEW HOME WAS A LOT MORE COMFORTABLE THAN THE BOARDING HOUSE. I SHARED JULIE'S ROOM.
DO YOU WANT ME TO GO WORK SOMEWHERE ELSE?
STAY PUT, I JUST CAME BY TO GET MY JACKET.
WOULD YOU BELIEVE I HAVE A DATE WITH ERNST, THE OWNER OF CAFÉ SCHELTER.
THE OWNER?
BUT HOW OLD IS THIS OWNER?
TWENTY-SIX.
TWENTY-SIX??
YES ... MATURE, THE WAY I LIKE THEM.
OK, I'M OFF.
DID YOU DO YOUR HOMEWORK?
BYE, MOM!
JULIE, WHERE ARE YOU GOING?
AND THE SISTERS WHO FOUND ME INSOLENT ... IF ONLY THEY'D SEEN JULIE.
IN MY CULTURE, PARENTS WERE SACRED. WE AT LEAST OWED THEM AN ANSWER.
ARMELLE, WOULD YOU LIKE A CUP OF TEA?
YES.
TO BEHAVE LIKE THIS TOWARD ONE'S OWN MOTHER MADE ME INDIGNANT.

181

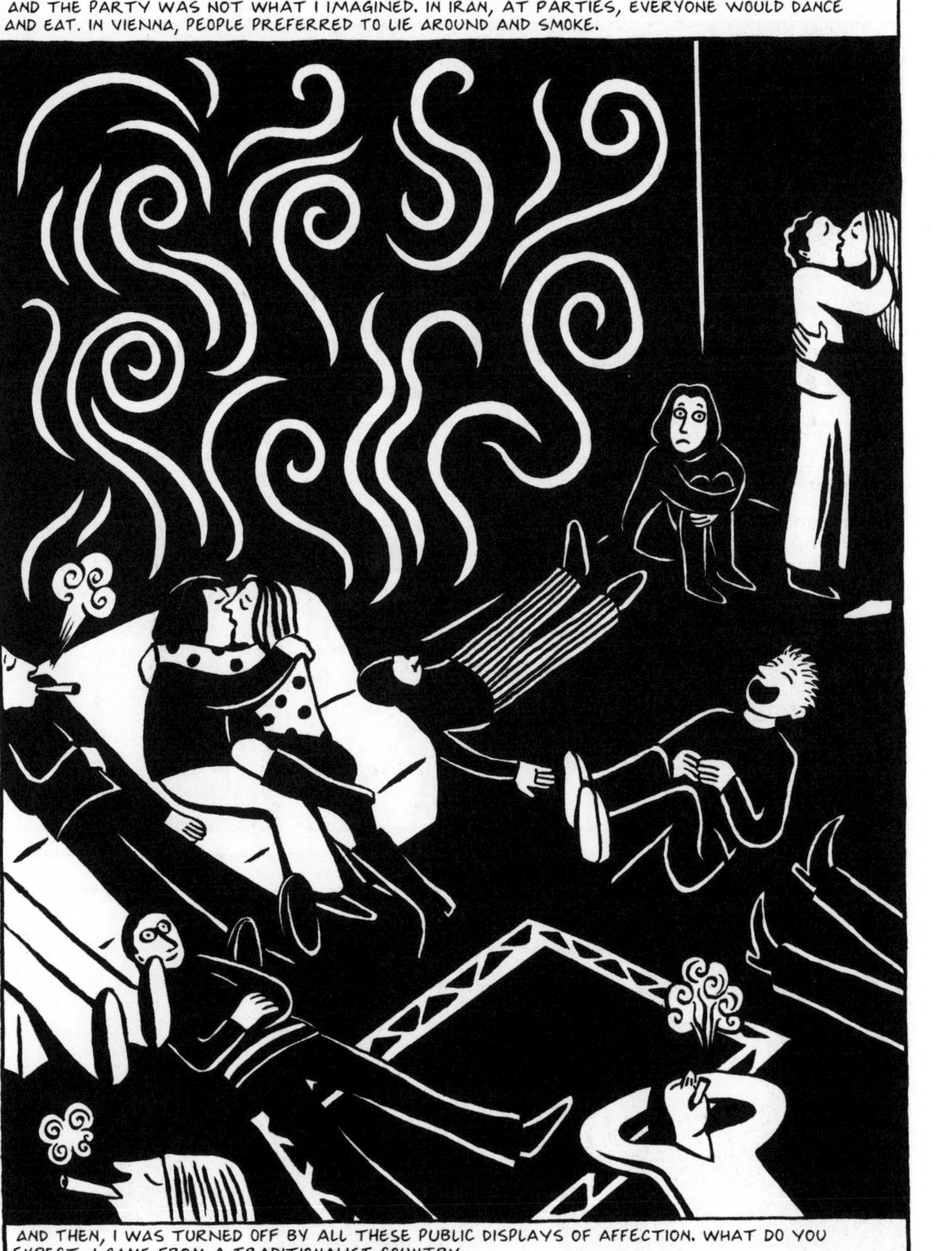
AND THE PARTY WAS NOT WHAT I IMAGINED. IN IRAN, AT PARTIES, EVERYONE WOULD DANCE AND EAT. IN VIENNA, PEOPLE PREFERRED TO LIE AROUND AND SMOKE.
AND THEN, I WAS TURNED OFF BY ALL THESE PUBLIC DISPLAYS OF AFFECTION. WHAT DO YOU EXPECT, I CAME FROM A TRADITIONALIST COUNTRY.

I RUSHED TO THE LIVING ROOM TO PROTECT MYSELF FROM I DON'T KNOW WHAT, BEHIND MY BEST FRIEND, A BOOK.

IT GOES WITHOUT SAYING THAT I DIDN'T UNDERSTAND A WORD I READ.

SEVERAL MINUTES LATER, I MADE OUT IN THE DARK THE SILHOUETTE OF A NAKED MAN,

FOLLOWED BY ONE OF A NAKED WOMAN,

THEN A MAN AND WOMAN HALF-NAKED!

HELLO!

HI!

UH...

I COULDN'T BELIEVE MY EYES...

...I'D NEVER SEEN THAT!

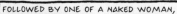

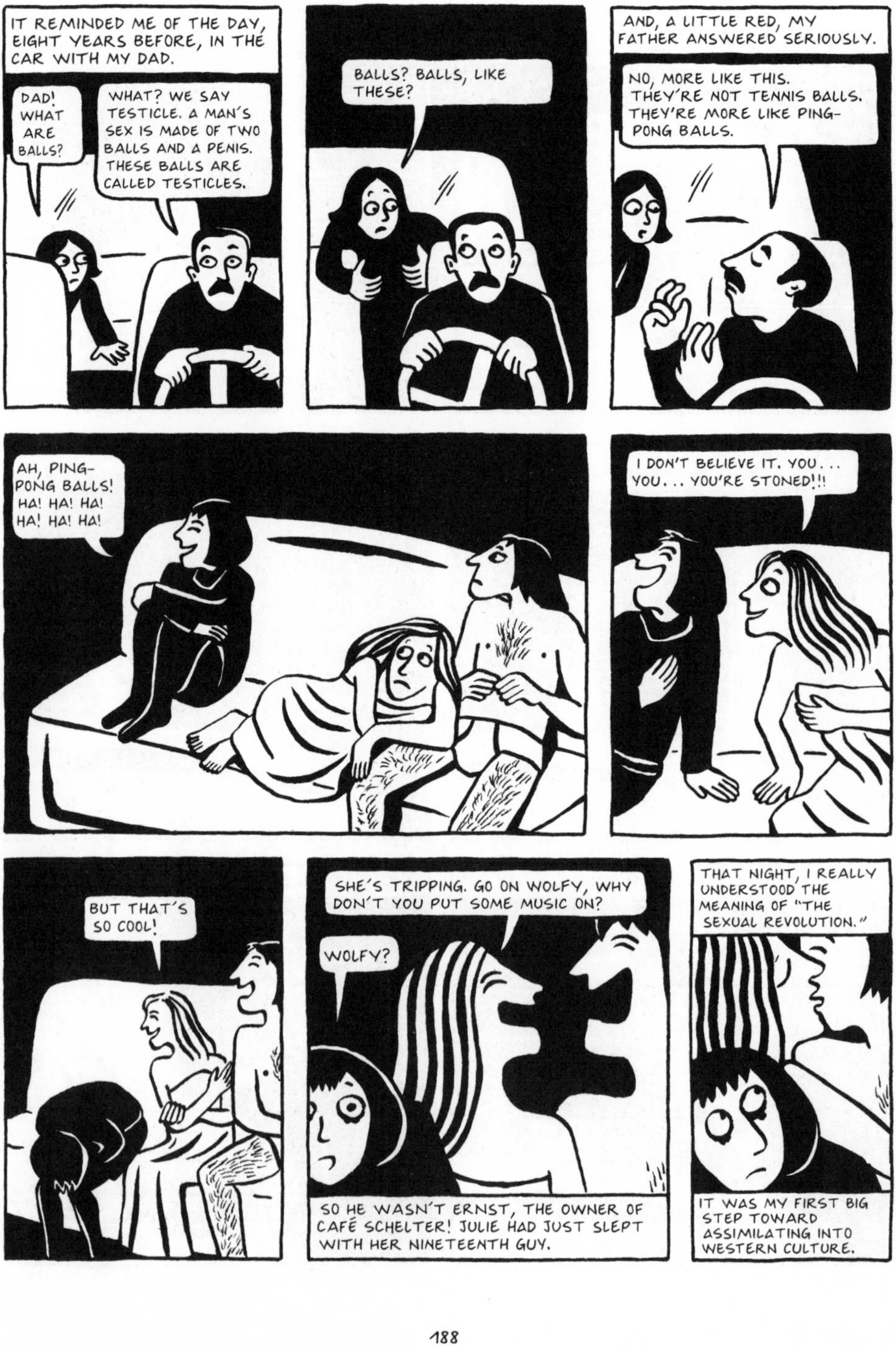

IT REMINDED ME OF THE DAY, EIGHT YEARS BEFORE, IN THE CAR WITH MY DAD.
DAD! WHAT ARE BALLS?
WHAT? WE SAY TESTICLE. A MAN'S SEX IS MADE OF TWO BALLS AND A PENIS. THESE BALLS ARE CALLED TESTICLES.
BALLS? BALLS, LIKE THESE?
AND, A LITTLE RED, MY FATHER ANSWERED SERIOUSLY.
NO, MORE LIKE THIS. THEY'RE NOT TENNIS BALLS. THEY'RE MORE LIKE PING-PONG BALLS.
AH, PING-PONG BALLS! HA! HA! HA! HA! HA! HA!
I DON'T BELIEVE IT. YOU... YOU... YOU'RE STONED!!!
BUT THAT'S SO COOL!
SHE'S TRIPPING. GO ON WOLFY, WHY DON'T YOU PUT SOME MUSIC ON?
WOLFY?
SO HE WASN'T ERNST, THE OWNER OF CAFÉ SCHELTER! JULIE HAD JUST SLEPT WITH HER NINETEENTH GUY.
THAT NIGHT, I REALLY UNDERSTOOD THE MEANING OF "THE SEXUAL REVOLUTION."
IT WAS MY FIRST BIG STEP TOWARD ASSIMILATING INTO WESTERN CULTURE.

THE VEGETABLE

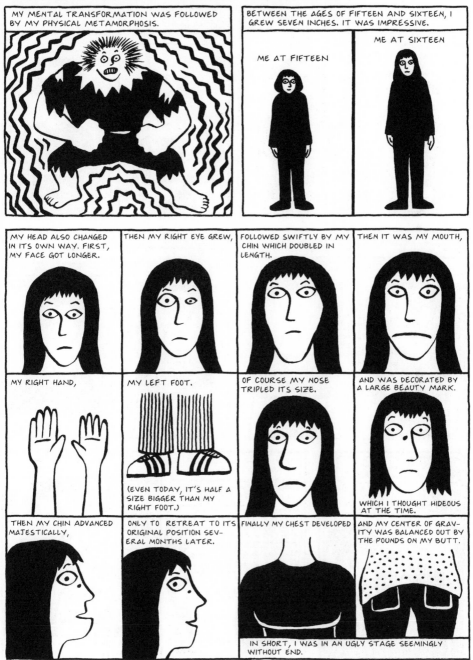

MY MENTAL TRANSFORMATION WAS FOLLOWED BY MY PHYSICAL METAMORPHOSIS.

BETWEEN THE AGES OF FIFTEEN AND SIXTEEN, I GREW SEVEN INCHES. IT WAS IMPRESSIVE.

ME AT FIFTEEN

ME AT SIXTEEN

MY HEAD ALSO CHANGED IN ITS OWN WAY. FIRST, MY FACE GOT LONGER.

THEN MY RIGHT EYE GREW,

FOLLOWED SWIFTLY BY MY CHIN WHICH DOUBLED IN LENGTH.

THEN IT WAS MY MOUTH,

MY RIGHT HAND,

MY LEFT FOOT.

(EVEN TODAY, IT'S HALF A SIZE BIGGER THAN MY RIGHT FOOT.)

OF COURSE MY NOSE TRIPLED ITS SIZE.

AND WAS DECORATED BY A LARGE BEAUTY MARK.

WHICH I THOUGHT HIDEOUS AT THE TIME.

THEN MY CHIN ADVANCED MAJESTICALLY,

ONLY TO RETREAT TO ITS ORIGINAL POSITION SEVERAL MONTHS LATER.

FINALLY MY CHEST DEVELOPED

AND MY CENTER OF GRAVITY WAS BALANCED OUT BY THE POUNDS ON MY BUTT.

IN SHORT, I WAS IN AN UGLY STAGE SEEMINGLY WITHOUT END.

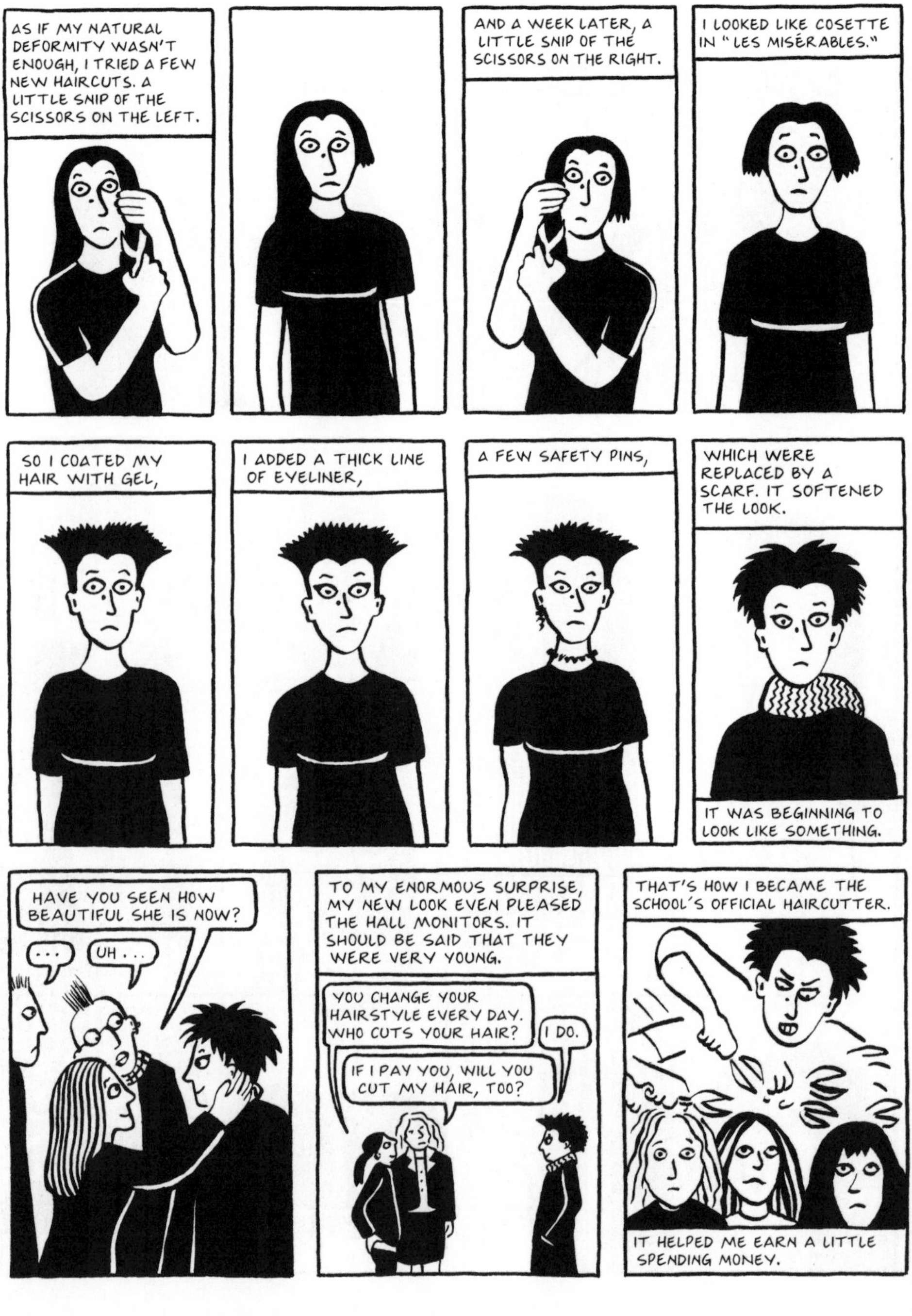

AS IF MY NATURAL DEFORMITY WASN'T ENOUGH, I TRIED A FEW NEW HAIRCUTS. A LITTLE SNIP OF THE SCISSORS ON THE LEFT.
AND A WEEK LATER, A LITTLE SNIP OF THE SCISSORS ON THE RIGHT.
I LOOKED LIKE COSETTE IN "LES MISÉRABLES."
SO I COATED MY HAIR WITH GEL,
I ADDED A THICK LINE OF EYELINER,
A FEW SAFETY PINS,
WHICH WERE REPLACED BY A SCARF. IT SOFTENED THE LOOK.
IT WAS BEGINNING TO LOOK LIKE SOMETHING.
HAVE YOU SEEN HOW BEAUTIFUL SHE IS NOW?
...
UH ...
TO MY ENORMOUS SURPRISE, MY NEW LOOK EVEN PLEASED THE HALL MONITORS. IT SHOULD BE SAID THAT THEY WERE VERY YOUNG.
YOU CHANGE YOUR HAIRSTYLE EVERY DAY. WHO CUTS YOUR HAIR?
I DO.
IF I PAY YOU, WILL YOU CUT MY HAIR, TOO?
THAT'S HOW I BECAME THE SCHOOL'S OFFICIAL HAIRCUTTER.
IT HELPED ME EARN A LITTLE SPENDING MONEY.

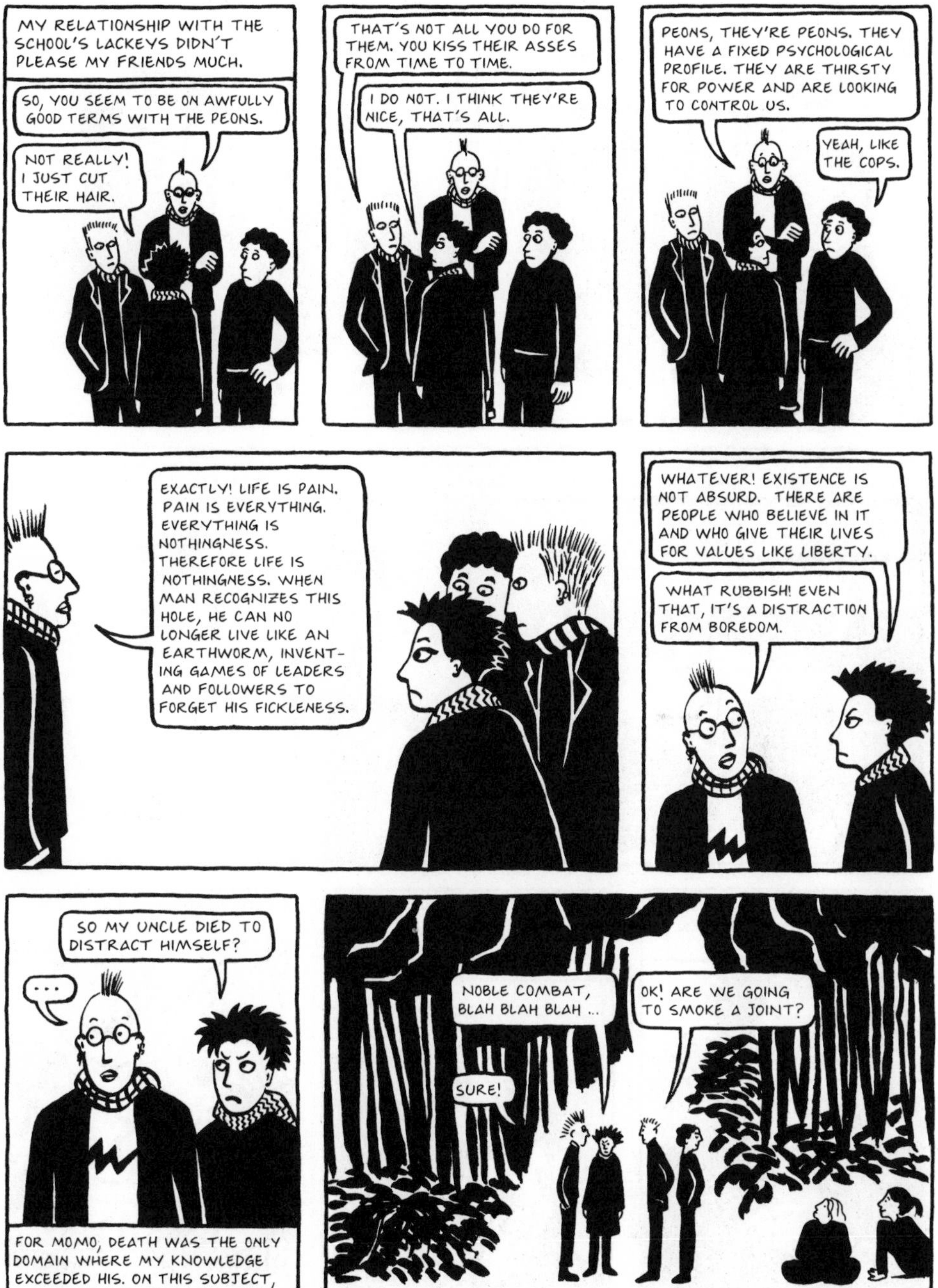
MY RELATIONSHIP WITH THE SCHOOL'S LACKEYS DIDN'T PLEASE MY FRIENDS MUCH.
SO, YOU SEEM TO BE ON AWFULLY GOOD TERMS WITH THE PEONS.
NOT REALLY! I JUST CUT THEIR HAIR.
THAT'S NOT ALL YOU DO FOR THEM. YOU KISS THEIR ASSES FROM TIME TO TIME.
I DO NOT. I THINK THEY'RE NICE, THAT'S ALL.
PEONS, THEY'RE PEONS. THEY HAVE A FIXED PSYCHOLOGICAL PROFILE. THEY ARE THIRSTY FOR POWER AND ARE LOOKING TO CONTROL US.
YEAH, LIKE THE COPS.
EXACTLY! LIFE IS PAIN. PAIN IS EVERYTHING. EVERYTHING IS NOTHINGNESS. THEREFORE LIFE IS NOTHINGNESS. WHEN MAN RECOGNIZES THIS HOLE, HE CAN NO LONGER LIVE LIKE AN EARTHWORM, INVENTING GAMES OF LEADERS AND FOLLOWERS TO FORGET HIS FICKLENESS.
WHATEVER! EXISTENCE IS NOT ABSURD. THERE ARE PEOPLE WHO BELIEVE IN IT AND WHO GIVE THEIR LIVES FOR VALUES LIKE LIBERTY.
WHAT RUBBISH! EVEN THAT, IT'S A DISTRACTION FROM BOREDOM.
SO MY UNCLE DIED TO DISTRACT HIMSELF?
...
FOR MOMO, DEATH WAS THE ONLY DOMAIN WHERE MY KNOWLEDGE EXCEEDED HIS. ON THIS SUBJECT, I ALWAYS HAD THE LAST WORD.
NOBLE COMBAT, BLAH BLAH BLAH ...
OK! ARE WE GOING TO SMOKE A JOINT?
SURE!

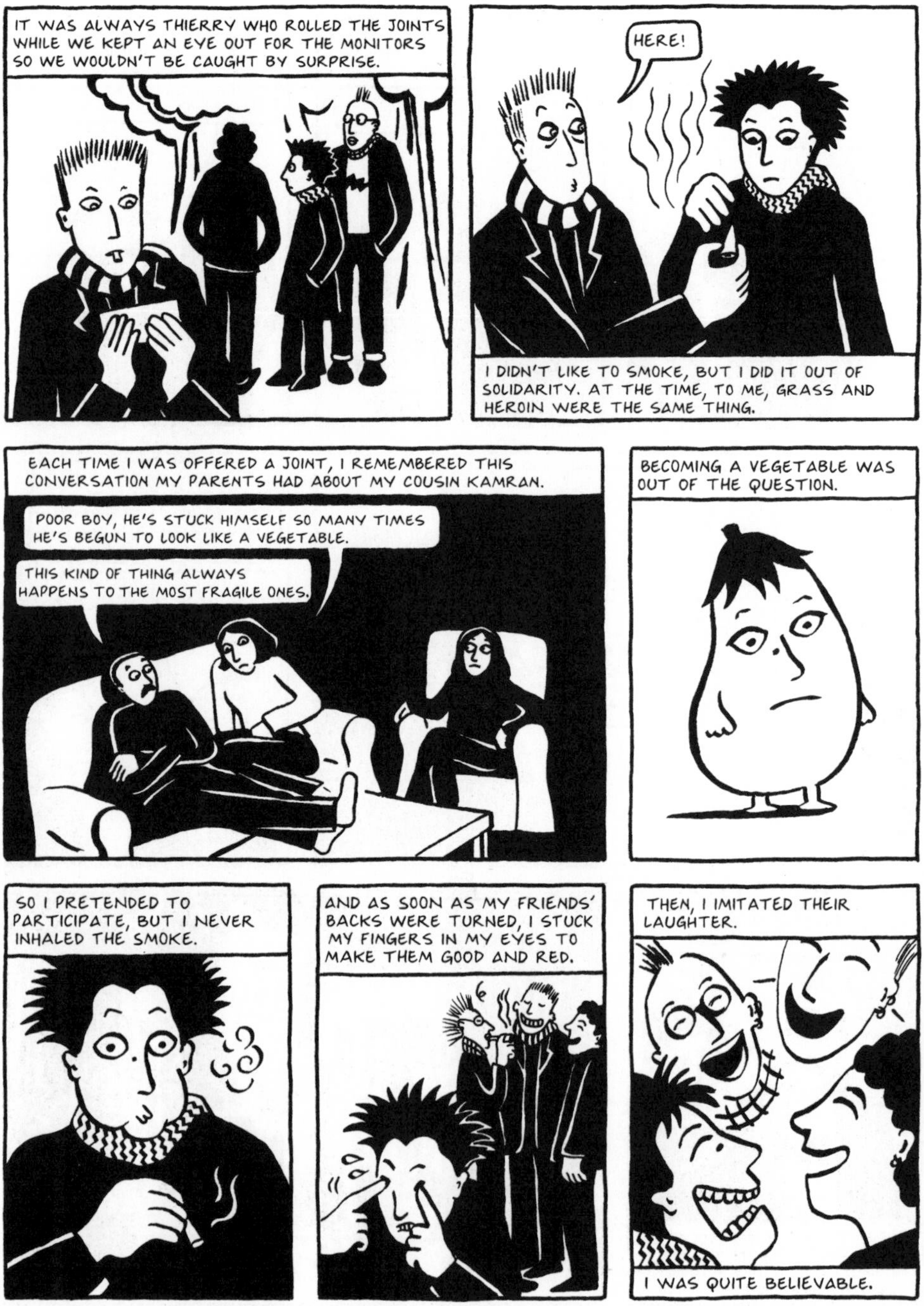
IT WAS ALWAYS THIERRY WHO ROLLED THE JOINTS WHILE WE KEPT AN EYE OUT FOR THE MONITORS SO WE WOULDN'T BE CAUGHT BY SURPRISE.
HERE!
I DIDN'T LIKE TO SMOKE, BUT I DID IT OUT OF SOLIDARITY. AT THE TIME, TO ME, GRASS AND HEROIN WERE THE SAME THING.
EACH TIME I WAS OFFERED A JOINT, I REMEMBERED THIS CONVERSATION MY PARENTS HAD ABOUT MY COUSIN KAMRAN.
POOR BOY, HE'S STUCK HIMSELF SO MANY TIMES HE'S BEGUN TO LOOK LIKE A VEGETABLE.
THIS KIND OF THING ALWAYS HAPPENS TO THE MOST FRAGILE ONES.
BECOMING A VEGETABLE WAS OUT OF THE QUESTION.
SO I PRETENDED TO PARTICIPATE, BUT I NEVER INHALED THE SMOKE.
AND AS SOON AS MY FRIENDS' BACKS WERE TURNED, I STUCK MY FINGERS IN MY EYES TO MAKE THEM GOOD AND RED.
THEN, I IMITATED THEIR LAUGHTER.
I WAS QUITE BELIEVABLE.

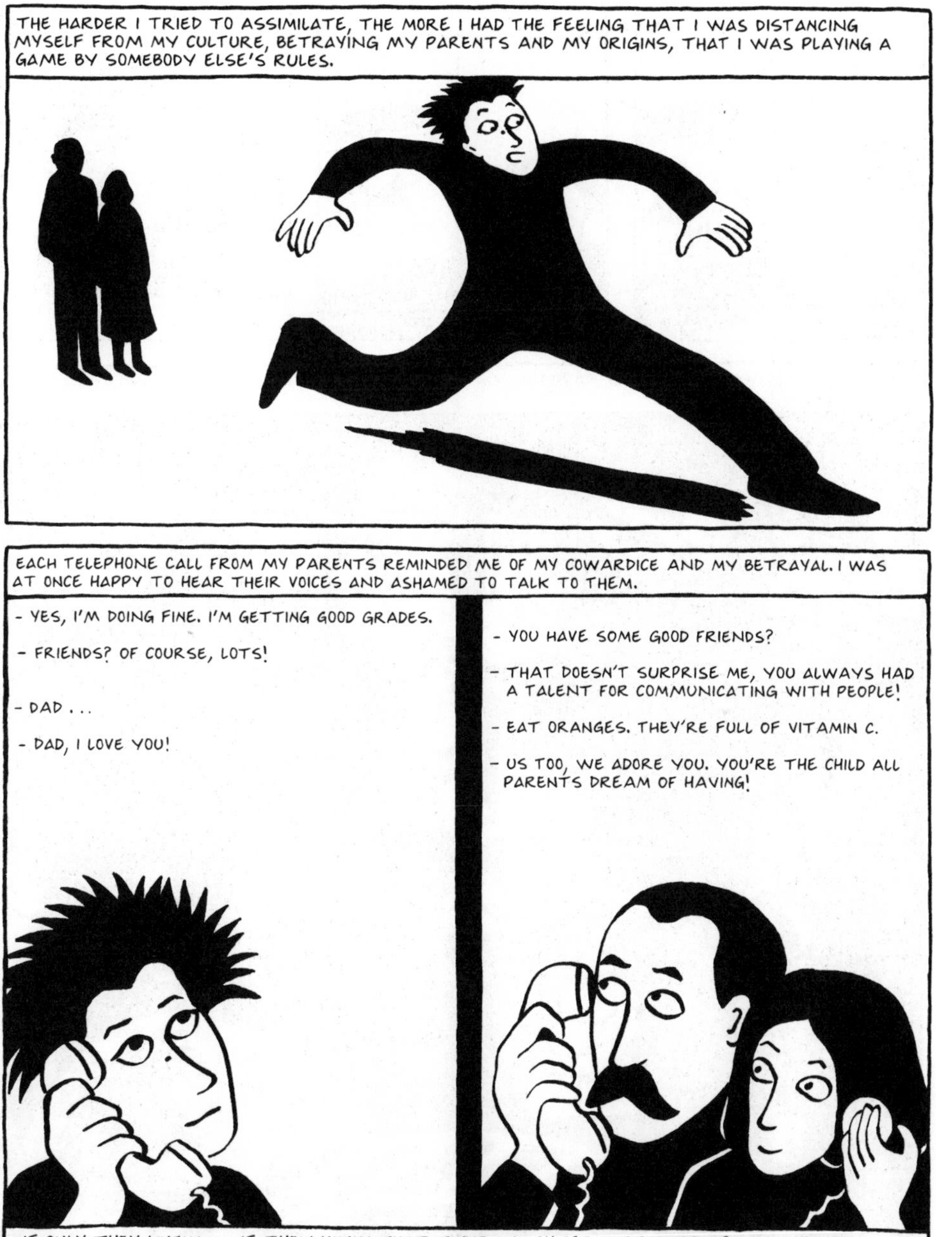
THE HARDER I TRIED TO ASSIMILATE, THE MORE I HAD THE FEELING THAT I WAS DISTANCING MYSELF FROM MY CULTURE, BETRAYING MY PARENTS AND MY ORIGINS, THAT I WAS PLAYING A GAME BY SOMEBODY ELSE'S RULES.
EACH TELEPHONE CALL FROM MY PARENTS REMINDED ME OF MY COWARDICE AND MY BETRAYAL. I WAS AT ONCE HAPPY TO HEAR THEIR VOICES AND ASHAMED TO TALK TO THEM.
- YES, I'M DOING FINE. I'M GETTING GOOD GRADES.
- YOU HAVE SOME GOOD FRIENDS?
- FRIENDS? OF COURSE, LOTS!
- THAT DOESN'T SURPRISE ME, YOU ALWAYS HAD A TALENT FOR COMMUNICATING WITH PEOPLE!
- DAD . . .
- EAT ORANGES. THEY'RE FULL OF VITAMIN C.
- DAD, I LOVE YOU!
- US TOO, WE ADORE YOU. YOU'RE THE CHILD ALL PARENTS DREAM OF HAVING!
IF ONLY THEY KNEW . . . IF THEY KNEW THAT THEIR DAUGHTER WAS MADE UP LIKE A PUNK, THAT SHE SMOKED JOINTS TO MAKE A GOOD IMPRESSION, THAT SHE HAD SEEN MEN IN THEIR UNDERWEAR WHILE THEY WERE BEING BOMBED EVERY DAY, THEY WOULDN'T CALL ME THEIR DREAM CHILD.

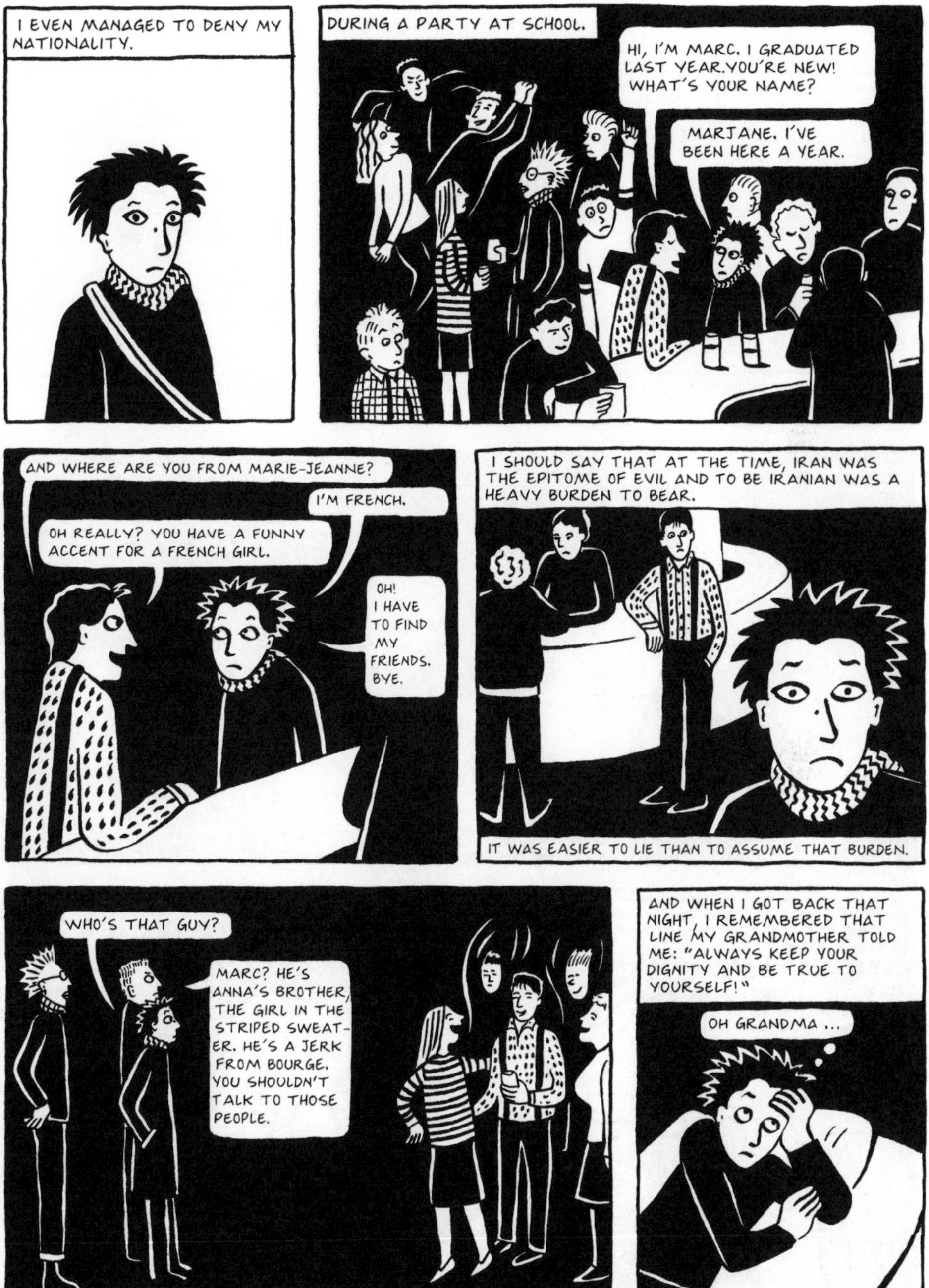
I EVEN MANAGED TO DENY MY NATIONALITY.
DURING A PARTY AT SCHOOL.
HI, I'M MARC. I GRADUATED LAST YEAR. YOU'RE NEW! WHAT'S YOUR NAME?
MARJANE. I'VE BEEN HERE A YEAR.
AND WHERE ARE YOU FROM MARIE-JEANNE?
I'M FRENCH.
OH REALLY? YOU HAVE A FUNNY ACCENT FOR A FRENCH GIRL.
OH! I HAVE TO FIND MY FRIENDS. BYE.
I SHOULD SAY THAT AT THE TIME, IRAN WAS THE EPITOME OF EVIL AND TO BE IRANIAN WAS A HEAVY BURDEN TO BEAR.
IT WAS EASIER TO LIE THAN TO ASSUME THAT BURDEN.
WHO'S THAT GUY?
MARC? HE'S ANNA'S BROTHER, THE GIRL IN THE STRIPED SWEAT-ER. HE'S A JERK FROM BOURGE. YOU SHOULDN'T TALK TO THOSE PEOPLE.
AND WHEN I GOT BACK THAT NIGHT, I REMEMBERED THAT LINE MY GRANDMOTHER TOLD ME: "ALWAYS KEEP YOUR DIGNITY AND BE TRUE TO YOURSELF!"
OH GRANDMA ...

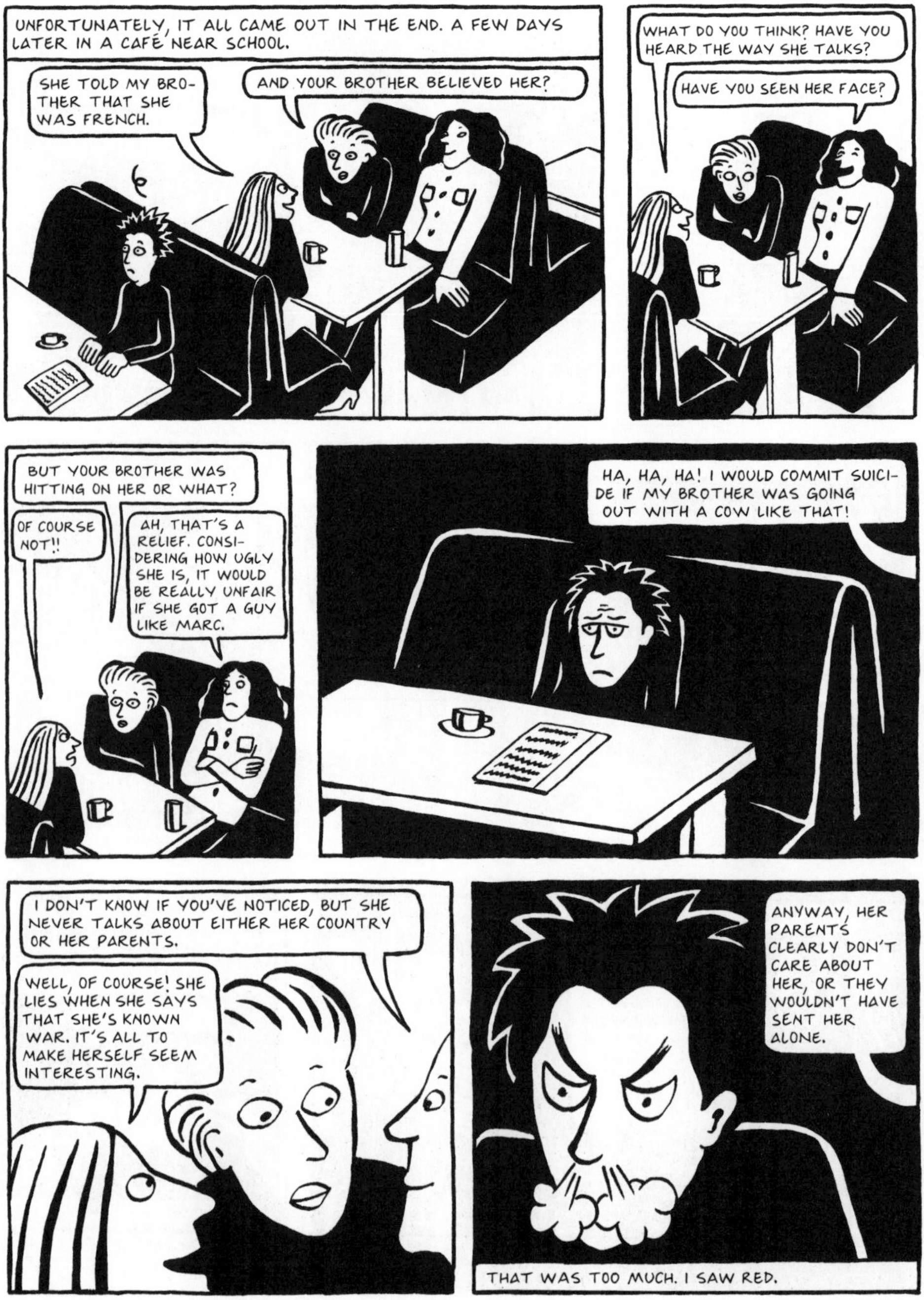
UNFORTUNATELY, IT ALL CAME OUT IN THE END. A FEW DAYS LATER IN A CAFÉ NEAR SCHOOL.
SHE TOLD MY BROTHER THAT SHE WAS FRENCH.
AND YOUR BROTHER BELIEVED HER?
WHAT DO YOU THINK? HAVE YOU HEARD THE WAY SHE TALKS?
HAVE YOU SEEN HER FACE?
BUT YOUR BROTHER WAS HITTING ON HER OR WHAT?
OF COURSE NOT!!
AH, THAT'S A RELIEF. CONSIDERING HOW UGLY SHE IS, IT WOULD BE REALLY UNFAIR IF SHE GOT A GUY LIKE MARC.
HA, HA, HA! I WOULD COMMIT SUICIDE IF MY BROTHER WAS GOING OUT WITH A COW LIKE THAT!
I DON'T KNOW IF YOU'VE NOTICED, BUT SHE NEVER TALKS ABOUT EITHER HER COUNTRY OR HER PARENTS.
WELL, OF COURSE! SHE LIES WHEN SHE SAYS THAT SHE'S KNOWN WAR. IT'S ALL TO MAKE HERSELF SEEM INTERESTING.
ANYWAY, HER PARENTS CLEARLY DON'T CARE ABOUT HER, OR THEY WOULDN'T HAVE SENT HER ALONE.
THAT WAS TOO MUCH. I SAW RED.

THE HORSE

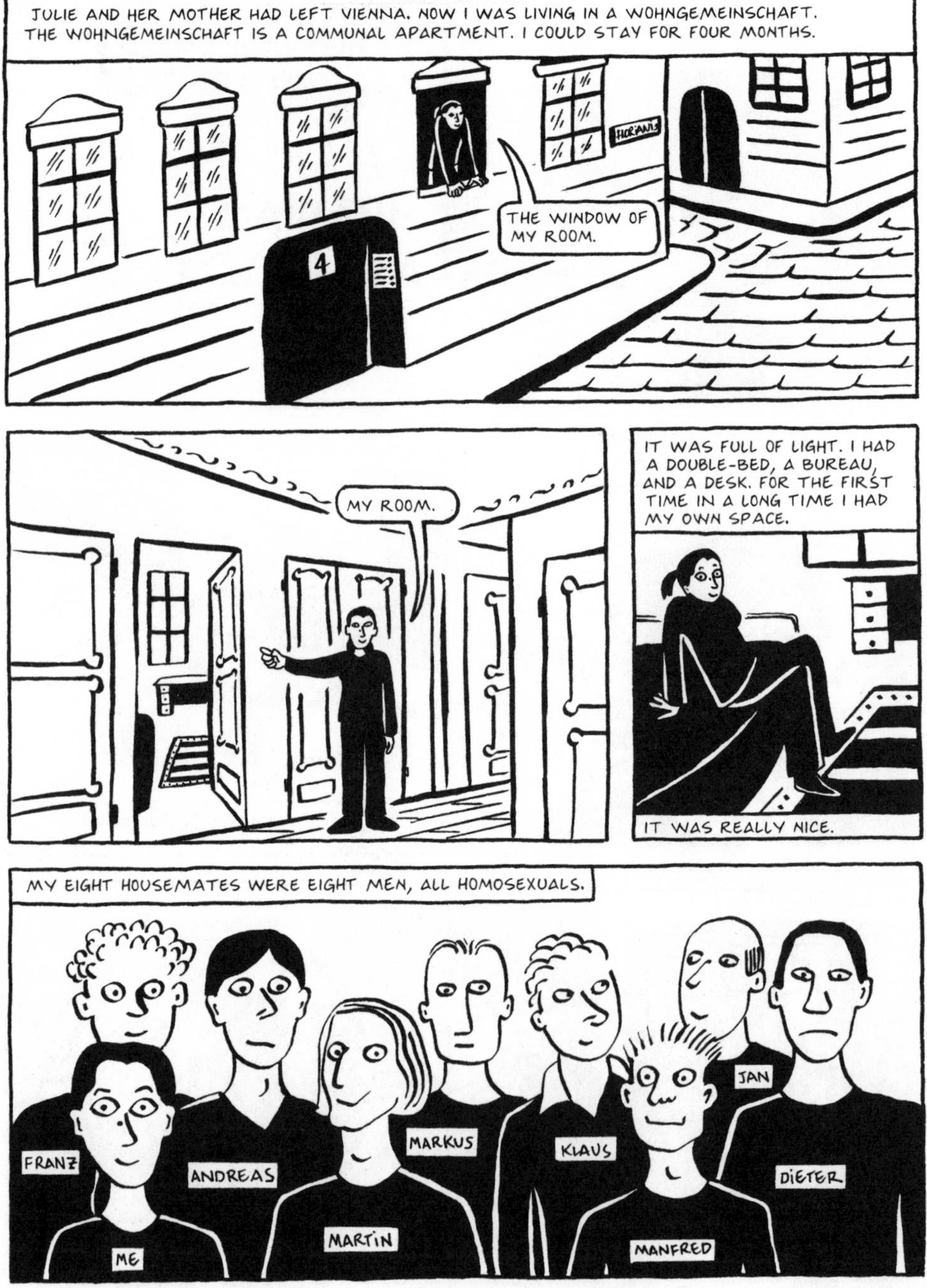
JULIE AND HER MOTHER HAD LEFT VIENNA. NOW I WAS LIVING IN A WOHNGEMEINSCHAFT. THE WOHNGEMEINSCHAFT IS A COMMUNAL APARTMENT. I COULD STAY FOR FOUR MONTHS.
4
THE WINDOW OF MY ROOM.
MY ROOM.
IT WAS FULL OF LIGHT. I HAD A DOUBLE-BED, A BUREAU, AND A DESK. FOR THE FIRST TIME IN A LONG TIME I HAD MY OWN SPACE.
IT WAS REALLY NICE.
MY EIGHT HOUSEMATES WERE EIGHT MEN, ALL HOMOSEXUALS.
FRANZ
ANDREAS
MARKUS
KLAUS
JAN
DIETER
ME
MARTIN
MANFRED

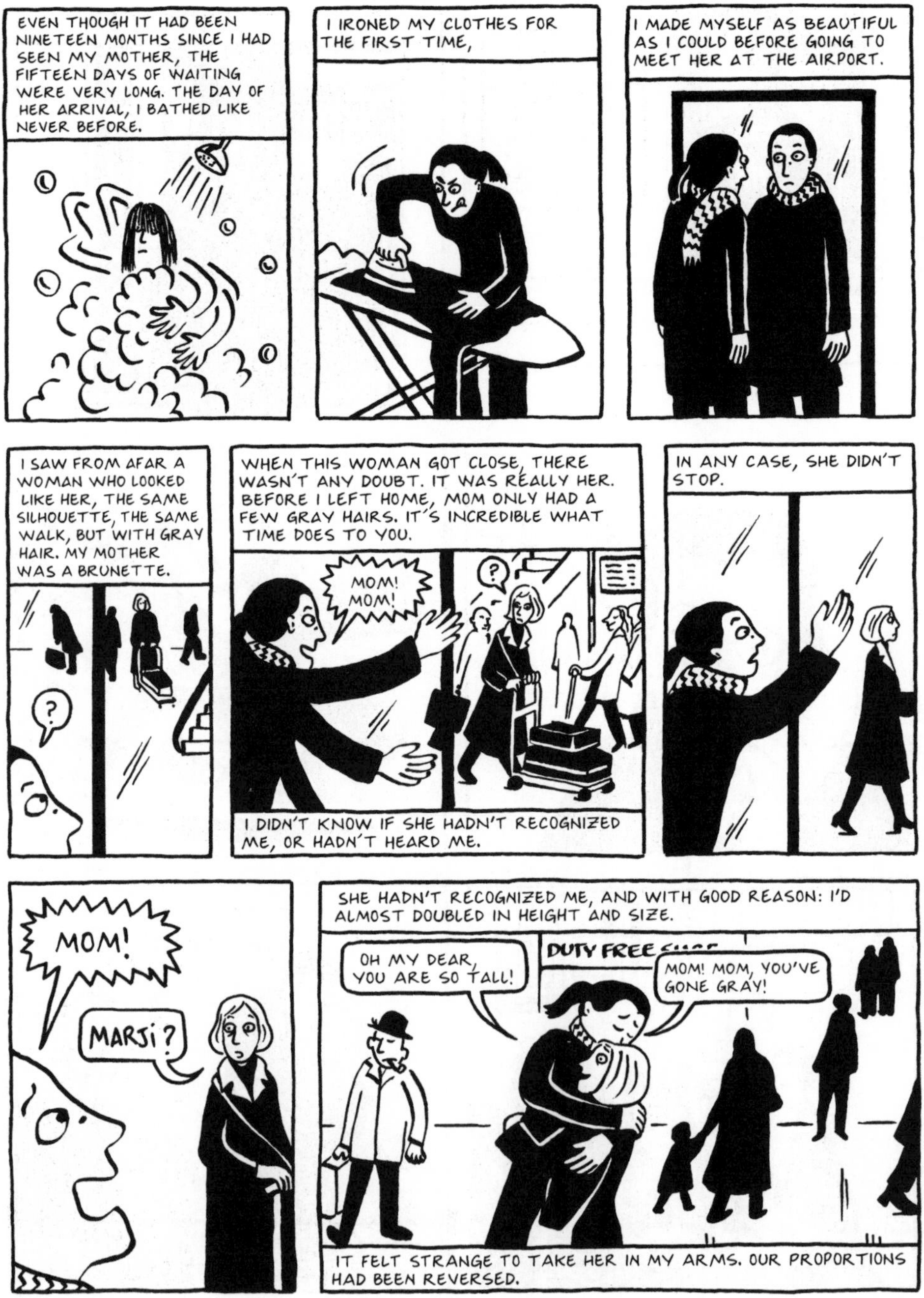
EVEN THOUGH IT HAD BEEN NINETEEN MONTHS SINCE I HAD SEEN MY MOTHER, THE FIFTEEN DAYS OF WAITING WERE VERY LONG. THE DAY OF HER ARRIVAL, I BATHED LIKE NEVER BEFORE.
I IRONED MY CLOTHES FOR THE FIRST TIME,
I MADE MYSELF AS BEAUTIFUL AS I COULD BEFORE GOING TO MEET HER AT THE AIRPORT.
I SAW FROM AFAR A WOMAN WHO LOOKED LIKE HER, THE SAME SILHOUETTE, THE SAME WALK, BUT WITH GRAY HAIR. MY MOTHER WAS A BRUNETTE.
?
WHEN THIS WOMAN GOT CLOSE, THERE WASN'T ANY DOUBT. IT WAS REALLY HER. BEFORE I LEFT HOME, MOM ONLY HAD A FEW GRAY HAIRS. IT'S INCREDIBLE WHAT TIME DOES TO YOU.
MOM! MOM!
?
I DIDN'T KNOW IF SHE HADN'T RECOGNIZED ME, OR HADN'T HEARD ME.
IN ANY CASE, SHE DIDN'T STOP.
MOM!
MARJI?
SHE HADN'T RECOGNIZED ME, AND WITH GOOD REASON: I'D ALMOST DOUBLED IN HEIGHT AND SIZE.
DUTY FREE
OH MY DEAR, YOU ARE SO TALL!
MOM! MOM, YOU'VE GONE GRAY!
IT FELT STRANGE TO TAKE HER IN MY ARMS. OUR PROPORTIONS HAD BEEN REVERSED.

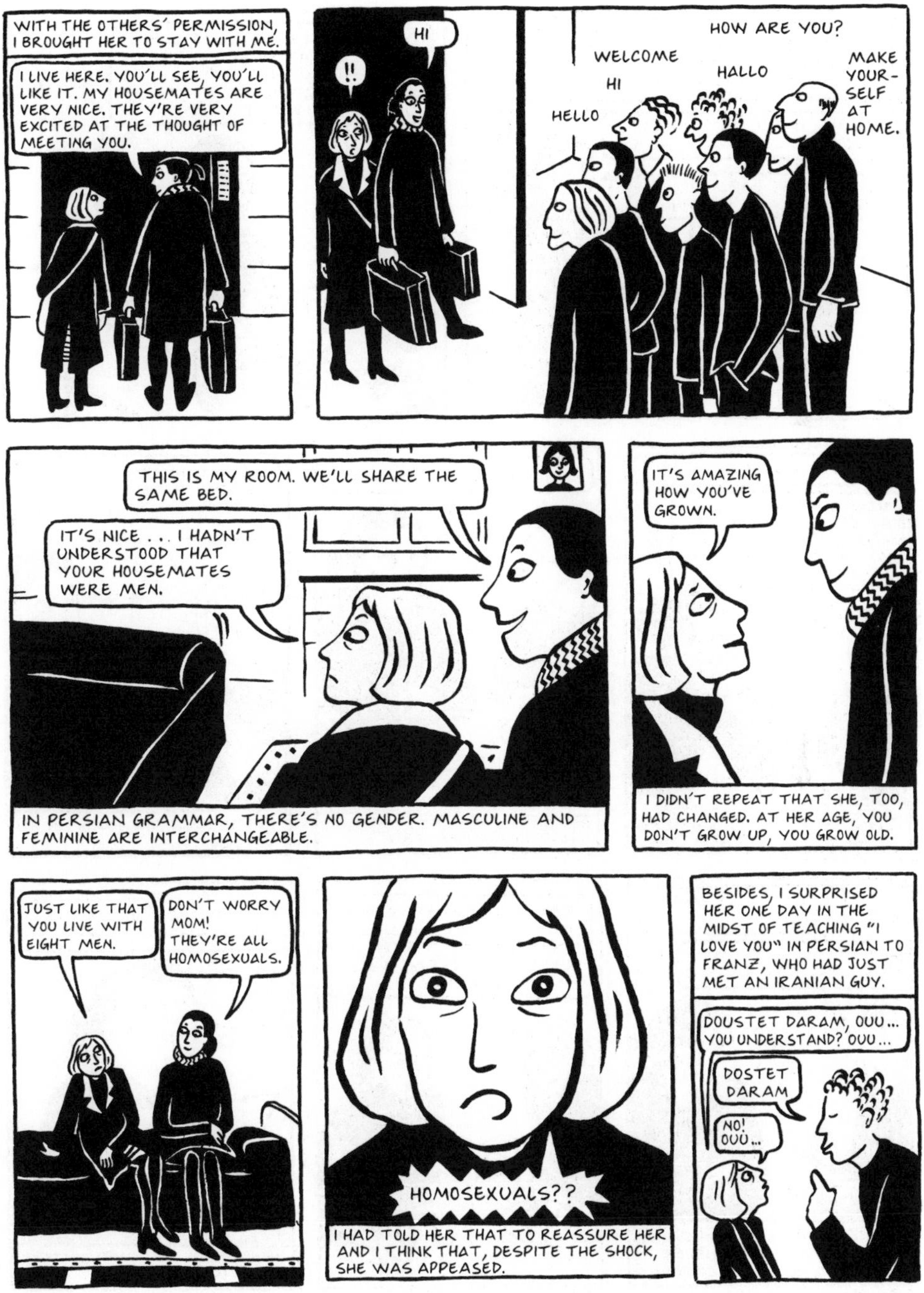

WITH THE OTHERS' PERMISSION, I BROUGHT HER TO STAY WITH ME.
I LIVE HERE. YOU'LL SEE, YOU'LL LIKE IT. MY HOUSEMATES ARE VERY NICE. THEY'RE VERY EXCITED AT THE THOUGHT OF MEETING YOU.
!!
HI
HOW ARE YOU?
WELCOME
HI
HALLO
MAKE YOURSELF AT HOME.
HELLO
THIS IS MY ROOM. WE'LL SHARE THE SAME BED.
IT'S NICE . . . I HADN'T UNDERSTOOD THAT YOUR HOUSEMATES WERE MEN.
IN PERSIAN GRAMMAR, THERE'S NO GENDER. MASCULINE AND FEMININE ARE INTERCHANGEABLE.
IT'S AMAZING HOW YOU'VE GROWN.
I DIDN'T REPEAT THAT SHE, TOO, HAD CHANGED. AT HER AGE, YOU DON'T GROW UP, YOU GROW OLD.
JUST LIKE THAT YOU LIVE WITH EIGHT MEN.
DON'T WORRY MOM! THEY'RE ALL HOMOSEXUALS.
HOMOSEXUALS??
I HAD TOLD HER THAT TO REASSURE HER AND I THINK THAT, DESPITE THE SHOCK, SHE WAS APPEASED.
BESIDES, I SURPRISED HER ONE DAY IN THE MIDST OF TEACHING "I LOVE YOU" IN PERSIAN TO FRANZ, WHO HAD JUST MET AN IRANIAN GUY.
DOUSTET DARAM, OUU... YOU UNDERSTAND? OUU...
DOSTET DARAM
NO! OUU...

WE OFTEN WENT WALKING, MY MOTHER AND I.

HOW'S OUR COUNTRY DOING?

SIGH! STILL THE SAME, BOMBINGS, ARRESTS, WE'RE SO USED TO IT THAT THE CALM HERE MAKES ME A LITTLE NERVOUS.

DO YOU REMEMBER OUR NEIGHBORS, THE KIANIS? THEY BOUGHT A HOUSE IN DEMAVEND.* WHEN WE HEAR THAT THERE'S GOING TO BE AN AIR STRIKE, WE TAKE REFUGE AT THEIR HOUSE. THE AIR IS VERY PURE UP THERE. WE HAVE A GOOD TIME.

HOW GOOD IT FEELS TO WALK WITHOUT A VEIL ON MY HEAD, WITHOUT THE WORRY OF BEING ARRESTED OVER TWO LOCKS OF HAIR OR MY NAIL POLISH.

SHE NEVER ASKED ME ANY QUESTIONS ABOUT MY SITUATION. CERTAINLY OUT OF A SENSE OF RESTRAINT AND ALSO BECAUSE SHE WAS SCARED OF THE ANSWERS. IF SHE HAD SACRIFICED HERSELF SO THAT I COULD LIVE FREELY, THE LEAST I COULD DO WAS BEHAVE WELL.

* A MOUNTAINOUS CITY NORTH OF TEHRAN.

SO WHEN WORDS FAILED US, GESTURES CAME TO OUR AID.

I LOVE MY MOM.

SHE LOVES YOU, TOO.

I'M HAPPY TO SEE YOU SO WELL-SETTLED HERE. NOW YOU MUST MAKE AN EFFORT, YOU MUST BECOME SOMEBODY. I DON'T CARE WHAT YOU DO LATER, ONLY TRY TO BE THE BEST. EVEN IF YOU BECOME A CABARET DANCER, BETTER THAT YOU DANCE AT THE LIDO THAN IN A HOLE IN THE WALL.

WHILE WE'RE ON THE SUBJECT, DID YOU KNOW YOUR UNCLE MASSOUD IS LIVING IN GERMANY?

IN GERMANY? BUT THAT'S NEXT DOOR. HE DIDN'T WANT TO COME VISIT US?

HE'S VERY DEPRESSED. IN IRAN, HE WAS SOMEBODY: "MR. CHARTERED ACCOUNTANT!" IN GERMANY, THEY THINK HE'S A TURK . . . AT OUR AGE, IT'S DIFFICULT TO START OVER AT ZERO.

I REMEMBER THE DAYS WHEN WE TRAVELED AROUND EUROPE. IT WAS ENOUGH TO CARRY AN IRANIAN PASSPORT; THEY ROLLED OUT THE RED CARPET. WE WERE RICH BEFORE. NOW AS SOON AS THEY LEARN OUR NATIONALITY, THEY GO THROUGH EVERYTHING, AS THOUGH WE WERE ALL TERRORISTS. THEY TREAT US AS THOUGH WE HAVE THE PLAGUE.

MY STAY AT THE WOHNGE-MEINSCHAFT WAS TEMPORARY. I HAD TO FIND NEW LODGINGS.

MARJI, I PASSED BY THE UNIVERSITY. I SAW AN AD FOR A ROOM IN THE THIRTEENTH QUARTER.

WE WENT THERE THAT AFTERNOON. HANSE NIESE WEG 1.

HALLO! I'M FRAU DOCTOR HELLER.

MRS. SATRAPI.

* SHE'S SO FAT!

HERE... THE RENT IS TWO THOUSAND SHILLINGS*. SHE CAN USE THE KITCHEN AND THE BATHROOM WHICH SHE'LL SHARE WITH THREE ROOMMATES, TWO ENGLISH MUSICIANS AND AN AMERICAN ARCHITECTURE STUDENT.

* 150 DOLLARS.

ALL THE TERMS SUITED US.

TAKE GOOD CARE OF MY DAUGHTER.

OF COURSE, MRS. SATRAPI, OF COURSE.

AND AT THE TRAM STOP.

WHAT DID YOU THINK OF THE TEA?

LIKE HORSE PISS!

HER TOO, SHE LOOKED LIKE A HORSE!

MPFRR

MMF

HORSE PISS FROM A HORSE-FACE!!

EVEN TODAY THIS INFANTILE JOKE BRINGS TEARS TO OUR EYES.

205

HIDE AND SEEK

FRAU DOCTOR HELLER'S HOUSE WAS AN OLD VILLA, BUILT BY HER FATHER, A 1930S SCULPTOR OF SOME RENOWN. THE BIG TERRACE THAT LOOKED OUT ON THE GARDEN WAS MY FAVORITE PLACE. I SPENT SOME VERY PLEASANT MOMENTS THERE.

ONLY THE EXCREMENT OF VICTOR, FRAU DOCTOR HELLER'S DOG, DISTURBED THIS HARMONY.

ON AVERAGE, HE DEFECATED ONCE A WEEK ON MY BED.

DOCTOR HELLER!

DO YOU HAVE ANY IDEA? IT'S THE FIFTH TIME IN A MONTH! IT'S UNACCEPTABLE! WHY DON'T YOU TRAIN HIM?

YES, WELL! I'M GOING TO HAVE THE SHEETS CHANGED.

I OFTEN FORGOT THAT HE WAS TOO OLD TO LEARN ANYTHING.

YOU ARE REALLY VERY UPTIGHT!

?!

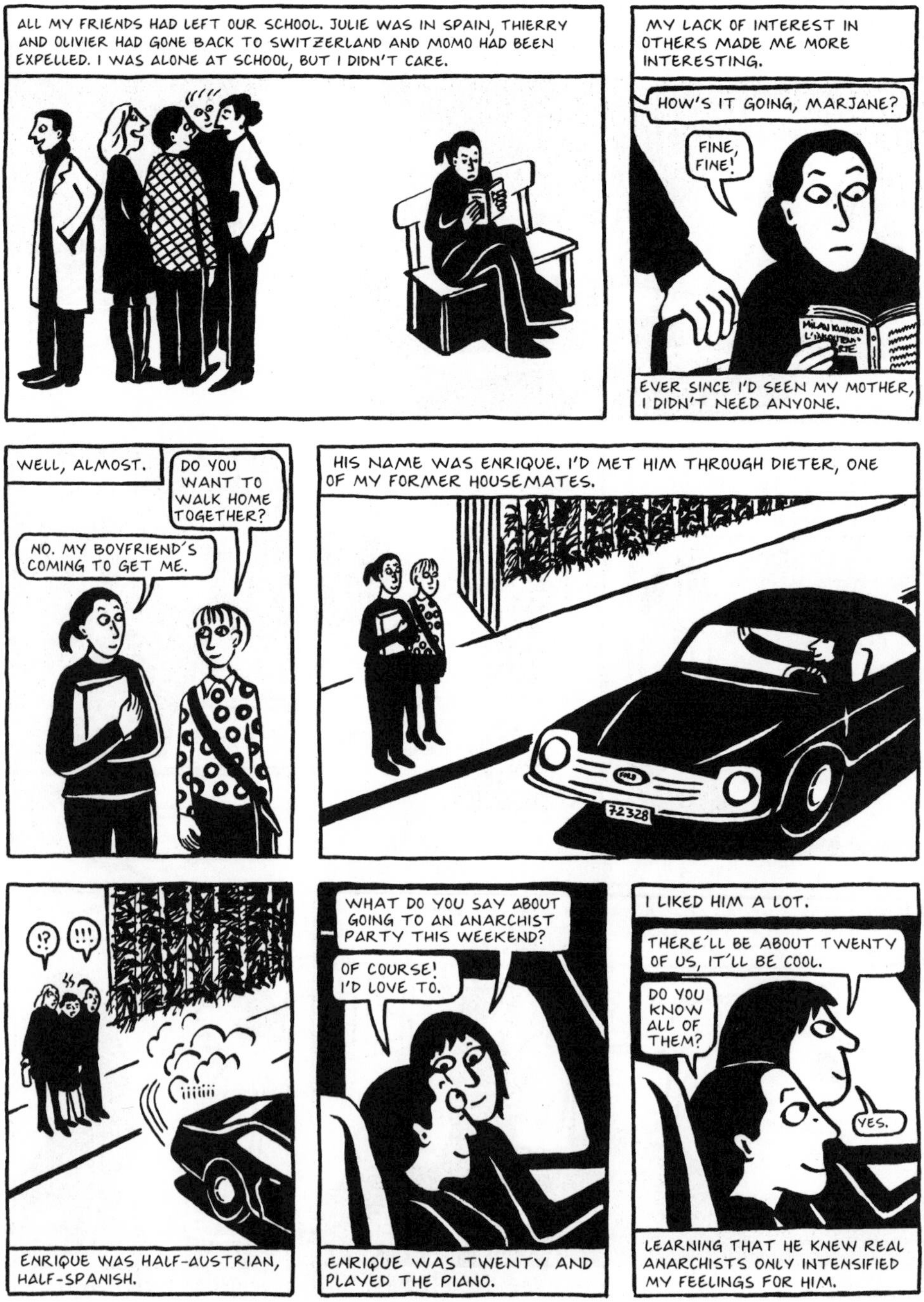
ALL MY FRIENDS HAD LEFT OUR SCHOOL. JULIE WAS IN SPAIN, THIERRY AND OLIVIER HAD GONE BACK TO SWITZERLAND AND MOMO HAD BEEN EXPELLED. I WAS ALONE AT SCHOOL, BUT I DIDN'T CARE.
MY LACK OF INTEREST IN OTHERS MADE ME MORE INTERESTING.
HOW'S IT GOING, MARJANE?
FINE, FINE!
EVER SINCE I'D SEEN MY MOTHER, I DIDN'T NEED ANYONE.
WELL, ALMOST.
DO YOU WANT TO WALK HOME TOGETHER?
NO. MY BOYFRIEND'S COMING TO GET ME.
HIS NAME WAS ENRIQUE. I'D MET HIM THROUGH DIETER, ONE OF MY FORMER HOUSEMATES.
72328
!?
!!!
ENRIQUE WAS HALF-AUSTRIAN, HALF-SPANISH.
WHAT DO YOU SAY ABOUT GOING TO AN ANARCHIST PARTY THIS WEEKEND?
OF COURSE! I'D LOVE TO.
ENRIQUE WAS TWENTY AND PLAYED THE PIANO.
I LIKED HIM A LOT.
THERE'LL BE ABOUT TWENTY OF US, IT'LL BE COOL.
DO YOU KNOW ALL OF THEM?
YES.
LEARNING THAT HE KNEW REAL ANARCHISTS ONLY INTENSIFIED MY FEELINGS FOR HIM.

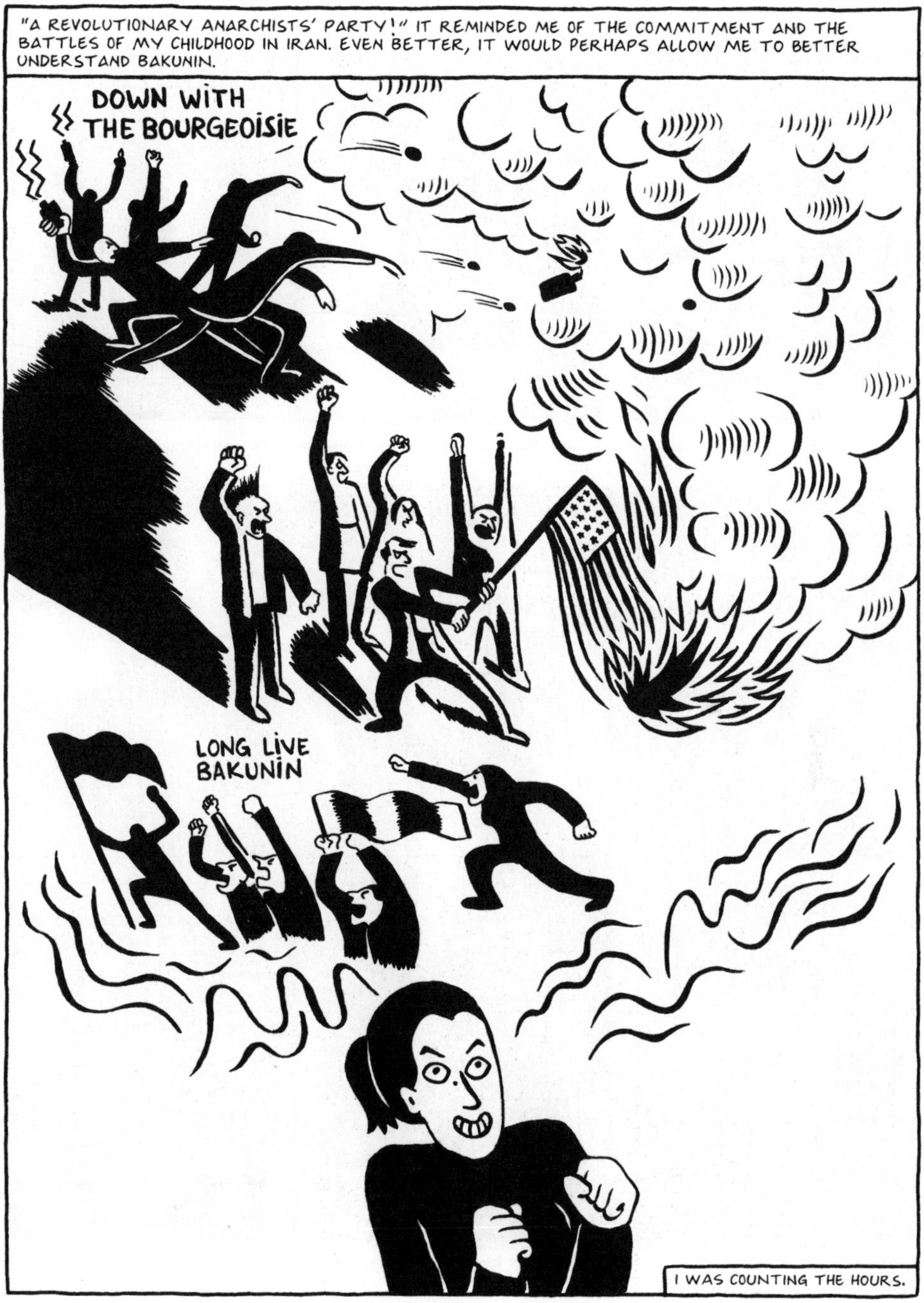
"A REVOLUTIONARY ANARCHISTS' PARTY!" IT REMINDED ME OF THE COMMITMENT AND THE BATTLES OF MY CHILDHOOD IN IRAN. EVEN BETTER, IT WOULD PERHAPS ALLOW ME TO BETTER UNDERSTAND BAKUNIN.
DOWN WITH THE BOURGEOISIE
LONG LIVE BAKUNIN
I WAS COUNTING THE HOURS.

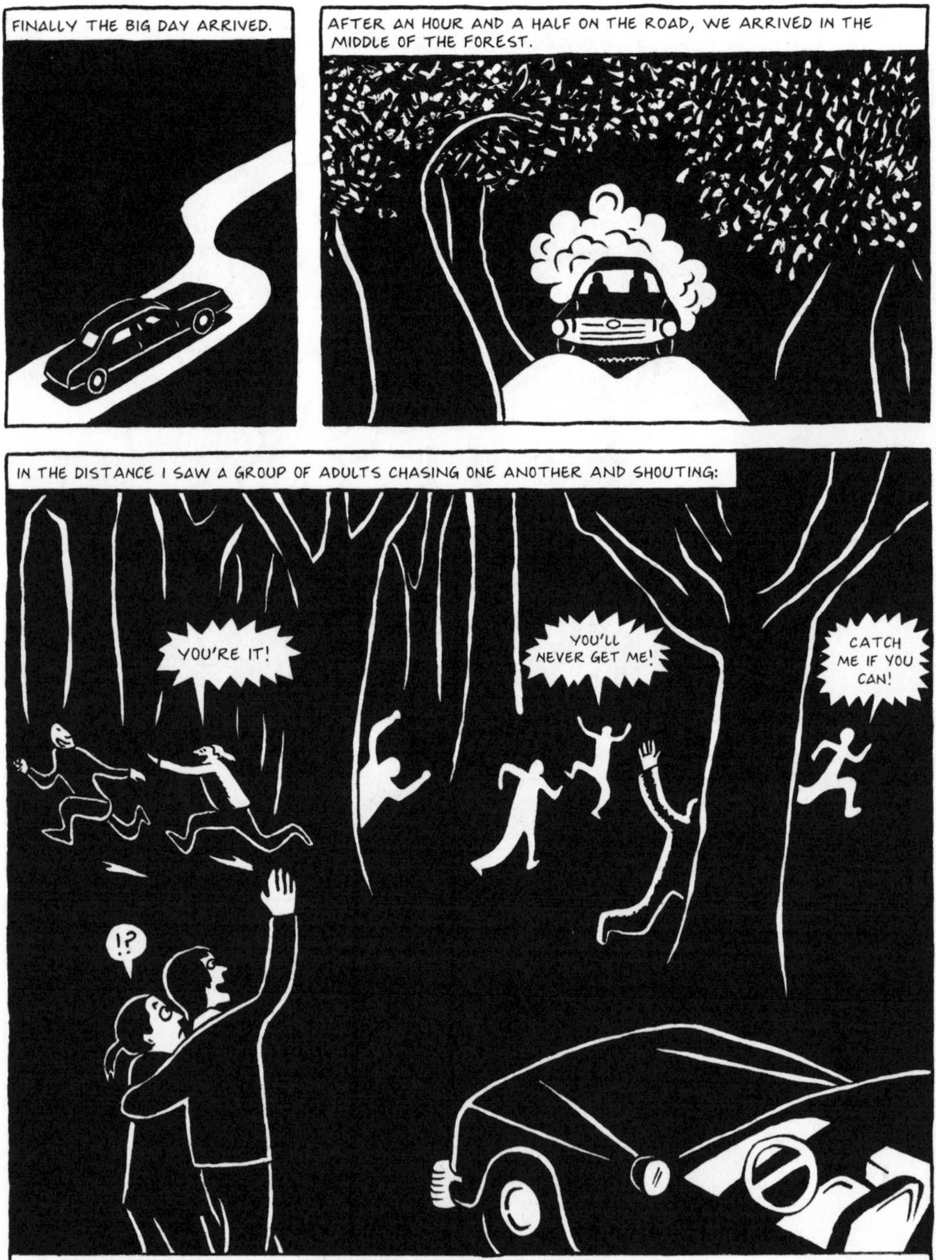
FINALLY THE BIG DAY ARRIVED.
AFTER AN HOUR AND A HALF ON THE ROAD, WE ARRIVED IN THE MIDDLE OF THE FOREST.
IN THE DISTANCE I SAW A GROUP OF ADULTS CHASING ONE ANOTHER AND SHOUTING:
YOU'RE IT!
YOU'LL NEVER GET ME!
CATCH ME IF YOU CAN!
!?
WHAT A DISAPPOINTMENT... MY ENTHUSIASM WAS QUICKLY REPLACED BY A FEELING OF DISGUST AND PROFOUND CONTEMPT.

THEN WE WENT INSIDE TO GO TO SLEEP.

GOOD NIGHT ALL.

SWEET DREAMS!

WE'RE ALL GOING TO SLEEP HERE?

IT EMBARRASSED ME TO SLEEP WITH ENRIQUE IN FRONT OF ALL THESE PEOPLE. I CAME FROM A CULTURE WHERE EVEN KISSING IN PUBLIC WAS CONSIDERED A SEXUAL ACT.

HERE, MARJANE, LET ME INTRODUCE YOU TO INGRID.

DELIGHTED TO MEET YOU, MARJANE. THERE'S A ROOM UPSTAIRS. YOU CAN SLEEP THERE IF YOU LIKE.

YES, THANKS, THAT'S KIND OF YOU.

SHE'S VERY CUTE, YOUR GIRLFRIEND.

I KNOW.

GOOD NIGHT, LOVE-BIRDS.

UNTIL THAT NIGHT, MY RELATION-SHIP WITH ENRIQUE WAS STRICTLY PLATONIC. I HAD GROWN UP IN A COUNTRY WHERE THE SEX ACT WAS NEVER CONSUMMATED UNTIL AFTER MARRIAGE. FOR ENRIQUE, IT WASN'T A PROBLEM. WE SATIS-FIED OURSELVES WITH TENDER KISSES.

BUT THIS NIGHT WAS DIFFERENT. I FELT READY TO LOSE MY INNOCENCE.

AND TOO BAD IF NO IRANIAN EVER MARRIES ME. I LIVE IN EUROPE AND I'LL MARRY A EUROPEAN!

I DIDN'T WANT TO BE A TIMID VIRGIN ANY LONGER.

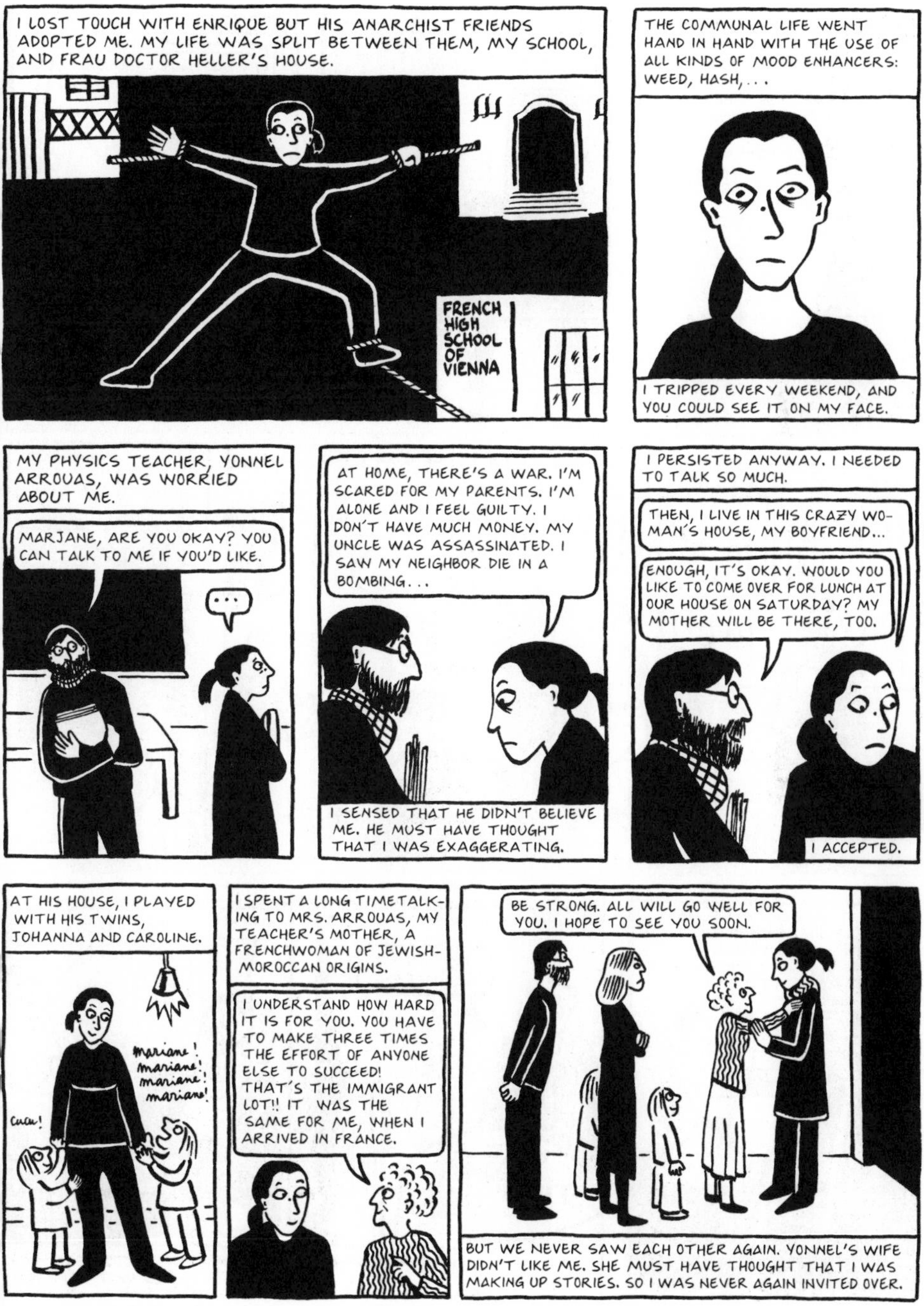
I LOST TOUCH WITH ENRIQUE BUT HIS ANARCHIST FRIENDS ADOPTED ME. MY LIFE WAS SPLIT BETWEEN THEM, MY SCHOOL, AND FRAU DOCTOR HELLER'S HOUSE.
FRENCH HIGH SCHOOL OF VIENNA
THE COMMUNAL LIFE WENT HAND IN HAND WITH THE USE OF ALL KINDS OF MOOD ENHANCERS: WEED, HASH, . . .
I TRIPPED EVERY WEEKEND, AND YOU COULD SEE IT ON MY FACE.
MY PHYSICS TEACHER, YONNEL ARROUAS, WAS WORRIED ABOUT ME.
MARJANE, ARE YOU OKAY? YOU CAN TALK TO ME IF YOU'D LIKE.
...
AT HOME, THERE'S A WAR. I'M SCARED FOR MY PARENTS. I'M ALONE AND I FEEL GUILTY. I DON'T HAVE MUCH MONEY. MY UNCLE WAS ASSASSINATED. I SAW MY NEIGHBOR DIE IN A BOMBING. . .
I SENSED THAT HE DIDN'T BELIEVE ME. HE MUST HAVE THOUGHT THAT I WAS EXAGGERATING.
I PERSISTED ANYWAY. I NEEDED TO TALK SO MUCH.
THEN, I LIVE IN THIS CRAZY WOMAN'S HOUSE, MY BOYFRIEND...
ENOUGH, IT'S OKAY. WOULD YOU LIKE TO COME OVER FOR LUNCH AT OUR HOUSE ON SATURDAY? MY MOTHER WILL BE THERE, TOO.
I ACCEPTED.
AT HIS HOUSE, I PLAYED WITH HIS TWINS, JOHANNA AND CAROLINE.
mariane! mariane! mariane! mariane!
Cucu!
I SPENT A LONG TIME TALKING TO MRS. ARROUAS, MY TEACHER'S MOTHER, A FRENCHWOMAN OF JEWISH-MOROCCAN ORIGINS.
I UNDERSTAND HOW HARD IT IS FOR YOU. YOU HAVE TO MAKE THREE TIMES THE EFFORT OF ANYONE ELSE TO SUCCEED! THAT'S THE IMMIGRANT LOT!! IT WAS THE SAME FOR ME, WHEN I ARRIVED IN FRANCE.
BE STRONG. ALL WILL GO WELL FOR YOU. I HOPE TO SEE YOU SOON.
BUT WE NEVER SAW EACH OTHER AGAIN. YONNEL'S WIFE DIDN'T LIKE ME. SHE MUST HAVE THOUGHT THAT I WAS MAKING UP STORIES. SO I WAS NEVER AGAIN INVITED OVER.

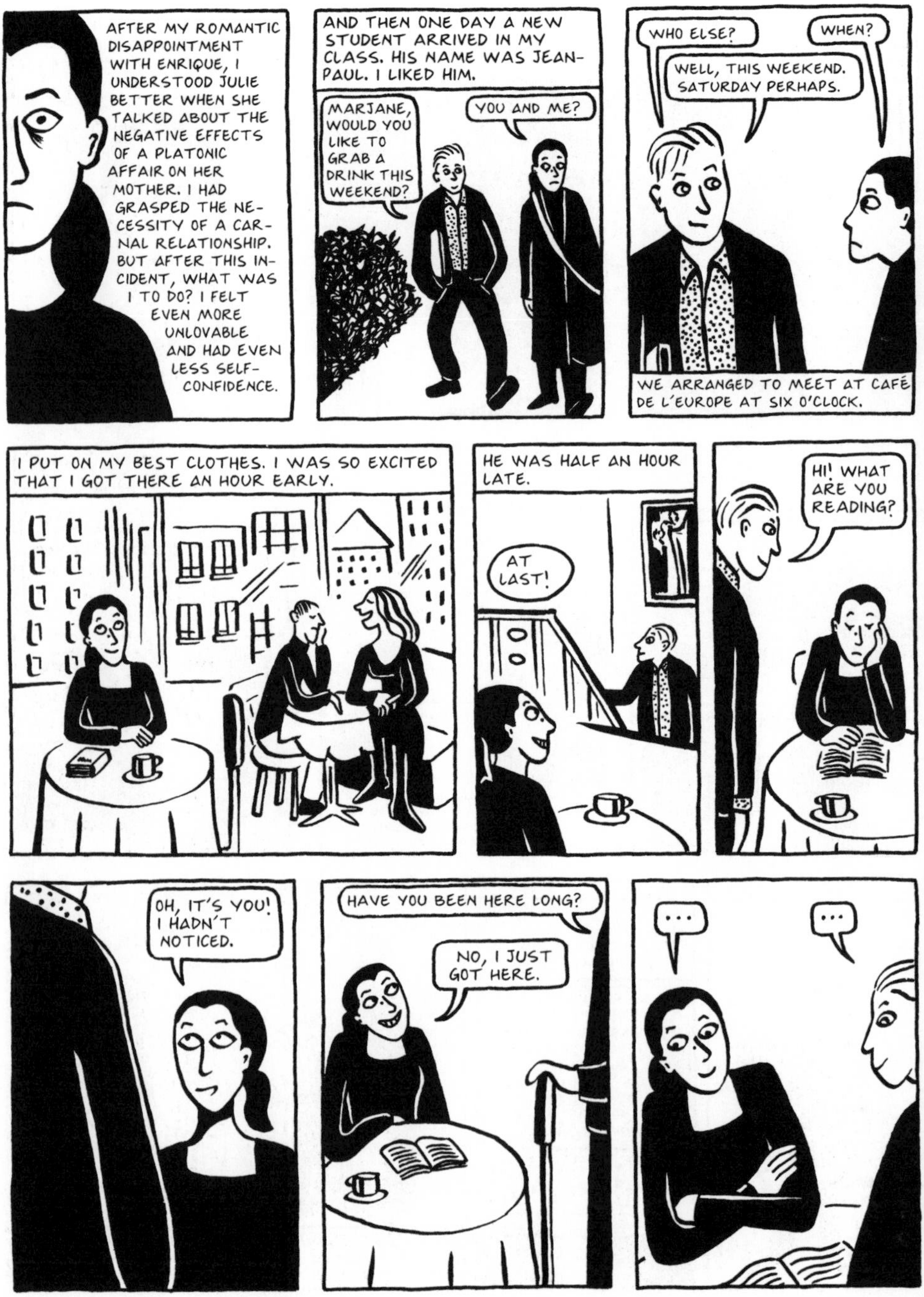
AFTER MY ROMANTIC DISAPPOINTMENT WITH ENRIQUE, I UNDERSTOOD JULIE BETTER WHEN SHE TALKED ABOUT THE NEGATIVE EFFECTS OF A PLATONIC AFFAIR ON HER MOTHER. I HAD GRASPED THE NECESSITY OF A CARNAL RELATIONSHIP. BUT AFTER THIS INCIDENT, WHAT WAS I TO DO? I FELT EVEN MORE UNLOVABLE AND HAD EVEN LESS SELF-CONFIDENCE.
AND THEN ONE DAY A NEW STUDENT ARRIVED IN MY CLASS. HIS NAME WAS JEAN-PAUL. I LIKED HIM.
MARJANE, WOULD YOU LIKE TO GRAB A DRINK THIS WEEKEND?
YOU AND ME?
WHO ELSE?
WHEN?
WELL, THIS WEEKEND. SATURDAY PERHAPS.
WE ARRANGED TO MEET AT CAFÉ DE L'EUROPE AT SIX O'CLOCK.
I PUT ON MY BEST CLOTHES. I WAS SO EXCITED THAT I GOT THERE AN HOUR EARLY.
HE WAS HALF AN HOUR LATE.
AT LAST!
HI! WHAT ARE YOU READING?
OH, IT'S YOU! I HADN'T NOTICED.
HAVE YOU BEEN HERE LONG?
NO, I JUST GOT HERE.
...
...

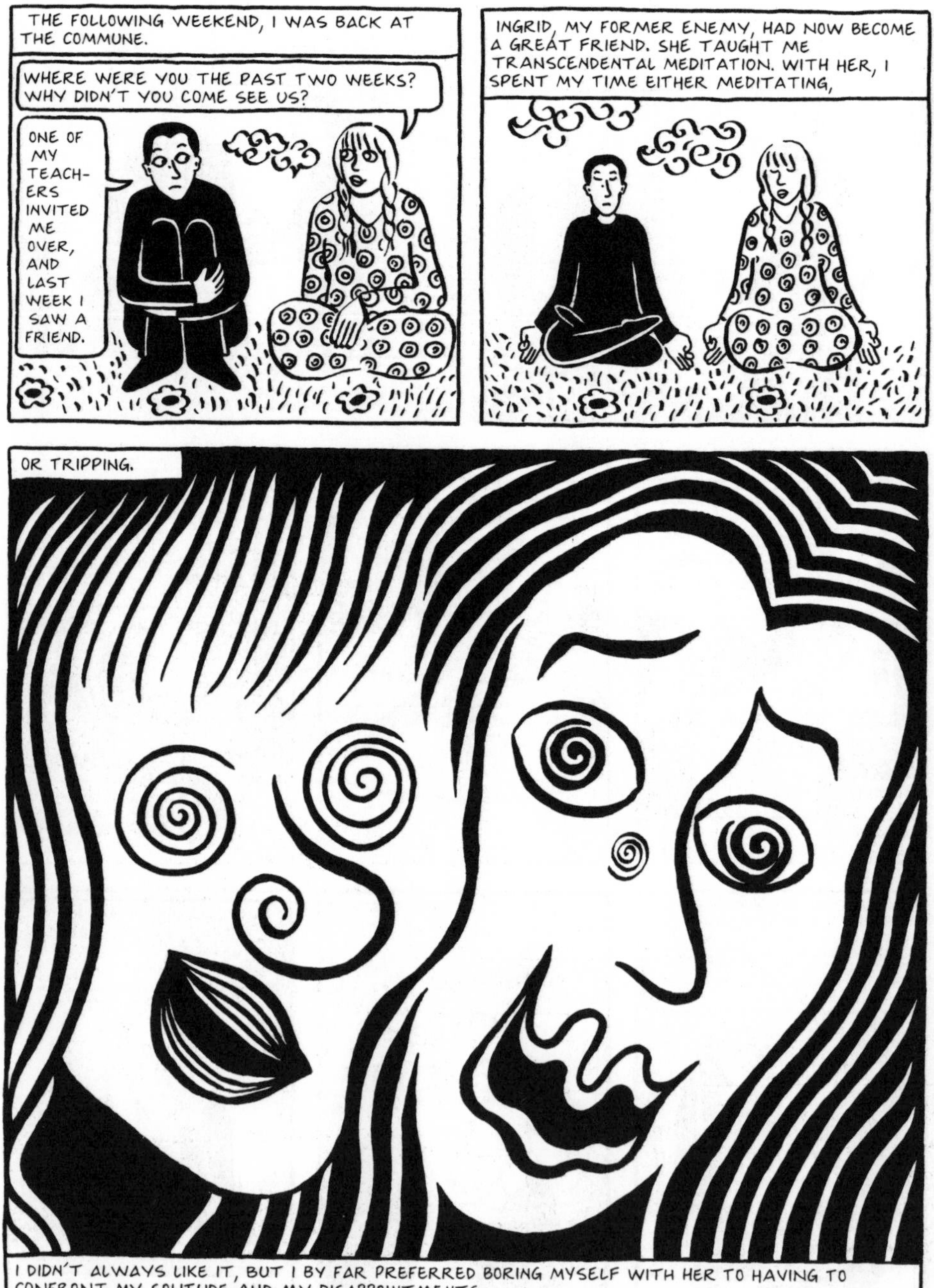
THE FOLLOWING WEEKEND, I WAS BACK AT THE COMMUNE.
WHERE WERE YOU THE PAST TWO WEEKS? WHY DIDN'T YOU COME SEE US?
ONE OF MY TEACHERS INVITED ME OVER, AND LAST WEEK I SAW A FRIEND.
INGRID, MY FORMER ENEMY, HAD NOW BECOME A GREAT FRIEND. SHE TAUGHT ME TRANSCENDENTAL MEDITATION. WITH HER, I SPENT MY TIME EITHER MEDITATING,
OR TRIPPING.
I DIDN'T ALWAYS LIKE IT, BUT I BY FAR PREFERRED BORING MYSELF WITH HER TO HAVING TO CONFRONT MY SOLITUDE AND MY DISAPPOINTMENTS.

LITTLE BY LITTLE, I BECAME THE PORTRAIT OF DORIAN GRAY. THE MORE TIME PASSED, THE MORE I WAS MARKED.

BUT THIS KIND OF DECADENCE WAS PLEASING TO SOME. AND THAT'S HOW I MET THE FIRST GREAT LOVE OF MY LIFE.

HEY! MARJANE!

HIS NAME WAS MARKUS. HE WAS STUDYING LITERATURE. AT LEAST I WAS SURE THAT HE DIDN'T WANT TO SEE ME BE-CAUSE OF HIS MATH PROBLEMS.

WHAT ARE YOU DOING ON SATURDAY?

I'M GOING TO SEE MY FRIENDS IN THE COUNTRY. WHY?

DO YOU WANT TO GO TO A CLUB?

SURE, WHY NOT?

THIS TIME I DIDN'T MAKE ANY EFFORT AT ALL: I DIDN'T PUT ON MY BEST CLOTHES AND I ARRIVED AN HOUR LATE.

I HAD GIVEN UP. I THOUGHT THAT YOU WOULDN'T COME. I'M HAPPY THAT YOU'RE HERE. DO YOU WANT TO DANCE?

NO, I DON'T LIKE DANCING. ACTUALLY, I DON'T LIKE CLUBS.

WE DANCED ANYWAY.

YOU'RE SO BEAUTIFUL TONIGHT!

WHAT A LIAR.

ASIDE FROM THE FACT THAT WE WERE BOTH ONLY CHILDREN, WE DIDN'T HAVE ANYTHING IN COMMON. I WAS UNCOMFORTABLE.

HAPPILY, THIS PATHETIC SITUA-TION DIDN'T LAST LONG. THE CLUB CLOSED AT 2:30 IN THE MORNING.

IF YOU WANT, I CAN TAKE YOU HOME, BUT I NEED TO FILL UP FIRST. SHALL WE SPLIT IT?

OKAY.

NOTHING SURPRISED ME ANYMORE. EVEN PAYING FOR GAS SO THAT MY WHITE KNIGHT COULD DRIVE ME HOME SEEMED COMPLETELY NORMAL.

YOU KNOW WHAT I LOVE ABOUT YOU, YOUR REBELLIOUS SIDE AND YOUR NATURAL NONCHALANCE.

THANKS

THEN . . .

THINGS ALWAYS HAPPEN WHEN YOU LEAST EXPECT. IT WAS HAPPINESS.

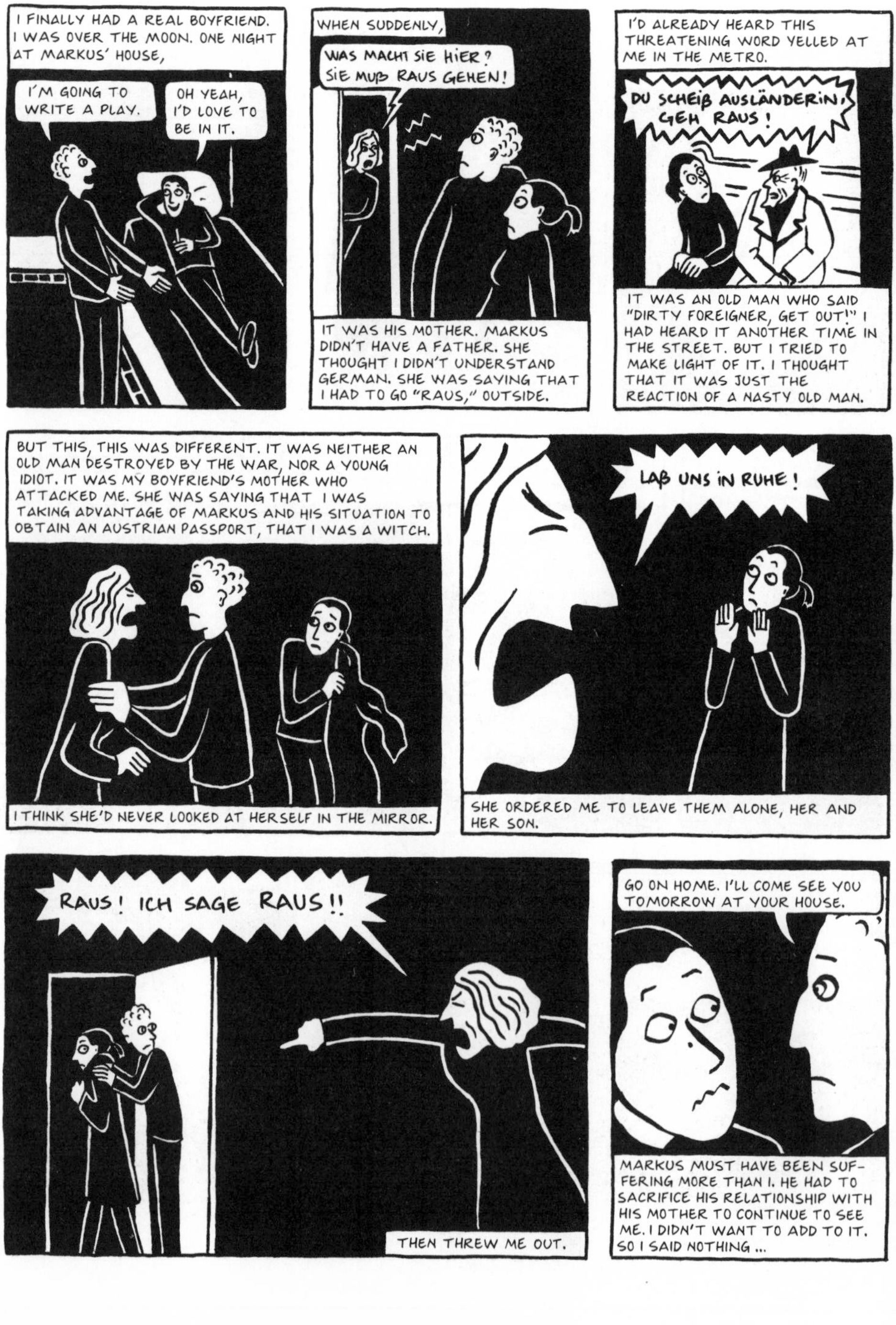
I FINALLY HAD A REAL BOYFRIEND. I WAS OVER THE MOON. ONE NIGHT AT MARKUS' HOUSE,
I'M GOING TO WRITE A PLAY.
OH YEAH, I'D LOVE TO BE IN IT.
WHEN SUDDENLY,
WAS MACHT SIE HIER? SIE MUß RAUS GEHEN!
IT WAS HIS MOTHER. MARKUS DIDN'T HAVE A FATHER. SHE THOUGHT I DIDN'T UNDERSTAND GERMAN. SHE WAS SAYING THAT I HAD TO GO "RAUS," OUTSIDE.
I'D ALREADY HEARD THIS THREATENING WORD YELLED AT ME IN THE METRO.
DU SCHEIß AUSLÄNDERIN, GEH RAUS!
IT WAS AN OLD MAN WHO SAID "DIRTY FOREIGNER, GET OUT!" I HAD HEARD IT ANOTHER TIME IN THE STREET. BUT I TRIED TO MAKE LIGHT OF IT. I THOUGHT THAT IT WAS JUST THE REACTION OF A NASTY OLD MAN.
BUT THIS, THIS WAS DIFFERENT. IT WAS NEITHER AN OLD MAN DESTROYED BY THE WAR, NOR A YOUNG IDIOT. IT WAS MY BOYFRIEND'S MOTHER WHO ATTACKED ME. SHE WAS SAYING THAT I WAS TAKING ADVANTAGE OF MARKUS AND HIS SITUATION TO OBTAIN AN AUSTRIAN PASSPORT, THAT I WAS A WITCH.
I THINK SHE'D NEVER LOOKED AT HERSELF IN THE MIRROR.
LAß UNS IN RUHE!
SHE ORDERED ME TO LEAVE THEM ALONE, HER AND HER SON.
RAUS! ICH SAGE RAUS!!
THEN THREW ME OUT.
GO ON HOME. I'LL COME SEE YOU TOMORROW AT YOUR HOUSE.
MARKUS MUST HAVE BEEN SUFFERING MORE THAN I. HE HAD TO SACRIFICE HIS RELATIONSHIP WITH HIS MOTHER TO CONTINUE TO SEE ME. I DIDN'T WANT TO ADD TO IT. SO I SAID NOTHING ...

* THIS ISN'T A BORDELLO.

* I HAD JUST READ HIS THREE ESSAYS ON THE THEORY OF SEXUALITY.

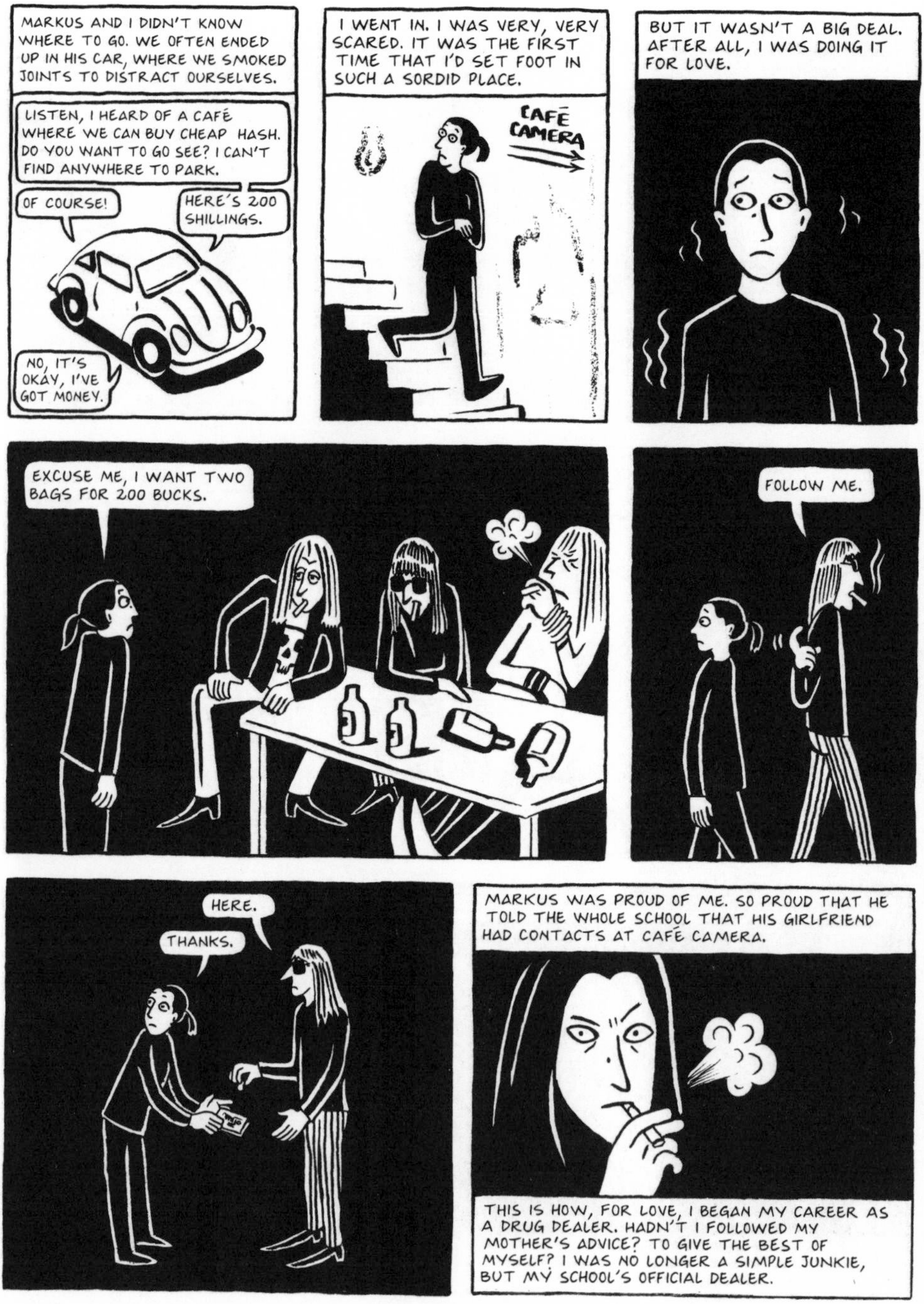
MARKUS AND I DIDN'T KNOW WHERE TO GO. WE OFTEN ENDED UP IN HIS CAR, WHERE WE SMOKED JOINTS TO DISTRACT OURSELVES.
LISTEN, I HEARD OF A CAFÉ WHERE WE CAN BUY CHEAP HASH. DO YOU WANT TO GO SEE? I CAN'T FIND ANYWHERE TO PARK.
OF COURSE!
HERE'S 200 SHILLINGS.
NO, IT'S OKAY, I'VE GOT MONEY.
I WENT IN. I WAS VERY, VERY SCARED. IT WAS THE FIRST TIME THAT I'D SET FOOT IN SUCH A SORDID PLACE.
CAFÉ CAMERA
BUT IT WASN'T A BIG DEAL. AFTER ALL, I WAS DOING IT FOR LOVE.
EXCUSE ME, I WANT TWO BAGS FOR 200 BUCKS.
FOLLOW ME.
HERE.
THANKS.
MARKUS WAS PROUD OF ME. SO PROUD THAT HE TOLD THE WHOLE SCHOOL THAT HIS GIRLFRIEND HAD CONTACTS AT CAFÉ CAMERA.
THIS IS HOW, FOR LOVE, I BEGAN MY CAREER AS A DRUG DEALER. HADN'T I FOLLOWED MY MOTHER'S ADVICE? TO GIVE THE BEST OF MYSELF? I WAS NO LONGER A SIMPLE JUNKIE, BUT MY SCHOOL'S OFFICIAL DEALER.

THE CROISSANT

LUCKILY, I HAD BENEFITED ENOUGH FROM A SOLID EDUCATION TO NEVER DRIFT TOO FAR. IT WAS THE END OF MY LAST YEAR. I WAS GOING TO TAKE THE FRENCH BACCALAUREATE.

WHEN I STUDIED WITH THE OTHERS, I REALIZED THAT I HAD MANY GAPS. I NEEDED A MIRACLE TO PASS.

AND THIS MIRACLE HAPPENED ONE NIGHT IN JUNE, DURING MY SLEEP.

HEY, MARJI, THE SUBJECT ON THE BAC, IT WILL BE MONTESQUIEU'S "SLAVERY OF THE NEGROES."

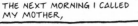

THE NEXT MORNING I CALLED MY MOTHER,

WHO CALLED GOD, WHO IN TURN SENT HIS MESSAGE TO THE EXAMINER.

EACH TIME THAT I ASKED MY MOTHER TO PRAY FOR ME, MY WISH WAS GRANTED.

DO YOU LIKE THE 18TH CENTURY?

YES.

DO YOU LIKE MONTESQUIEU?

YES.

YOU HAVE THIRTY MINUTES TO PREPARE "SLAVERY OF THE NEGROES."

I GOT A 17, THE BEST GRADE IN SCHOOL.

THEN CAME SUMMER. TO BE TRUTHFUL, I WASN'T MAKING ANYTHING BY DEALING BECAUSE I WAS DOING IT AS A FAVOR. SO I SET OUT TO FIND SOME ODD JOBS.

IT WAS SOMETIMES BORING.

SOMETIMES FUN.

ONE DAY I SAW AN AD IN A NEWSPAPER: "CAFÉ SOLE IS LOOKING FOR A WAITRESS, THREE EUROPEAN LANGUAGES REQUIRED."

YOU SPEAK GERMAN, ENGLISH AND FRENCH. THAT'S GOOD. HAVE YOU EVER WORKED IN A BAR?

YES*

GOOD! YOU START TOMORROW. BUT WATCH OUT! THE CUSTOMER IS ALWAYS RIGHT!!

CAFÉ SOLE WAS LOCATED IN THE BEST NEIGHBORHOOD IN VIENNA, I WAS PAID DECENTLY, BUT IT WASN'T ALWAYS EASY WITH THE CUSTOMERS. SOMETIMES, I REALLY WANTED TO SLAP THEM.

"THE CUSTOMER IS ALWAYS RIGHT." "THE CUSTOMER IS ALWAYS RIGHT"...

* I LIED.

NONETHELESS, I HAD AN ALLY. IT WAS SVETLANA, THE YUGOSLAVIAN CHEF.

WHAT'S THE MATTER, SWEETIE?

SOME MORON PINCHED MY BUTT.

TELL ME, WHAT DID HE ORDER, THIS SON-OF-A-BITCH?

A WIENER SCHNITZEL.

GOD FORGIVE ME!

RAAK PTOUH!

THERE! JUSTICE IS DONE.

SHE REALLY MADE ME LAUGH. THANKS TO HER, I WAS ABLE TO WORK THERE WITHOUT HAVING TO INJURE A FEW MEN WHERE IT COUNTS.

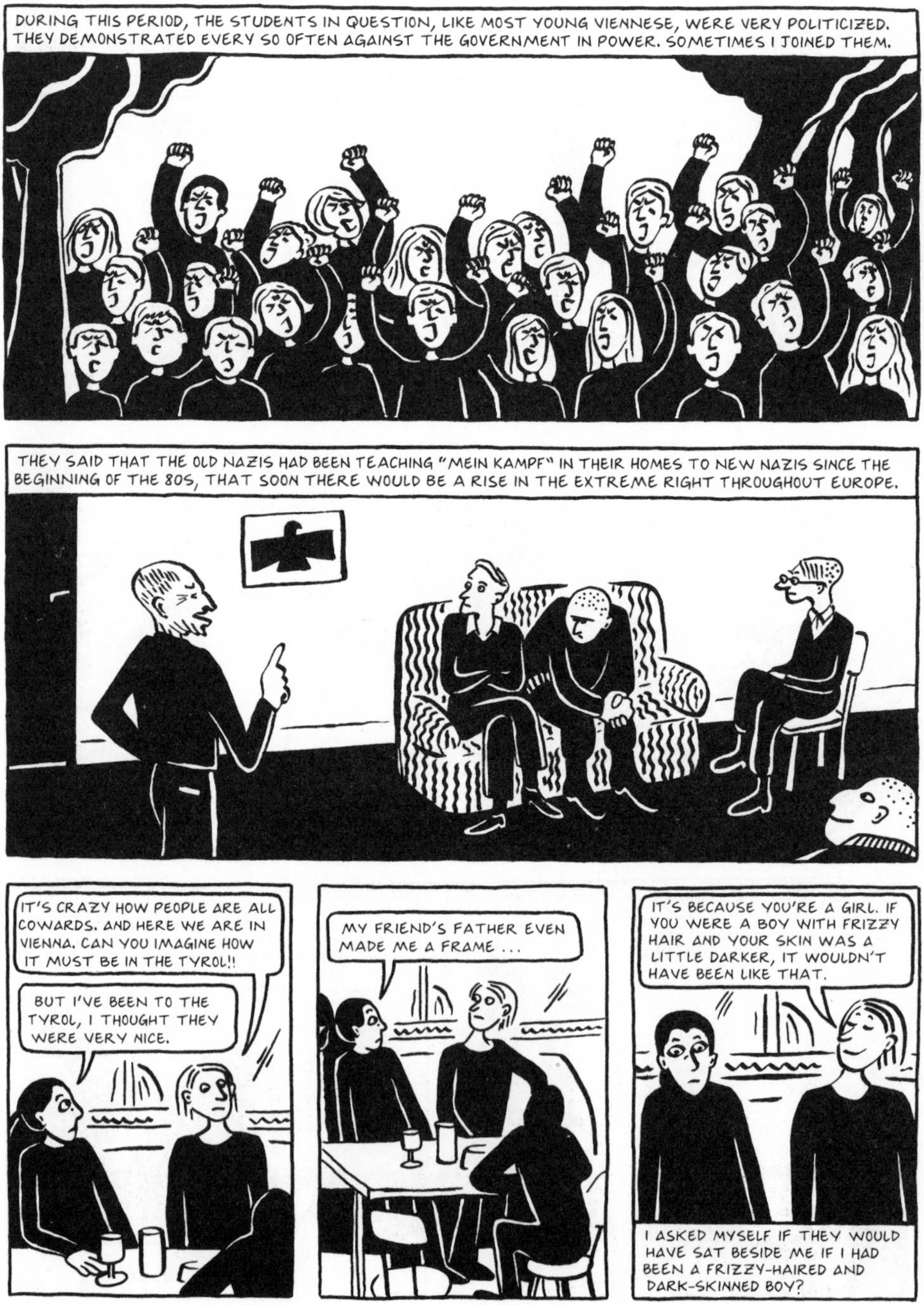
DURING THIS PERIOD, THE STUDENTS IN QUESTION, LIKE MOST YOUNG VIENNESE, WERE VERY POLITICIZED. THEY DEMONSTRATED EVERY SO OFTEN AGAINST THE GOVERNMENT IN POWER. SOMETIMES I JOINED THEM.
THEY SAID THAT THE OLD NAZIS HAD BEEN TEACHING "MEIN KAMPF" IN THEIR HOMES TO NEW NAZIS SINCE THE BEGINNING OF THE 80S, THAT SOON THERE WOULD BE A RISE IN THE EXTREME RIGHT THROUGHOUT EUROPE.
IT'S CRAZY HOW PEOPLE ARE ALL COWARDS. AND HERE WE ARE IN VIENNA. CAN YOU IMAGINE HOW IT MUST BE IN THE TYROL!!
BUT I'VE BEEN TO THE TYROL, I THOUGHT THEY WERE VERY NICE.
MY FRIEND'S FATHER EVEN MADE ME A FRAME ...
IT'S BECAUSE YOU'RE A GIRL. IF YOU WERE A BOY WITH FRIZZY HAIR AND YOUR SKIN WAS A LITTLE DARKER, IT WOULDN'T HAVE BEEN LIKE THAT.
I ASKED MYSELF IF THEY WOULD HAVE SAT BESIDE ME IF I HAD BEEN A FRIZZY-HAIRED AND DARK-SKINNED BOY?

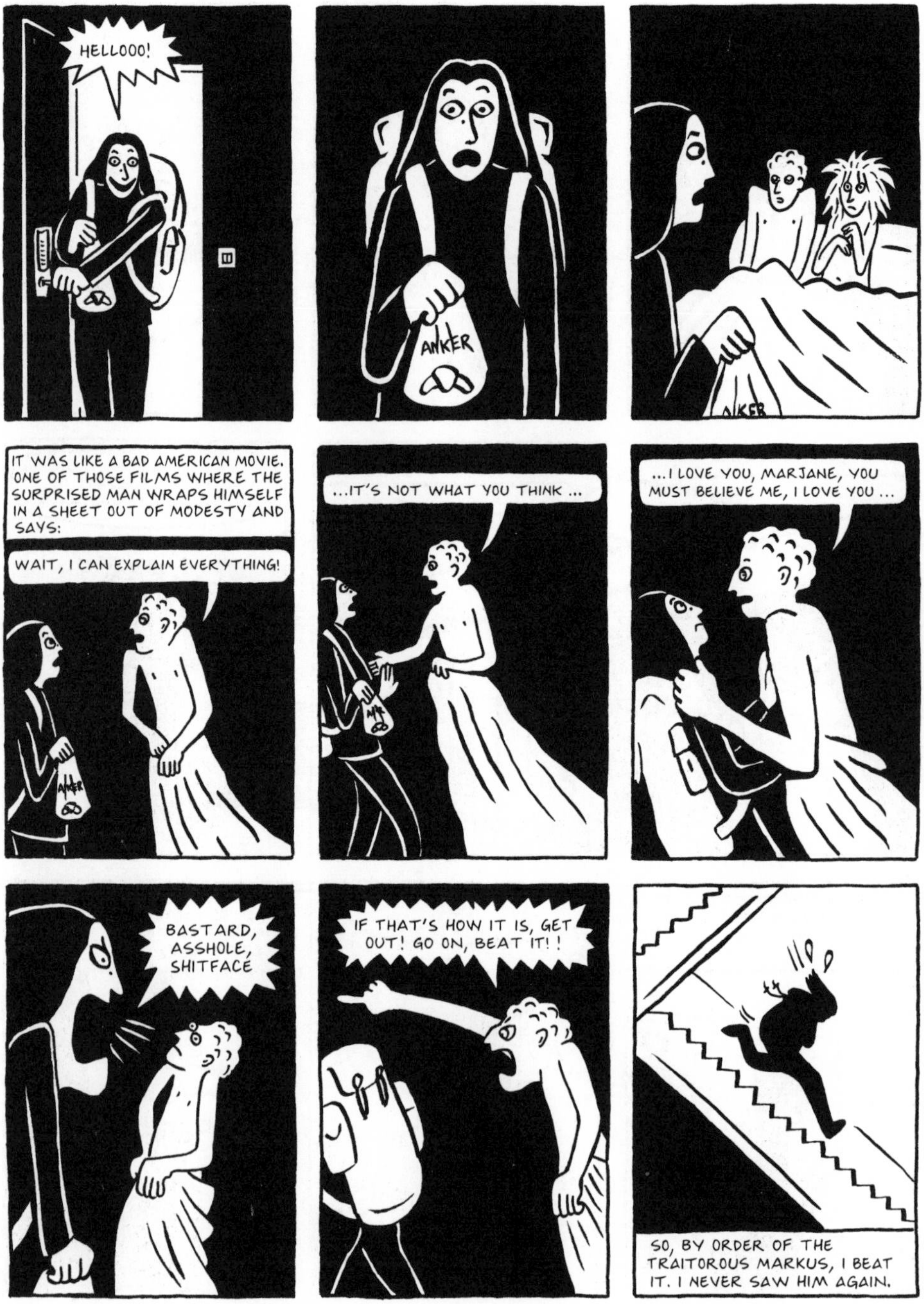
HELLOOO!
ANKER
ANKER
IT WAS LIKE A BAD AMERICAN MOVIE. ONE OF THOSE FILMS WHERE THE SURPRISED MAN WRAPS HIMSELF IN A SHEET OUT OF MODESTY AND SAYS:
WAIT, I CAN EXPLAIN EVERYTHING!
...IT'S NOT WHAT YOU THINK ...
...I LOVE YOU, MARJANE, YOU MUST BELIEVE ME, I LOVE YOU ...
BASTARD, ASSHOLE, SHITFACE
IF THAT'S HOW IT IS, GET OUT! GO ON, BEAT IT!!
SO, BY ORDER OF THE TRAITOROUS MARKUS, I BEAT IT. I NEVER SAW HIM AGAIN.

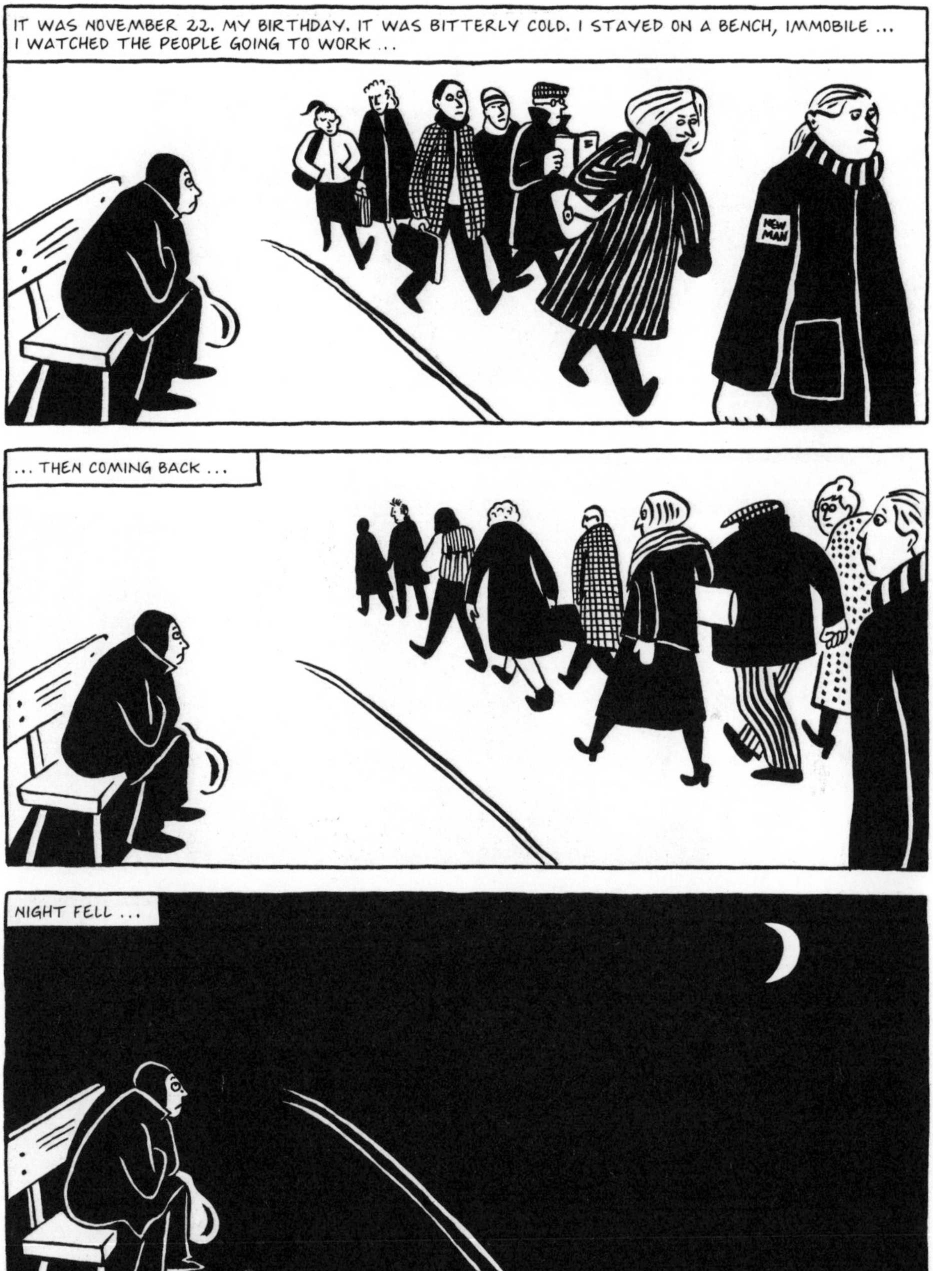
IT WAS NOVEMBER 22. MY BIRTHDAY. IT WAS BITTERLY COLD. I STAYED ON A BENCH, IMMOBILE ... I WATCHED THE PEOPLE GOING TO WORK ...
NEW MAN
... THEN COMING BACK ...
NIGHT FELL ...
"NIGHT BRINGS GOOD COUNSEL," MY GRANDMOTHER ALWAYS TOLD ME.

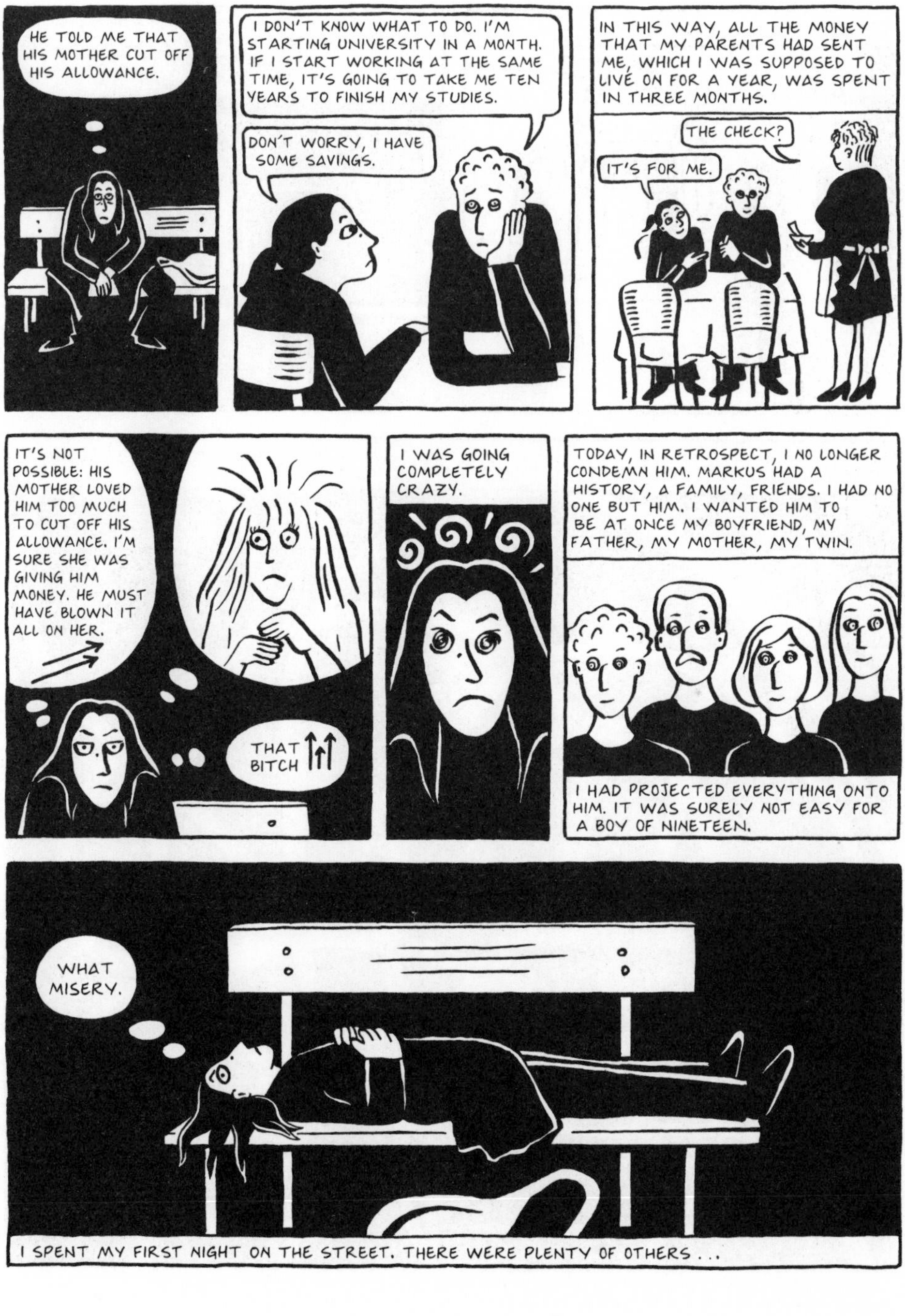
HE TOLD ME THAT HIS MOTHER CUT OFF HIS ALLOWANCE.
I DON'T KNOW WHAT TO DO. I'M STARTING UNIVERSITY IN A MONTH. IF I START WORKING AT THE SAME TIME, IT'S GOING TO TAKE ME TEN YEARS TO FINISH MY STUDIES.
DON'T WORRY, I HAVE SOME SAVINGS.
IN THIS WAY, ALL THE MONEY THAT MY PARENTS HAD SENT ME, WHICH I WAS SUPPOSED TO LIVE ON FOR A YEAR, WAS SPENT IN THREE MONTHS.
THE CHECK?
IT'S FOR ME.
IT'S NOT POSSIBLE: HIS MOTHER LOVED HIM TOO MUCH TO CUT OFF HIS ALLOWANCE. I'M SURE SHE WAS GIVING HIM MONEY. HE MUST HAVE BLOWN IT ALL ON HER.
THAT BITCH
I WAS GOING COMPLETELY CRAZY.
TODAY, IN RETROSPECT, I NO LONGER CONDEMN HIM. MARKUS HAD A HISTORY, A FAMILY, FRIENDS. I HAD NO ONE BUT HIM. I WANTED HIM TO BE AT ONCE MY BOYFRIEND, MY FATHER, MY MOTHER, MY TWIN.
I HAD PROJECTED EVERYTHING ONTO HIM. IT WAS SURELY NOT EASY FOR A BOY OF NINETEEN.
WHAT MISERY.
I SPENT MY FIRST NIGHT ON THE STREET. THERE WERE PLENTY OF OTHERS . . .

IN THE MORNING, I TOOK THE TRAM.

INSIDE, THERE WERE TWO SPOTS THAT WERE VERY WARM, BECAUSE THEY WERE ABOVE THE MOTOR. I FELL ASLEEP ON ONE OF THESE SEATS. IT WAS PEACEFUL.

FOR ALMOST A MONTH, I LIVED AT THIS RHYTHM: THE NIGHT PROSTRATE AND THE DAY LETTING MYSELF BE CARRIED ACROSS VIENNA BY SLEEP AND THE TRAMWAY.

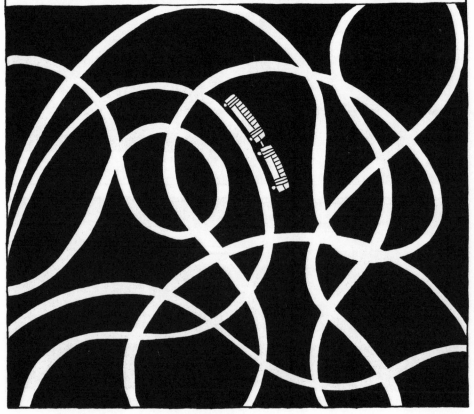

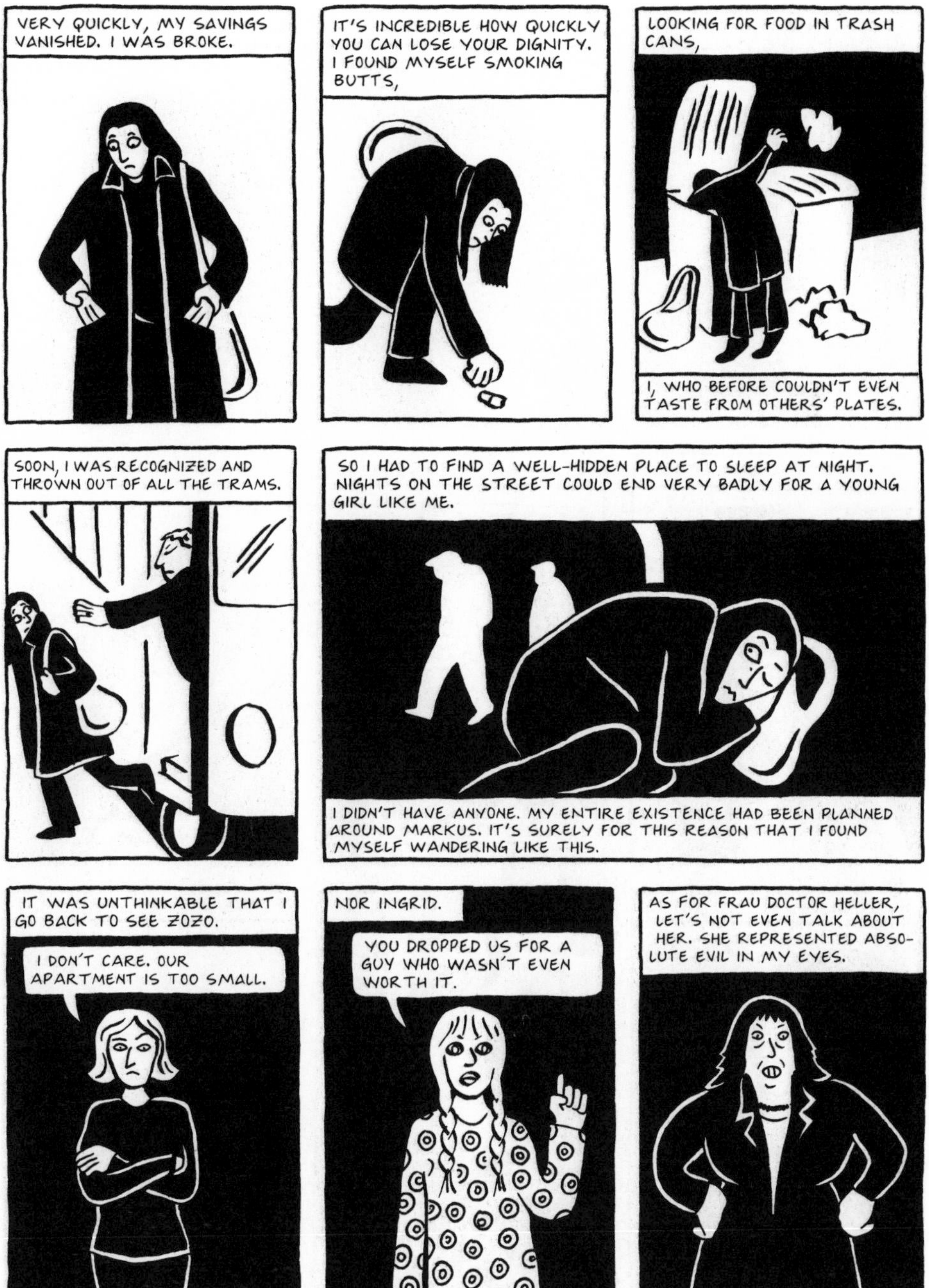
VERY QUICKLY, MY SAVINGS VANISHED. I WAS BROKE.
IT'S INCREDIBLE HOW QUICKLY YOU CAN LOSE YOUR DIGNITY. I FOUND MYSELF SMOKING BUTTS,
LOOKING FOR FOOD IN TRASH CANS,
I, WHO BEFORE COULDN'T EVEN TASTE FROM OTHERS' PLATES.
SOON, I WAS RECOGNIZED AND THROWN OUT OF ALL THE TRAMS.
SO I HAD TO FIND A WELL-HIDDEN PLACE TO SLEEP AT NIGHT. NIGHTS ON THE STREET COULD END VERY BADLY FOR A YOUNG GIRL LIKE ME.
I DIDN'T HAVE ANYONE. MY ENTIRE EXISTENCE HAD BEEN PLANNED AROUND MARKUS. IT'S SURELY FOR THIS REASON THAT I FOUND MYSELF WANDERING LIKE THIS.
IT WAS UNTHINKABLE THAT I GO BACK TO SEE ZOZO.
I DON'T CARE. OUR APARTMENT IS TOO SMALL.
NOR INGRID.
YOU DROPPED US FOR A GUY WHO WASN'T EVEN WORTH IT.
AS FOR FRAU DOCTOR HELLER, LET'S NOT EVEN TALK ABOUT HER. SHE REPRESENTED ABSOLUTE EVIL IN MY EYES.

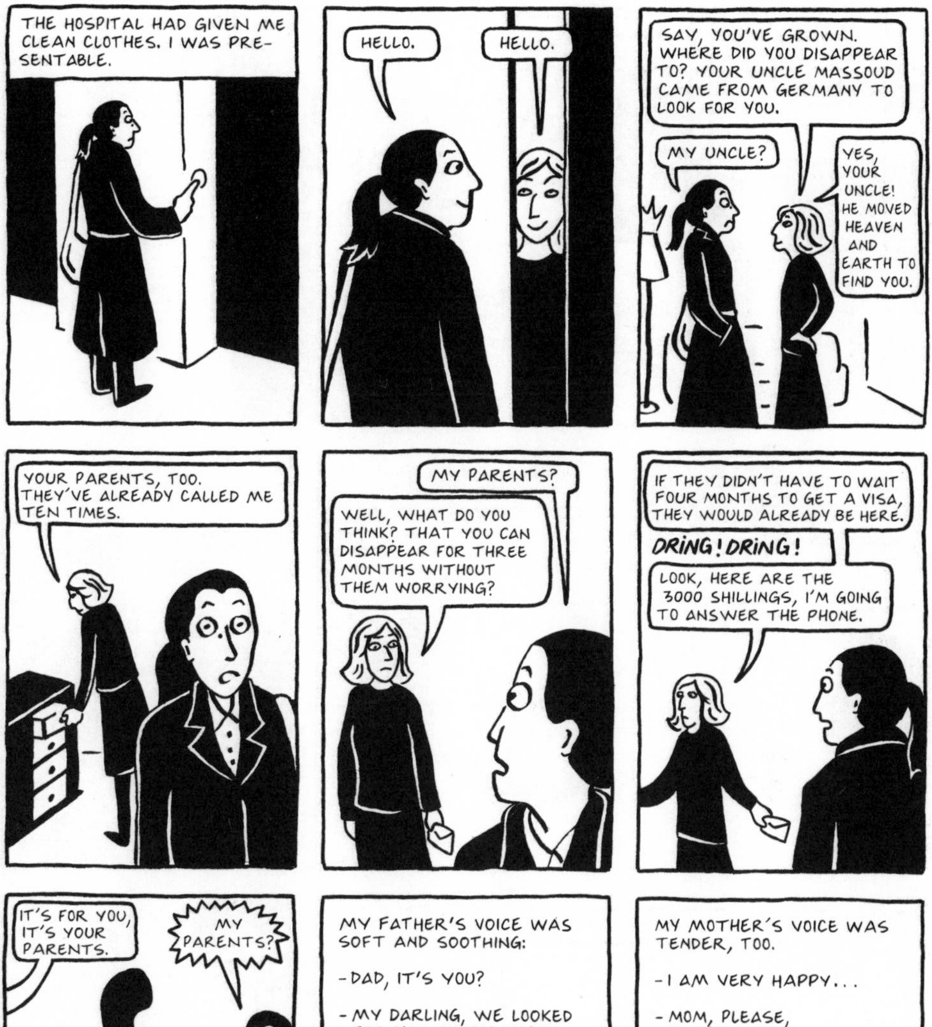
THE HOSPITAL HAD GIVEN ME CLEAN CLOTHES. I WAS PRESENTABLE.
HELLO.
HELLO.
SAY, YOU'VE GROWN. WHERE DID YOU DISAPPEAR TO? YOUR UNCLE MASSOUD CAME FROM GERMANY TO LOOK FOR YOU.
MY UNCLE?
YES, YOUR UNCLE! HE MOVED HEAVEN AND EARTH TO FIND YOU.
YOUR PARENTS, TOO. THEY'VE ALREADY CALLED ME TEN TIMES.
MY PARENTS?
WELL, WHAT DO YOU THINK? THAT YOU CAN DISAPPEAR FOR THREE MONTHS WITHOUT THEM WORRYING?
IF THEY DIDN'T HAVE TO WAIT FOUR MONTHS TO GET A VISA, THEY WOULD ALREADY BE HERE.
DRING! DRING!
LOOK, HERE ARE THE 3000 SHILLINGS, I'M GOING TO ANSWER THE PHONE.
IT'S FOR YOU, IT'S YOUR PARENTS.
MY PARENTS?
ANOTHER MIRACLE HAD JUST OCCURRED.
MY FATHER'S VOICE WAS SOFT AND SOOTHING:
-DAD, IT'S YOU?
-MY DARLING, WE LOOKED FOR YOU EVERYWHERE.
-CAN I COME BACK?
-OF COURSE, WHAT A QUESTION.
-DAD, PROMISE ME TO NEVER ASK ME ANYTHING ABOUT THESE THREE MONTHS.
-I PROMISE YOU... HERE'S YOUR MOTHER.
MY MOTHER'S VOICE WAS TENDER, TOO.
-I AM VERY HAPPY...
-MOM, PLEASE, DON'T CRY.
-THESE ARE TEARS OF JOY.
-MOM...
-COME HOME, DARLING, WE ARE WAITING FOR YOU...
-MOM...
-NO ONE WILL ASK YOU ANY QUESTIONS. IT'S A PROMISE.

BEFORE MY DEPARTURE, I WENT BY FRAU DOCTOR HELLER'S.

I CAME TO GET MY THINGS.

HERE THEY ARE!

WHERE IS THE REST?

THERE IS NO REST. THE REST WILL COMPENSATE THE BROOCH THAT YOU STOLE FROM ME.

I DIDN'T SAY ANYTHING. IN ANY CASE, I COULDN'T TAKE FOUR YEARS OF MY LIFE BACK WITH ME.

I FOUND AN INEXPENSIVE HOTEL. I HAD FIVE DAYS AHEAD OF ME, BEFORE THE NEXT FLIGHT TO TEHRAN.

HOTEL TU iP

I FINALLY FOUND A PLACE OF MY OWN, SOME PRIVACY.

DESPITE THE DOCTOR'S ORDERS, I BOUGHT MYSELF SEVERAL CARTONS OF CIGARETTES.

YOU ARE PUTTING YOURSELF IN SERIOUS DANGER...

I THINK THAT I PREFERRED TO PUT MYSELF IN SERIOUS DANGER RATHER THAN CONFRONT MY SHAME. MY SHAME AT NOT HAVING BECOME SOMEONE, THE SHAME OF NOT HAVING MADE MY PARENTS PROUD AFTER ALL THE SACRIFICES THEY HAD MADE FOR ME. THE SHAME OF HAVING BECOME A MEDIOCRE NIHILIST.

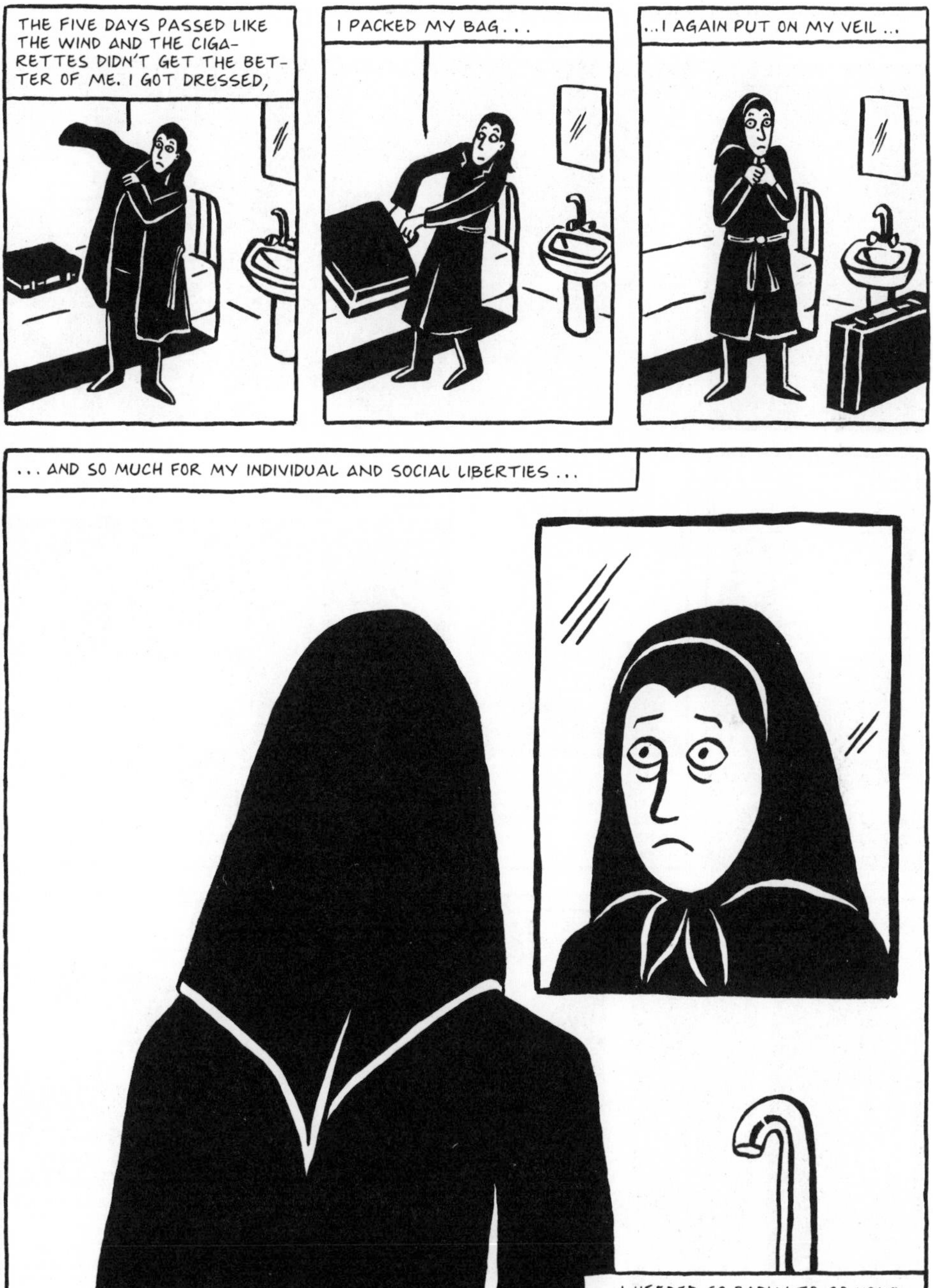
THE FIVE DAYS PASSED LIKE THE WIND AND THE CIGARETTES DIDN'T GET THE BETTER OF ME. I GOT DRESSED,
I PACKED MY BAG . . .
..I AGAIN PUT ON MY VEIL ...
. . . AND SO MUCH FOR MY INDIVIDUAL AND SOCIAL LIBERTIES . . .
. . . I NEEDED SO BADLY TO GO HOME.

THE RETURN

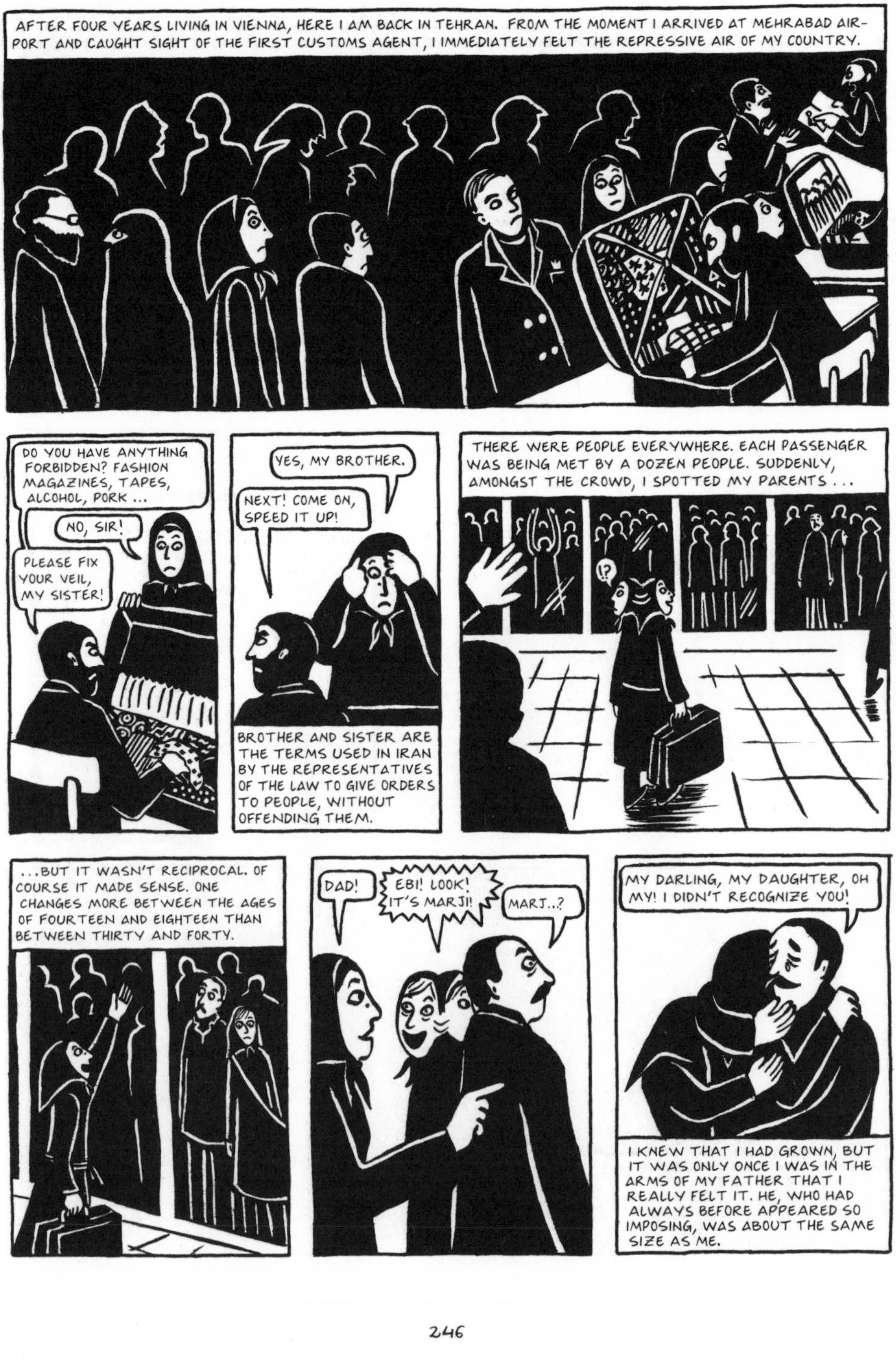
AFTER FOUR YEARS LIVING IN VIENNA, HERE I AM BACK IN TEHRAN. FROM THE MOMENT I ARRIVED AT MEHRABAD AIR-PORT AND CAUGHT SIGHT OF THE FIRST CUSTOMS AGENT, I IMMEDIATELY FELT THE REPRESSIVE AIR OF MY COUNTRY.
DO YOU HAVE ANYTHING FORBIDDEN? FASHION MAGAZINES, TAPES, ALCOHOL, PORK ...
NO, SIR!
PLEASE FIX YOUR VEIL, MY SISTER!
YES, MY BROTHER.
NEXT! COME ON, SPEED IT UP!
BROTHER AND SISTER ARE THE TERMS USED IN IRAN BY THE REPRESENTATIVES OF THE LAW TO GIVE ORDERS TO PEOPLE, WITHOUT OFFENDING THEM.
THERE WERE PEOPLE EVERYWHERE. EACH PASSENGER WAS BEING MET BY A DOZEN PEOPLE. SUDDENLY, AMONGST THE CROWD, I SPOTTED MY PARENTS . . .
!?
. . . BUT IT WASN'T RECIPROCAL. OF COURSE IT MADE SENSE. ONE CHANGES MORE BETWEEN THE AGES OF FOURTEEN AND EIGHTEEN THAN BETWEEN THIRTY AND FORTY.
DAD!
EBI! LOOK! IT'S MARJI!
MARJ...?
MY DARLING, MY DAUGHTER, OH MY! I DIDN'T RECOGNIZE YOU!
I KNEW THAT I HAD GROWN, BUT IT WAS ONLY ONCE I WAS IN THE ARMS OF MY FATHER THAT I REALLY FELT IT. HE, WHO HAD ALWAYS BEFORE APPEARED SO IMPOSING, WAS ABOUT THE SAME SIZE AS ME.

I CAN'T BELIEVE MY EYES! TELL US, ARE YOU HUNGRY?

DAD, YOU KNOW WHAT IT'S LIKE ON IRAN AIR. THEY FEED YOU AT LEAST FIFTY TIMES.

THEN WE GOT IN THE CAR.

MY FATHER DIDN'T HAVE HIS CADILLAC ANYMORE, BUT DROVE A RENAULT 5 INSTEAD. THAT SAME CADILLAC IN WHICH I WAS ASHAMED TO SIT BECAUSE IT WAS SO DIFFICULT TO ACCEPT BEING MORE COMFORTABLE THAN OTHERS. NOW THAT I MYSELF HAD UNDERSTOOD DISTRESS, I NO LONGER ASKED THESE KINDS OF QUESTIONS. I WOULD EVEN HAVE PREFERRED THAT HE COME GET ME WITH A BETTER CAR, AS A WAY TO REMIND ME OF A MORE GLORIOUS TIME.

I DIDN'T FEEL LIKE TALKING. I PRETENDED TO LOOK AT THE CITY, EVEN THOUGH IT WAS TOO DARK TO SEE ANYTHING.

WELCOME HOME!

THEY WERE THE MOST COMFORTING WORDS THAT I HAD HEARD IN A LONG TIME.

I WENT STRAIGHT TO THE LIVING ROOM. THERE WAS STILL THAT SOFA ON WHICH MY PARENTS HAD ANNOUNCED THAT THEY WERE SENDING ME TO AUSTRIA.

ENTERING INTO A CONVERSATION ABOUT THIS SUBJECT SCARED ME SO MUCH THAT I HEADED FOR MY ROOM LIKE A BOOR WITHOUT SAYING GOOD NIGHT OR GOODBYE.

MY ROOM . . . MY ROOM!!

I WAS OVERJOYED TO FINALLY HAVE A PLACE OF MY OWN AND THIS REASSURED ME.

I DIDN'T WANT TO TURN ON THE LIGHT. I COULDN'T BEAR TO SEE EVERYTHING AGAIN SO QUICKLY.

I SPENT A GOOD PART OF THE NIGHT IN THE EMPTINESS, JUST HAPPY TO BE THERE.

247

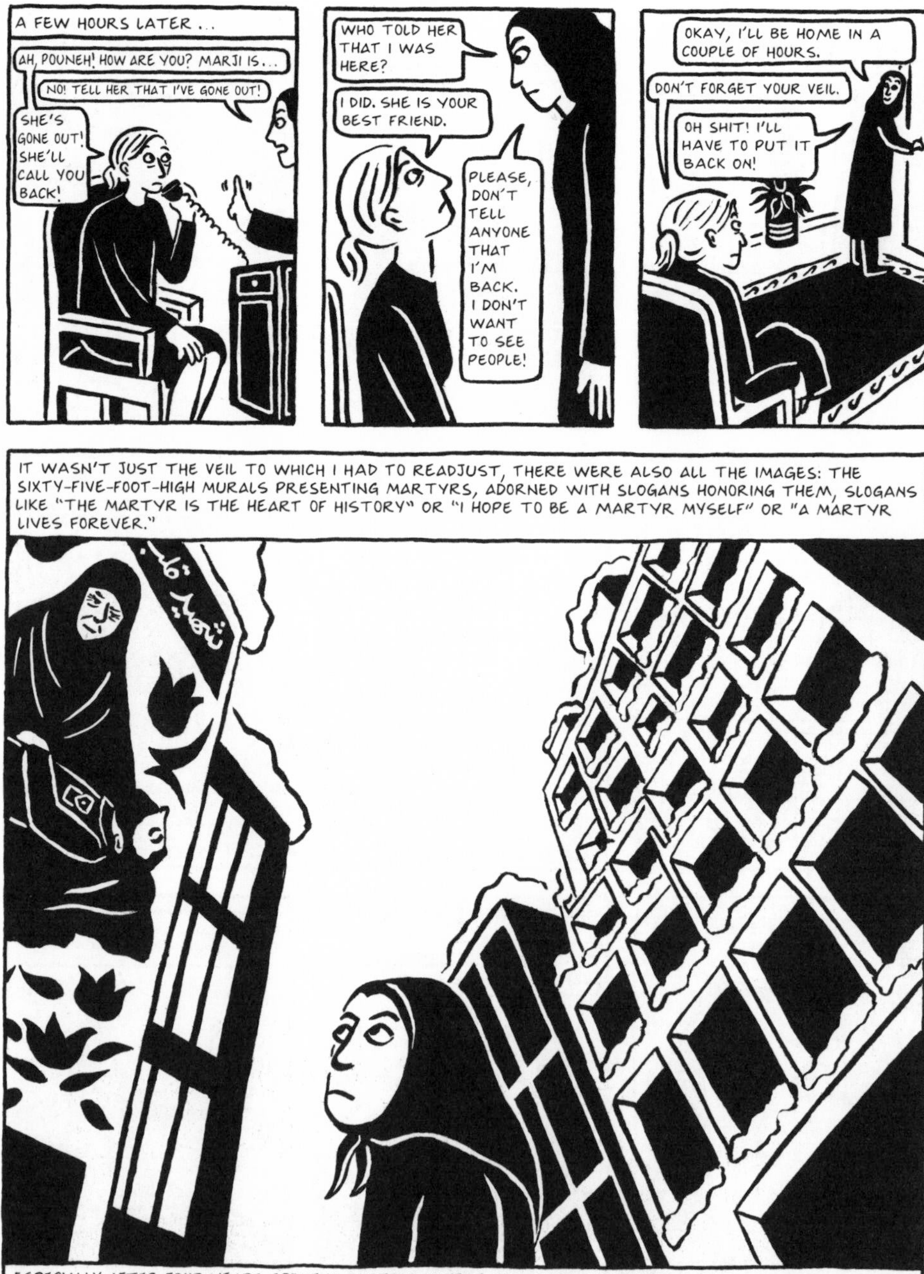

A FEW HOURS LATER . . .
AH, POUNEH! HOW ARE YOU? MARJI IS . . .
NO! TELL HER THAT I'VE GONE OUT!
SHE'S GONE OUT! SHE'LL CALL YOU BACK!
WHO TOLD HER THAT I WAS HERE?
I DID. SHE IS YOUR BEST FRIEND.
PLEASE, DON'T TELL ANYONE THAT I'M BACK. I DON'T WANT TO SEE PEOPLE!
OKAY, I'LL BE HOME IN A COUPLE OF HOURS.
DON'T FORGET YOUR VEIL.
OH SHIT! I'LL HAVE TO PUT IT BACK ON!
IT WASN'T JUST THE VEIL TO WHICH I HAD TO READJUST, THERE WERE ALSO ALL THE IMAGES: THE SIXTY-FIVE-FOOT-HIGH MURALS PRESENTING MARTYRS, ADORNED WITH SLOGANS HONORING THEM, SLOGANS LIKE "THE MARTYR IS THE HEART OF HISTORY" OR "I HOPE TO BE A MARTYR MYSELF" OR "A MARTYR LIVES FOREVER."
ESPECIALLY AFTER FOUR YEARS SPENT IN AUSTRIA, WHERE YOU WERE MORE LIKELY TO SEE ON THE WALLS "BEST SAUSAGES FOR 20 SHILLINGS," THE ROAD TO READJUSTMENT SEEMED VERY LONG TO ME.

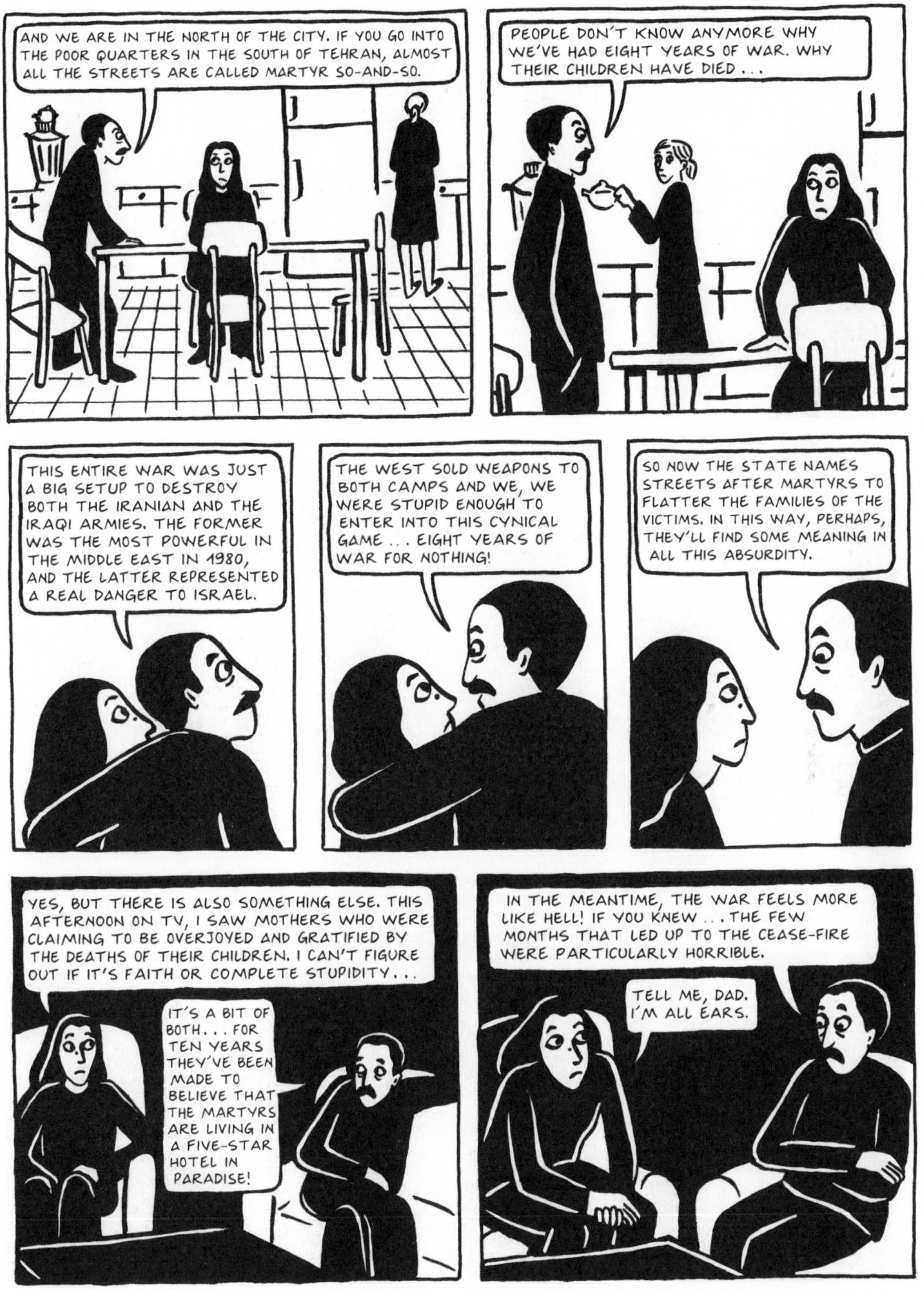
AND WE ARE IN THE NORTH OF THE CITY. IF YOU GO INTO THE POOR QUARTERS IN THE SOUTH OF TEHRAN, ALMOST ALL THE STREETS ARE CALLED MARTYR SO-AND-SO.
PEOPLE DON'T KNOW ANYMORE WHY WE'VE HAD EIGHT YEARS OF WAR. WHY THEIR CHILDREN HAVE DIED...
THIS ENTIRE WAR WAS JUST A BIG SETUP TO DESTROY BOTH THE IRANIAN AND THE IRAQI ARMIES. THE FORMER WAS THE MOST POWERFUL IN THE MIDDLE EAST IN 1980, AND THE LATTER REPRESENTED A REAL DANGER TO ISRAEL.
THE WEST SOLD WEAPONS TO BOTH CAMPS AND WE, WE WERE STUPID ENOUGH TO ENTER INTO THIS CYNICAL GAME... EIGHT YEARS OF WAR FOR NOTHING!
SO NOW THE STATE NAMES STREETS AFTER MARTYRS TO FLATTER THE FAMILIES OF THE VICTIMS. IN THIS WAY, PERHAPS, THEY'LL FIND SOME MEANING IN ALL THIS ABSURDITY.
YES, BUT THERE IS ALSO SOMETHING ELSE. THIS AFTERNOON ON TV, I SAW MOTHERS WHO WERE CLAIMING TO BE OVERJOYED AND GRATIFIED BY THE DEATHS OF THEIR CHILDREN. I CAN'T FIGURE OUT IF IT'S FAITH OR COMPLETE STUPIDITY...
IT'S A BIT OF BOTH... FOR TEN YEARS THEY'VE BEEN MADE TO BELIEVE THAT THE MARTYRS ARE LIVING IN A FIVE-STAR HOTEL IN PARADISE!
IN THE MEANTIME, THE WAR FEELS MORE LIKE HELL! IF YOU KNEW... THE FEW MONTHS THAT LED UP TO THE CEASE-FIRE WERE PARTICULARLY HORRIBLE.
TELL ME, DAD. I'M ALL EARS.

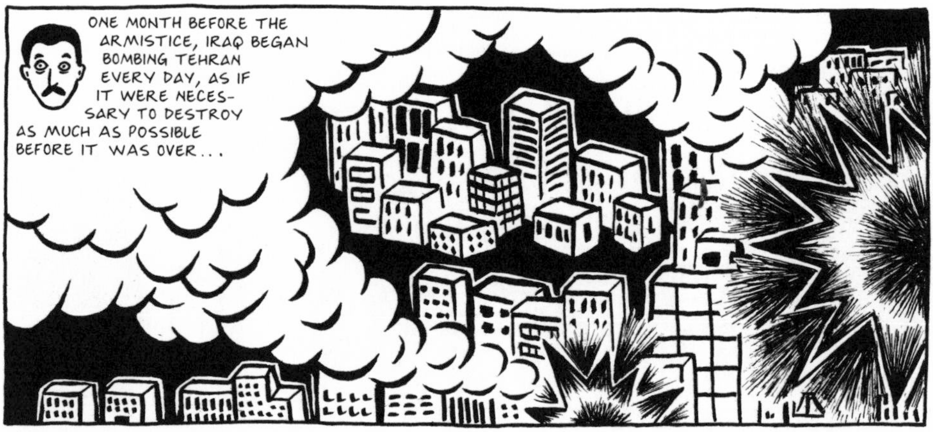
ONE MONTH BEFORE THE ARMISTICE, IRAQ BEGAN BOMBING TEHRAN EVERY DAY, AS IF IT WERE NECES-SARY TO DESTROY AS MUCH AS POSSIBLE BEFORE IT WAS OVER...

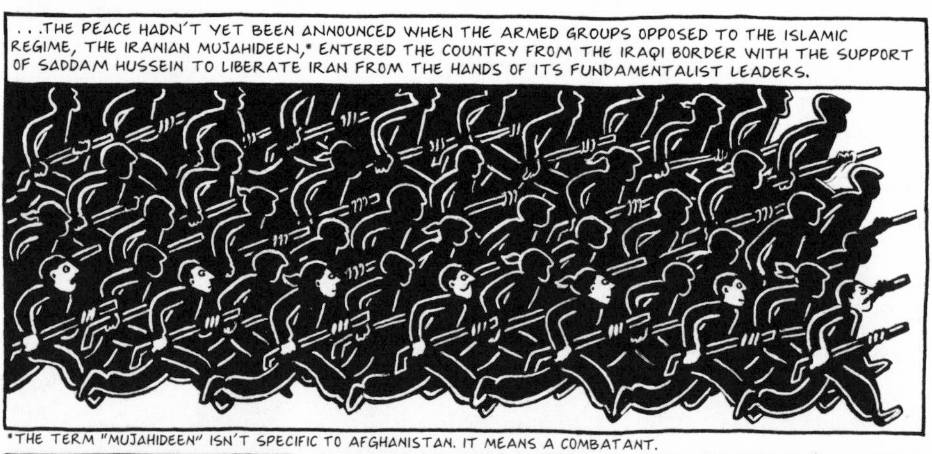
...THE PEACE HADN'T YET BEEN ANNOUNCED WHEN THE ARMED GROUPS OPPOSED TO THE ISLAMIC REGIME, THE IRANIAN MUJAHIDEEN,* ENTERED THE COUNTRY FROM THE IRAQI BORDER WITH THE SUPPORT OF SADDAM HUSSEIN TO LIBERATE IRAN FROM THE HANDS OF ITS FUNDAMENTALIST LEADERS.

*THE TERM "MUJAHIDEEN" ISN'T SPECIFIC TO AFGHANISTAN. IT MEANS A COMBATANT.

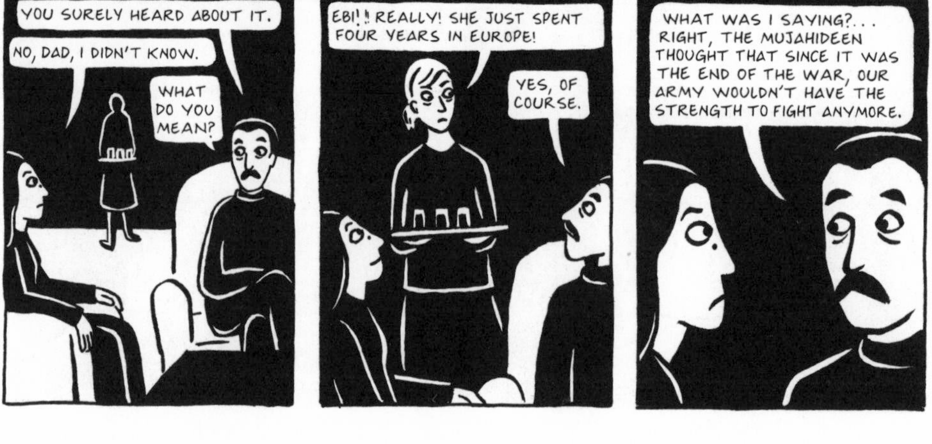
YOU SURELY HEARD ABOUT IT.
NO, DAD, I DIDN'T KNOW.
WHAT DO YOU MEAN?
EBI!! REALLY! SHE JUST SPENT FOUR YEARS IN EUROPE!
YES, OF COURSE.
WHAT WAS I SAYING?... RIGHT, THE MUJAHIDEEN THOUGHT THAT SINCE IT WAS THE END OF THE WAR, OUR ARMY WOULDN'T HAVE THE STRENGTH TO FIGHT ANYMORE.

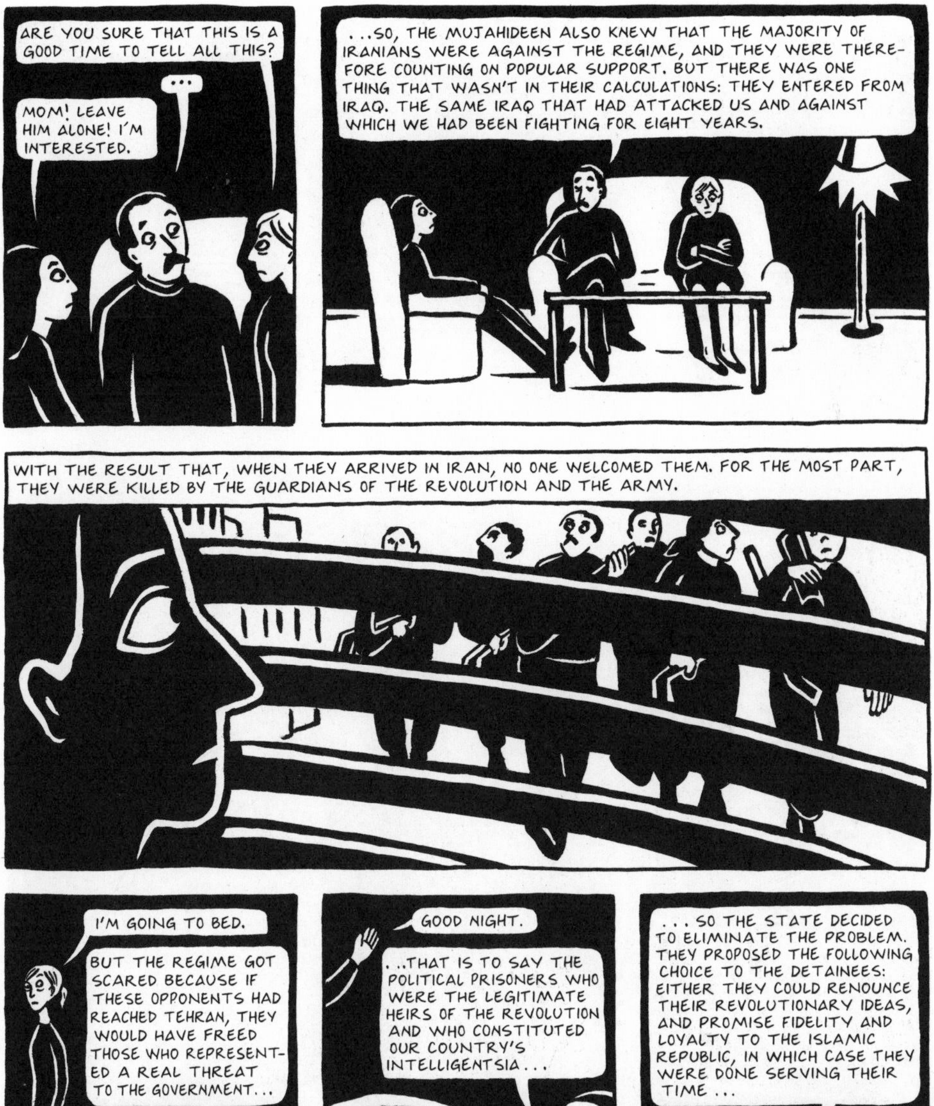
ARE YOU SURE THAT THIS IS A GOOD TIME TO TELL ALL THIS?
MOM! LEAVE HIM ALONE! I'M INTERESTED.
...
...SO, THE MUJAHIDEEN ALSO KNEW THAT THE MAJORITY OF IRANIANS WERE AGAINST THE REGIME, AND THEY WERE THEREFORE COUNTING ON POPULAR SUPPORT. BUT THERE WAS ONE THING THAT WASN'T IN THEIR CALCULATIONS: THEY ENTERED FROM IRAQ. THE SAME IRAQ THAT HAD ATTACKED US AND AGAINST WHICH WE HAD BEEN FIGHTING FOR EIGHT YEARS.
WITH THE RESULT THAT, WHEN THEY ARRIVED IN IRAN, NO ONE WELCOMED THEM. FOR THE MOST PART, THEY WERE KILLED BY THE GUARDIANS OF THE REVOLUTION AND THE ARMY.
I'M GOING TO BED.
BUT THE REGIME GOT SCARED BECAUSE IF THESE OPPONENTS HAD REACHED TEHRAN, THEY WOULD HAVE FREED THOSE WHO REPRESENTED A REAL THREAT TO THE GOVERNMENT...
GOOD NIGHT.
...THAT IS TO SAY THE POLITICAL PRISONERS WHO WERE THE LEGITIMATE HEIRS OF THE REVOLUTION AND WHO CONSTITUTED OUR COUNTRY'S INTELLIGENTSIA...
...SO THE STATE DECIDED TO ELIMINATE THE PROBLEM. THEY PROPOSED THE FOLLOWING CHOICE TO THE DETAINEES: EITHER THEY COULD RENOUNCE THEIR REVOLUTIONARY IDEAS, AND PROMISE FIDELITY AND LOYALTY TO THE ISLAMIC REPUBLIC, IN WHICH CASE THEY WERE DONE SERVING THEIR TIME ...

257

THE JOKE

I HAD BEEN IN TEHRAN FOR TEN DAYS. DESPITE MY RELUCTANCE, IN THE END MY ENTIRE FAMILY CAME TO SEE ME. I DIDN'T KNOW WHETHER OR NOT THEY KNEW ABOUT MY EUROPEAN FAILURE. I WAS SCARED THAT THEY WOULD BE DISAPPOINTED.

YOU MUST SPEAK GOOD GERMAN NOW.

I KNOW HOW TO SAY "ICH LIEBE DICH" HEE HEE HEE!

YES, I SPEAK A LITTLE.

THANK YOU FOR THE FLOWERS.

THIS IS UNCLE ARDESHIR, MY MOTHER'S UNCLE. HE'S RETIRED FROM THE NATIONAL EDUCATION SYSTEM.

WHEN I THINK OF VIENNA, I IMMEDIATELY THINK OF SISSI. YOU MUST HAVE SEEN THE FILM STARRING ROMY!

YES.

THAT'S MINA, MY FIRST COUSIN. SHE'S AN IMBECILE. SHE TALKS ABOUT ROMY SCHNEIDER AS IF SHE WERE HER BEST FRIEND.

MARJANE, THE STARS SHINE IN THE SKY AND YOU IN MY HEART...

THESE ARE OUR NEIGHBORS. THEY'RE THE INCARNATION OF THE PERFECT FAMILY.

EVEN THOUGH I KNEW THAT THEY WERE COMING TO SEE ME OUT OF FRIEND-SHIP AND KINDNESS, I'D QUICKLY HAD ENOUGH OF RECEIVING THEM EVERY DAY.

BUT THERE WAS NOTHING TO BE DONE, THE VISITS CONTINUED...

ASIDE FROM MY PARENTS, THE ONLY PERSON TO WHOM I REALLY WANTED TO TALK WAS MY GRANDMOTHER. BUT SHE CAME AFTER EVERYONE ELSE.

GRANDMA, WHERE WERE YOU?

I WAS WAITING FOR THE TRIBE TO GO FIRST! OH MY!! HOW YOU'VE GROWN. SOON YOU'LL BE CATCHING THE LORD'S BALLS.

SHE WAS STILL HER OLD SELF.

AFTER MY FAMILY, IT WAS MY FRIENDS' TURN. I HAD FEWER APPREHENSIONS ABOUT THEM: WE WERE THE SAME AGE, WHICH SHOULD MAKE IT EASIER TO CONNECT.

HI!

HOW ARE YOU?

UHHH . . .

I WAS WRONG. THEY ALL LOOKED LIKE THE HEROINES OF AMERICAN TV SERIES, READY TO GET MARRIED AT THE DROP OF A HAT, IF THE OPPORTUNITY PRESENTED ITSELF.

WHY DO YOU LOOK LIKE A NUN? NO ONE WOULD EVER GUESS THAT YOU'D LIVED IN EUROPE.

OH, REALLY?

COMPARED TO HER FASHIONABLE MAKEUP, I REALLY DID EXUDE ALL THE ALLURE OF A NUN.

COME ON, TALK TO US! YOU MUST HAVE A MILLION THINGS TO TELL US ABOUT.

I DON'T KNOW . . .

WELL, WHY DON'T YOU TELL US WHAT THE NIGHTCLUBS IN VIENNA WERE LIKE?

IT'S JUST THAT... I DIDN'T GO THAT OFTEN ... I DON'T REALLY LIKE THEM MUCH.

WHAT?

OH STOP PRETENDING TO BE SO SHOCKED! DON'T YOU REMEMBER HOW SHE WAS? ALWAYS GIVING LESSONS!! SHE'S A "REBEL," THIS ONE!

IF THERE WERE STILL NIGHTCLUBS IN TEHRAN, I'D BE THERE EVERY NIGHT!

HEE! HEE! HEE! HEE! ME TOO!

I HAD A HARD TIME REMEMBERING WHAT HAD BROUGHT US TOGETHER BEFORE.

A PART OF ME UNDERSTOOD THEM. WHEN SOMETHING IS FORBIDDEN, IT TAKES ON A DISPROPORTIONATE IMPORTANCE. MUCH LATER, I LEARNED THAT MAKING THEMSELVES UP AND WANTING TO FOLLOW WESTERN WAYS WAS AN ACT OF RESISTANCE ON THEIR PART.

NEVERTHELESS, I FELT TERRIBLY ALONE.

259

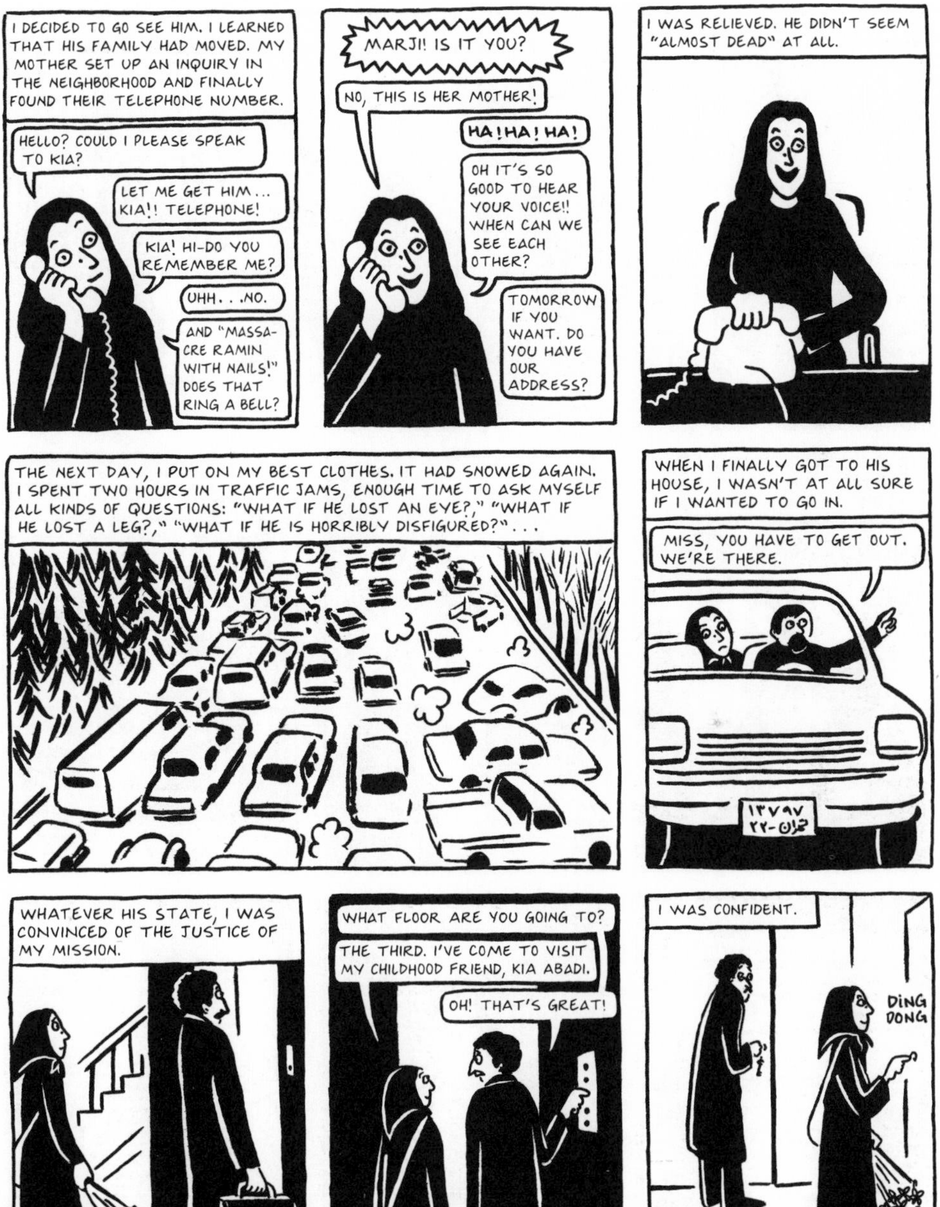
I DECIDED TO GO SEE HIM. I LEARNED THAT HIS FAMILY HAD MOVED. MY MOTHER SET UP AN INQUIRY IN THE NEIGHBORHOOD AND FINALLY FOUND THEIR TELEPHONE NUMBER.
HELLO? COULD I PLEASE SPEAK TO KIA?
LET ME GET HIM... KIA!! TELEPHONE!
KIA! HI-DO YOU REMEMBER ME?
UHH. . .NO.
AND "MASSACRE RAMIN WITH NAILS!" DOES THAT RING A BELL?
MARJI! IS IT YOU?
NO, THIS IS HER MOTHER!
HA!HA!HA!
OH IT'S SO GOOD TO HEAR YOUR VOICE!! WHEN CAN WE SEE EACH OTHER?
TOMORROW IF YOU WANT. DO YOU HAVE OUR ADDRESS?
I WAS RELIEVED. HE DIDN'T SEEM "ALMOST DEAD" AT ALL.
THE NEXT DAY, I PUT ON MY BEST CLOTHES. IT HAD SNOWED AGAIN. I SPENT TWO HOURS IN TRAFFIC JAMS, ENOUGH TIME TO ASK MYSELF ALL KINDS OF QUESTIONS: "WHAT IF HE LOST AN EYE?," "WHAT IF HE LOST A LEG?," "WHAT IF HE IS HORRIBLY DISFIGURED?" . . .
WHEN I FINALLY GOT TO HIS HOUSE, I WASN'T AT ALL SURE IF I WANTED TO GO IN.
MISS, YOU HAVE TO GET OUT. WE'RE THERE.
WHATEVER HIS STATE, I WAS CONVINCED OF THE JUSTICE OF MY MISSION.
WHAT FLOOR ARE YOU GOING TO?
THE THIRD. I'VE COME TO VISIT MY CHILDHOOD FRIEND, KIA ABADI.
OH! THAT'S GREAT!
THE NEIGHBOR'S "THAT'S GREAT" CALMED ME DOWN EVEN MORE. IF SOMETHING REALLY SERIOUS HAD HAPPENED, HE CERTAINLY WOULDN'T HAVE SAID THAT.
I WAS CONFIDENT.
DING DONG

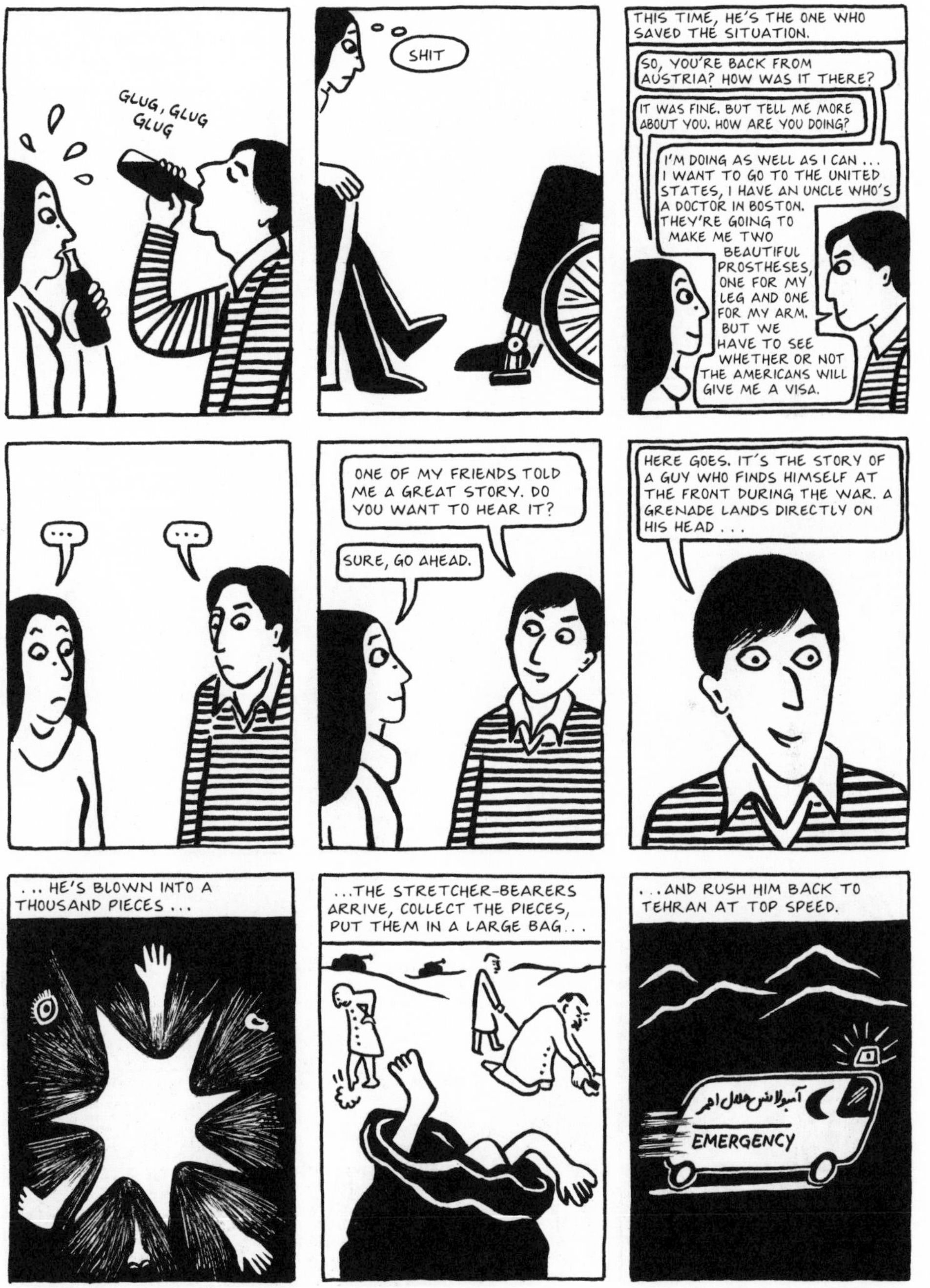
GLUG, GLUG
GLUG
SHIT
THIS TIME, HE'S THE ONE WHO SAVED THE SITUATION.
SO, YOU'RE BACK FROM AUSTRIA? HOW WAS IT THERE?
IT WAS FINE. BUT TELL ME MORE ABOUT YOU. HOW ARE YOU DOING?
I'M DOING AS WELL AS I CAN... I WANT TO GO TO THE UNITED STATES, I HAVE AN UNCLE WHO'S A DOCTOR IN BOSTON. THEY'RE GOING TO MAKE ME TWO BEAUTIFUL PROSTHESES, ONE FOR MY LEG AND ONE FOR MY ARM. BUT WE HAVE TO SEE WHETHER OR NOT THE AMERICANS WILL GIVE ME A VISA.
...
...
ONE OF MY FRIENDS TOLD ME A GREAT STORY. DO YOU WANT TO HEAR IT?
SURE, GO AHEAD.
HERE GOES. IT'S THE STORY OF A GUY WHO FINDS HIMSELF AT THE FRONT DURING THE WAR. A GRENADE LANDS DIRECTLY ON HIS HEAD...
...HE'S BLOWN INTO A THOUSAND PIECES...
...THE STRETCHER-BEARERS ARRIVE, COLLECT THE PIECES, PUT THEM IN A LARGE BAG...
...AND RUSH HIM BACK TO TEHRAN AT TOP SPEED.
آمبولانس هلال احمر
EMERGENCY

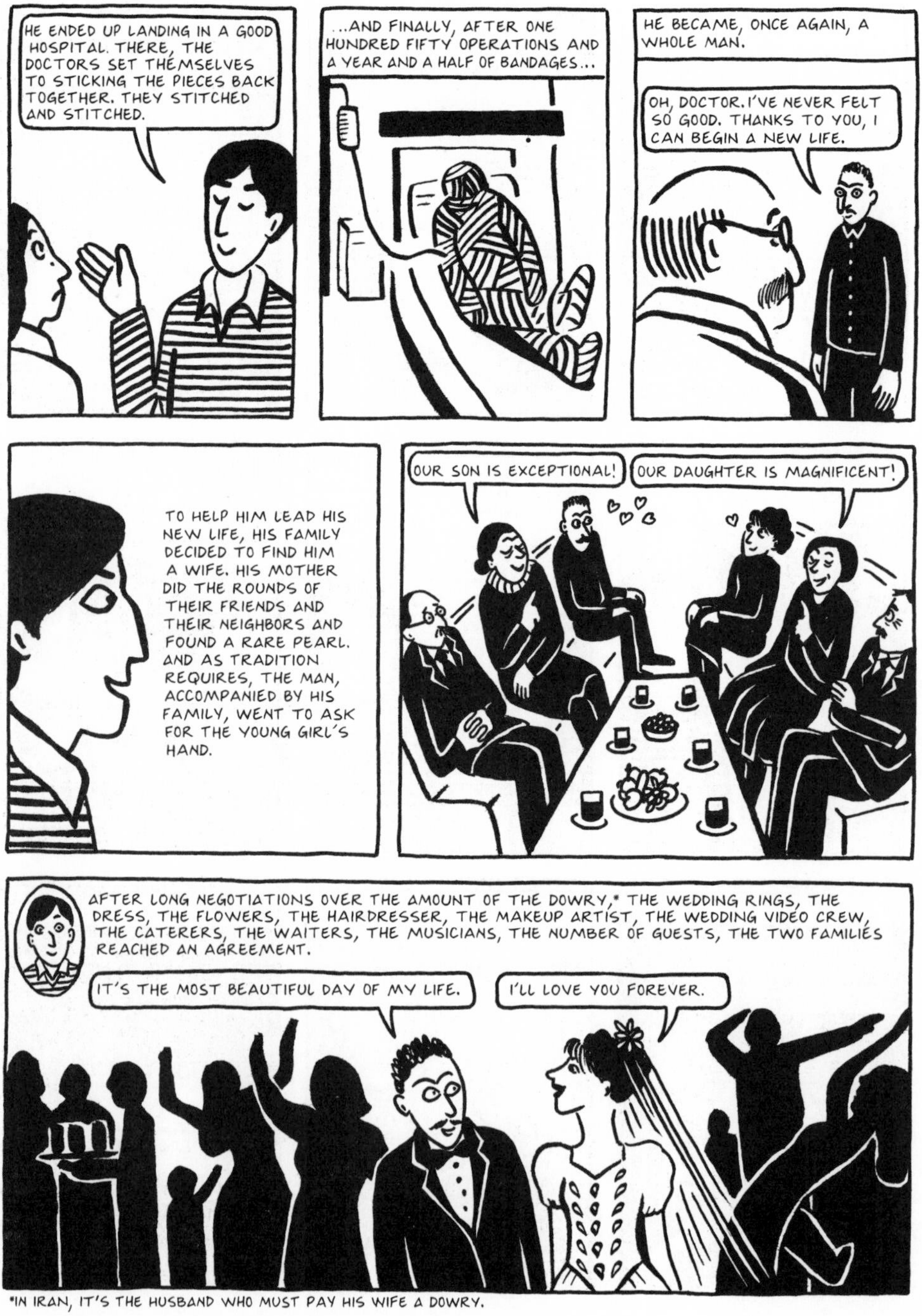
HE ENDED UP LANDING IN A GOOD HOSPITAL. THERE, THE DOCTORS SET THEMSELVES TO STICKING THE PIECES BACK TOGETHER. THEY STITCHED AND STITCHED.
...AND FINALLY, AFTER ONE HUNDRED FIFTY OPERATIONS AND A YEAR AND A HALF OF BANDAGES...
HE BECAME, ONCE AGAIN, A WHOLE MAN.
OH, DOCTOR. I'VE NEVER FELT SO GOOD. THANKS TO YOU, I CAN BEGIN A NEW LIFE.
TO HELP HIM LEAD HIS NEW LIFE, HIS FAMILY DECIDED TO FIND HIM A WIFE. HIS MOTHER DID THE ROUNDS OF THEIR FRIENDS AND THEIR NEIGHBORS AND FOUND A RARE PEARL. AND AS TRADITION REQUIRES, THE MAN, ACCOMPANIED BY HIS FAMILY, WENT TO ASK FOR THE YOUNG GIRL'S HAND.
OUR SON IS EXCEPTIONAL!
OUR DAUGHTER IS MAGNIFICENT!
AFTER LONG NEGOTIATIONS OVER THE AMOUNT OF THE DOWRY,* THE WEDDING RINGS, THE DRESS, THE FLOWERS, THE HAIRDRESSER, THE MAKEUP ARTIST, THE WEDDING VIDEO CREW, THE CATERERS, THE WAITERS, THE MUSICIANS, THE NUMBER OF GUESTS, THE TWO FAMILIES REACHED AN AGREEMENT.
IT'S THE MOST BEAUTIFUL DAY OF MY LIFE.
I'LL LOVE YOU FOREVER.

*IN IRAN, IT'S THE HUSBAND WHO MUST PAY HIS WIFE A DOWRY.

265

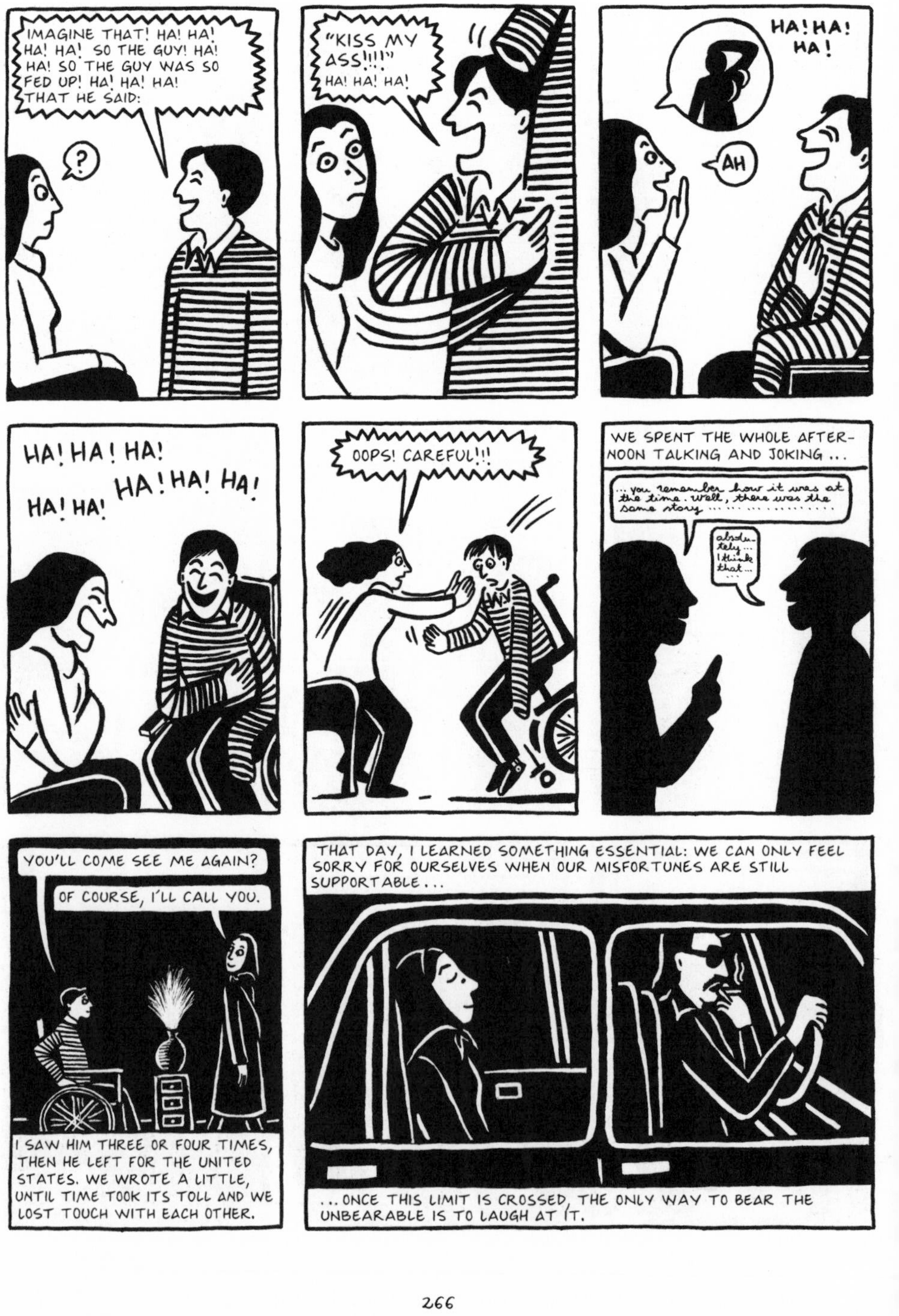
IMAGINE THAT! HA! HA! HA! HA! SO THE GUY! HA! HA! SO THE GUY WAS SO FED UP! HA! HA! HA! THAT HE SAID:
?
"KISS MY ASS!!!!" HA! HA! HA!
HA! HA! HA!
AH
HA! HA! HA!
HA! HA!
HA! HA! HA!
OOPS! CAREFUL!!!
WE SPENT THE WHOLE AFTERNOON TALKING AND JOKING...
... you remember how it was at the time. Well, there was the same story ...
absolutely... I think that...
YOU'LL COME SEE ME AGAIN?
OF COURSE, I'LL CALL YOU.
I SAW HIM THREE OR FOUR TIMES, THEN HE LEFT FOR THE UNITED STATES. WE WROTE A LITTLE, UNTIL TIME TOOK ITS TOLL AND WE LOST TOUCH WITH EACH OTHER.
THAT DAY, I LEARNED SOMETHING ESSENTIAL: WE CAN ONLY FEEL SORRY FOR OURSELVES WHEN OUR MISFORTUNES ARE STILL SUPPORTABLE...
...ONCE THIS LIMIT IS CROSSED, THE ONLY WAY TO BEAR THE UNBEARABLE IS TO LAUGH AT IT.

SKIING

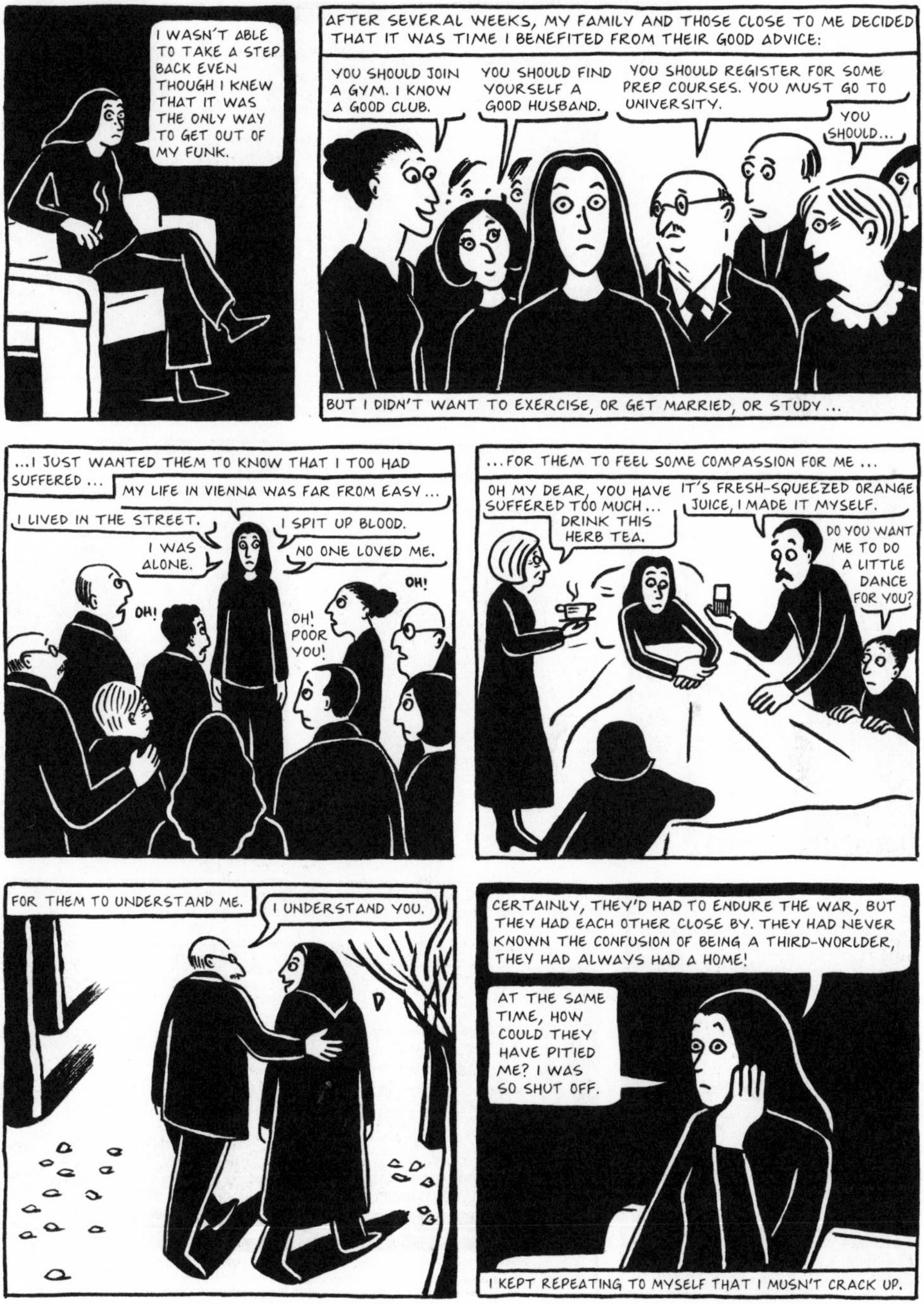

I WASN'T ABLE TO TAKE A STEP BACK EVEN THOUGH I KNEW THAT IT WAS THE ONLY WAY TO GET OUT OF MY FUNK.
AFTER SEVERAL WEEKS, MY FAMILY AND THOSE CLOSE TO ME DECIDED THAT IT WAS TIME I BENEFITED FROM THEIR GOOD ADVICE:
YOU SHOULD JOIN A GYM. I KNOW A GOOD CLUB.
YOU SHOULD FIND YOURSELF A GOOD HUSBAND.
YOU SHOULD REGISTER FOR SOME PREP COURSES. YOU MUST GO TO UNIVERSITY.
YOU SHOULD...
BUT I DIDN'T WANT TO EXERCISE, OR GET MARRIED, OR STUDY...
...I JUST WANTED THEM TO KNOW THAT I TOO HAD SUFFERED...
MY LIFE IN VIENNA WAS FAR FROM EASY...
I LIVED IN THE STREET.
I SPIT UP BLOOD.
I WAS ALONE.
NO ONE LOVED ME.
OH!
OH!
OH! POOR YOU!
...FOR THEM TO FEEL SOME COMPASSION FOR ME...
OH MY DEAR, YOU HAVE SUFFERED TOO MUCH... DRINK THIS HERB TEA.
IT'S FRESH-SQUEEZED ORANGE JUICE, I MADE IT MYSELF.
DO YOU WANT ME TO DO A LITTLE DANCE FOR YOU?
FOR THEM TO UNDERSTAND ME.
I UNDERSTAND YOU.
CERTAINLY, THEY'D HAD TO ENDURE THE WAR, BUT THEY HAD EACH OTHER CLOSE BY. THEY HAD NEVER KNOWN THE CONFUSION OF BEING A THIRD-WORLDER, THEY HAD ALWAYS HAD A HOME!
AT THE SAME TIME, HOW COULD THEY HAVE PITIED ME? I WAS SO SHUT OFF.
I KEPT REPEATING TO MYSELF THAT I MUSN'T CRACK UP.

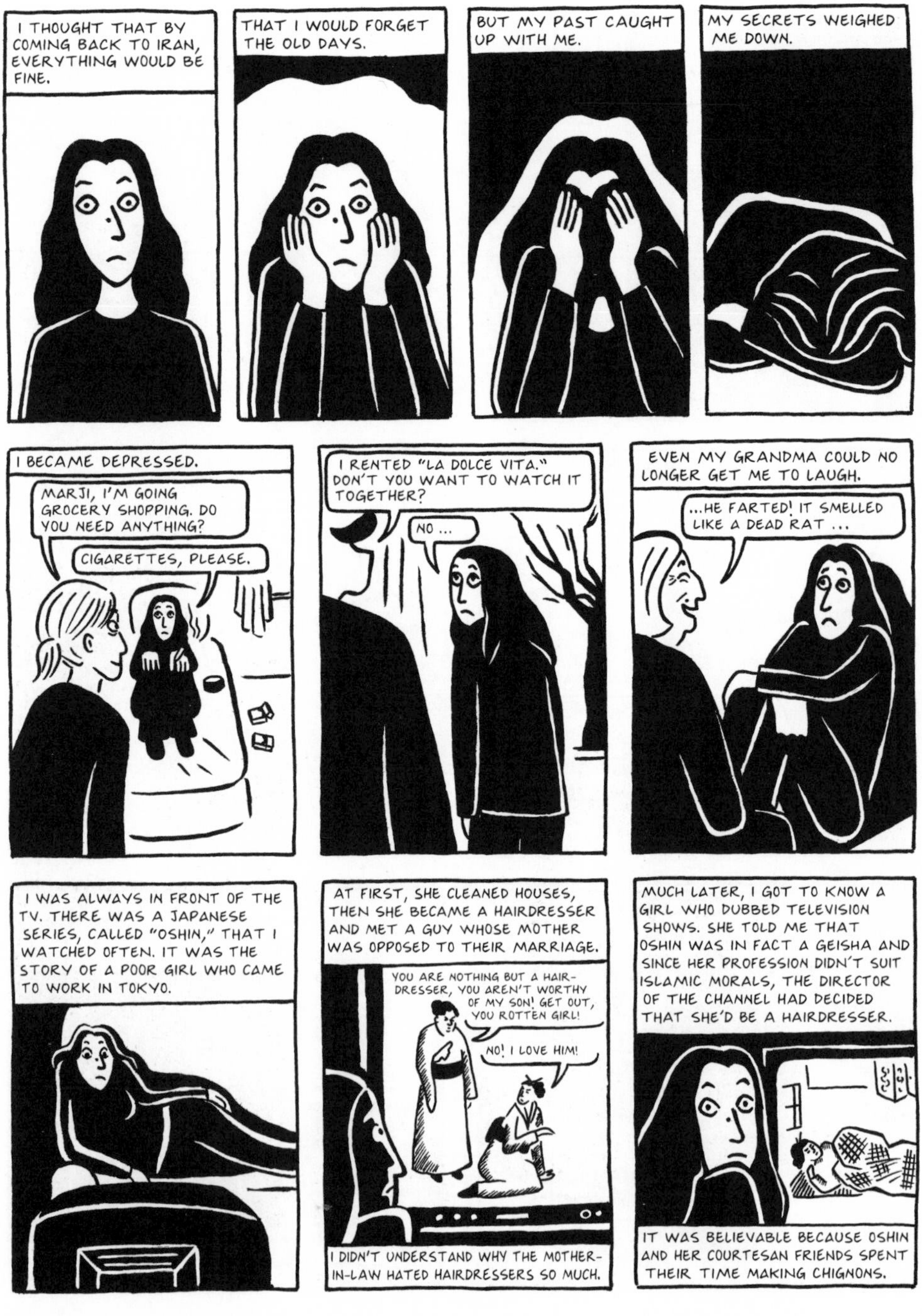
I THOUGHT THAT BY COMING BACK TO IRAN, EVERYTHING WOULD BE FINE.
THAT I WOULD FORGET THE OLD DAYS.
BUT MY PAST CAUGHT UP WITH ME.
MY SECRETS WEIGHED ME DOWN.
I BECAME DEPRESSED.
MARJI, I'M GOING GROCERY SHOPPING. DO YOU NEED ANYTHING?
CIGARETTES, PLEASE.
I RENTED "LA DOLCE VITA." DON'T YOU WANT TO WATCH IT TOGETHER?
NO ...
EVEN MY GRANDMA COULD NO LONGER GET ME TO LAUGH.
...HE FARTED! IT SMELLED LIKE A DEAD RAT ...
I WAS ALWAYS IN FRONT OF THE TV. THERE WAS A JAPANESE SERIES, CALLED "OSHIN," THAT I WATCHED OFTEN. IT WAS THE STORY OF A POOR GIRL WHO CAME TO WORK IN TOKYO.
AT FIRST, SHE CLEANED HOUSES, THEN SHE BECAME A HAIRDRESSER AND MET A GUY WHOSE MOTHER WAS OPPOSED TO THEIR MARRIAGE.
YOU ARE NOTHING BUT A HAIR-DRESSER, YOU AREN'T WORTHY OF MY SON! GET OUT, YOU ROTTEN GIRL!
NO! I LOVE HIM!
I DIDN'T UNDERSTAND WHY THE MOTHER-IN-LAW HATED HAIRDRESSERS SO MUCH.
MUCH LATER, I GOT TO KNOW A GIRL WHO DUBBED TELEVISION SHOWS. SHE TOLD ME THAT OSHIN WAS IN FACT A GEISHA AND SINCE HER PROFESSION DIDN'T SUIT ISLAMIC MORALS, THE DIRECTOR OF THE CHANNEL HAD DECIDED THAT SHE'D BE A HAIRDRESSER.
IT WAS BELIEVABLE BECAUSE OSHIN AND HER COURTESAN FRIENDS SPENT THEIR TIME MAKING CHIGNONS.

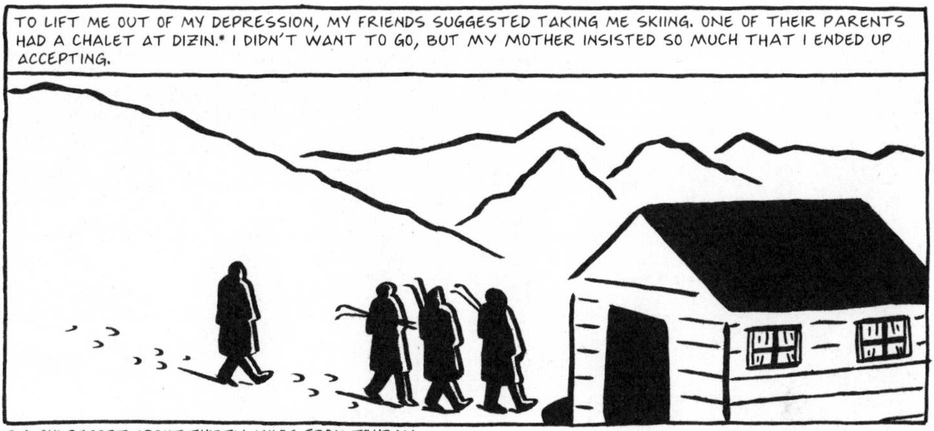
TO LIFT ME OUT OF MY DEPRESSION, MY FRIENDS SUGGESTED TAKING ME SKIING. ONE OF THEIR PARENTS HAD A CHALET AT DIZIN.* I DIDN'T WANT TO GO, BUT MY MOTHER INSISTED SO MUCH THAT I ENDED UP ACCEPTING.

* A SKI RESORT ABOUT THIRTY MILES FROM TEHRAN.

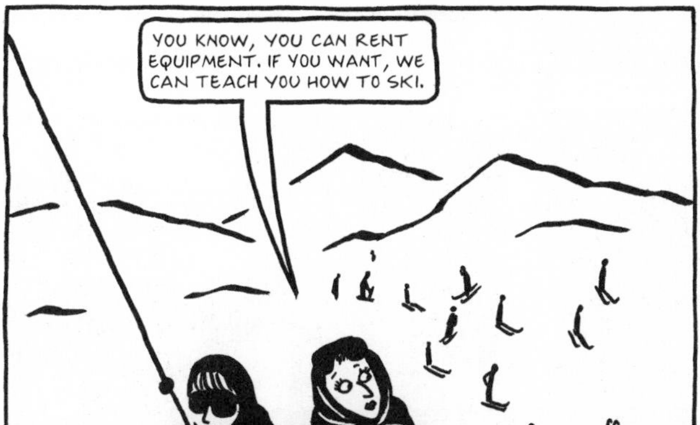
YOU KNOW, YOU CAN RENT EQUIPMENT. IF YOU WANT, WE CAN TEACH YOU HOW TO SKI.
NO, THANKS, I AM VERY HAPPY LIKE THIS.

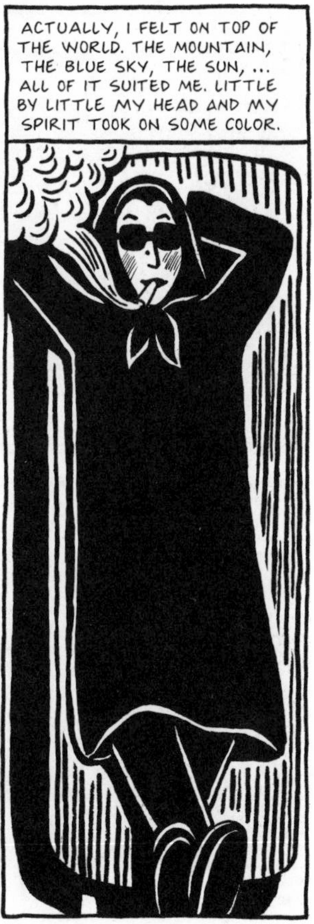
ACTUALLY, I FELT ON TOP OF THE WORLD. THE MOUNTAIN, THE BLUE SKY, THE SUN, ... ALL OF IT SUITED ME. LITTLE BY LITTLE MY HEAD AND MY SPIRIT TOOK ON SOME COLOR.

270

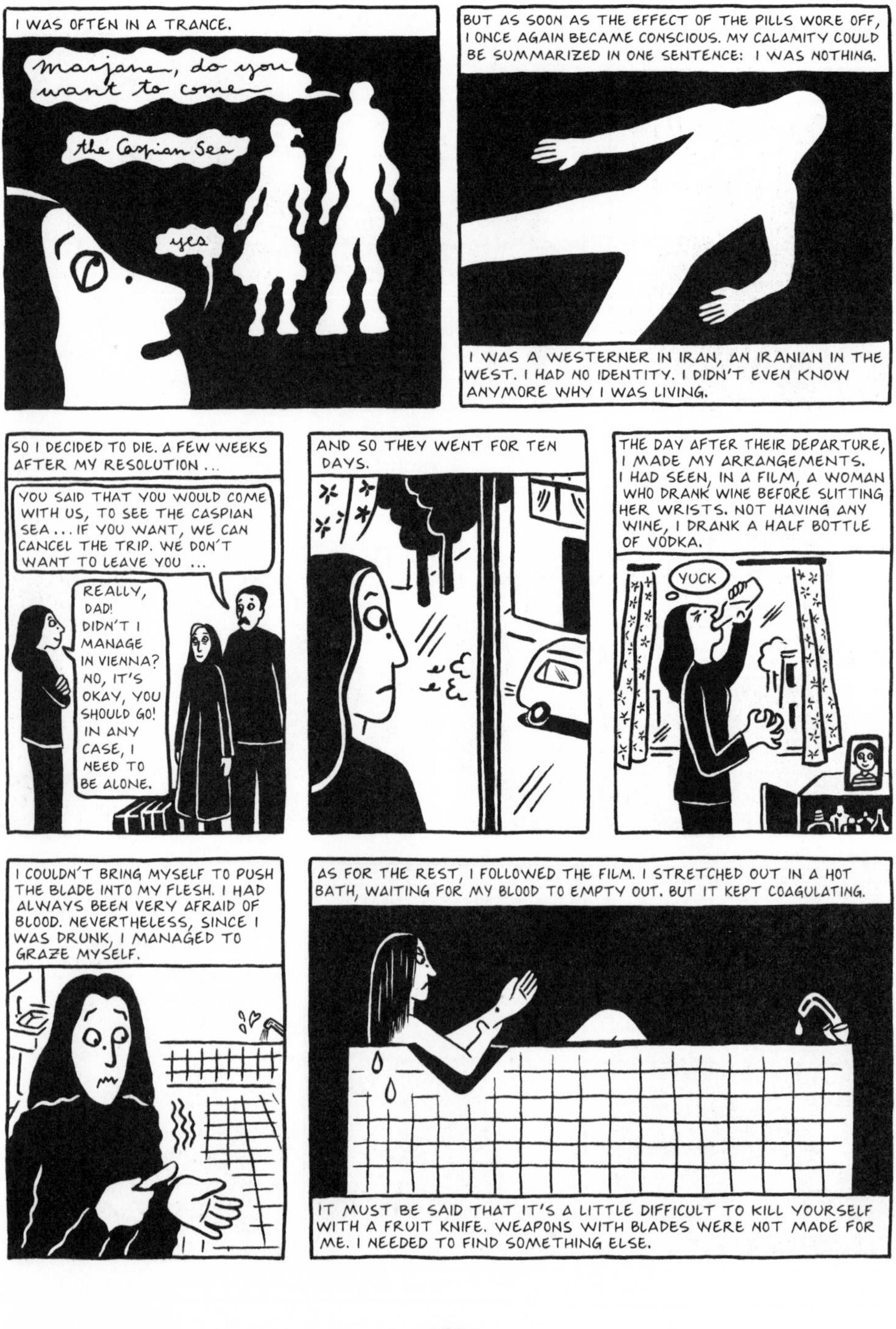
I WAS OFTEN IN A TRANCE.
marjane, do you want to come
the Caspian Sea
yes
BUT AS SOON AS THE EFFECT OF THE PILLS WORE OFF, I ONCE AGAIN BECAME CONSCIOUS. MY CALAMITY COULD BE SUMMARIZED IN ONE SENTENCE: I WAS NOTHING.
I WAS A WESTERNER IN IRAN, AN IRANIAN IN THE WEST. I HAD NO IDENTITY. I DIDN'T EVEN KNOW ANYMORE WHY I WAS LIVING.
SO I DECIDED TO DIE. A FEW WEEKS AFTER MY RESOLUTION ...
YOU SAID THAT YOU WOULD COME WITH US, TO SEE THE CASPIAN SEA ... IF YOU WANT, WE CAN CANCEL THE TRIP. WE DON'T WANT TO LEAVE YOU ...
REALLY, DAD! DIDN'T I MANAGE IN VIENNA? NO, IT'S OKAY, YOU SHOULD GO! IN ANY CASE, I NEED TO BE ALONE.
AND SO THEY WENT FOR TEN DAYS.
THE DAY AFTER THEIR DEPARTURE, I MADE MY ARRANGEMENTS. I HAD SEEN, IN A FILM, A WOMAN WHO DRANK WINE BEFORE SLITTING HER WRISTS. NOT HAVING ANY WINE, I DRANK A HALF BOTTLE OF VODKA.
YUCK
I COULDN'T BRING MYSELF TO PUSH THE BLADE INTO MY FLESH. I HAD ALWAYS BEEN VERY AFRAID OF BLOOD. NEVERTHELESS, SINCE I WAS DRUNK, I MANAGED TO GRAZE MYSELF.
AS FOR THE REST, I FOLLOWED THE FILM. I STRETCHED OUT IN A HOT BATH, WAITING FOR MY BLOOD TO EMPTY OUT. BUT IT KEPT COAGULATING.
IT MUST BE SAID THAT IT'S A LITTLE DIFFICULT TO KILL YOURSELF WITH A FRUIT KNIFE. WEAPONS WITH BLADES WERE NOT MADE FOR ME. I NEEDED TO FIND SOMETHING ELSE.

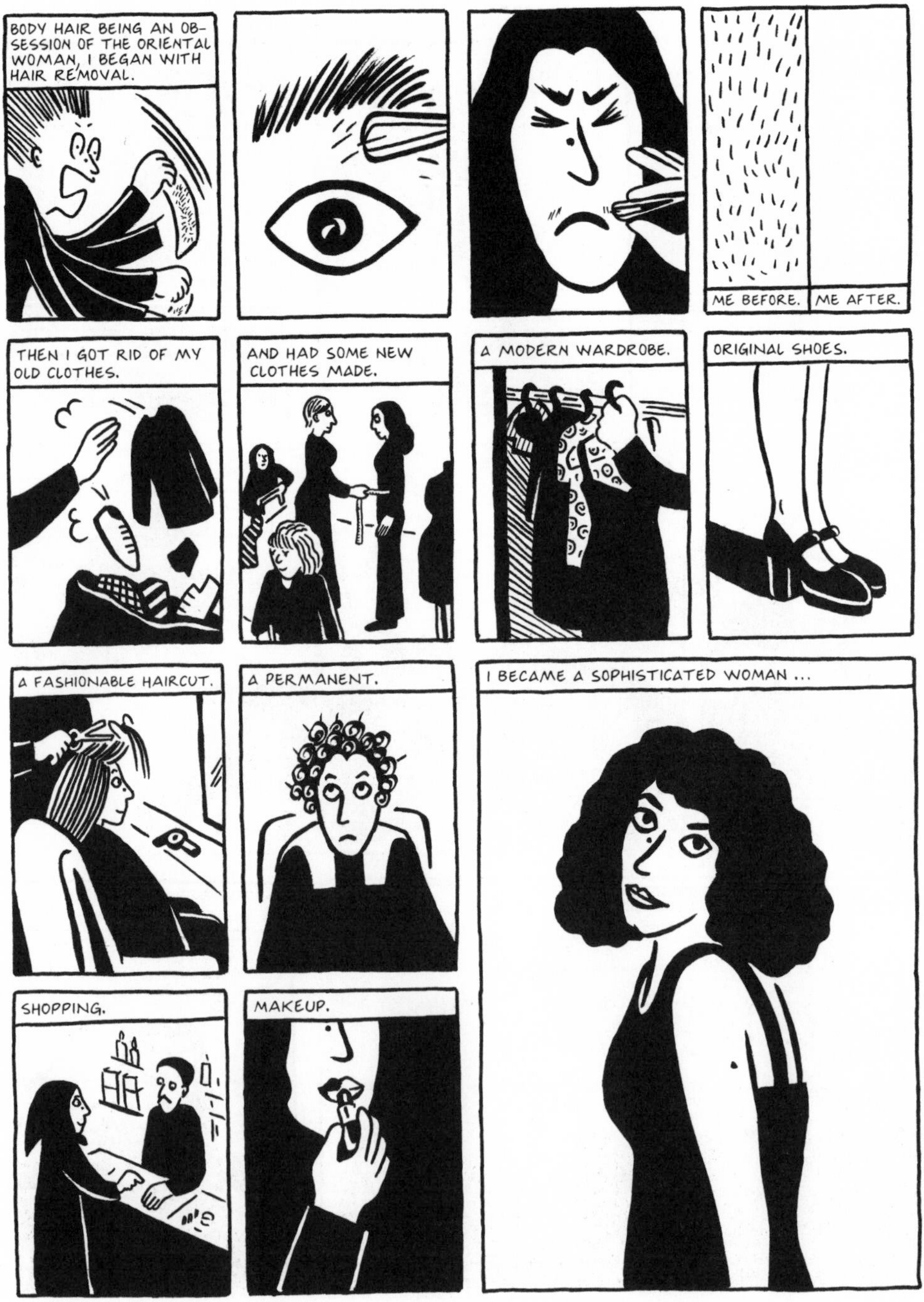
BODY HAIR BEING AN OBSESSION OF THE ORIENTAL WOMAN, I BEGAN WITH HAIR REMOVAL.
ME BEFORE.
ME AFTER.
THEN I GOT RID OF MY OLD CLOTHES.
AND HAD SOME NEW CLOTHES MADE.
A MODERN WARDROBE.
ORIGINAL SHOES.
A FASHIONABLE HAIRCUT.
A PERMANENT.
I BECAME A SOPHISTICATED WOMAN ...
SHOPPING.
MAKEUP.

THE EXAM

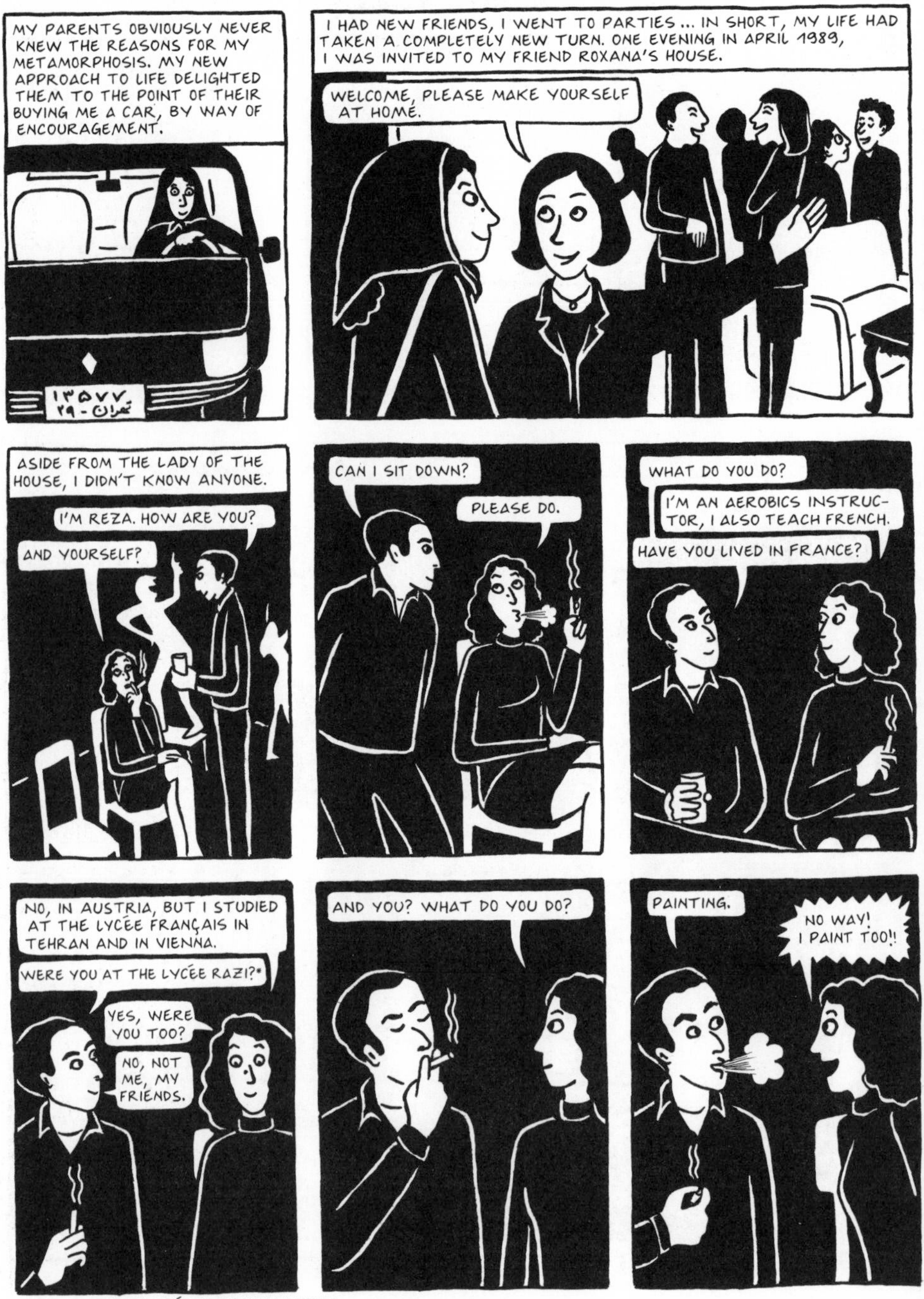

MY PARENTS OBVIOUSLY NEVER KNEW THE REASONS FOR MY METAMORPHOSIS. MY NEW APPROACH TO LIFE DELIGHTED THEM TO THE POINT OF THEIR BUYING ME A CAR, BY WAY OF ENCOURAGEMENT.
۱۳۵۷۷
تهران - ۲۹
I HAD NEW FRIENDS, I WENT TO PARTIES ... IN SHORT, MY LIFE HAD TAKEN A COMPLETELY NEW TURN. ONE EVENING IN APRIL 1989, I WAS INVITED TO MY FRIEND ROXANA'S HOUSE.
WELCOME, PLEASE MAKE YOURSELF AT HOME.
ASIDE FROM THE LADY OF THE HOUSE, I DIDN'T KNOW ANYONE.
I'M REZA. HOW ARE YOU?
AND YOURSELF?
CAN I SIT DOWN?
PLEASE DO.
WHAT DO YOU DO?
I'M AN AEROBICS INSTRUCTOR, I ALSO TEACH FRENCH.
HAVE YOU LIVED IN FRANCE?
NO, IN AUSTRIA, BUT I STUDIED AT THE LYCÉE FRANÇAIS IN TEHRAN AND IN VIENNA.
WERE YOU AT THE LYCÉE RAZI?*
YES, WERE YOU TOO?
NO, NOT ME, MY FRIENDS.
AND YOU? WHAT DO YOU DO?
PAINTING.
NO WAY! I PAINT TOO!!

*THE NAME OF THE LYCÉE FRANÇAIS IN TEHRAN.

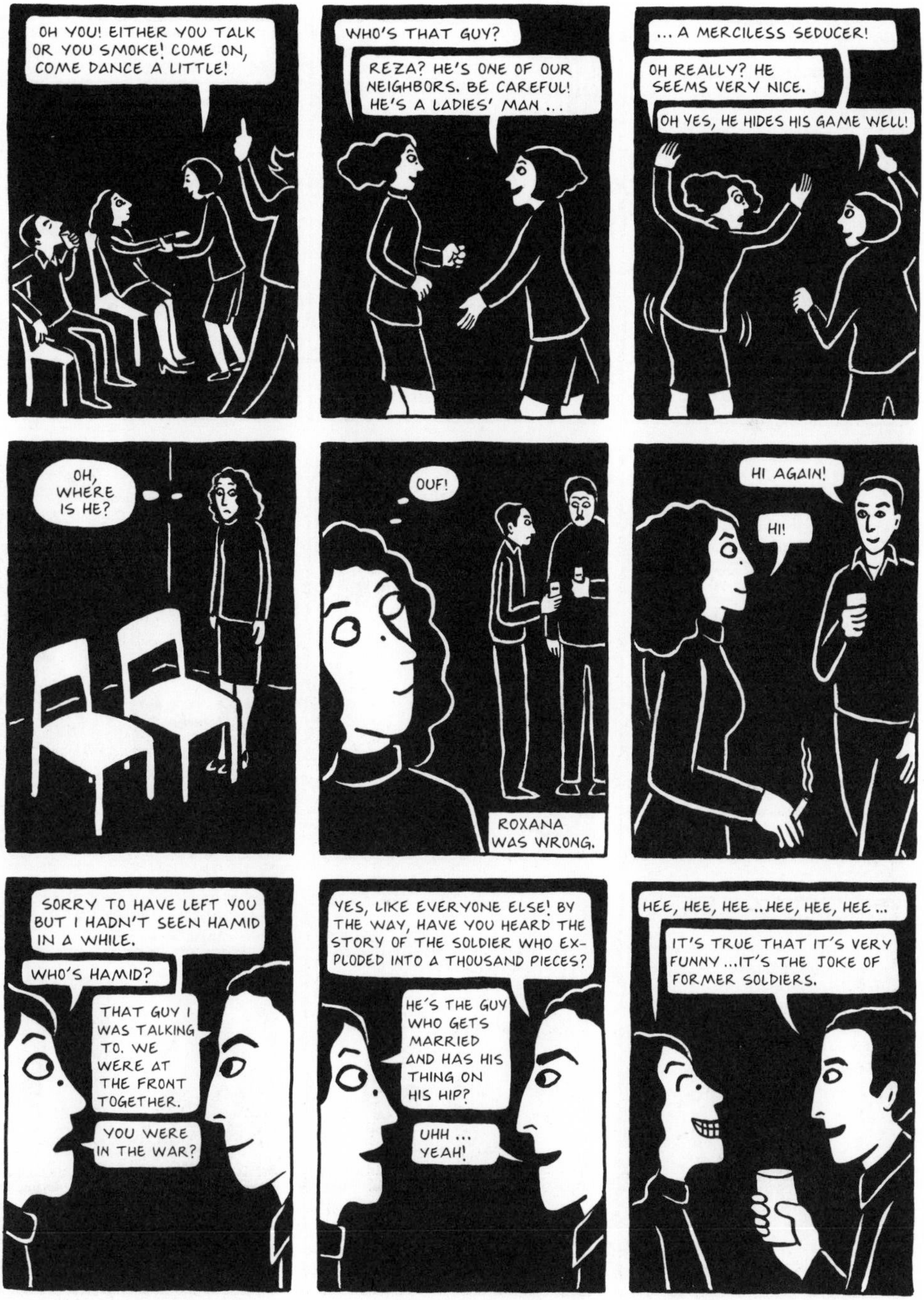
OH YOU! EITHER YOU TALK OR YOU SMOKE! COME ON, COME DANCE A LITTLE!
WHO'S THAT GUY?
REZA? HE'S ONE OF OUR NEIGHBORS. BE CAREFUL! HE'S A LADIES' MAN ...
... A MERCILESS SEDUCER!
OH REALLY? HE SEEMS VERY NICE.
OH YES, HE HIDES HIS GAME WELL!
OH, WHERE IS HE?
OUF!
ROXANA WAS WRONG.
HI AGAIN!
HI!
SORRY TO HAVE LEFT YOU BUT I HADN'T SEEN HAMID IN A WHILE.
WHO'S HAMID?
THAT GUY I WAS TALKING TO. WE WERE AT THE FRONT TOGETHER.
YOU WERE IN THE WAR?
YES, LIKE EVERYONE ELSE! BY THE WAY, HAVE YOU HEARD THE STORY OF THE SOLDIER WHO EXPLODED INTO A THOUSAND PIECES?
HE'S THE GUY WHO GETS MARRIED AND HAS HIS THING ON HIS HIP?
UHH ... YEAH!
HEE, HEE, HEE ..HEE, HEE, HEE ...
IT'S TRUE THAT IT'S VERY FUNNY ...IT'S THE JOKE OF FORMER SOLDIERS.

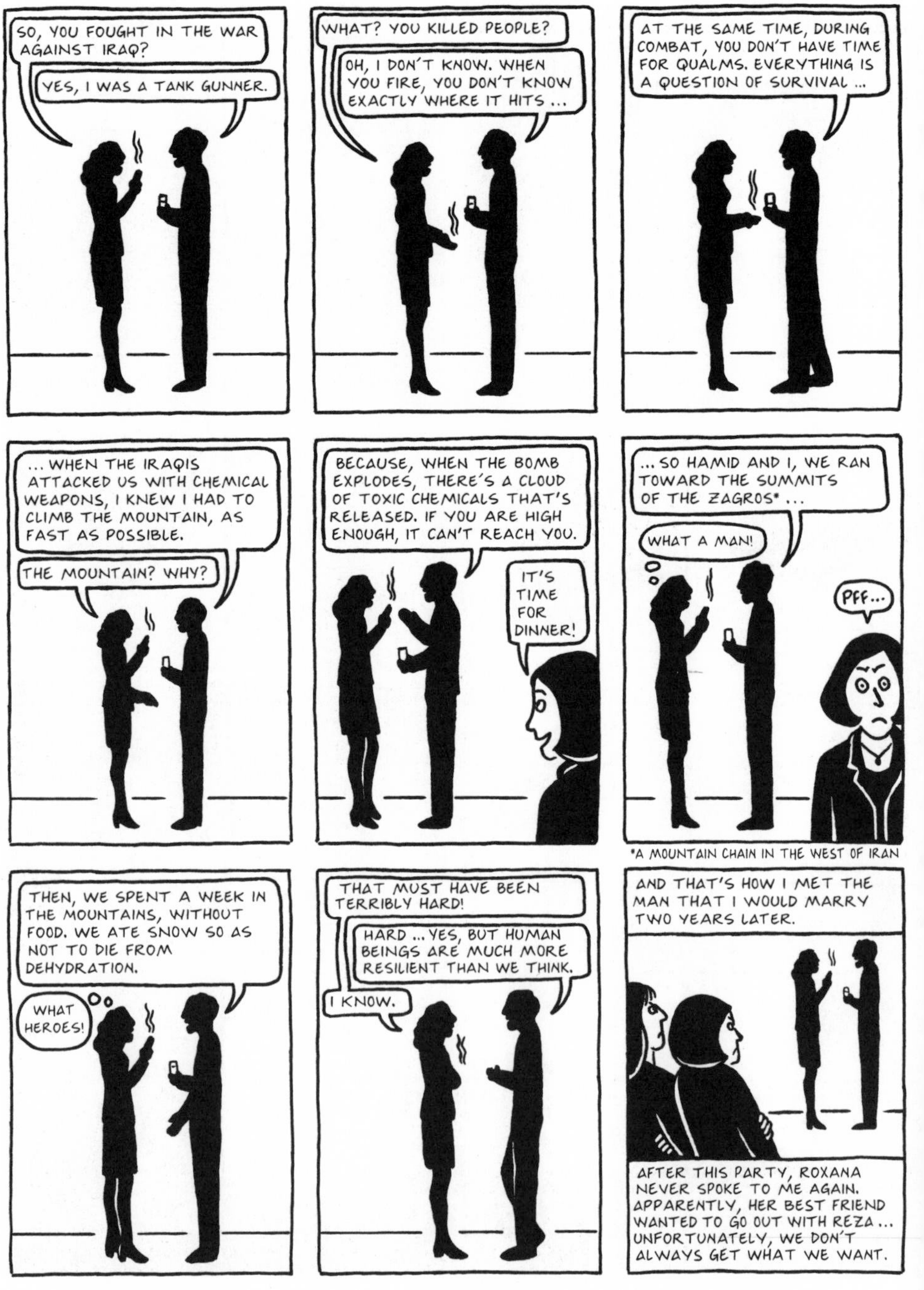
SO, YOU FOUGHT IN THE WAR AGAINST IRAQ?
YES, I WAS A TANK GUNNER.
WHAT? YOU KILLED PEOPLE?
OH, I DON'T KNOW. WHEN YOU FIRE, YOU DON'T KNOW EXACTLY WHERE IT HITS ...
AT THE SAME TIME, DURING COMBAT, YOU DON'T HAVE TIME FOR QUALMS. EVERYTHING IS A QUESTION OF SURVIVAL ...
... WHEN THE IRAQIS ATTACKED US WITH CHEMICAL WEAPONS, I KNEW I HAD TO CLIMB THE MOUNTAIN, AS FAST AS POSSIBLE.
THE MOUNTAIN? WHY?
BECAUSE, WHEN THE BOMB EXPLODES, THERE'S A CLOUD OF TOXIC CHEMICALS THAT'S RELEASED. IF YOU ARE HIGH ENOUGH, IT CAN'T REACH YOU.
IT'S TIME FOR DINNER!
... SO HAMID AND I, WE RAN TOWARD THE SUMMITS OF THE ZAGROS* ...
WHAT A MAN!
PFF...
*A MOUNTAIN CHAIN IN THE WEST OF IRAN
THEN, WE SPENT A WEEK IN THE MOUNTAINS, WITHOUT FOOD. WE ATE SNOW SO AS NOT TO DIE FROM DEHYDRATION.
WHAT HEROES!
THAT MUST HAVE BEEN TERRIBLY HARD!
HARD ... YES, BUT HUMAN BEINGS ARE MUCH MORE RESILIENT THAN WE THINK.
I KNOW.
AND THAT'S HOW I MET THE MAN THAT I WOULD MARRY TWO YEARS LATER.
AFTER THIS PARTY, ROXANA NEVER SPOKE TO ME AGAIN. APPARENTLY, HER BEST FRIEND WANTED TO GO OUT WITH REZA ... UNFORTUNATELY, WE DON'T ALWAYS GET WHAT WE WANT.

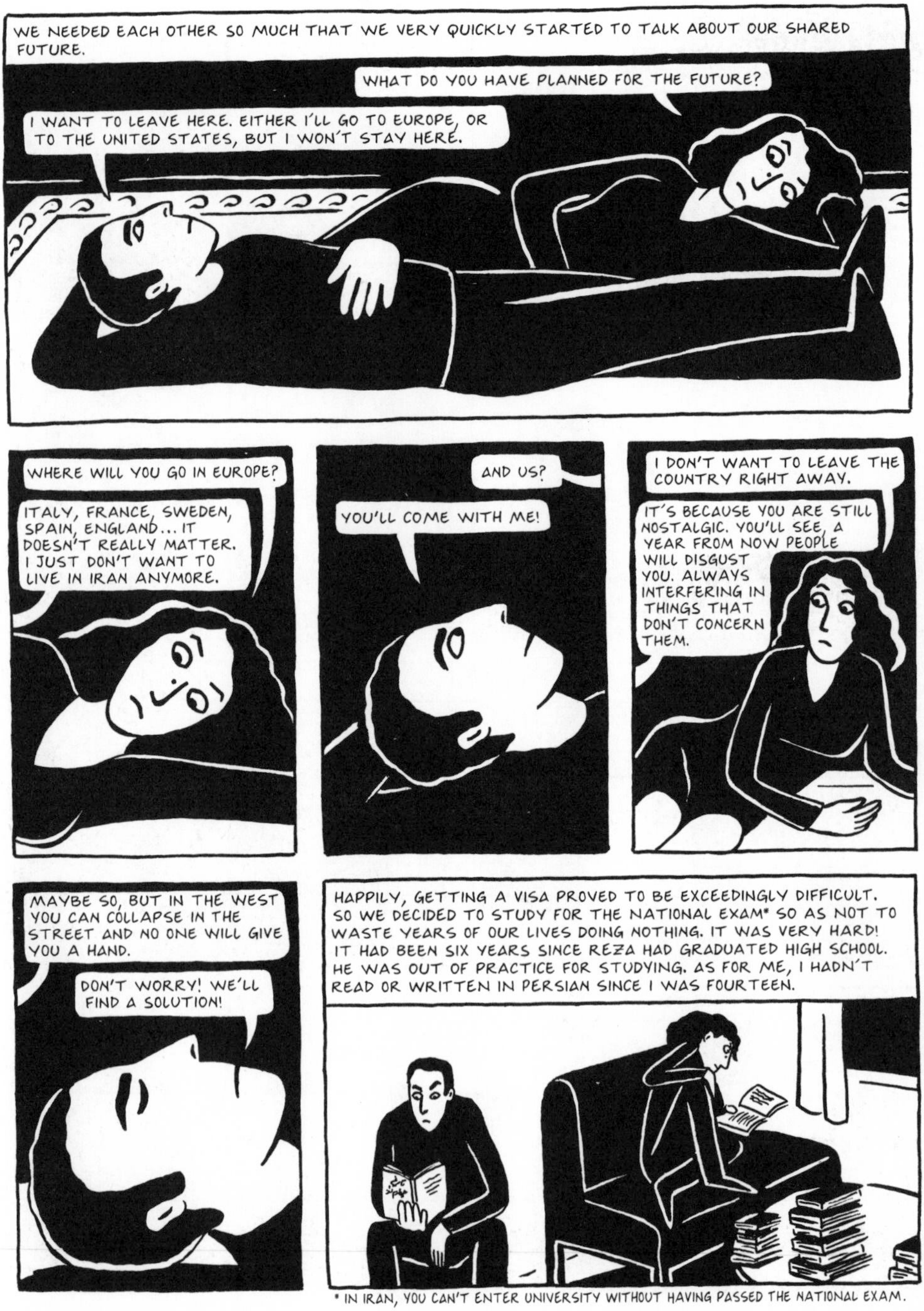
WE NEEDED EACH OTHER SO MUCH THAT WE VERY QUICKLY STARTED TO TALK ABOUT OUR SHARED FUTURE.
WHAT DO YOU HAVE PLANNED FOR THE FUTURE?
I WANT TO LEAVE HERE. EITHER I'LL GO TO EUROPE, OR TO THE UNITED STATES, BUT I WON'T STAY HERE.
WHERE WILL YOU GO IN EUROPE?
ITALY, FRANCE, SWEDEN, SPAIN, ENGLAND... IT DOESN'T REALLY MATTER. I JUST DON'T WANT TO LIVE IN IRAN ANYMORE.
AND US?
YOU'LL COME WITH ME!
I DON'T WANT TO LEAVE THE COUNTRY RIGHT AWAY.
IT'S BECAUSE YOU ARE STILL NOSTALGIC. YOU'LL SEE, A YEAR FROM NOW PEOPLE WILL DISGUST YOU. ALWAYS INTERFERING IN THINGS THAT DON'T CONCERN THEM.
MAYBE SO, BUT IN THE WEST YOU CAN COLLAPSE IN THE STREET AND NO ONE WILL GIVE YOU A HAND.
DON'T WORRY! WE'LL FIND A SOLUTION!
HAPPILY, GETTING A VISA PROVED TO BE EXCEEDINGLY DIFFICULT. SO WE DECIDED TO STUDY FOR THE NATIONAL EXAM* SO AS NOT TO WASTE YEARS OF OUR LIVES DOING NOTHING. IT WAS VERY HARD! IT HAD BEEN SIX YEARS SINCE REZA HAD GRADUATED HIGH SCHOOL. HE WAS OUT OF PRACTICE FOR STUDYING. AS FOR ME, I HADN'T READ OR WRITTEN IN PERSIAN SINCE I WAS FOURTEEN.

* IN IRAN, YOU CAN'T ENTER UNIVERSITY WITHOUT HAVING PASSED THE NATIONAL EXAM.

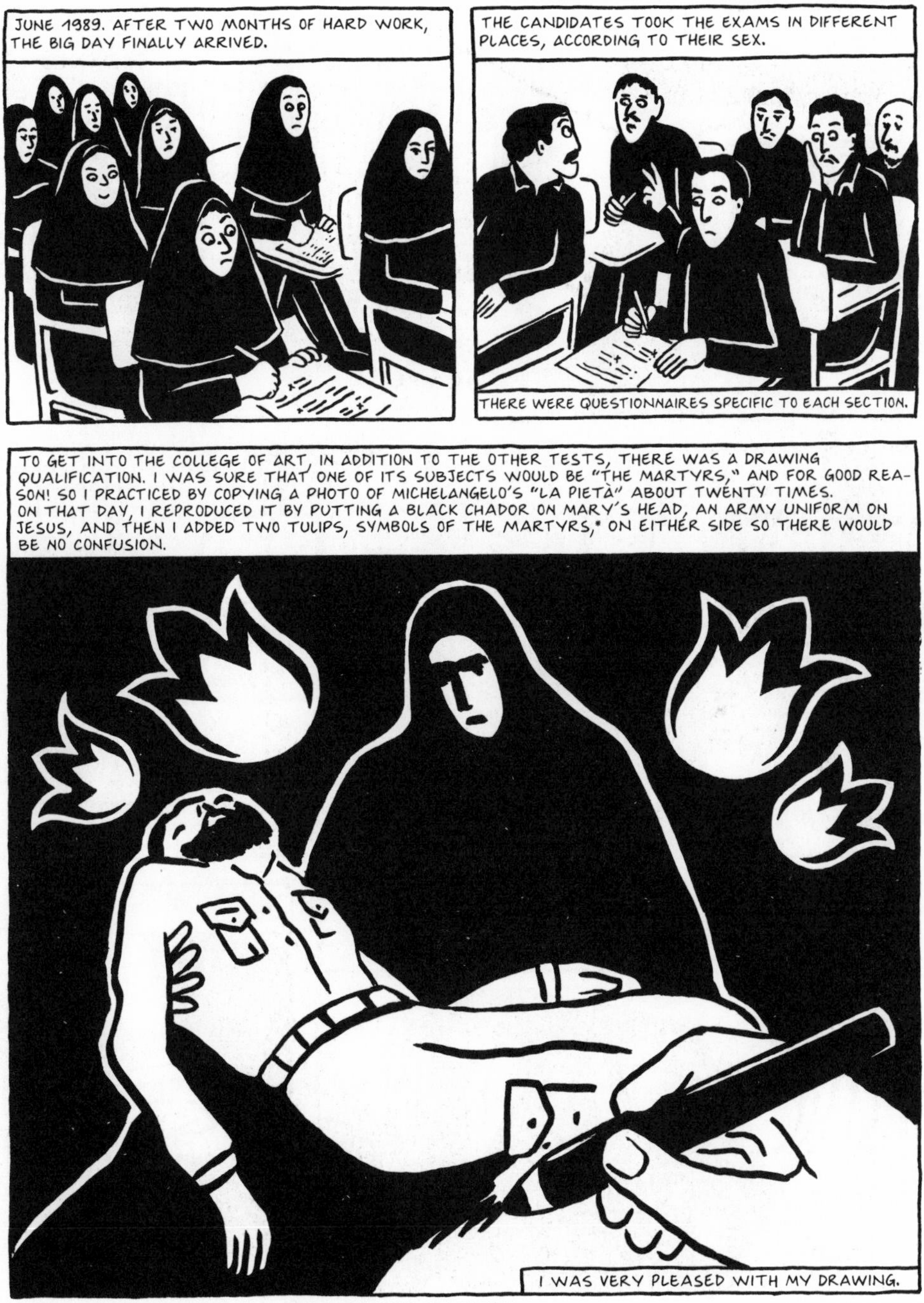
JUNE 1989. AFTER TWO MONTHS OF HARD WORK, THE BIG DAY FINALLY ARRIVED.
THE CANDIDATES TOOK THE EXAMS IN DIFFERENT PLACES, ACCORDING TO THEIR SEX.
THERE WERE QUESTIONNAIRES SPECIFIC TO EACH SECTION.
TO GET INTO THE COLLEGE OF ART, IN ADDITION TO THE OTHER TESTS, THERE WAS A DRAWING QUALIFICATION. I WAS SURE THAT ONE OF ITS SUBJECTS WOULD BE "THE MARTYRS," AND FOR GOOD REASON! SO I PRACTICED BY COPYING A PHOTO OF MICHELANGELO'S "LA PIETÀ" ABOUT TWENTY TIMES. ON THAT DAY, I REPRODUCED IT BY PUTTING A BLACK CHADOR ON MARY'S HEAD, AN ARMY UNIFORM ON JESUS, AND THEN I ADDED TWO TULIPS, SYMBOLS OF THE MARTYRS,* ON EITHER SIDE SO THERE WOULD BE NO CONFUSION.
I WAS VERY PLEASED WITH MY DRAWING.

*IT'S SAID THAT RED TULIPS GROW FROM THE BLOOD OF MARTYRS.

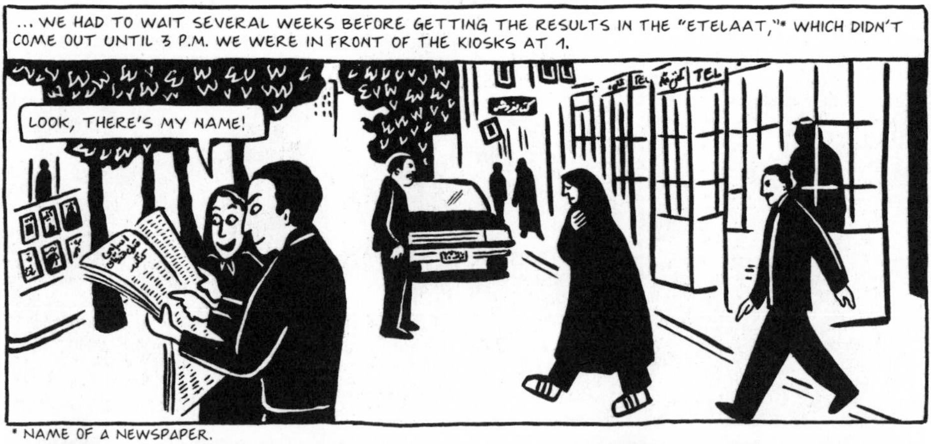
... WE HAD TO WAIT SEVERAL WEEKS BEFORE GETTING THE RESULTS IN THE "ETELAAT,"* WHICH DIDN'T COME OUT UNTIL 3 P.M. WE WERE IN FRONT OF THE KIOSKS AT 1.
LOOK, THERE'S MY NAME!
TEL

* NAME OF A NEWSPAPER.

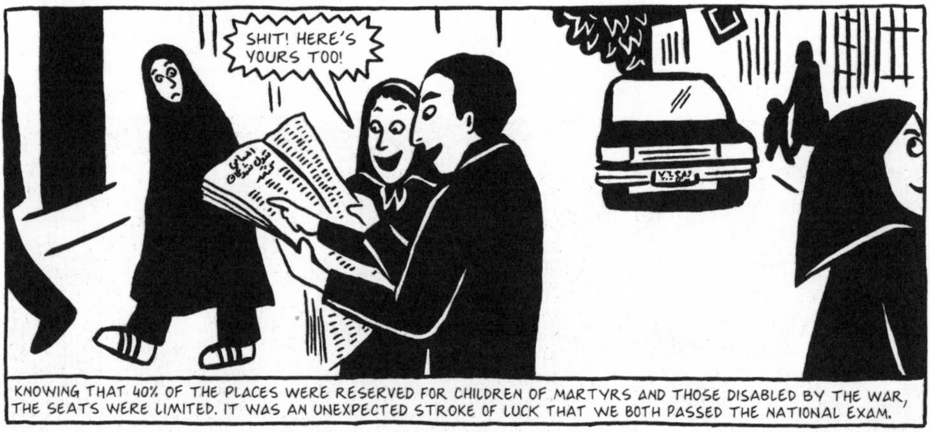
SHIT! HERE'S YOURS TOO!
KNOWING THAT 40% OF THE PLACES WERE RESERVED FOR CHILDREN OF MARTYRS AND THOSE DISABLED BY THE WAR, THE SEATS WERE LIMITED. IT WAS AN UNEXPECTED STROKE OF LUCK THAT WE BOTH PASSED THE NATIONAL EXAM.

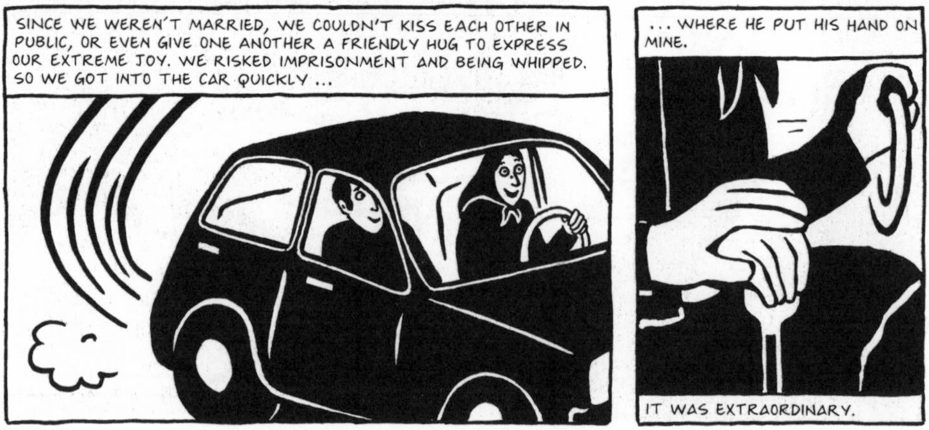
SINCE WE WEREN'T MARRIED, WE COULDN'T KISS EACH OTHER IN PUBLIC, OR EVEN GIVE ONE ANOTHER A FRIENDLY HUG TO EXPRESS OUR EXTREME JOY. WE RISKED IMPRISONMENT AND BEING WHIPPED. SO WE GOT INTO THE CAR QUICKLY ...
... WHERE HE PUT HIS HAND ON MINE.
IT WAS EXTRAORDINARY.

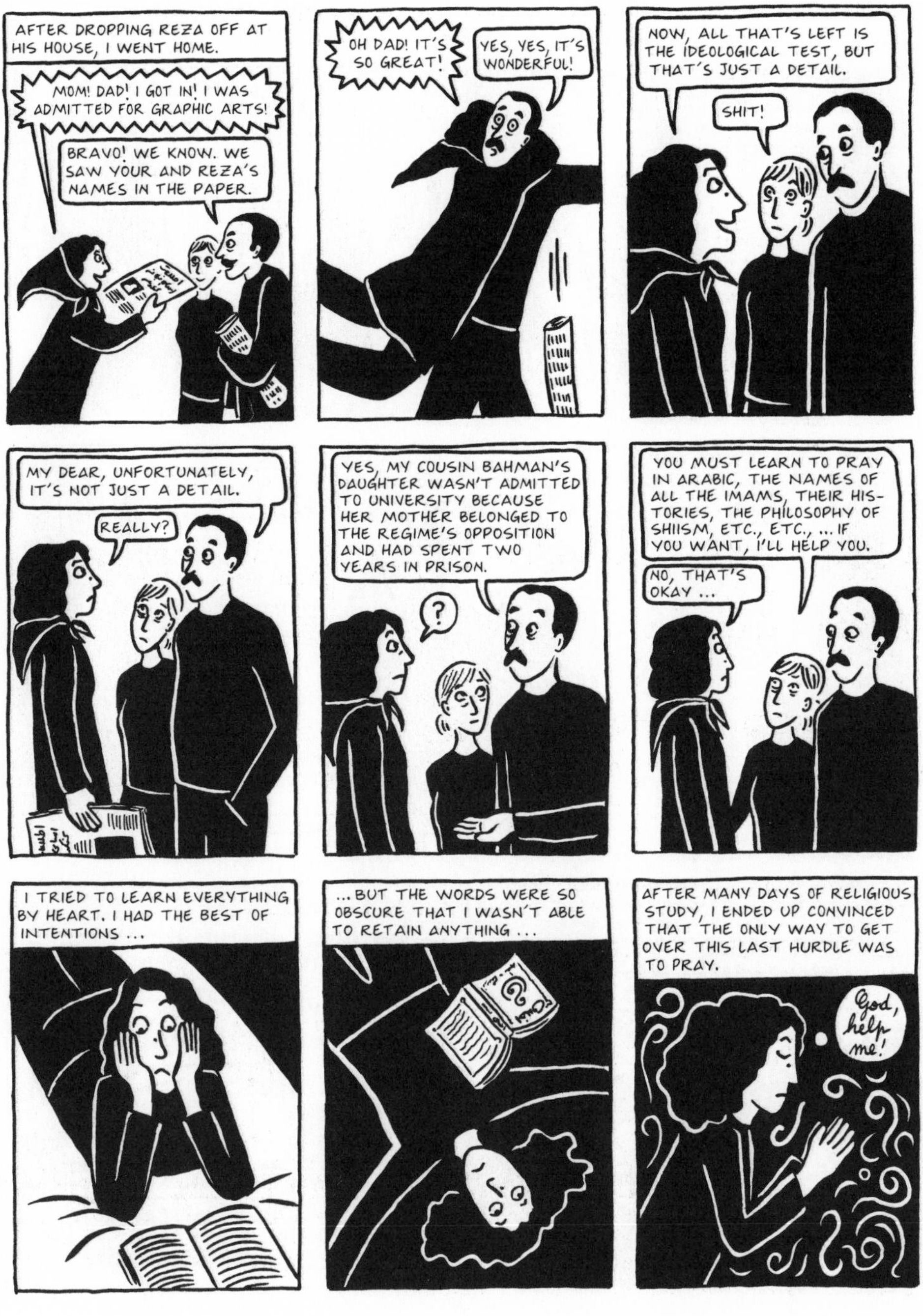
AFTER DROPPING REZA OFF AT HIS HOUSE, I WENT HOME.
MOM! DAD! I GOT IN! I WAS ADMITTED FOR GRAPHIC ARTS!
BRAVO! WE KNOW. WE SAW YOUR AND REZA'S NAMES IN THE PAPER.
OH DAD! IT'S SO GREAT!
YES, YES, IT'S WONDERFUL!
NOW, ALL THAT'S LEFT IS THE IDEOLOGICAL TEST, BUT THAT'S JUST A DETAIL.
SHIT!
MY DEAR, UNFORTUNATELY, IT'S NOT JUST A DETAIL.
REALLY?
YES, MY COUSIN BAHMAN'S DAUGHTER WASN'T ADMITTED TO UNIVERSITY BECAUSE HER MOTHER BELONGED TO THE REGIME'S OPPOSITION AND HAD SPENT TWO YEARS IN PRISON.
?
YOU MUST LEARN TO PRAY IN ARABIC, THE NAMES OF ALL THE IMAMS, THEIR HISTORIES, THE PHILOSOPHY OF SHIISM, ETC., ETC., ... IF YOU WANT, I'LL HELP YOU.
NO, THAT'S OKAY ...
I TRIED TO LEARN EVERYTHING BY HEART. I HAD THE BEST OF INTENTIONS ...
... BUT THE WORDS WERE SO OBSCURE THAT I WASN'T ABLE TO RETAIN ANYTHING ...
AFTER MANY DAYS OF RELIGIOUS STUDY, I ENDED UP CONVINCED THAT THE ONLY WAY TO GET OVER THIS LAST HURDLE WAS TO PRAY.
God, help me!

THE MAKEUP

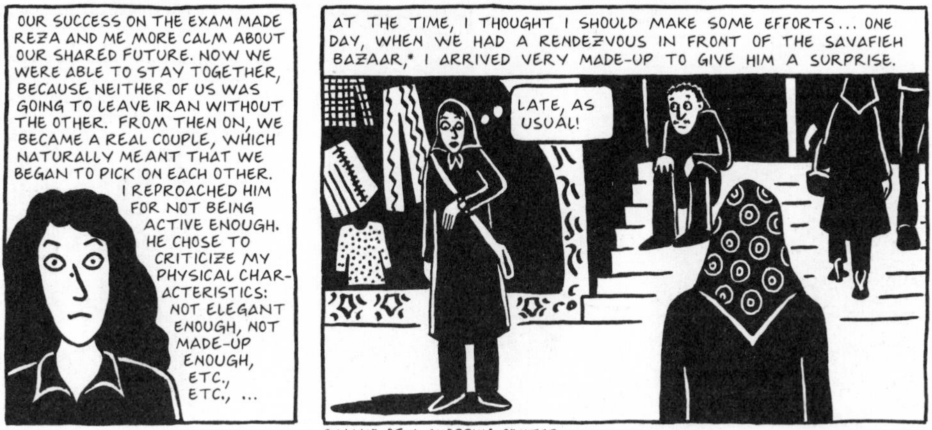
OUR SUCCESS ON THE EXAM MADE REZA AND ME MORE CALM ABOUT OUR SHARED FUTURE. NOW WE WERE ABLE TO STAY TOGETHER, BECAUSE NEITHER OF US WAS GOING TO LEAVE IRAN WITHOUT THE OTHER. FROM THEN ON, WE BECAME A REAL COUPLE, WHICH NATURALLY MEANT THAT WE BEGAN TO PICK ON EACH OTHER. I REPROACHED HIM FOR NOT BEING ACTIVE ENOUGH. HE CHOSE TO CRITICIZE MY PHYSICAL CHAR-ACTERISTICS: NOT ELEGANT ENOUGH, NOT MADE-UP ENOUGH, ETC., ETC., ...
AT THE TIME, I THOUGHT I SHOULD MAKE SOME EFFORTS... ONE DAY, WHEN WE HAD A RENDEZVOUS IN FRONT OF THE SAVAFIEH BAZAAR,* I ARRIVED VERY MADE-UP TO GIVE HIM A SURPRISE.
LATE, AS USUAL!

* NAME OF A SHOPPING CENTER

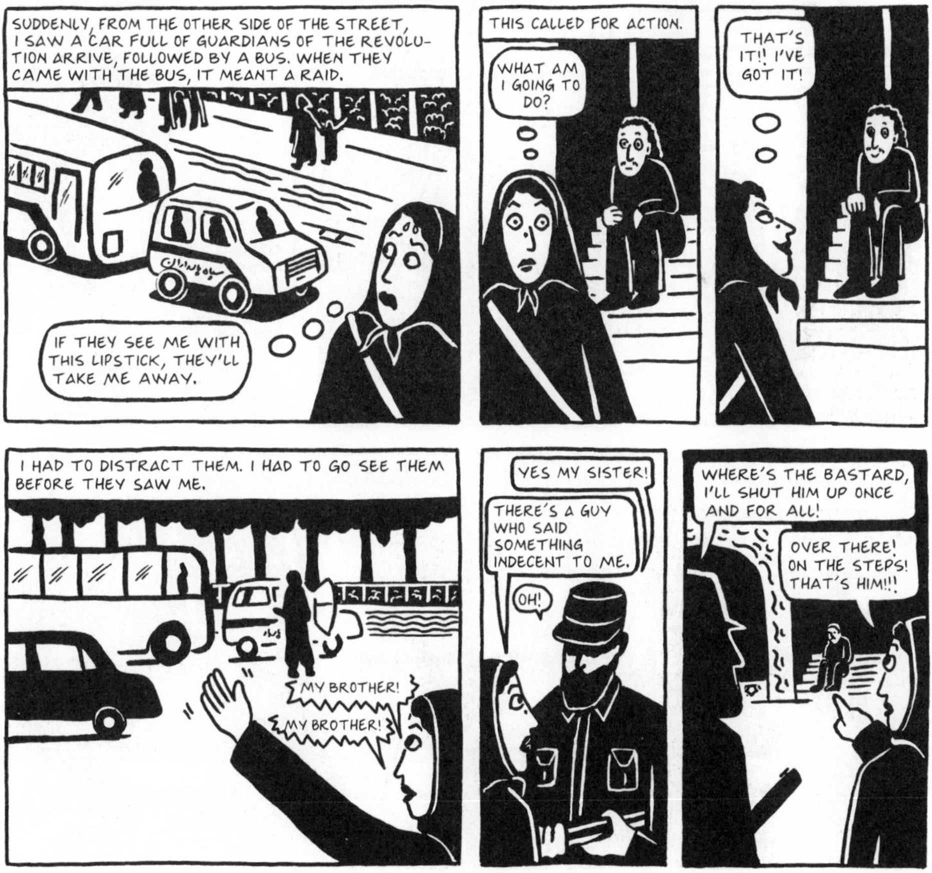
SUDDENLY, FROM THE OTHER SIDE OF THE STREET, I SAW A CAR FULL OF GUARDIANS OF THE REVOLU-TION ARRIVE, FOLLOWED BY A BUS. WHEN THEY CAME WITH THE BUS, IT MEANT A RAID.
IF THEY SEE ME WITH THIS LIPSTICK, THEY'LL TAKE ME AWAY.
THIS CALLED FOR ACTION.
WHAT AM I GOING TO DO?
THAT'S IT!! I'VE GOT IT!
I HAD TO DISTRACT THEM. I HAD TO GO SEE THEM BEFORE THEY SAW ME.
MY BROTHER!
MY BROTHER!
YES MY SISTER!
THERE'S A GUY WHO SAID SOMETHING INDECENT TO ME.
OH!
WHERE'S THE BASTARD, I'LL SHUT HIM UP ONCE AND FOR ALL!
OVER THERE! ON THE STEPS! THAT'S HIM!!!

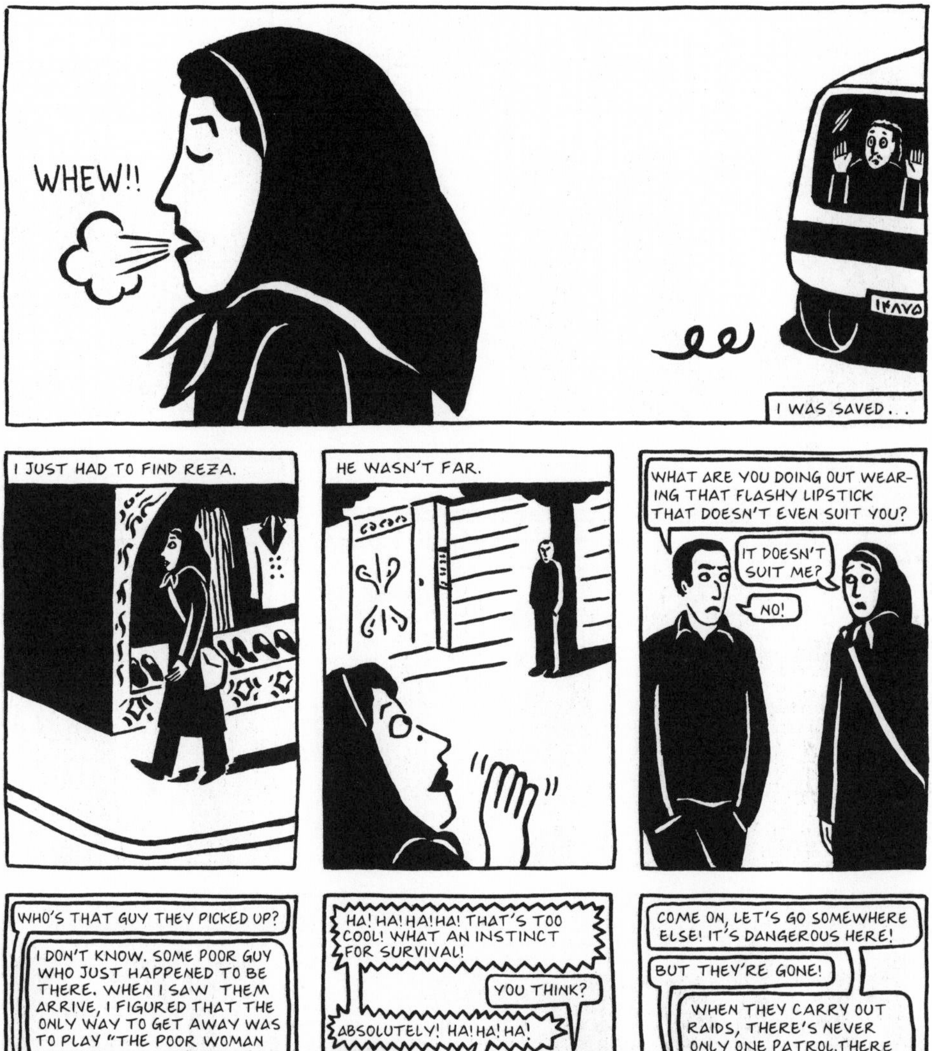
WHEW!!
I WAS SAVED...
I JUST HAD TO FIND REZA.
HE WASN'T FAR.
WHAT ARE YOU DOING OUT WEARING THAT FLASHY LIPSTICK THAT DOESN'T EVEN SUIT YOU?
IT DOESN'T SUIT ME?
NO!
WHO'S THAT GUY THEY PICKED UP?
I DON'T KNOW. SOME POOR GUY WHO JUST HAPPENED TO BE THERE. WHEN I SAW THEM ARRIVE, I FIGURED THAT THE ONLY WAY TO GET AWAY WAS TO PLAY "THE POOR WOMAN WHO NEEDS PROTECTION." SO I TOLD THEM THAT THAT GUY HAD SPOKEN INDECENTLY TO ME AND THEY ARRESTED HIM.
YOU DID THAT??!!
HA! HA! HA! HA! THAT'S TOO COOL! WHAT AN INSTINCT FOR SURVIVAL!
YOU THINK?
ABSOLUTELY! HA! HA! HA!
COME ON, LET'S GO SOMEWHERE ELSE! IT'S DANGEROUS HERE!
BUT THEY'RE GONE!
WHEN THEY CARRY OUT RAIDS, THERE'S NEVER ONLY ONE PATROL. THERE WILL BE OTHERS.

IT MUST BE SAID THAT DURING THIS PERIOD, YOUNG COUPLES WHO SHOWED THEMSELVES IN PUBLIC WERE RUNNING A RISK.

IF THEY WERE MARRIED, THERE OBVIOUSLY WOULDN'T HAVE BEEN A PROBLEM...

MY BROTHER, WHAT IS YOUR RELATIONSHIP TO THIS WOMAN?

SHE'S MY WIFE.

BUT IT WAS PREFERABLE TO HAVE A PHOTOCOPY OF YOUR MARRIAGE CERTIFICATE ON YOU.

OKAY, IT'S FINE!

THE TROUBLES BEGAN IF THE TWO YOUNG PEOPLE WERE NOT UNITED BY SACRED TIES.

WHAT IS YOUR RELATIONSHIP TO THIS MAN?

HE'S MY COUSIN.

ESPECIALLY IF THEY HAD JUST MET.

WHAT'S YOUR MOTHER'S NAME?

AZAM KOLAHDOUZ

WHAT'S HIS MOTHER'S NAME?

I FORGOT.

WHAT'S THAT? HE'S YOUR COUSIN, RIGHT? YOU MUST KNOW THE NAME OF YOUR AUNT!

COME ON, GET IN THE CAR!

THEY TOOK THEM TO THE COMMITTEE.* THEN THEY CALLED THEIR PARENTS WHO CAME TO FREE THEIR CHILDREN, BY PAYING A FINE.

SIR, YOUR DAUGHTER IS AT THE COMMITTEE OF SAAD ABAD, ACCOMPANIED BY A YOUNG MAN...A CERTAIN SAID! THEY WERE WALKING TOGETHER IN THE PARK. IT'S AN ACT AGAINST THE RELIGIOUS MORAL CODE AND THE VALUES OF OUR REPUBLIC. YOU CAN COME GET HER IN EXCHANGE FOR 20,000 TUMANS** IN CASH, OTHERWISE SHE WILL BE WHIPPED.

SORRY! SORRY!

SORRY

*THE COMMISSARIAT OF THE GUARDIANS OF THE REVOLUTION.
**AT THE TIME, THE MONTHLY SALARY OF A GOVERNMENT WORKER.

288

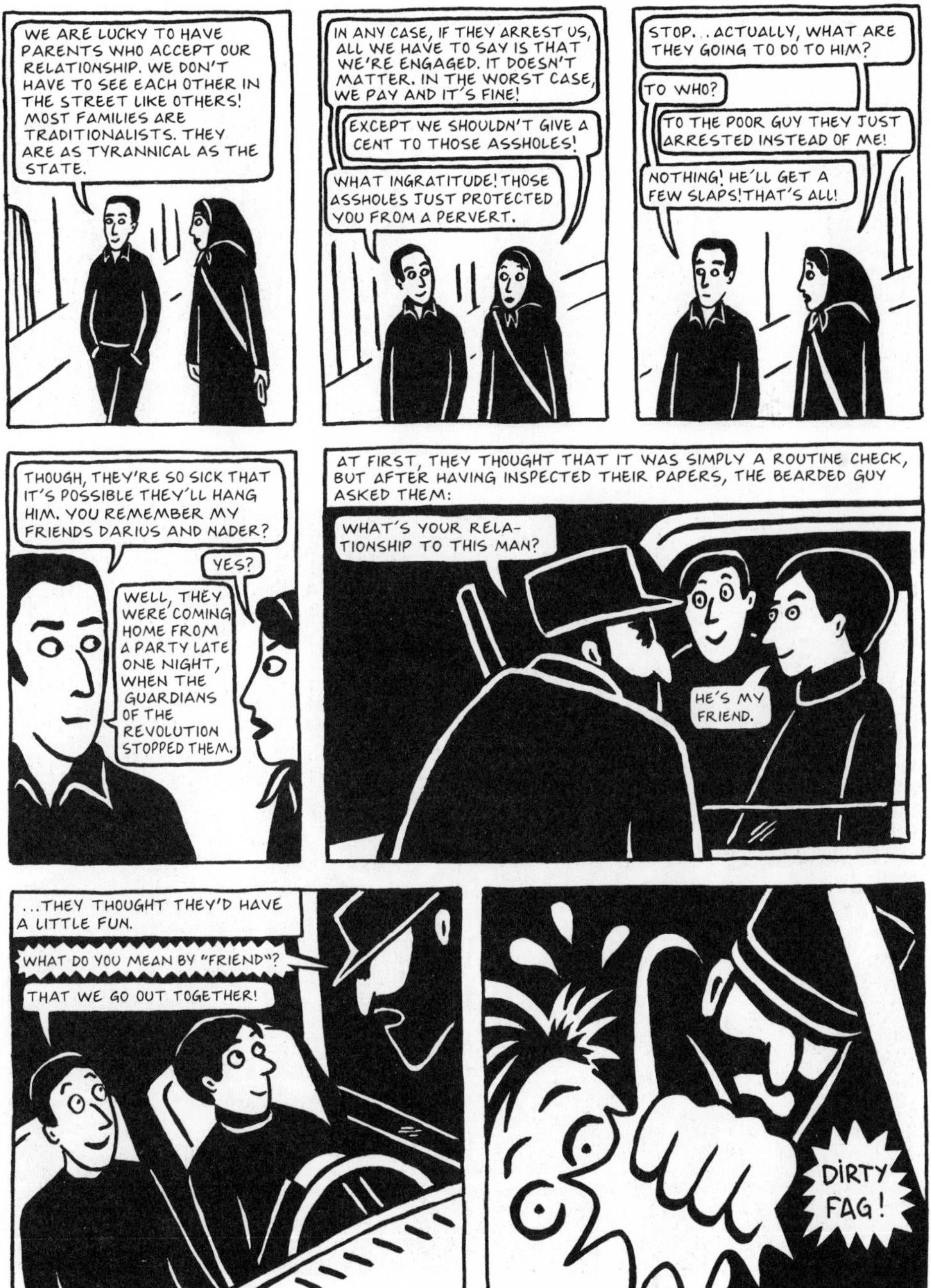

WE ARE LUCKY TO HAVE PARENTS WHO ACCEPT OUR RELATIONSHIP. WE DON'T HAVE TO SEE EACH OTHER IN THE STREET LIKE OTHERS! MOST FAMILIES ARE TRADITIONALISTS. THEY ARE AS TYRANNICAL AS THE STATE.
IN ANY CASE, IF THEY ARREST US, ALL WE HAVE TO SAY IS THAT WE'RE ENGAGED. IT DOESN'T MATTER. IN THE WORST CASE, WE PAY AND IT'S FINE!
EXCEPT WE SHOULDN'T GIVE A CENT TO THOSE ASSHOLES!
WHAT INGRATITUDE! THOSE ASSHOLES JUST PROTECTED YOU FROM A PERVERT.
STOP... ACTUALLY, WHAT ARE THEY GOING TO DO TO HIM?
TO WHO?
TO THE POOR GUY THEY JUST ARRESTED INSTEAD OF ME!
NOTHING! HE'LL GET A FEW SLAPS! THAT'S ALL!
THOUGH, THEY'RE SO SICK THAT IT'S POSSIBLE THEY'LL HANG HIM. YOU REMEMBER MY FRIENDS DARIUS AND NADER?
YES?
WELL, THEY WERE COMING HOME FROM A PARTY LATE ONE NIGHT, WHEN THE GUARDIANS OF THE REVOLUTION STOPPED THEM.
AT FIRST, THEY THOUGHT THAT IT WAS SIMPLY A ROUTINE CHECK, BUT AFTER HAVING INSPECTED THEIR PAPERS, THE BEARDED GUY ASKED THEM:
WHAT'S YOUR RELATIONSHIP TO THIS MAN?
HE'S MY FRIEND.
...THEY THOUGHT THEY'D HAVE A LITTLE FUN.
WHAT DO YOU MEAN BY "FRIEND"?
THAT WE GO OUT TOGETHER!
DIRTY FAG!

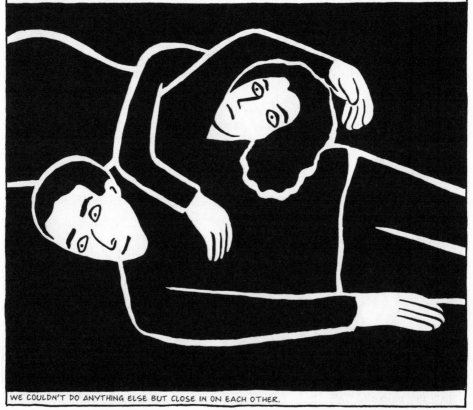

THE OUTSIDE BEING DANGEROUS, WE OFTEN FOUND OURSELVES INSIDE, AT HIS HOUSE OR AT MY HOUSE. THIS SITUATION WAS SUFFOCATING ME.

WE COULDN'T DO ANYTHING ELSE BUT CLOSE IN ON EACH OTHER.

THE CONVOCATION

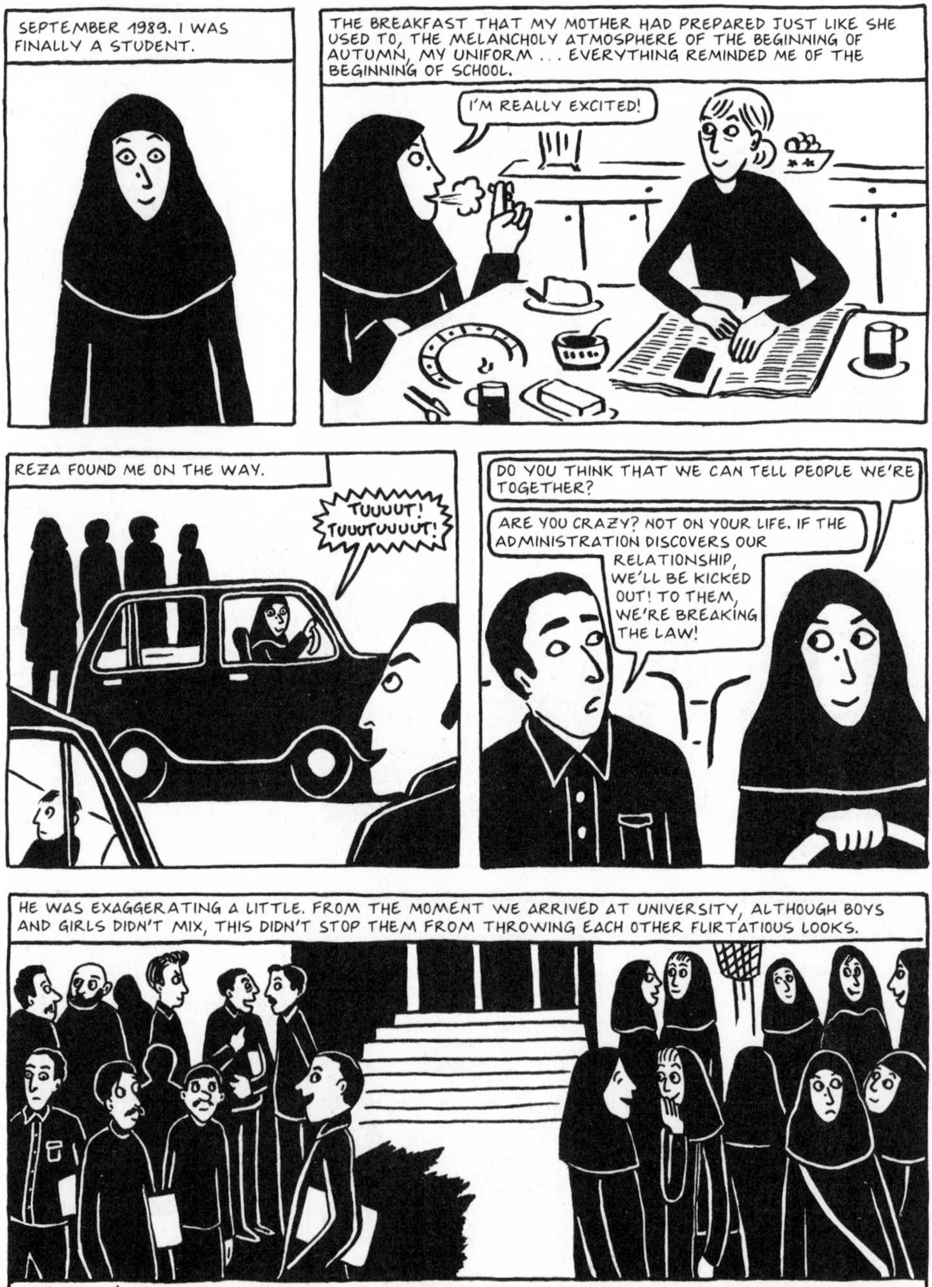
SEPTEMBER 1989. I WAS FINALLY A STUDENT.
THE BREAKFAST THAT MY MOTHER HAD PREPARED JUST LIKE SHE USED TO, THE MELANCHOLY ATMOSPHERE OF THE BEGINNING OF AUTUMN, MY UNIFORM . . . EVERYTHING REMINDED ME OF THE BEGINNING OF SCHOOL.
I'M REALLY EXCITED!
REZA FOUND ME ON THE WAY.
TUUUUT! TUUUTUUUUT!
DO YOU THINK THAT WE CAN TELL PEOPLE WE'RE TOGETHER?
ARE YOU CRAZY? NOT ON YOUR LIFE. IF THE ADMINISTRATION DISCOVERS OUR RELATIONSHIP, WE'LL BE KICKED OUT! TO THEM, WE'RE BREAKING THE LAW!
HE WAS EXAGGERATING A LITTLE. FROM THE MOMENT WE ARRIVED AT UNIVERSITY, ALTHOUGH BOYS AND GIRLS DIDN'T MIX, THIS DIDN'T STOP THEM FROM THROWING EACH OTHER FLIRTATIOUS LOOKS.
NATURALLY! AFTER ALL, LAW OR NO LAW, THESE WERE HUMAN BEINGS.

MANY OF THE STUDENTS KNEW ONE ANOTHER ALREADY. IN LISTENING TO THEM, I UNDERSTOOD THAT THEY'D TAKEN THE PREPARATORY CLASSES TOGETHER. OUR FIRST LESSON WAS "ART HISTORY."

WHAT IS GENERALLY KNOWN AS ARAB ART AND ARCHITECTURE SHOULD IN FACT BE CALLED THE ART OF THE ISLAMIC EMPIRE, WHICH STRETCHED FROM CHINA TO SPAIN. THIS ART IS A CROSS BETWEEN INDIAN, PERSIAN, AND MESOPOTAMIAN ART. THOSE WHOM WE CONSIDER, LIKE AVICENNA, TO BE "ARAB SCHOLARS" ARE FOR THE MOST PART ANYTHING BUT ARABS. EVEN THE FIRST BOOK OF ARABIC GRAMMAR WAS WRITTEN BY AN IRANIAN.

IT WAS FUNNY TO SEE TO WHAT EXTENT THE ISLAMIC REPUBLIC WAS NOT ABLE TO PUT AN END TO OUR CHAUVINISM. TO THE CONTRARY! PEOPLE OFTEN COMPARED THE OBSCURANTISM OF THE NEW REGIME TO THE ARAB INVASION. ACCORDING TO THIS LOGIC, "BEING PERSIAN" MEANT "NOT BEING A FANATIC." BUT THIS PARALLEL WENT ONLY SO FAR CONSIDERING THE FACT THAT OUR GOVERNMENT WASN'T COMPOSED OF ARAB INVADERS BUT PERSIAN FUNDAMENTALISTS.

AT LUNCH TIME.

THE PROFESSOR IS VERY INTERESTING, BUT OH MY! DOES HIS MOUTH SMELL. EVEN THIRTY FEET AWAY YOU CAN SMELL HIS JACKAL'S BREATH!

AMONG THE GUYS, A FEW EVEN HAVE HAIR CUTS!!! MY GOD!

HA! HA! HA!

HEY! LOOK, THE GUY IN THE BLUE SHIRT... HE'S REALLY NOT BAD!

DESPITE THEIR UPTIGHT APPEARANCE, THE GIRLS IN MY CLASS SEEMED TO BE QUITE THE COMEDIANS.

THEY WERE TALKING ABOUT REZA. I SUDDENLY FOUND THEM A LOT LESS FUNNY.

HI, I'M SHOUKA.

AND I'M NIYOOSHA.

NICE TO MEET YOU. I'M MARJANE.

YOU'VE LIVED ABROAD?

YES, HOW DID YOU KNOW?

BECAUSE OF YOUR MAGHNAEH.* YOU WEAR IT LIKE A BEGINNER.

IT'S TRUE THAT WEARING THE VEIL WAS A REAL SCIENCE. YOU HAD TO MAKE A SPECIAL FOLD, LIKE THIS:

NOT A HAIR SHOWS IN PROFILE.

BUT YOU SEE TUFTS FROM THE FRONT.

NIYOOSHA HAD VERY GREEN EYES WHICH MADE HER THE MOST SOUGHT AFTER GIRL AT THE COLLEGE. (THE MAJORITY OF IRANIANS HAVE BLACK EYES.)

SHOUKA WAS VERY FUNNY. UNFORTUNATELY, WHEN SHE GOT MARRIED TWO YEARS LATER, HER HUSBAND FORBADE HER FROM ASSOCIATING WITH ME. TO HIM, I WAS AN AMORAL PERSON.

*HOODED HEAD-SCARF

NEVERTHELESS, THINGS WERE EVOLVING... YEAR BY YEAR, WOMEN WERE WINNING AN EIGHTH OF AN INCH OF HAIR AND LOSING AN EIGHTH OF AN INCH OF VEIL.

WITH PRACTICE, EVEN THOUGH THEY WERE COVERED FROM HEAD TO FOOT, YOU GOT TO THE POINT WHERE YOU COULD GUESS THEIR SHAPE, THE WAY THEY WORE THEIR HAIR AND EVEN THEIR POLITICAL OPINIONS. OBVIOUSLY, THE MORE A WOMAN SHOWED, THE MORE PROGRESSIVE AND MODERN SHE WAS.

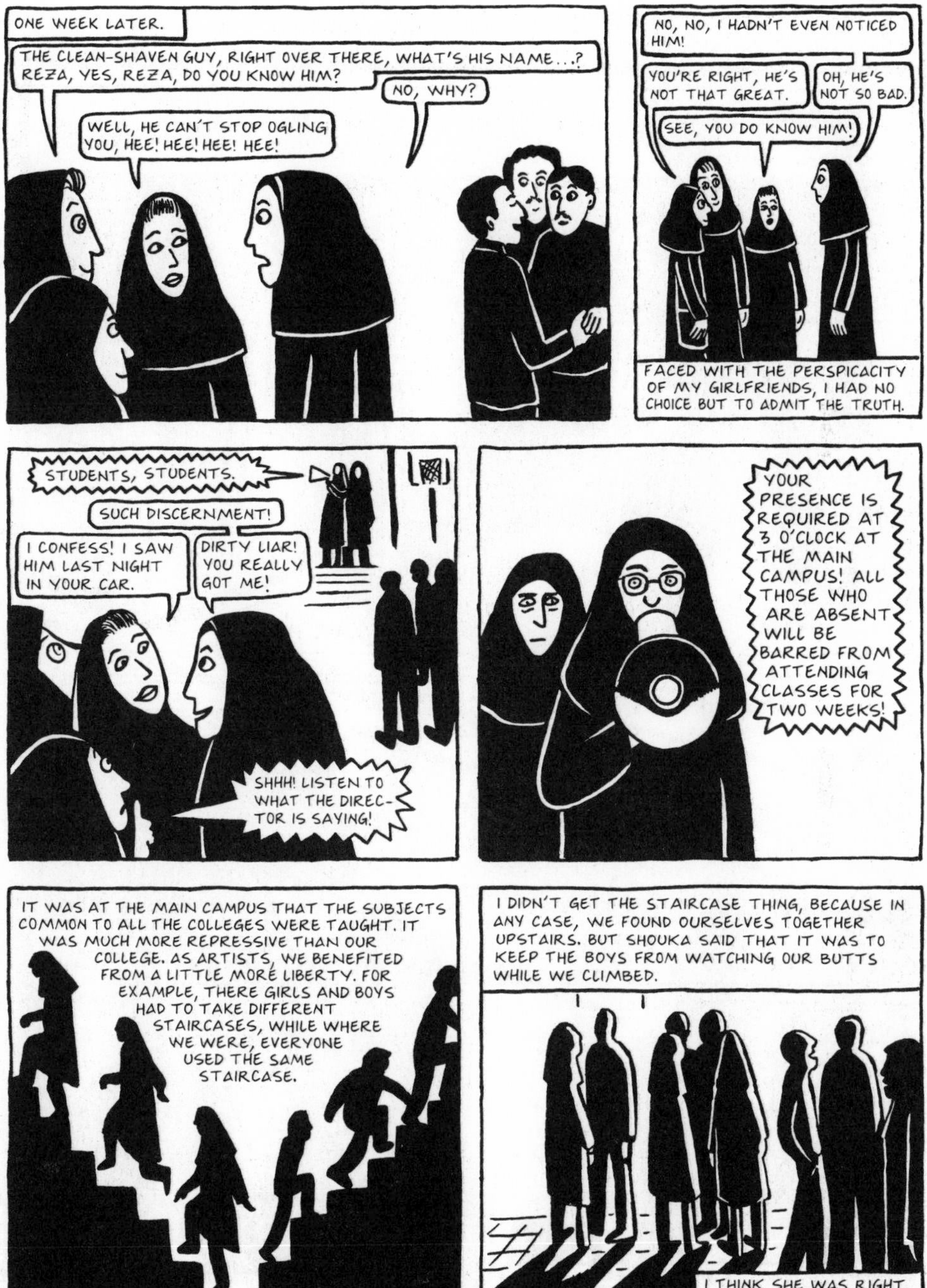

ONE WEEK LATER.
THE CLEAN-SHAVEN GUY, RIGHT OVER THERE, WHAT'S HIS NAME...? REZA, YES, REZA, DO YOU KNOW HIM?
NO, WHY?
WELL, HE CAN'T STOP OGLING YOU, HEE! HEE! HEE! HEE!
NO, NO, I HADN'T EVEN NOTICED HIM!
YOU'RE RIGHT, HE'S NOT THAT GREAT.
OH, HE'S NOT SO BAD.
SEE, YOU DO KNOW HIM!
FACED WITH THE PERSPICACITY OF MY GIRLFRIENDS, I HAD NO CHOICE BUT TO ADMIT THE TRUTH.
STUDENTS, STUDENTS.
SUCH DISCERNMENT!
I CONFESS! I SAW HIM LAST NIGHT IN YOUR CAR.
DIRTY LIAR! YOU REALLY GOT ME!
SHHH! LISTEN TO WHAT THE DIRECTOR IS SAYING!
YOUR PRESENCE IS REQUIRED AT 3 O'CLOCK AT THE MAIN CAMPUS! ALL THOSE WHO ARE ABSENT WILL BE BARRED FROM ATTENDING CLASSES FOR TWO WEEKS!
IT WAS AT THE MAIN CAMPUS THAT THE SUBJECTS COMMON TO ALL THE COLLEGES WERE TAUGHT. IT WAS MUCH MORE REPRESSIVE THAN OUR COLLEGE. AS ARTISTS, WE BENEFITED FROM A LITTLE MORE LIBERTY. FOR EXAMPLE, THERE GIRLS AND BOYS HAD TO TAKE DIFFERENT STAIRCASES, WHILE WHERE WE WERE, EVERYONE USED THE SAME STAIRCASE.
I DIDN'T GET THE STAIRCASE THING, BECAUSE IN ANY CASE, WE FOUND OURSELVES TOGETHER UPSTAIRS. BUT SHOUKA SAID THAT IT WAS TO KEEP THE BOYS FROM WATCHING OUR BUTTS WHILE WE CLIMBED.
I THINK SHE WAS RIGHT.

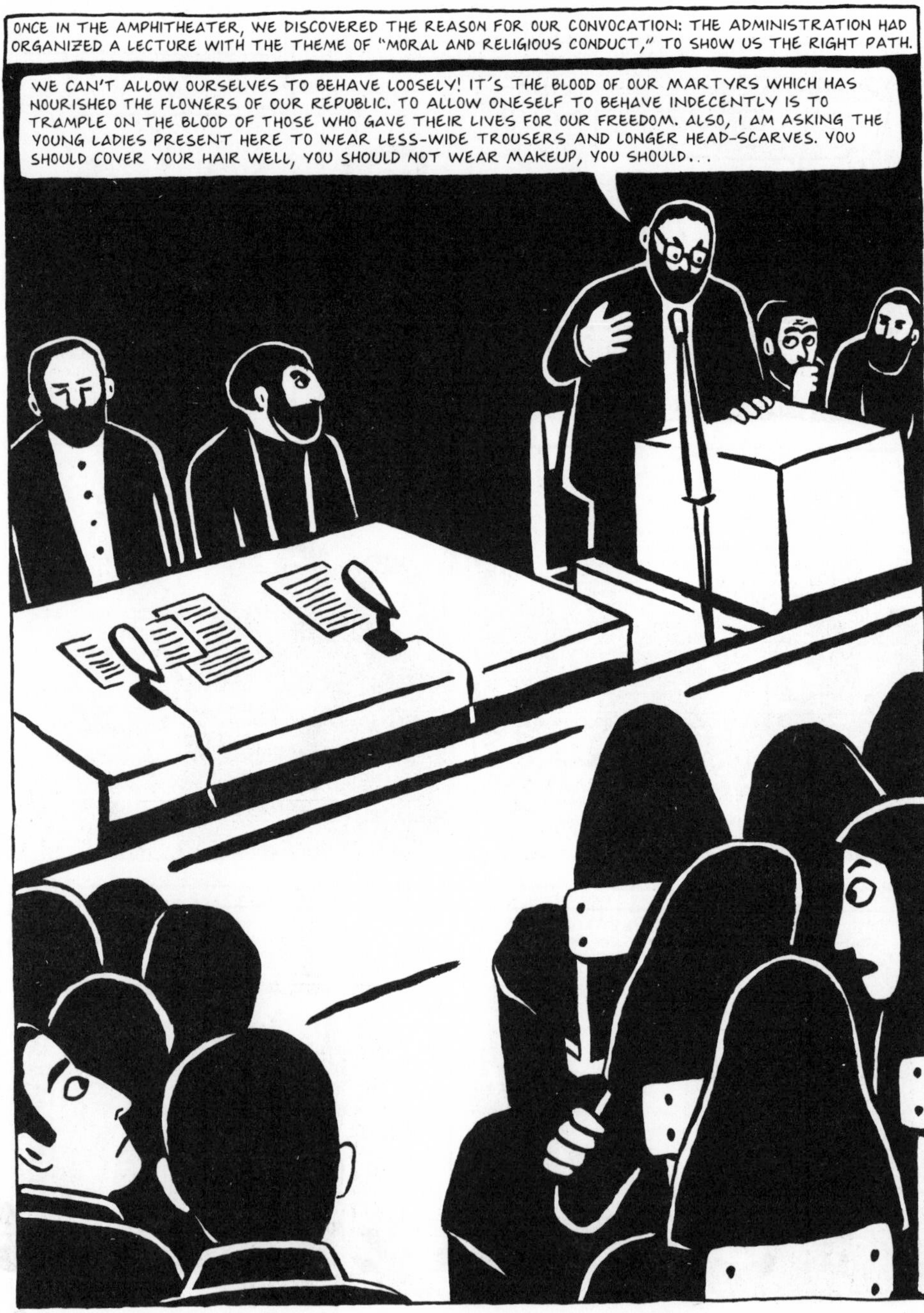
ONCE IN THE AMPHITHEATER, WE DISCOVERED THE REASON FOR OUR CONVOCATION: THE ADMINISTRATION HAD ORGANIZED A LECTURE WITH THE THEME OF "MORAL AND RELIGIOUS CONDUCT," TO SHOW US THE RIGHT PATH.
WE CAN'T ALLOW OURSELVES TO BEHAVE LOOSELY! IT'S THE BLOOD OF OUR MARTYRS WHICH HAS NOURISHED THE FLOWERS OF OUR REPUBLIC. TO ALLOW ONESELF TO BEHAVE INDECENTLY IS TO TRAMPLE ON THE BLOOD OF THOSE WHO GAVE THEIR LIVES FOR OUR FREEDOM. ALSO, I AM ASKING THE YOUNG LADIES PRESENT HERE TO WEAR LESS-WIDE TROUSERS AND LONGER HEAD-SCARVES. YOU SHOULD COVER YOUR HAIR WELL, YOU SHOULD NOT WEAR MAKEUP, YOU SHOULD. . .

297

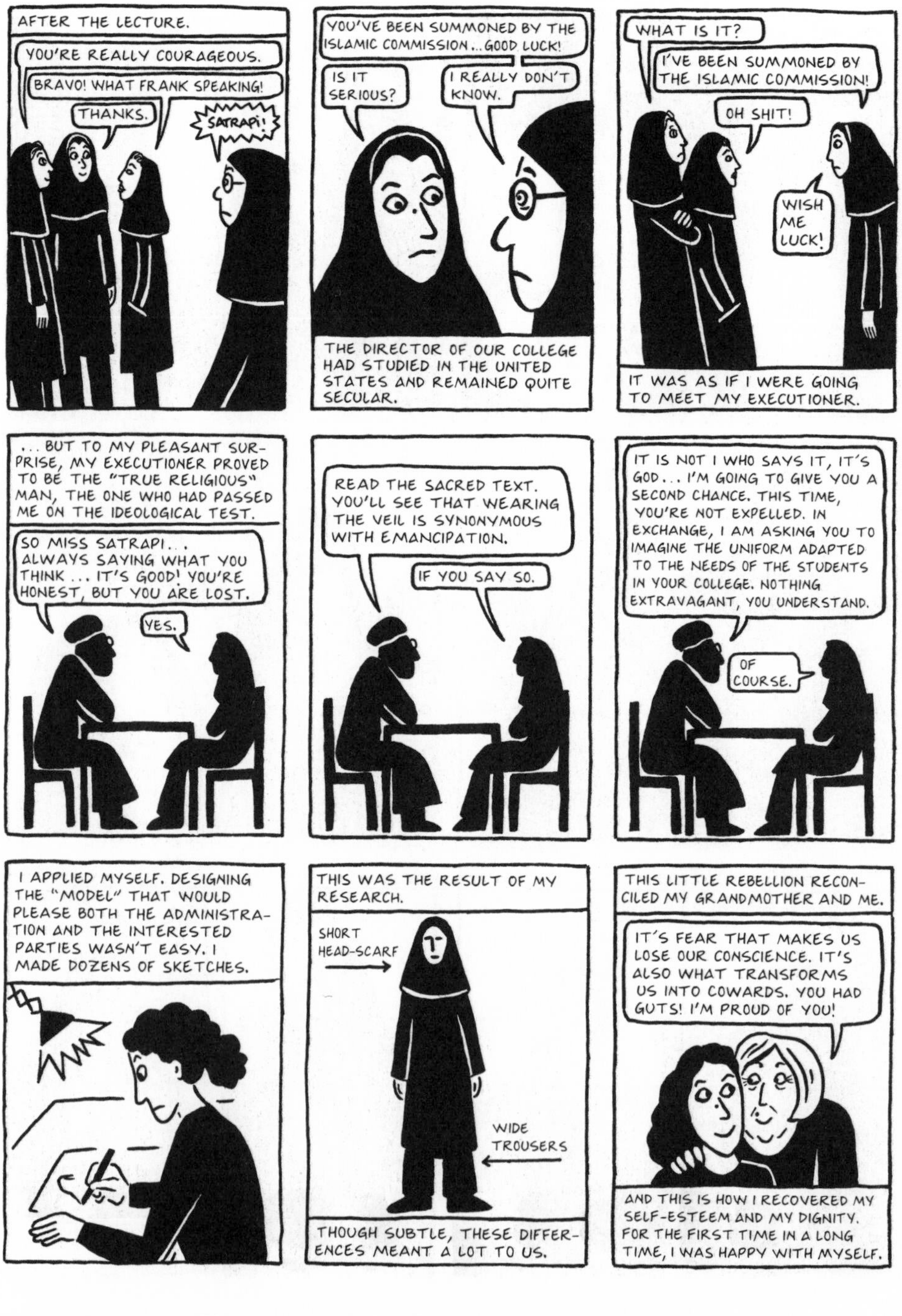
AFTER THE LECTURE.
YOU'RE REALLY COURAGEOUS.
BRAVO! WHAT FRANK SPEAKING!
THANKS.
SATRAPI!
YOU'VE BEEN SUMMONED BY THE ISLAMIC COMMISSION... GOOD LUCK!
IS IT SERIOUS?
I REALLY DON'T KNOW.
THE DIRECTOR OF OUR COLLEGE HAD STUDIED IN THE UNITED STATES AND REMAINED QUITE SECULAR.
WHAT IS IT?
I'VE BEEN SUMMONED BY THE ISLAMIC COMMISSION!
OH SHIT!
WISH ME LUCK!
IT WAS AS IF I WERE GOING TO MEET MY EXECUTIONER.
... BUT TO MY PLEASANT SURPRISE, MY EXECUTIONER PROVED TO BE THE "TRUE RELIGIOUS" MAN, THE ONE WHO HAD PASSED ME ON THE IDEOLOGICAL TEST.
SO MISS SATRAPI... ALWAYS SAYING WHAT YOU THINK... IT'S GOOD! YOU'RE HONEST, BUT YOU ARE LOST.
YES.
READ THE SACRED TEXT. YOU'LL SEE THAT WEARING THE VEIL IS SYNONYMOUS WITH EMANCIPATION.
IF YOU SAY SO.
IT IS NOT I WHO SAYS IT, IT'S GOD... I'M GOING TO GIVE YOU A SECOND CHANCE. THIS TIME, YOU'RE NOT EXPELLED. IN EXCHANGE, I AM ASKING YOU TO IMAGINE THE UNIFORM ADAPTED TO THE NEEDS OF THE STUDENTS IN YOUR COLLEGE. NOTHING EXTRAVAGANT, YOU UNDERSTAND.
OF COURSE.
I APPLIED MYSELF. DESIGNING THE "MODEL" THAT WOULD PLEASE BOTH THE ADMINISTRATION AND THE INTERESTED PARTIES WASN'T EASY. I MADE DOZENS OF SKETCHES.
THIS WAS THE RESULT OF MY RESEARCH.
SHORT HEAD-SCARF
WIDE TROUSERS
THOUGH SUBTLE, THESE DIFFERENCES MEANT A LOT TO US.
THIS LITTLE REBELLION RECONCILED MY GRANDMOTHER AND ME.
IT'S FEAR THAT MAKES US LOSE OUR CONSCIENCE. IT'S ALSO WHAT TRANSFORMS US INTO COWARDS. YOU HAD GUTS! I'M PROUD OF YOU!
AND THIS IS HOW I RECOVERED MY SELF-ESTEEM AND MY DIGNITY. FOR THE FIRST TIME IN A LONG TIME, I WAS HAPPY WITH MYSELF.

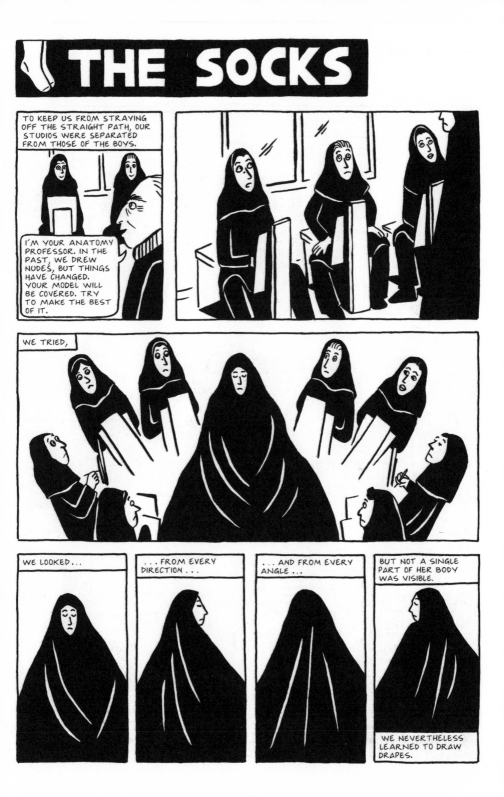

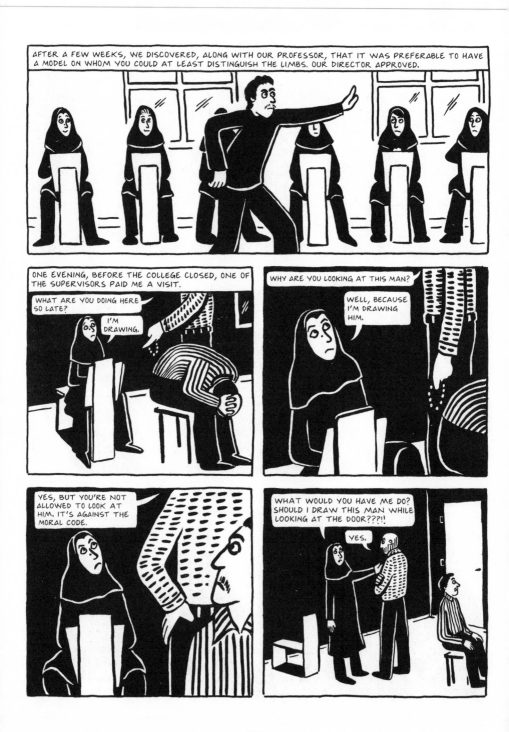

300

HAPPILY, THERE WAS STILL THE OTHER HALF. LITTLE BY LITTLE, I GOT TO KNOW THE STUDENTS WHO THOUGHT LIKE ME.

WE WOULD GO TO ONE ANOTHER'S HOUSES, WHERE WE POSED FOR EACH OTHER ... WE HAD AT LAST FOUND A PLACE OF FREEDOM.

AT FIRST THERE WERE ONLY FIVE OF US.

THEN ...

AND FINALLY ...

WE WERE MUCH MORE NUMEROUS THAN I WOULD HAVE BELIEVED.

OUR PROFESSOR WAS SO HAPPY TO SEE THE SKETCHES WE DID AT HOME.

BRAVO! AN ARTIST SHOULD DEFY THE LAW! I CONGRATULATE YOU!

THE MORE TIME PASSED, THE MORE I BECAME CONSCIOUS OF THE CONTRAST BETWEEN THE OFFICIAL REPRESENTATION OF MY COUNTRY AND THE REAL LIFE OF THE PEOPLE, THE ONE THAT WENT ON BEHIND THE WALLS.

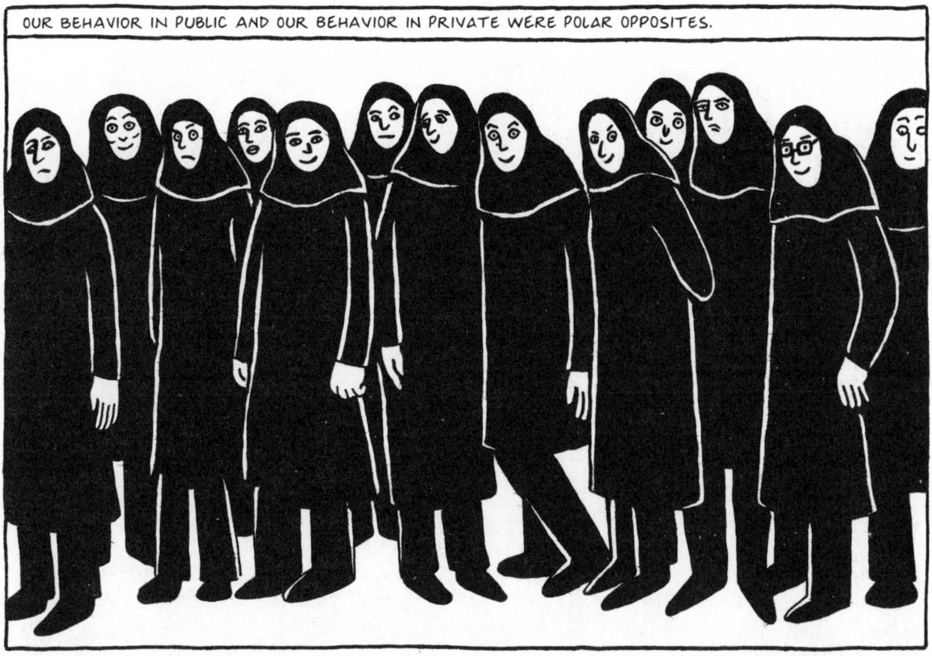
OUR BEHAVIOR IN PUBLIC AND OUR BEHAVIOR IN PRIVATE WERE POLAR OPPOSITES.

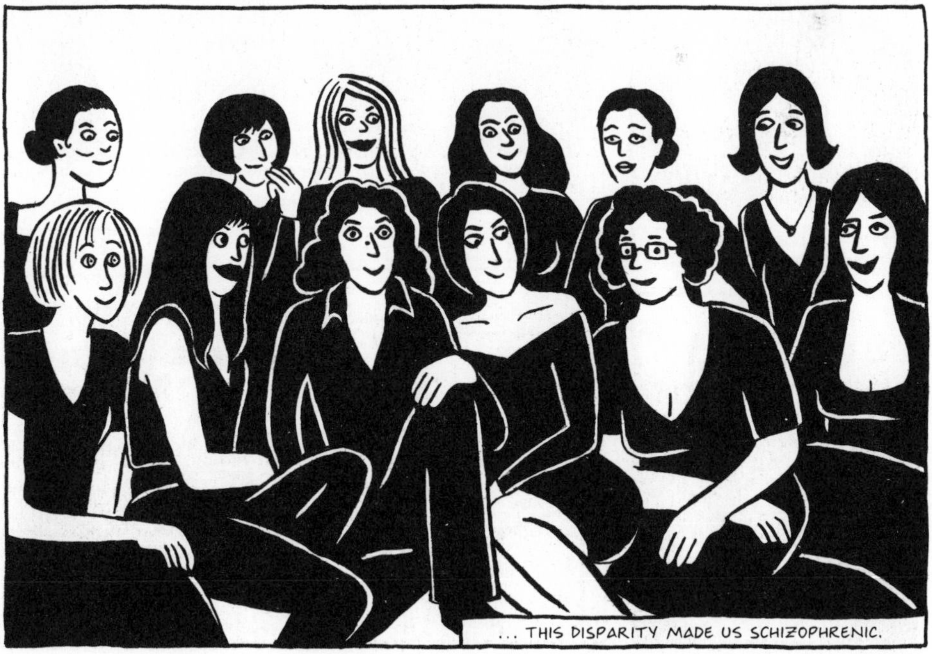
... THIS DISPARITY MADE US SCHIZOPHRENIC.

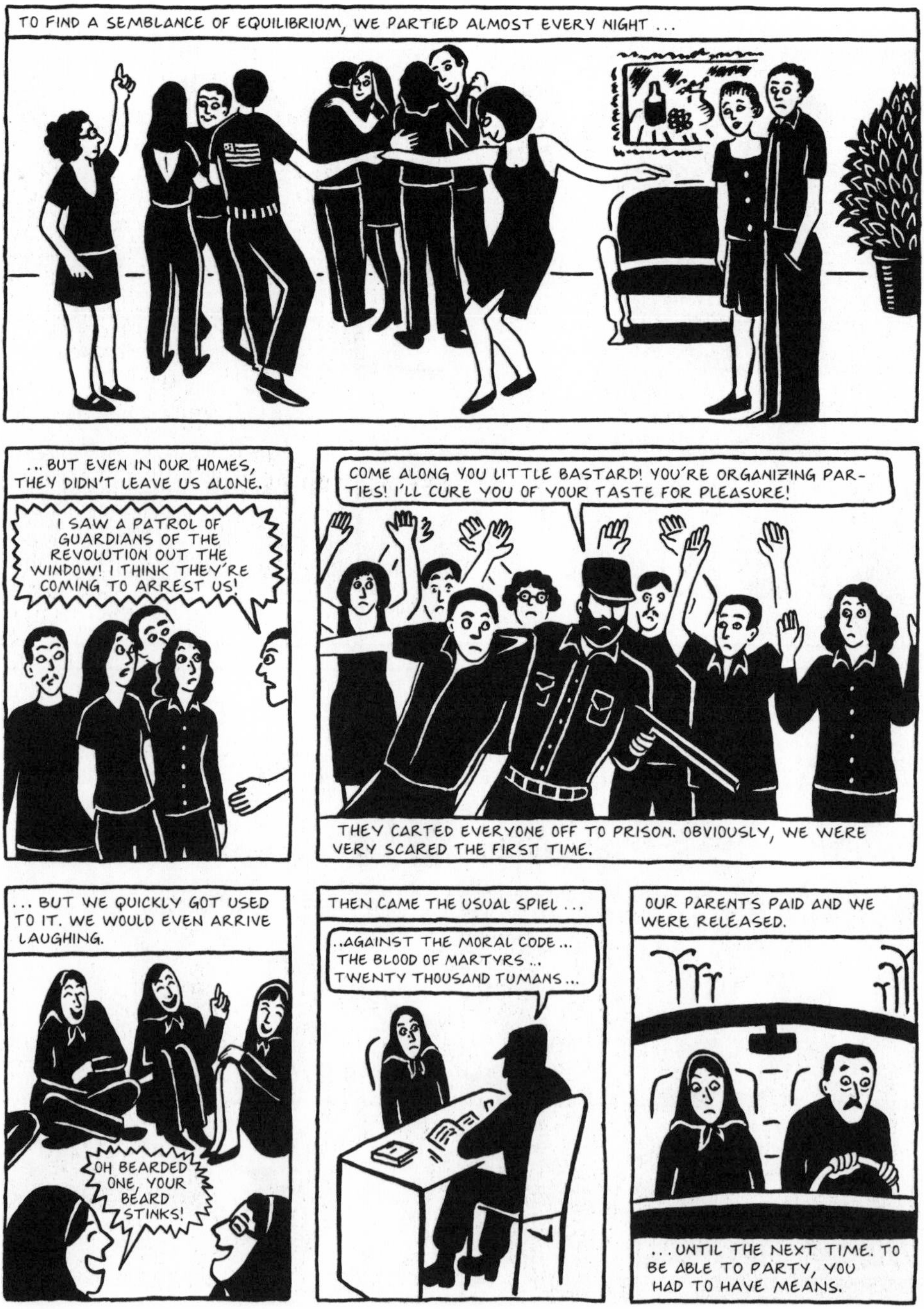
TO FIND A SEMBLANCE OF EQUILIBRIUM, WE PARTIED ALMOST EVERY NIGHT ...
... BUT EVEN IN OUR HOMES, THEY DIDN'T LEAVE US ALONE.
I SAW A PATROL OF GUARDIANS OF THE REVOLUTION OUT THE WINDOW! I THINK THEY'RE COMING TO ARREST US!
COME ALONG YOU LITTLE BASTARD! YOU'RE ORGANIZING PARTIES! I'LL CURE YOU OF YOUR TASTE FOR PLEASURE!
THEY CARTED EVERYONE OFF TO PRISON. OBVIOUSLY, WE WERE VERY SCARED THE FIRST TIME.
... BUT WE QUICKLY GOT USED TO IT. WE WOULD EVEN ARRIVE LAUGHING.
OH BEARDED ONE, YOUR BEARD STINKS!
THEN CAME THE USUAL SPIEL ...
..AGAINST THE MORAL CODE... THE BLOOD OF MARTYRS... TWENTY THOUSAND TUMANS...
OUR PARENTS PAID AND WE WERE RELEASED.
... UNTIL THE NEXT TIME. TO BE ABLE TO PARTY, YOU HAD TO HAVE MEANS.

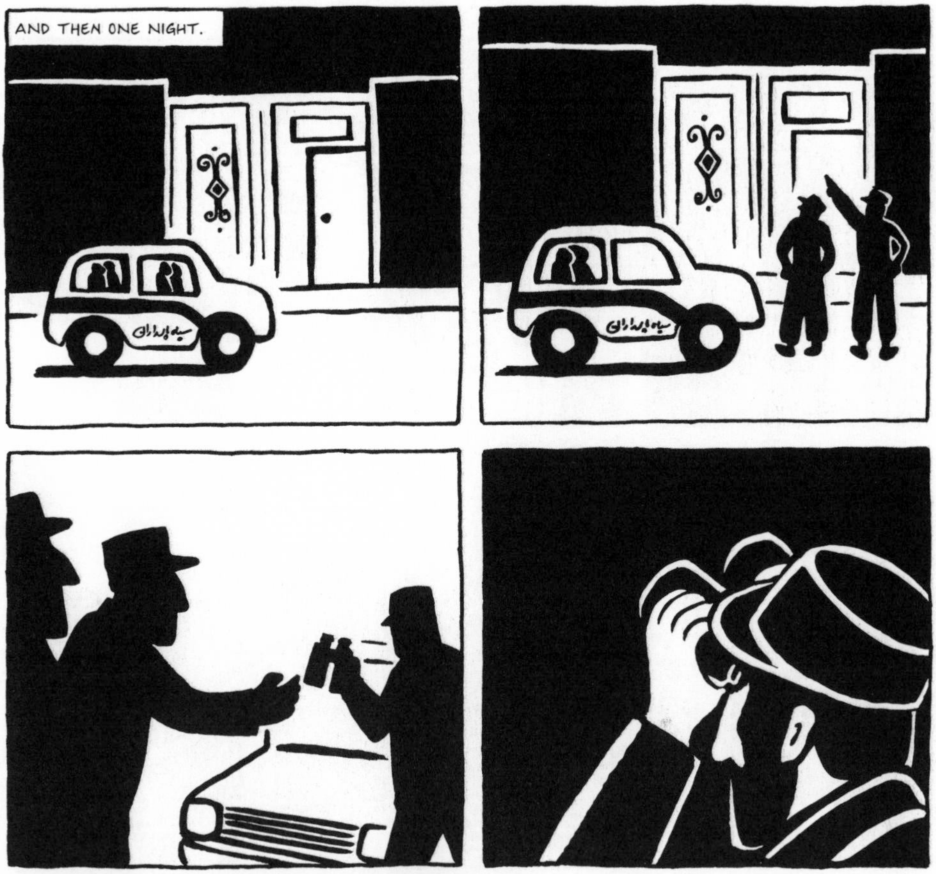

AND THEN ONE NIGHT.

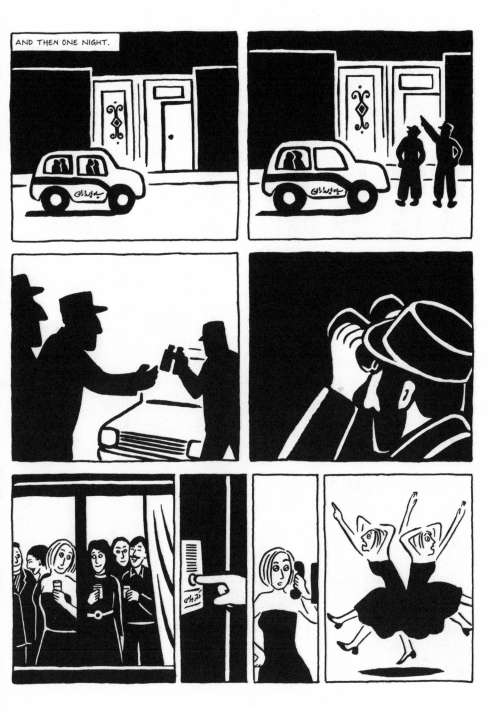

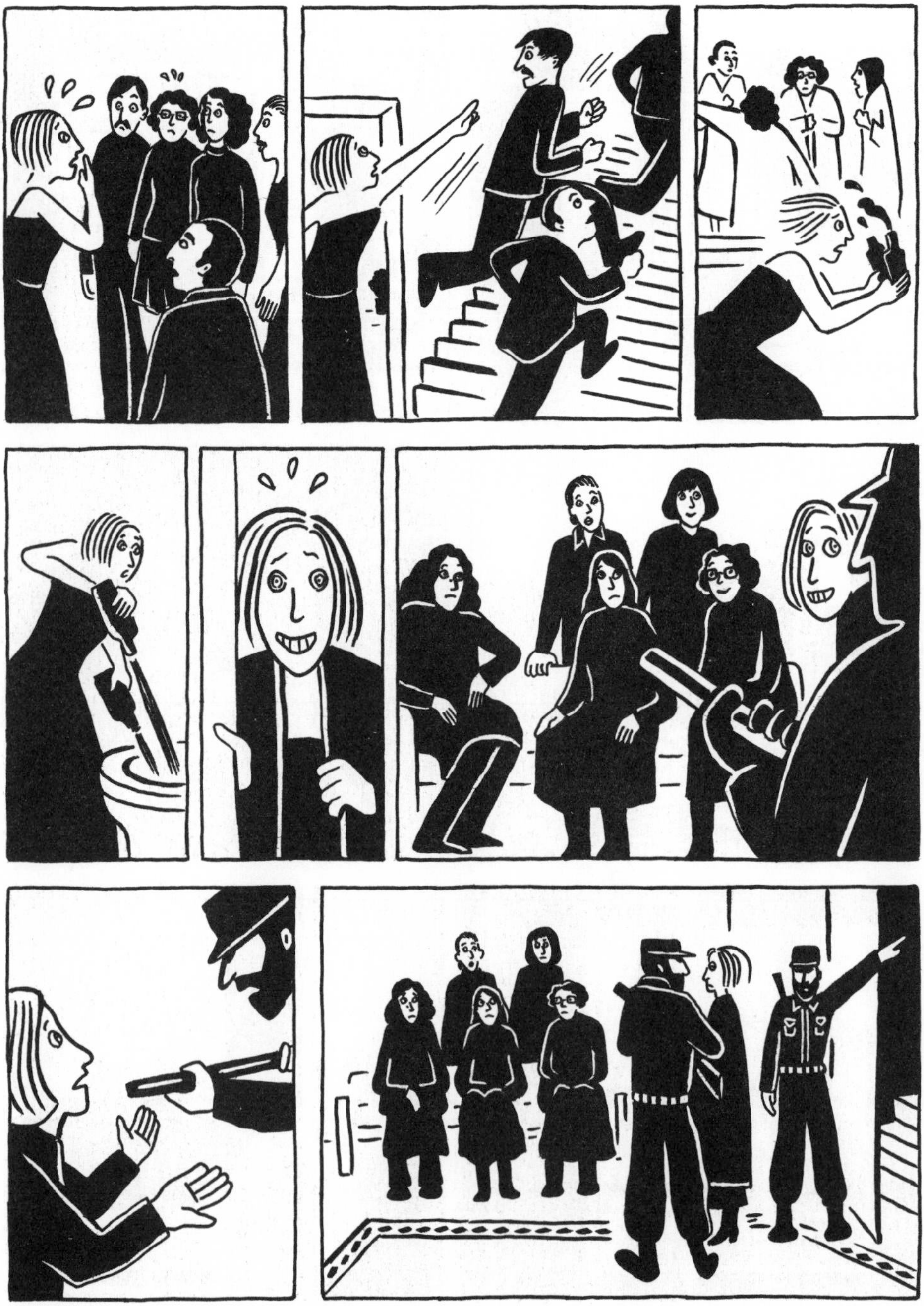

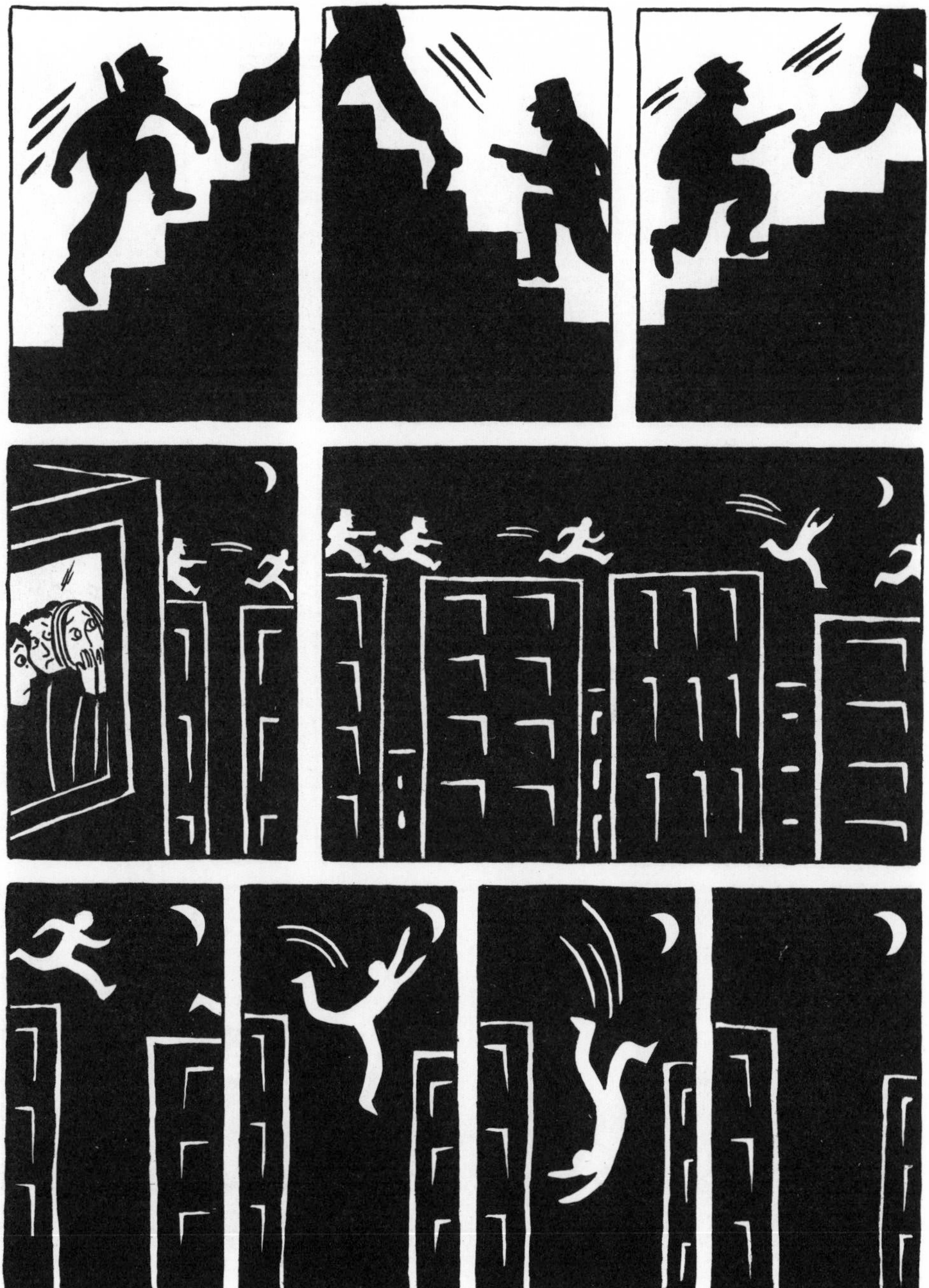

THE WEDDING

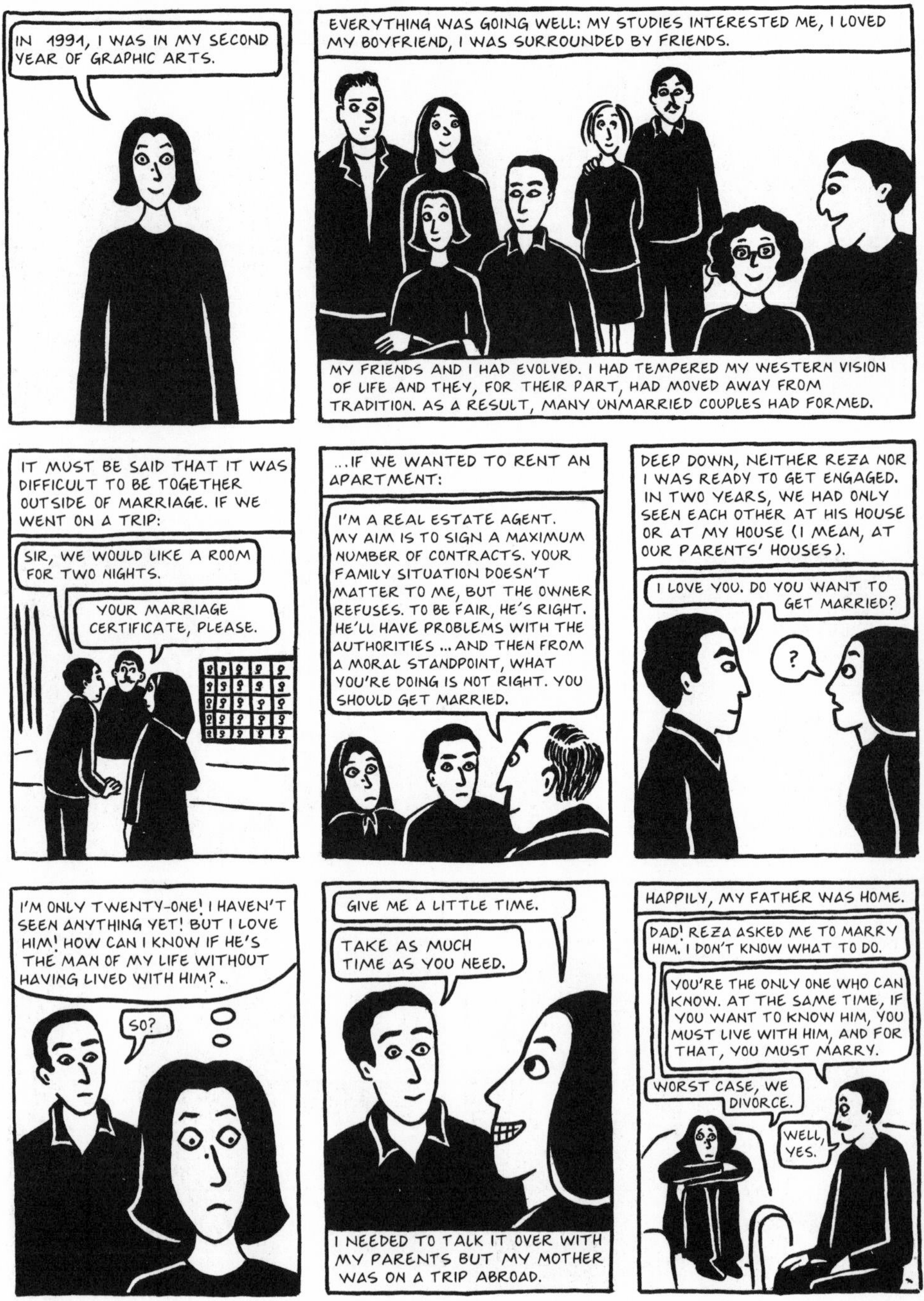
IN 1991, I WAS IN MY SECOND YEAR OF GRAPHIC ARTS.
EVERYTHING WAS GOING WELL: MY STUDIES INTERESTED ME, I LOVED MY BOYFRIEND, I WAS SURROUNDED BY FRIENDS.
MY FRIENDS AND I HAD EVOLVED. I HAD TEMPERED MY WESTERN VISION OF LIFE AND THEY, FOR THEIR PART, HAD MOVED AWAY FROM TRADITION. AS A RESULT, MANY UNMARRIED COUPLES HAD FORMED.
IT MUST BE SAID THAT IT WAS DIFFICULT TO BE TOGETHER OUTSIDE OF MARRIAGE. IF WE WENT ON A TRIP:
SIR, WE WOULD LIKE A ROOM FOR TWO NIGHTS.
YOUR MARRIAGE CERTIFICATE, PLEASE.
...IF WE WANTED TO RENT AN APARTMENT:
I'M A REAL ESTATE AGENT. MY AIM IS TO SIGN A MAXIMUM NUMBER OF CONTRACTS. YOUR FAMILY SITUATION DOESN'T MATTER TO ME, BUT THE OWNER REFUSES. TO BE FAIR, HE'S RIGHT. HE'LL HAVE PROBLEMS WITH THE AUTHORITIES ... AND THEN FROM A MORAL STANDPOINT, WHAT YOU'RE DOING IS NOT RIGHT. YOU SHOULD GET MARRIED.
DEEP DOWN, NEITHER REZA NOR I WAS READY TO GET ENGAGED. IN TWO YEARS, WE HAD ONLY SEEN EACH OTHER AT HIS HOUSE OR AT MY HOUSE (I MEAN, AT OUR PARENTS' HOUSES).
I LOVE YOU. DO YOU WANT TO GET MARRIED?
?
I'M ONLY TWENTY-ONE! I HAVEN'T SEEN ANYTHING YET! BUT I LOVE HIM! HOW CAN I KNOW IF HE'S THE MAN OF MY LIFE WITHOUT HAVING LIVED WITH HIM?..
SO?
GIVE ME A LITTLE TIME.
TAKE AS MUCH TIME AS YOU NEED.
I NEEDED TO TALK IT OVER WITH MY PARENTS BUT MY MOTHER WAS ON A TRIP ABROAD.
HAPPILY, MY FATHER WAS HOME.
DAD! REZA ASKED ME TO MARRY HIM. I DON'T KNOW WHAT TO DO.
YOU'RE THE ONLY ONE WHO CAN KNOW. AT THE SAME TIME, IF YOU WANT TO KNOW HIM, YOU MUST LIVE WITH HIM, AND FOR THAT, YOU MUST MARRY.
WORST CASE, WE DIVORCE.
WELL, YES.

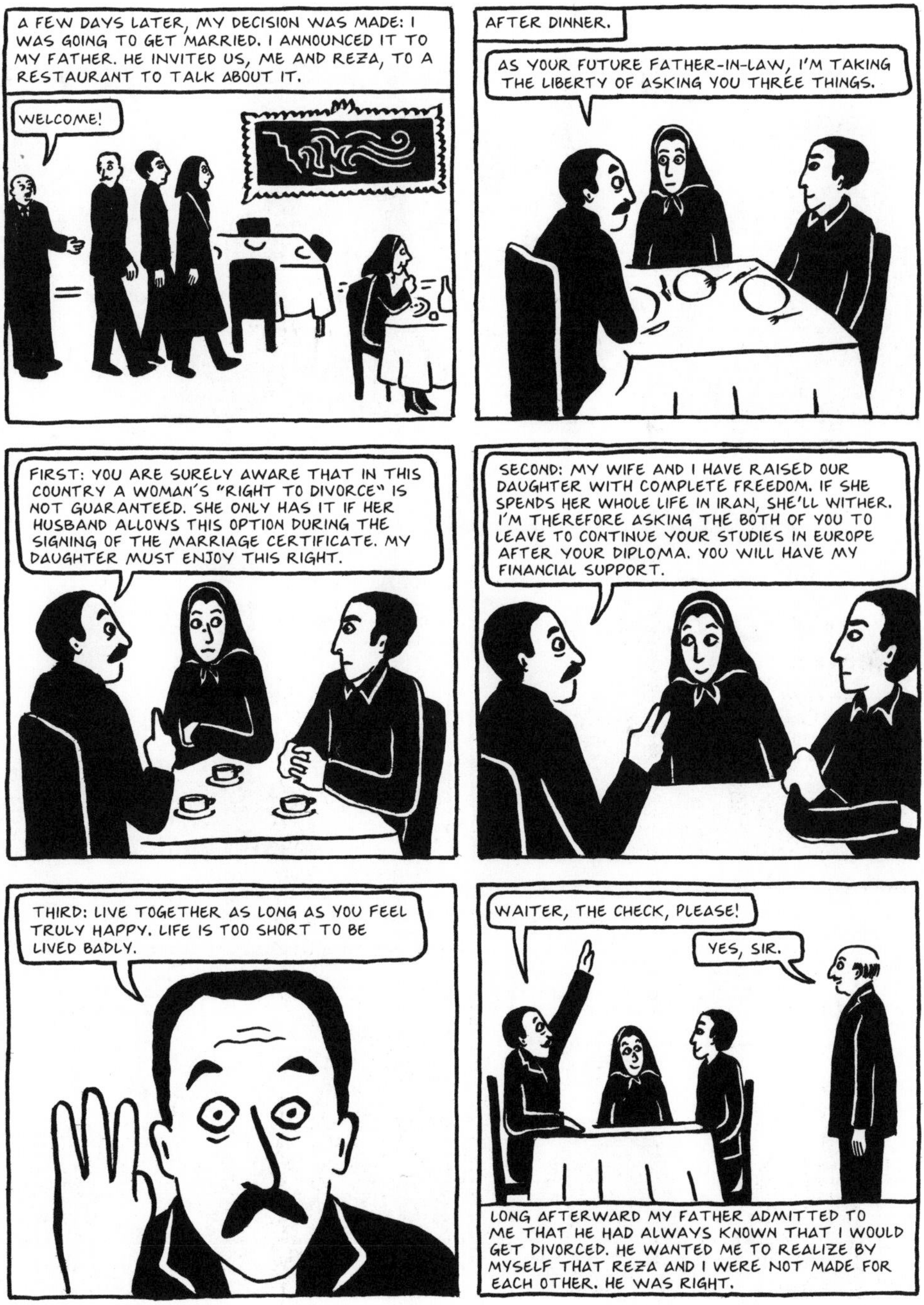
A FEW DAYS LATER, MY DECISION WAS MADE: I WAS GOING TO GET MARRIED. I ANNOUNCED IT TO MY FATHER. HE INVITED US, ME AND REZA, TO A RESTAURANT TO TALK ABOUT IT.
WELCOME!
AFTER DINNER.
AS YOUR FUTURE FATHER-IN-LAW, I'M TAKING THE LIBERTY OF ASKING YOU THREE THINGS.
FIRST: YOU ARE SURELY AWARE THAT IN THIS COUNTRY A WOMAN'S "RIGHT TO DIVORCE" IS NOT GUARANTEED. SHE ONLY HAS IT IF HER HUSBAND ALLOWS THIS OPTION DURING THE SIGNING OF THE MARRIAGE CERTIFICATE. MY DAUGHTER MUST ENJOY THIS RIGHT.
SECOND: MY WIFE AND I HAVE RAISED OUR DAUGHTER WITH COMPLETE FREEDOM. IF SHE SPENDS HER WHOLE LIFE IN IRAN, SHE'LL WITHER. I'M THEREFORE ASKING THE BOTH OF YOU TO LEAVE TO CONTINUE YOUR STUDIES IN EUROPE AFTER YOUR DIPLOMA. YOU WILL HAVE MY FINANCIAL SUPPORT.
THIRD: LIVE TOGETHER AS LONG AS YOU FEEL TRULY HAPPY. LIFE IS TOO SHORT TO BE LIVED BADLY.
WAITER, THE CHECK, PLEASE!
YES, SIR.
LONG AFTERWARD MY FATHER ADMITTED TO ME THAT HE HAD ALWAYS KNOWN THAT I WOULD GET DIVORCED. HE WANTED ME TO REALIZE BY MYSELF THAT REZA AND I WERE NOT MADE FOR EACH OTHER. HE WAS RIGHT.

MOM, ARE YOU IN THERE?
NO!
HAVE YOU BEEN CRYING?
NO.
I HAD ONLY TO PUT MY HAND ON HER SHOULDER FOR HER TO START AGAIN.
I HAVE ALWAYS WANTED FOR YOU TO BECOME INDEPENDENT, EDUCATED, CULTURED ... AND HERE YOU ARE GETTING MARRIED AT TWENTY-ONE. I WANT YOU TO LEAVE IRAN, FOR YOU TO BE FREE AND EMANCIPATED ...
MY SWEET LITTLE MOM! TRUST ME. I KNOW WHAT I'M DOING.
THE REST OF THE EVENING ALTERNATED BETWEEN LAUGHTER AND TEARS BUT ESPECIALLY LOTS OF WEARINESS. FINALLY, AT TWO IN THE MORNING ...
GOODBYE!
BE HAPPY!
GOOD LUCK!
WE WENT HOME ...
... WHEN THE APARTMENT DOOR CLOSED, I HAD A BIZARRE FEELING.
...I WAS ALREADY SORRY! I HAD SUDDENLY BECOME "A MARRIED WOMAN." I HAD CONFORMED TO SOCIETY, WHILE I HAD ALWAYS WANTED TO REMAIN IN THE MARGINS. IN MY MIND, "A MARRIED WOMAN" WASN'T LIKE ME. IT REQUIRED TOO MANY COMPROMISES. I COULDN'T ACCEPT IT, BUT IT WAS TOO LATE.

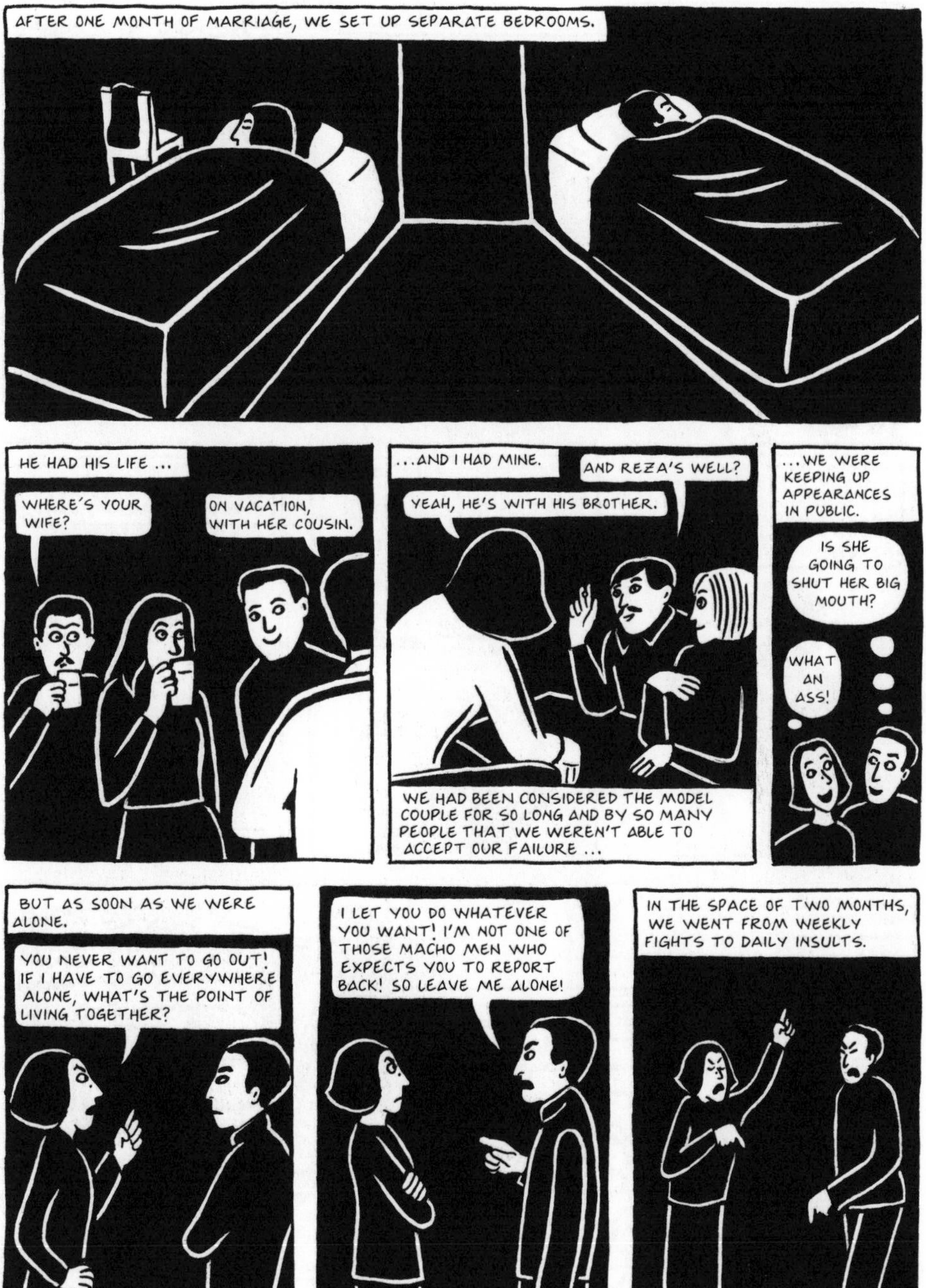
AFTER ONE MONTH OF MARRIAGE, WE SET UP SEPARATE BEDROOMS.
HE HAD HIS LIFE ...
WHERE'S YOUR WIFE?
ON VACATION, WITH HER COUSIN.
...AND I HAD MINE.
AND REZA'S WELL?
YEAH, HE'S WITH HIS BROTHER.
WE HAD BEEN CONSIDERED THE MODEL COUPLE FOR SO LONG AND BY SO MANY PEOPLE THAT WE WEREN'T ABLE TO ACCEPT OUR FAILURE ...
...WE WERE KEEPING UP APPEARANCES IN PUBLIC.
IS SHE GOING TO SHUT HER BIG MOUTH?
WHAT AN ASS!
BUT AS SOON AS WE WERE ALONE.
YOU NEVER WANT TO GO OUT! IF I HAVE TO GO EVERYWHERE ALONE, WHAT'S THE POINT OF LIVING TOGETHER?
I LET YOU DO WHATEVER YOU WANT! I'M NOT ONE OF THOSE MACHO MEN WHO EXPECTS YOU TO REPORT BACK! SO LEAVE ME ALONE!
IN THE SPACE OF TWO MONTHS, WE WENT FROM WEEKLY FIGHTS TO DAILY INSULTS.

THE SATELLITE

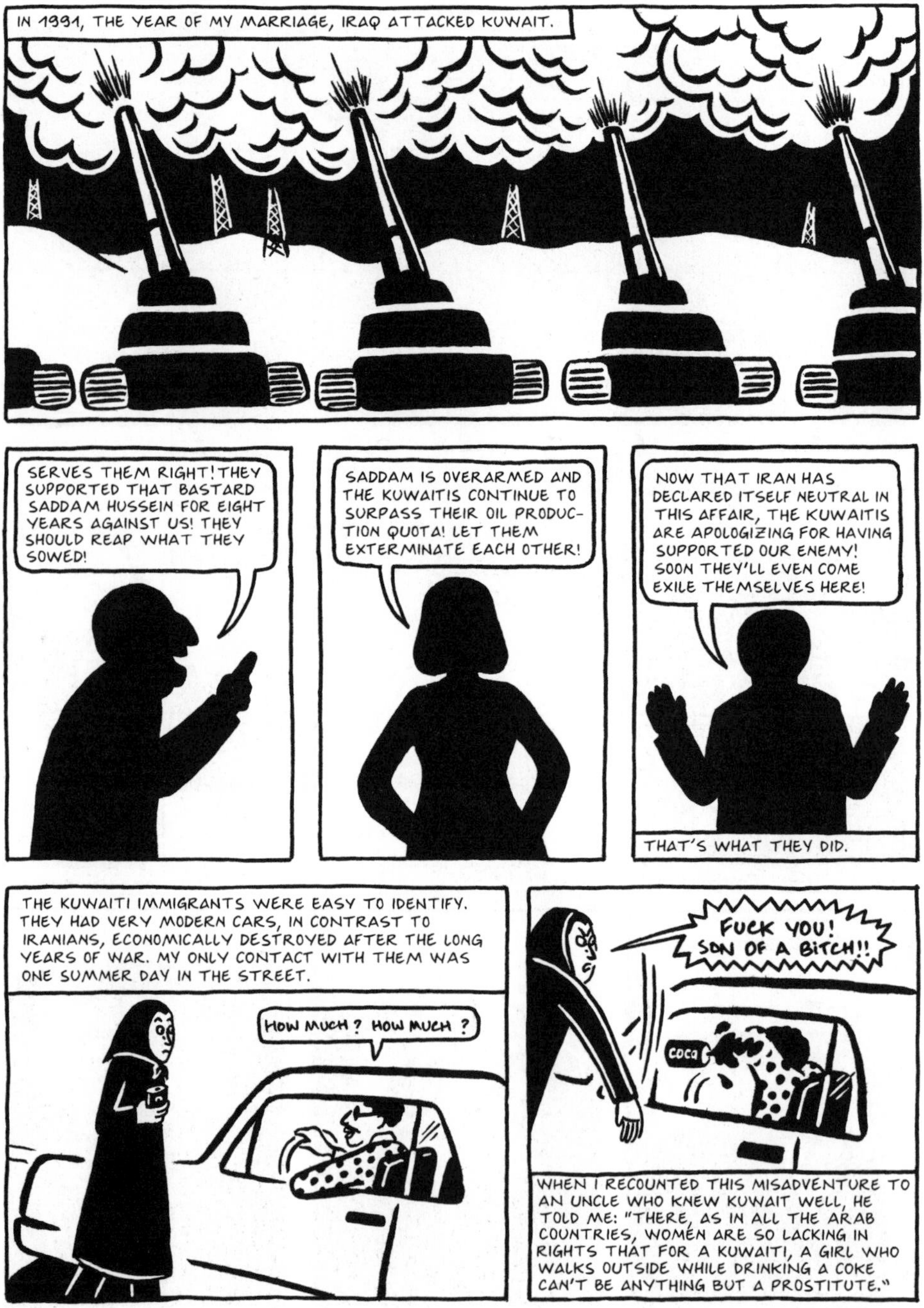
IN 1991, THE YEAR OF MY MARRIAGE, IRAQ ATTACKED KUWAIT.
SERVES THEM RIGHT! THEY SUPPORTED THAT BASTARD SADDAM HUSSEIN FOR EIGHT YEARS AGAINST US! THEY SHOULD REAP WHAT THEY SOWED!
SADDAM IS OVERARMED AND THE KUWAITIS CONTINUE TO SURPASS THEIR OIL PRODUCTION QUOTA! LET THEM EXTERMINATE EACH OTHER!
NOW THAT IRAN HAS DECLARED ITSELF NEUTRAL IN THIS AFFAIR, THE KUWAITIS ARE APOLOGIZING FOR HAVING SUPPORTED OUR ENEMY! SOON THEY'LL EVEN COME EXILE THEMSELVES HERE!
THAT'S WHAT THEY DID.
THE KUWAITI IMMIGRANTS WERE EASY TO IDENTIFY. THEY HAD VERY MODERN CARS, IN CONTRAST TO IRANIANS, ECONOMICALLY DESTROYED AFTER THE LONG YEARS OF WAR. MY ONLY CONTACT WITH THEM WAS ONE SUMMER DAY IN THE STREET.
HOW MUCH? HOW MUCH?
FUCK YOU! SON OF A BITCH!!
COCA
WHEN I RECOUNTED THIS MISADVENTURE TO AN UNCLE WHO KNEW KUWAIT WELL, HE TOLD ME: "THERE, AS IN ALL THE ARAB COUNTRIES, WOMEN ARE SO LACKING IN RIGHTS THAT FOR A KUWAITI, A GIRL WHO WALKS OUTSIDE WHILE DRINKING A COKE CAN'T BE ANYTHING BUT A PROSTITUTE."

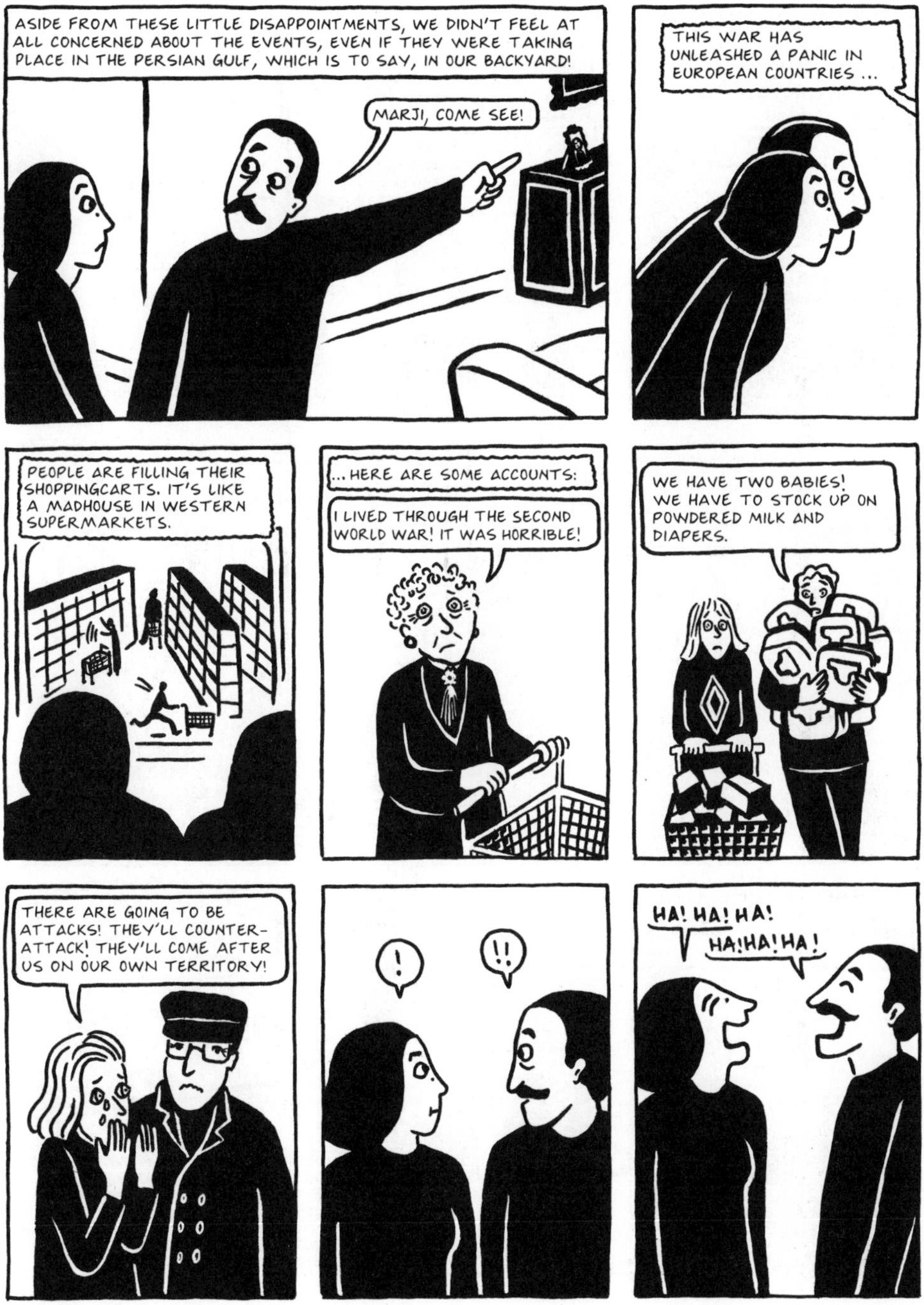
ASIDE FROM THESE LITTLE DISAPPOINTMENTS, WE DIDN'T FEEL AT ALL CONCERNED ABOUT THE EVENTS, EVEN IF THEY WERE TAKING PLACE IN THE PERSIAN GULF, WHICH IS TO SAY, IN OUR BACKYARD!
MARJI, COME SEE!
THIS WAR HAS UNLEASHED A PANIC IN EUROPEAN COUNTRIES ...
PEOPLE ARE FILLING THEIR SHOPPINGCARTS. IT'S LIKE A MADHOUSE IN WESTERN SUPERMARKETS.
... HERE ARE SOME ACCOUNTS:
I LIVED THROUGH THE SECOND WORLD WAR! IT WAS HORRIBLE!
WE HAVE TWO BABIES! WE HAVE TO STOCK UP ON POWDERED MILK AND DIAPERS.
THERE ARE GOING TO BE ATTACKS! THEY'LL COUNTER-ATTACK! THEY'LL COME AFTER US ON OUR OWN TERRITORY!
!
!!
HA! HA! HA!
HA! HA! HA!

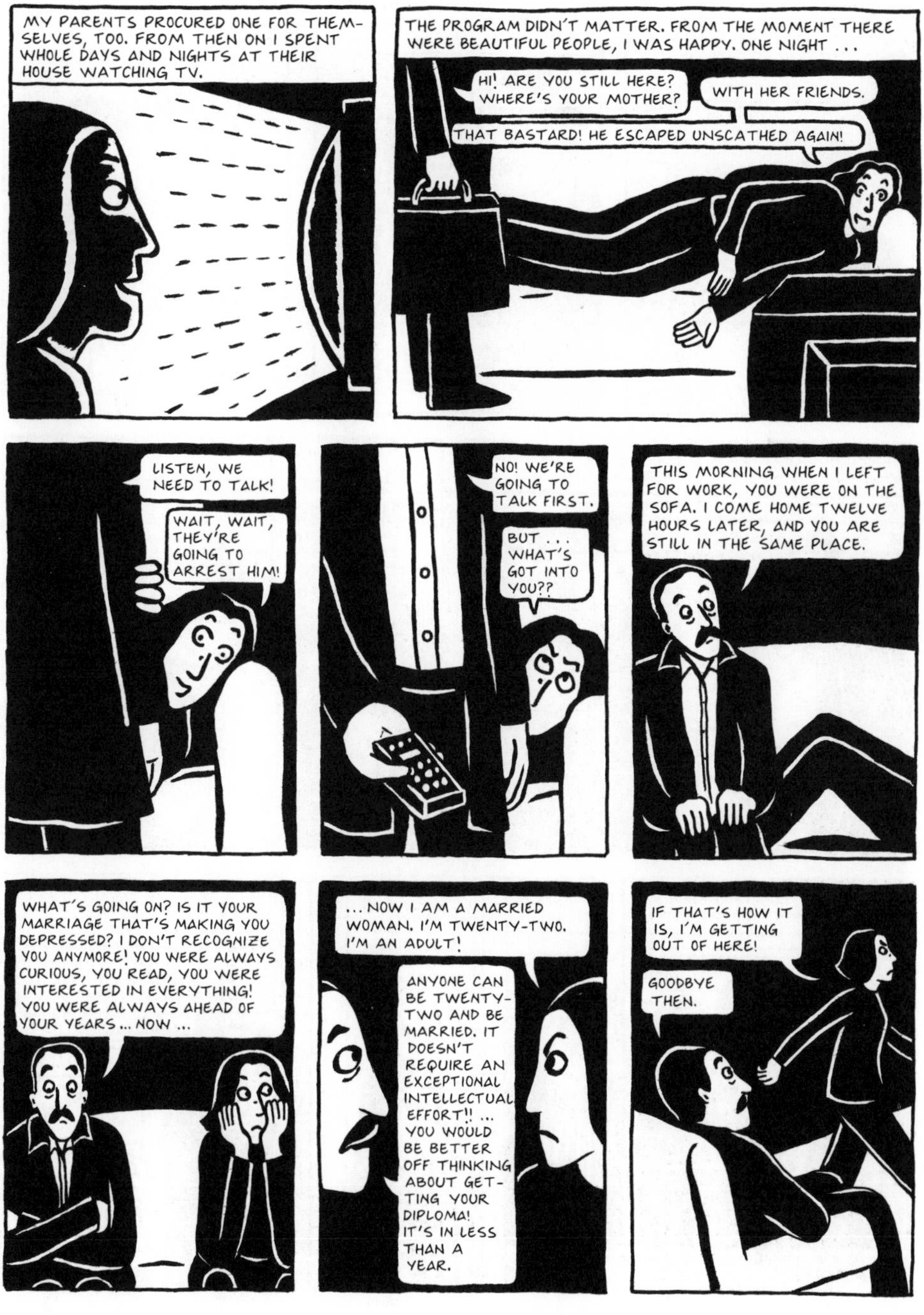
MY PARENTS PROCURED ONE FOR THEMSELVES, TOO. FROM THEN ON I SPENT WHOLE DAYS AND NIGHTS AT THEIR HOUSE WATCHING TV.
THE PROGRAM DIDN'T MATTER. FROM THE MOMENT THERE WERE BEAUTIFUL PEOPLE, I WAS HAPPY. ONE NIGHT . . .
HI! ARE YOU STILL HERE? WHERE'S YOUR MOTHER?
WITH HER FRIENDS.
THAT BASTARD! HE ESCAPED UNSCATHED AGAIN!
LISTEN, WE NEED TO TALK!
WAIT, WAIT, THEY'RE GOING TO ARREST HIM!
NO! WE'RE GOING TO TALK FIRST.
BUT . . . WHAT'S GOT INTO YOU??
THIS MORNING WHEN I LEFT FOR WORK, YOU WERE ON THE SOFA. I COME HOME TWELVE HOURS LATER, AND YOU ARE STILL IN THE SAME PLACE.
WHAT'S GOING ON? IS IT YOUR MARRIAGE THAT'S MAKING YOU DEPRESSED? I DON'T RECOGNIZE YOU ANYMORE! YOU WERE ALWAYS CURIOUS, YOU READ, YOU WERE INTERESTED IN EVERYTHING! YOU WERE ALWAYS AHEAD OF YOUR YEARS ... NOW ...
... NOW I AM A MARRIED WOMAN. I'M TWENTY-TWO. I'M AN ADULT!
ANYONE CAN BE TWENTY-TWO AND BE MARRIED. IT DOESN'T REQUIRE AN EXCEPTIONAL INTELLECTUAL EFFORT!! ... YOU WOULD BE BETTER OFF THINKING ABOUT GETTING YOUR DIPLOMA! IT'S IN LESS THAN A YEAR.
IF THAT'S HOW IT IS, I'M GETTING OUT OF HERE!
GOODBYE THEN.

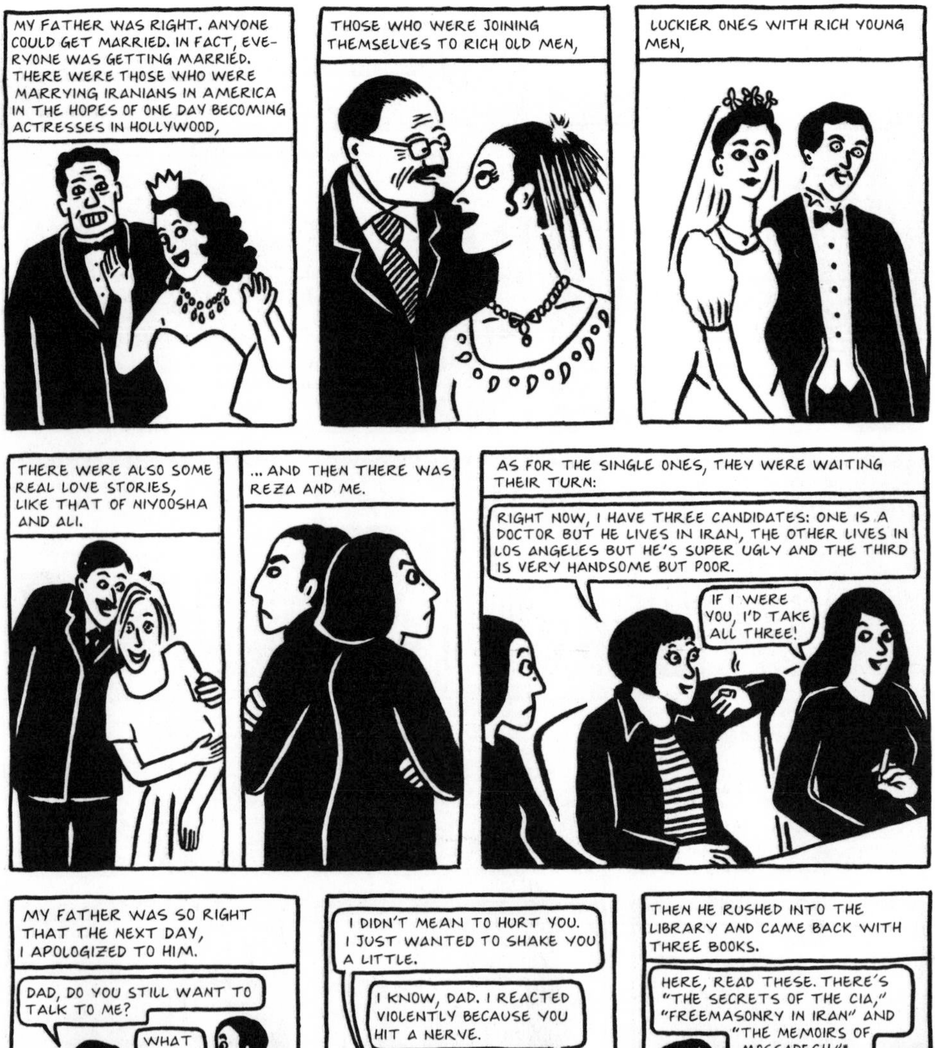
MY FATHER WAS RIGHT. ANYONE COULD GET MARRIED. IN FACT, EVERYONE WAS GETTING MARRIED. THERE WERE THOSE WHO WERE MARRYING IRANIANS IN AMERICA IN THE HOPES OF ONE DAY BECOMING ACTRESSES IN HOLLYWOOD,
THOSE WHO WERE JOINING THEMSELVES TO RICH OLD MEN,
LUCKIER ONES WITH RICH YOUNG MEN,
THERE WERE ALSO SOME REAL LOVE STORIES, LIKE THAT OF NIYOOSHA AND ALI.
...AND THEN THERE WAS REZA AND ME.
AS FOR THE SINGLE ONES, THEY WERE WAITING THEIR TURN:
RIGHT NOW, I HAVE THREE CANDIDATES: ONE IS A DOCTOR BUT HE LIVES IN IRAN, THE OTHER LIVES IN LOS ANGELES BUT HE'S SUPER UGLY AND THE THIRD IS VERY HANDSOME BUT POOR.
IF I WERE YOU, I'D TAKE ALL THREE!
MY FATHER WAS SO RIGHT THAT THE NEXT DAY, I APOLOGIZED TO HIM.
DAD, DO YOU STILL WANT TO TALK TO ME?
WHAT DO YOU THINK?
I DIDN'T MEAN TO HURT YOU. I JUST WANTED TO SHAKE YOU A LITTLE.
I KNOW, DAD. I REACTED VIOLENTLY BECAUSE YOU HIT A NERVE.
THEN HE RUSHED INTO THE LIBRARY AND CAME BACK WITH THREE BOOKS.
HERE, READ THESE. THERE'S "THE SECRETS OF THE CIA," "FREEMASONRY IN IRAN" AND "THE MEMOIRS OF MOSSADEGH."*
OH GREAT! COOL!!
TO CATCH UP, I READ ALL OF THEM IN TEN DAYS. DESPITE MY ASSUMPTIONS, I FOUND THEM REALLY INTERESTING.

*IRANIAN PRIME MINISTER. HE NATIONALIZED THE OIL INDUSTRY IN 1951.

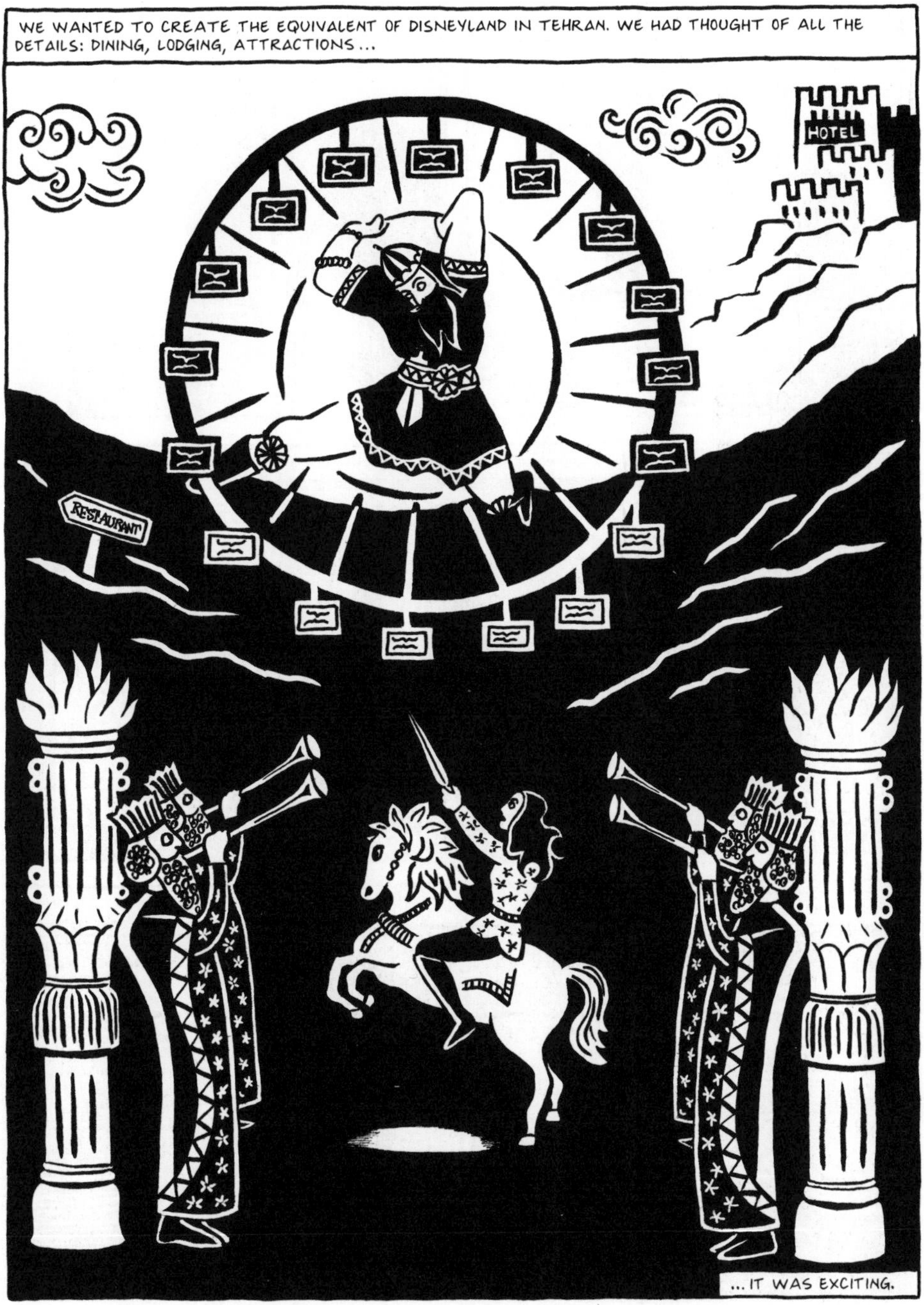
WE WANTED TO CREATE THE EQUIVALENT OF DISNEYLAND IN TEHRAN. WE HAD THOUGHT OF ALL THE DETAILS: DINING, LODGING, ATTRACTIONS...
HOTEL
RESTAURANT
... IT WAS EXCITING.

WE WORKED NIGHT AND DAY FOR SEVEN MONTHS.

FINALLY CAME THE DAY OF GRADUATION.

BEFORE THE JURY ARRIVED, OUR FRIENDS AND FAMILIES WERE GIVEN A CHANCE TO APPRECIATE OUR WORK UP CLOSE.

DR. M, THANK YOU FOR BEING HERE. I'M TRULY HONORED.

THE HONOR IS MINE.

SINCE I WAS A LOT MORE TALKATIVE THAN REZA, WE HAD DECIDED THAT I WOULD DEFEND OUR DISSERTATION.

OUR MYTHOLOGY IS ONE OF THE MOST COMPLEX MYTHOLOGIES ON EARTH, BUT WE HAVE NEVER KNOWN HOW TO MINE IT, FOR FEAR OF MAKING IT VULGAR. MANY THINGS, LIKE THE HOLY GRAIL, THE KNIGHTS OF THE ROUND TABLE, ETC., ETC., COME FROM IRAN. IN OUR COUNTRY, WE HAVE THEME PARKS, BUT THE MOTIFS ARE AMERICAN. WHICH IS THE REASON BEHIND OUR INITIATIVE.

WE GOT A TWENTY OUT OF TWEN-TY. AFTER THE DELIBERATION ...

BRAVO, MY CHILDREN! IT WAS PERFECT! THANKS TO YOUNG PEOPLE LIKE YOU, I STILL HAVE HOPE FOR THE FUTURE OF IRAN. YOU SHOULD PROPOSE YOUR PROJECT TO THE MAYOR OF TEHRAN. I PERSONALLY KNOW THE MAYOR'S DEPUTY. YOU CAN USE MY NAME.

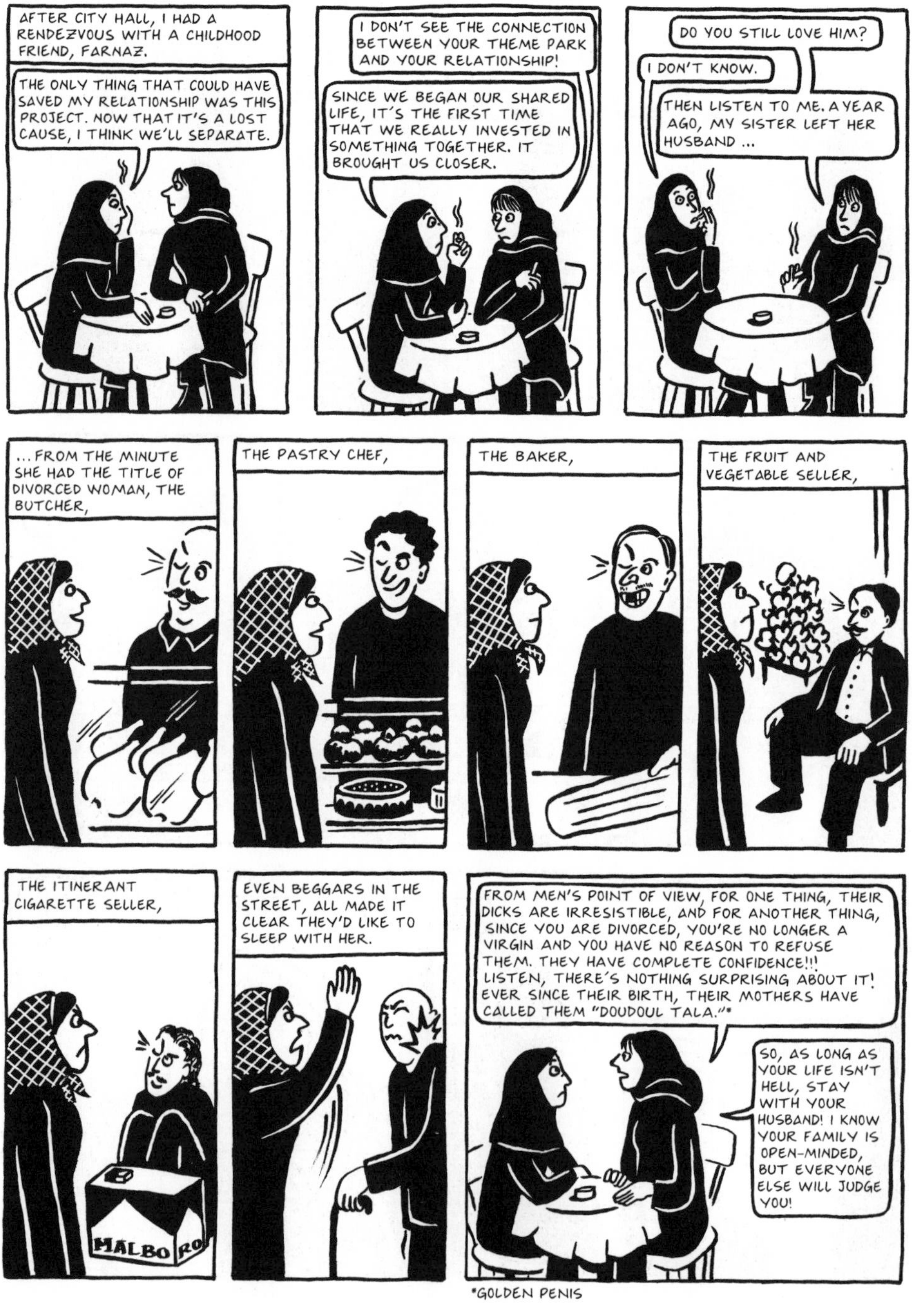
AFTER CITY HALL, I HAD A RENDEZVOUS WITH A CHILDHOOD FRIEND, FARNAZ.
THE ONLY THING THAT COULD HAVE SAVED MY RELATIONSHIP WAS THIS PROJECT. NOW THAT IT'S A LOST CAUSE, I THINK WE'LL SEPARATE.
I DON'T SEE THE CONNECTION BETWEEN YOUR THEME PARK AND YOUR RELATIONSHIP!
SINCE WE BEGAN OUR SHARED LIFE, IT'S THE FIRST TIME THAT WE REALLY INVESTED IN SOMETHING TOGETHER. IT BROUGHT US CLOSER.
DO YOU STILL LOVE HIM?
I DON'T KNOW.
THEN LISTEN TO ME. A YEAR AGO, MY SISTER LEFT HER HUSBAND ...
... FROM THE MINUTE SHE HAD THE TITLE OF DIVORCED WOMAN, THE BUTCHER,
THE PASTRY CHEF,
THE BAKER,
THE FRUIT AND VEGETABLE SELLER,
THE ITINERANT CIGARETTE SELLER,
MALBORO
EVEN BEGGARS IN THE STREET, ALL MADE IT CLEAR THEY'D LIKE TO SLEEP WITH HER.
FROM MEN'S POINT OF VIEW, FOR ONE THING, THEIR DICKS ARE IRRESISTIBLE, AND FOR ANOTHER THING, SINCE YOU ARE DIVORCED, YOU'RE NO LONGER A VIRGIN AND YOU HAVE NO REASON TO REFUSE THEM. THEY HAVE COMPLETE CONFIDENCE!!! LISTEN, THERE'S NOTHING SURPRISING ABOUT IT! EVER SINCE THEIR BIRTH, THEIR MOTHERS HAVE CALLED THEM "DOUDOUL TALA."*
SO, AS LONG AS YOUR LIFE ISN'T HELL, STAY WITH YOUR HUSBAND! I KNOW YOUR FAMILY IS OPEN-MINDED, BUT EVERYONE ELSE WILL JUDGE YOU!

*GOLDEN PENIS

333

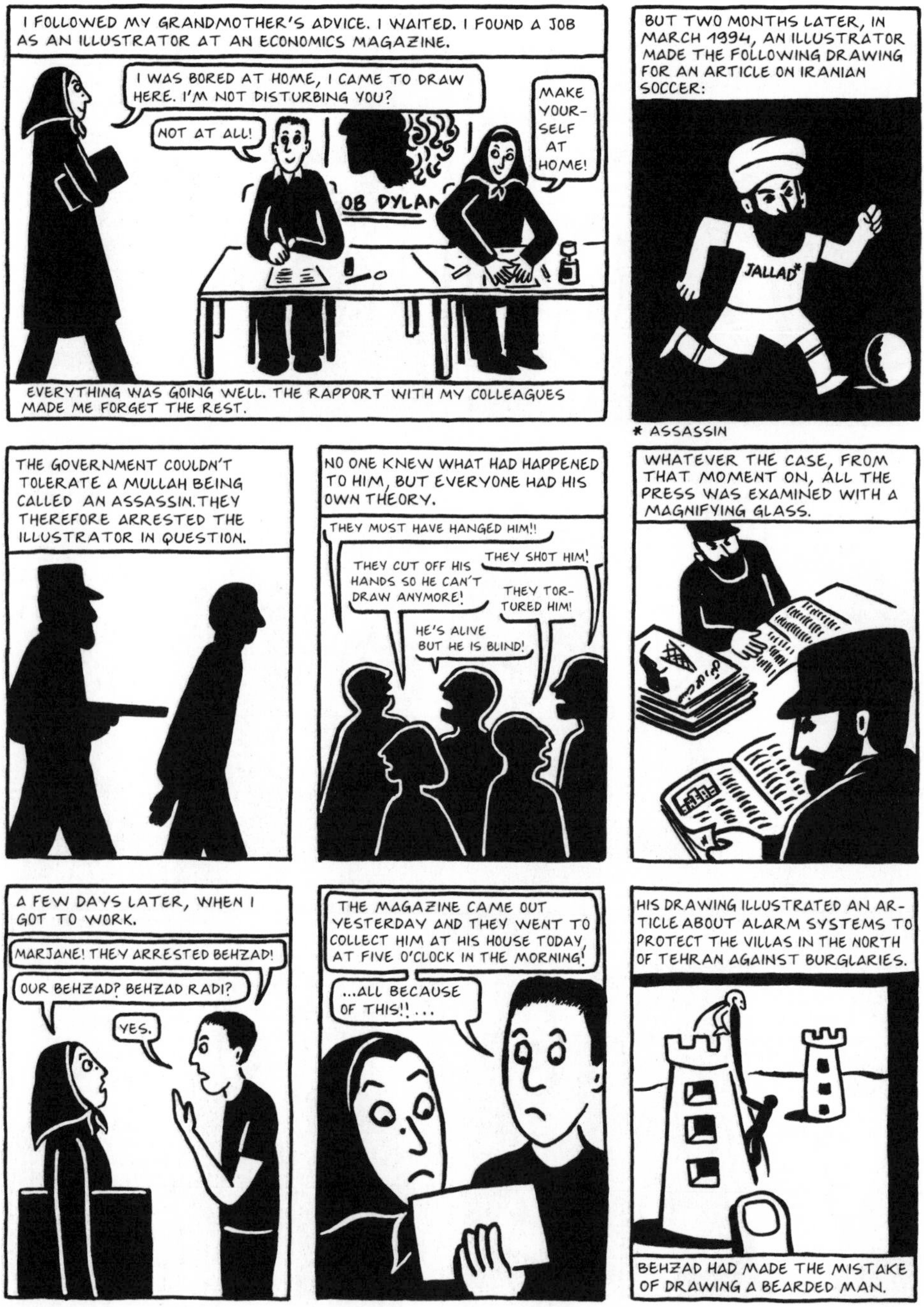
I FOLLOWED MY GRANDMOTHER'S ADVICE. I WAITED. I FOUND A JOB AS AN ILLUSTRATOR AT AN ECONOMICS MAGAZINE.
I WAS BORED AT HOME, I CAME TO DRAW HERE. I'M NOT DISTURBING YOU?
NOT AT ALL!
MAKE YOURSELF AT HOME!
OB DYLAN
EVERYTHING WAS GOING WELL. THE RAPPORT WITH MY COLLEAGUES MADE ME FORGET THE REST.
BUT TWO MONTHS LATER, IN MARCH 1994, AN ILLUSTRATOR MADE THE FOLLOWING DRAWING FOR AN ARTICLE ON IRANIAN SOCCER:
JALLAD*
* ASSASSIN
THE GOVERNMENT COULDN'T TOLERATE A MULLAH BEING CALLED AN ASSASSIN. THEY THEREFORE ARRESTED THE ILLUSTRATOR IN QUESTION.
NO ONE KNEW WHAT HAD HAPPENED TO HIM, BUT EVERYONE HAD HIS OWN THEORY.
THEY MUST HAVE HANGED HIM!!
THEY SHOT HIM!
THEY CUT OFF HIS HANDS SO HE CAN'T DRAW ANYMORE!
THEY TORTURED HIM!
HE'S ALIVE BUT HE IS BLIND!
WHATEVER THE CASE, FROM THAT MOMENT ON, ALL THE PRESS WAS EXAMINED WITH A MAGNIFYING GLASS.
A FEW DAYS LATER, WHEN I GOT TO WORK.
MARJANE! THEY ARRESTED BEHZAD!
OUR BEHZAD? BEHZAD RADI?
YES.
THE MAGAZINE CAME OUT YESTERDAY AND THEY WENT TO COLLECT HIM AT HIS HOUSE TODAY, AT FIVE O'CLOCK IN THE MORNING!
...ALL BECAUSE OF THIS!! ...
HIS DRAWING ILLUSTRATED AN ARTICLE ABOUT ALARM SYSTEMS TO PROTECT THE VILLAS IN THE NORTH OF TEHRAN AGAINST BURGLARIES.
BEHZAD HAD MADE THE MISTAKE OF DRAWING A BEARDED MAN.

337

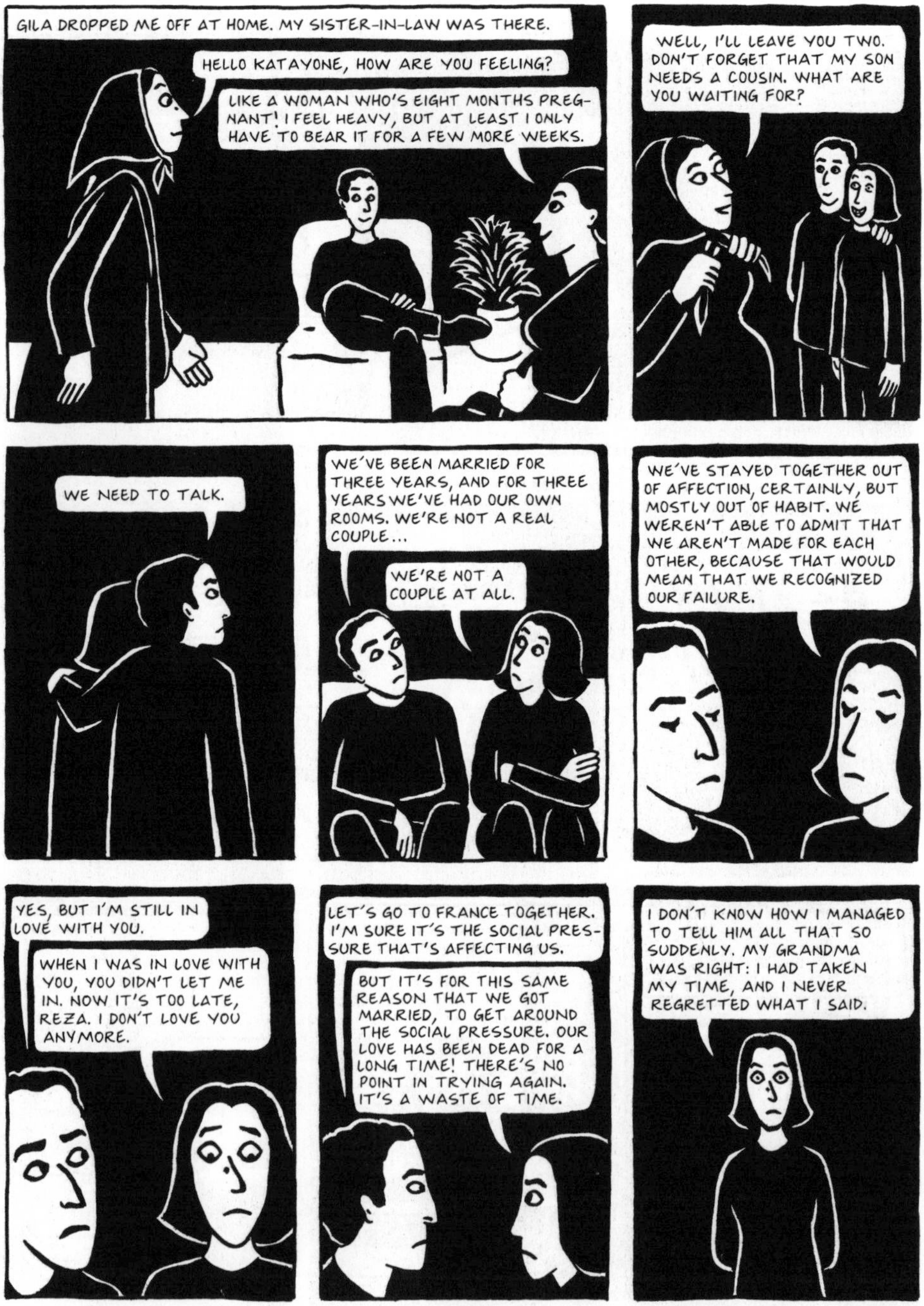
GILA DROPPED ME OFF AT HOME. MY SISTER-IN-LAW WAS THERE.
HELLO KATAYONE, HOW ARE YOU FEELING?
LIKE A WOMAN WHO'S EIGHT MONTHS PREGNANT! I FEEL HEAVY, BUT AT LEAST I ONLY HAVE TO BEAR IT FOR A FEW MORE WEEKS.
WELL, I'LL LEAVE YOU TWO. DON'T FORGET THAT MY SON NEEDS A COUSIN. WHAT ARE YOU WAITING FOR?
WE NEED TO TALK.
WE'VE BEEN MARRIED FOR THREE YEARS, AND FOR THREE YEARS WE'VE HAD OUR OWN ROOMS. WE'RE NOT A REAL COUPLE...
WE'RE NOT A COUPLE AT ALL.
WE'VE STAYED TOGETHER OUT OF AFFECTION, CERTAINLY, BUT MOSTLY OUT OF HABIT. WE WEREN'T ABLE TO ADMIT THAT WE AREN'T MADE FOR EACH OTHER, BECAUSE THAT WOULD MEAN THAT WE RECOGNIZED OUR FAILURE.
YES, BUT I'M STILL IN LOVE WITH YOU.
WHEN I WAS IN LOVE WITH YOU, YOU DIDN'T LET ME IN. NOW IT'S TOO LATE, REZA. I DON'T LOVE YOU ANYMORE.
LET'S GO TO FRANCE TOGETHER. I'M SURE IT'S THE SOCIAL PRESSURE THAT'S AFFECTING US.
BUT IT'S FOR THIS SAME REASON THAT WE GOT MARRIED, TO GET AROUND THE SOCIAL PRESSURE. OUR LOVE HAS BEEN DEAD FOR A LONG TIME! THERE'S NO POINT IN TRYING AGAIN. IT'S A WASTE OF TIME.
I DON'T KNOW HOW I MANAGED TO TELL HIM ALL THAT SO SUDDENLY. MY GRANDMA WAS RIGHT: I HAD TAKEN MY TIME, AND I NEVER REGRETTED WHAT I SAID.

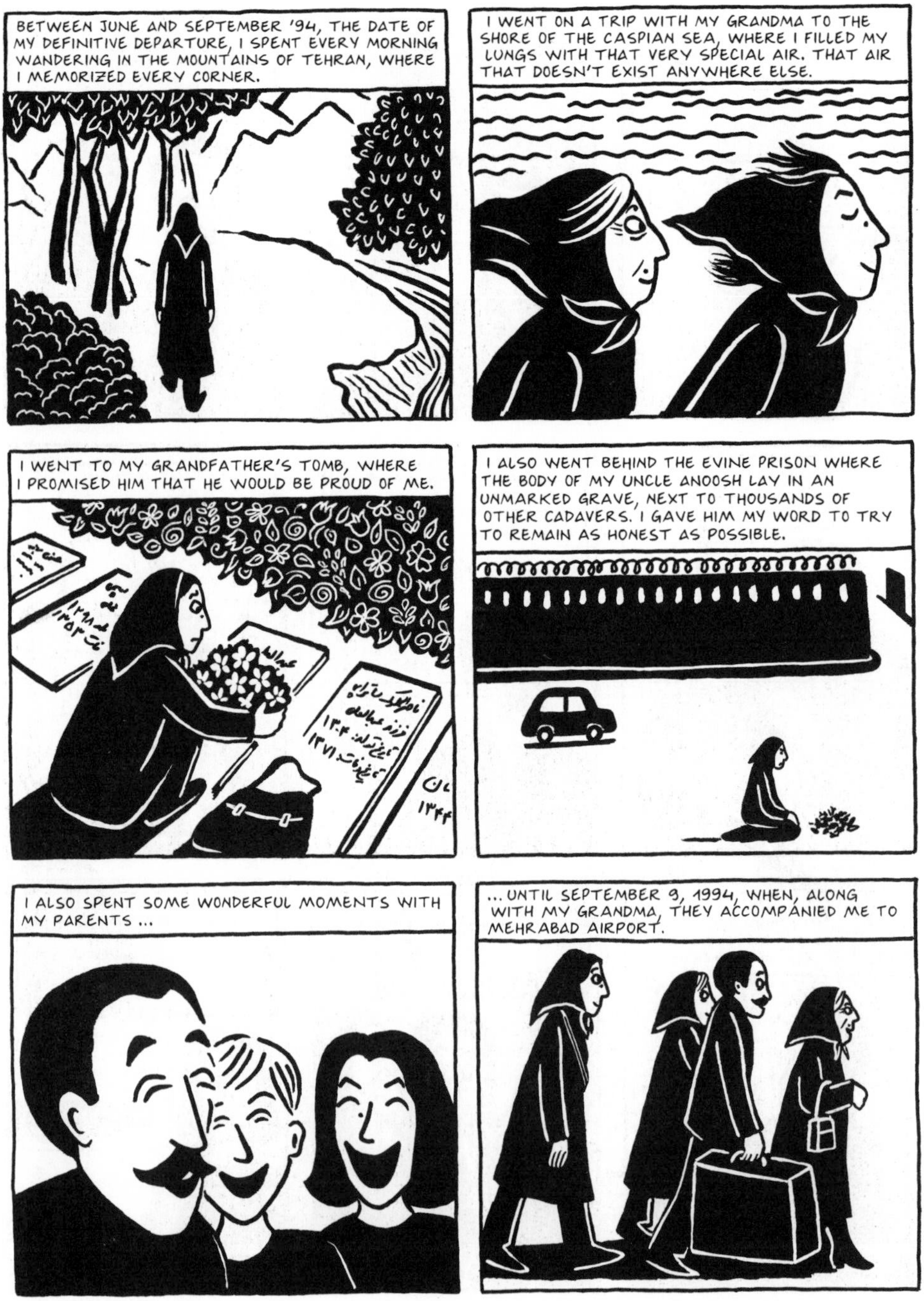
BETWEEN JUNE AND SEPTEMBER '94, THE DATE OF MY DEFINITIVE DEPARTURE, I SPENT EVERY MORNING WANDERING IN THE MOUNTAINS OF TEHRAN, WHERE I MEMORIZED EVERY CORNER.
I WENT ON A TRIP WITH MY GRANDMA TO THE SHORE OF THE CASPIAN SEA, WHERE I FILLED MY LUNGS WITH THAT VERY SPECIAL AIR. THAT AIR THAT DOESN'T EXIST ANYWHERE ELSE.
I WENT TO MY GRANDFATHER'S TOMB, WHERE I PROMISED HIM THAT HE WOULD BE PROUD OF ME.
I ALSO WENT BEHIND THE EVINE PRISON WHERE THE BODY OF MY UNCLE ANOOSH LAY IN AN UNMARKED GRAVE, NEXT TO THOUSANDS OF OTHER CADAVERS. I GAVE HIM MY WORD TO TRY TO REMAIN AS HONEST AS POSSIBLE.
I ALSO SPENT SOME WONDERFUL MOMENTS WITH MY PARENTS ...
... UNTIL SEPTEMBER 9, 1994, WHEN, ALONG WITH MY GRANDMA, THEY ACCOMPANIED ME TO MEHRABAD AIRPORT.

CREDITS

Translation of first part of *Persepolis*: Mattias Ripa
Translation of second part of *Persepolis*: Blake Ferris
Supervision of translation: Marjane Satrapi and Carol Bernstein
Lettering: Céline Merrien and Eve Deluze

THANKS TO

Anjali Singh
L'Association
David B.
Jean-Christophe Menu
Emile Bravo
Christophe Blain
Guillaume Dumora
Fanny Dalle-Rive
Nicolas Leroy
Matthieu Wahiche
Charlotte Miquel
Amber Hoover